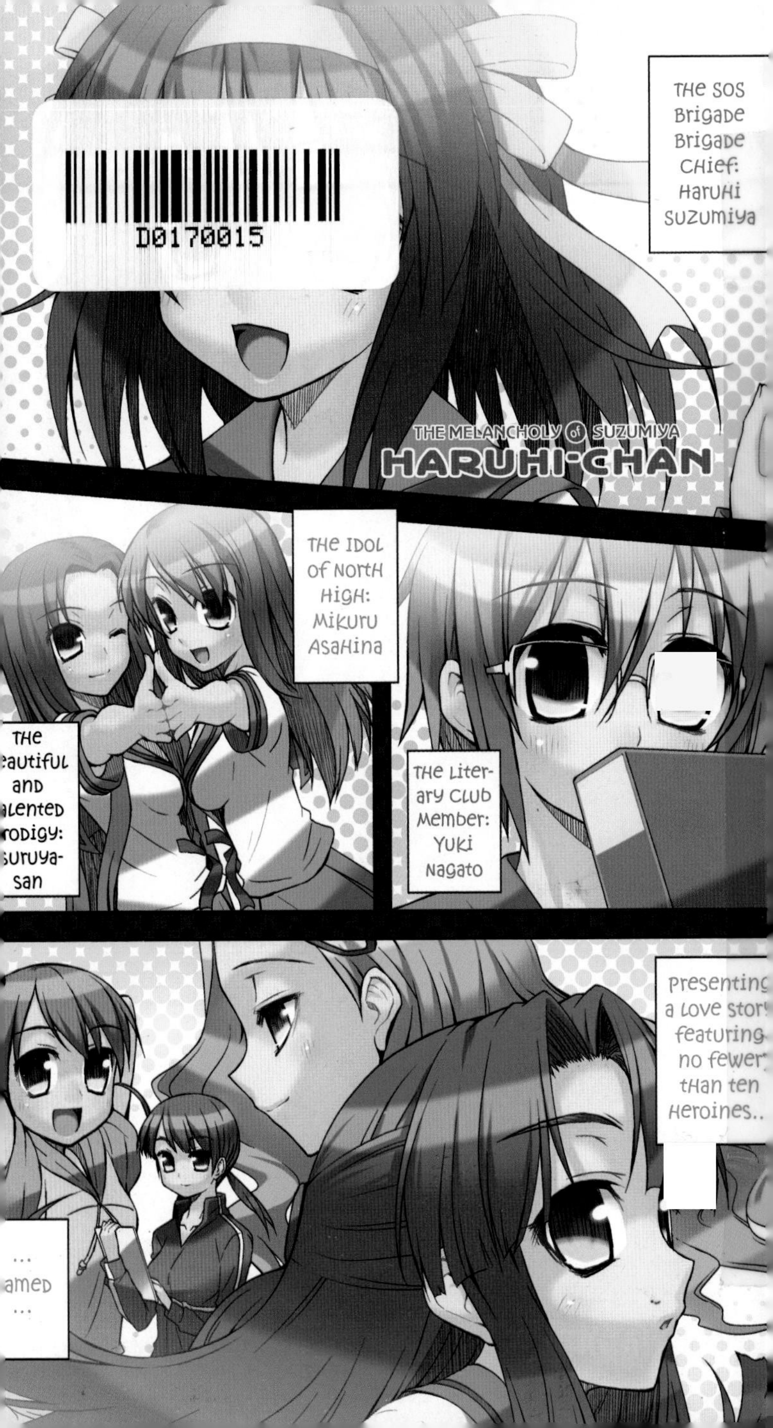

The SOS Brigade Brigade Chief: Haruhi Suzumiya
THE MELANCHOLY of SUZUMIYA
HARUHI-CHAN
The Literary Club Member: Yuki Nagato
The Idol of North High: Mikuru Asahina
THE eautiful and alented rodigy: suruya-san
Presentin a Love stor featuring no fewer than ten Heroines..
... amed ...

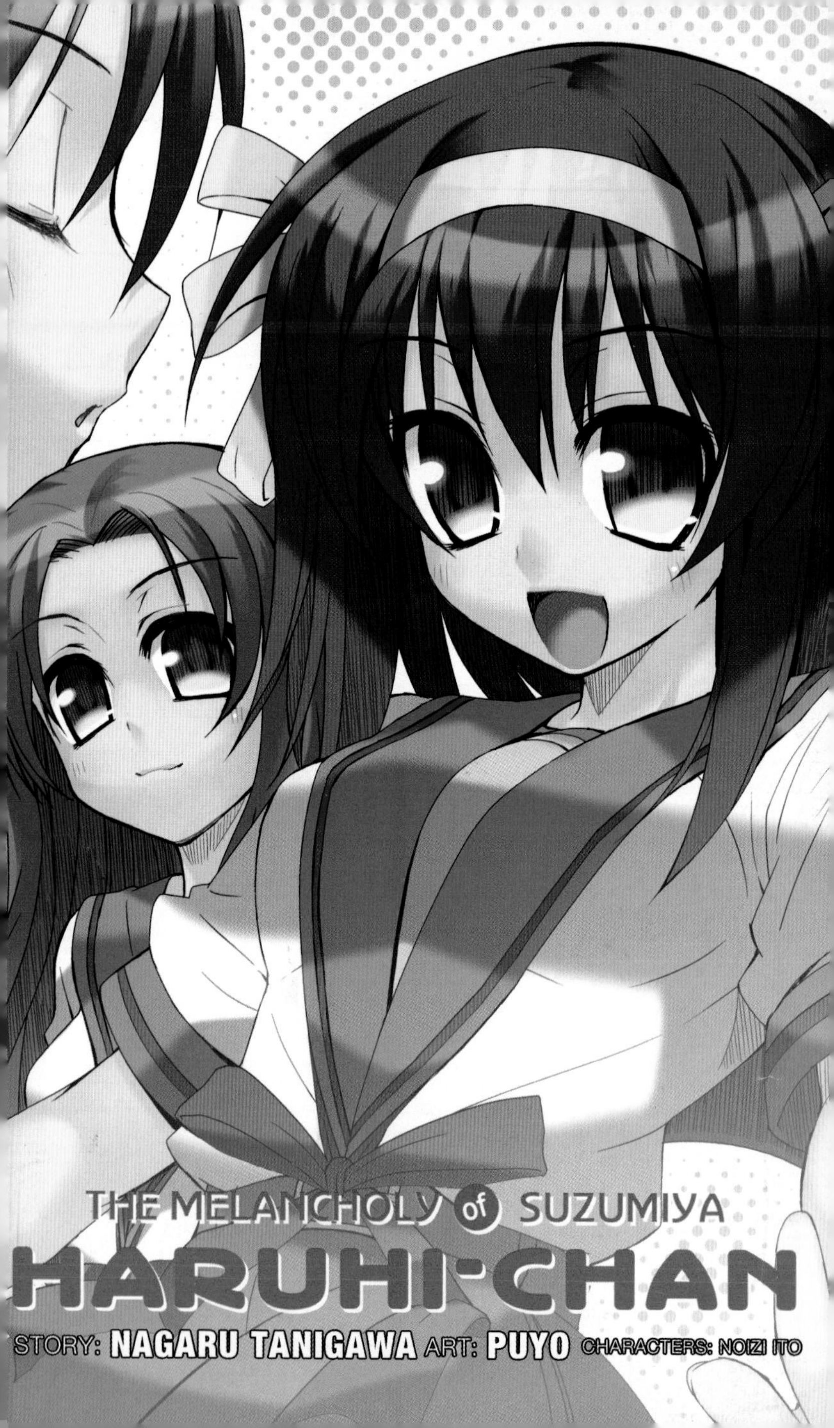
THE MELANCHOLY of SUZUMIYA
HARUHI-CHAN
STORY: NAGARU TANIGAWA ART: PUYO CHARACTERS: NOIZI ITO

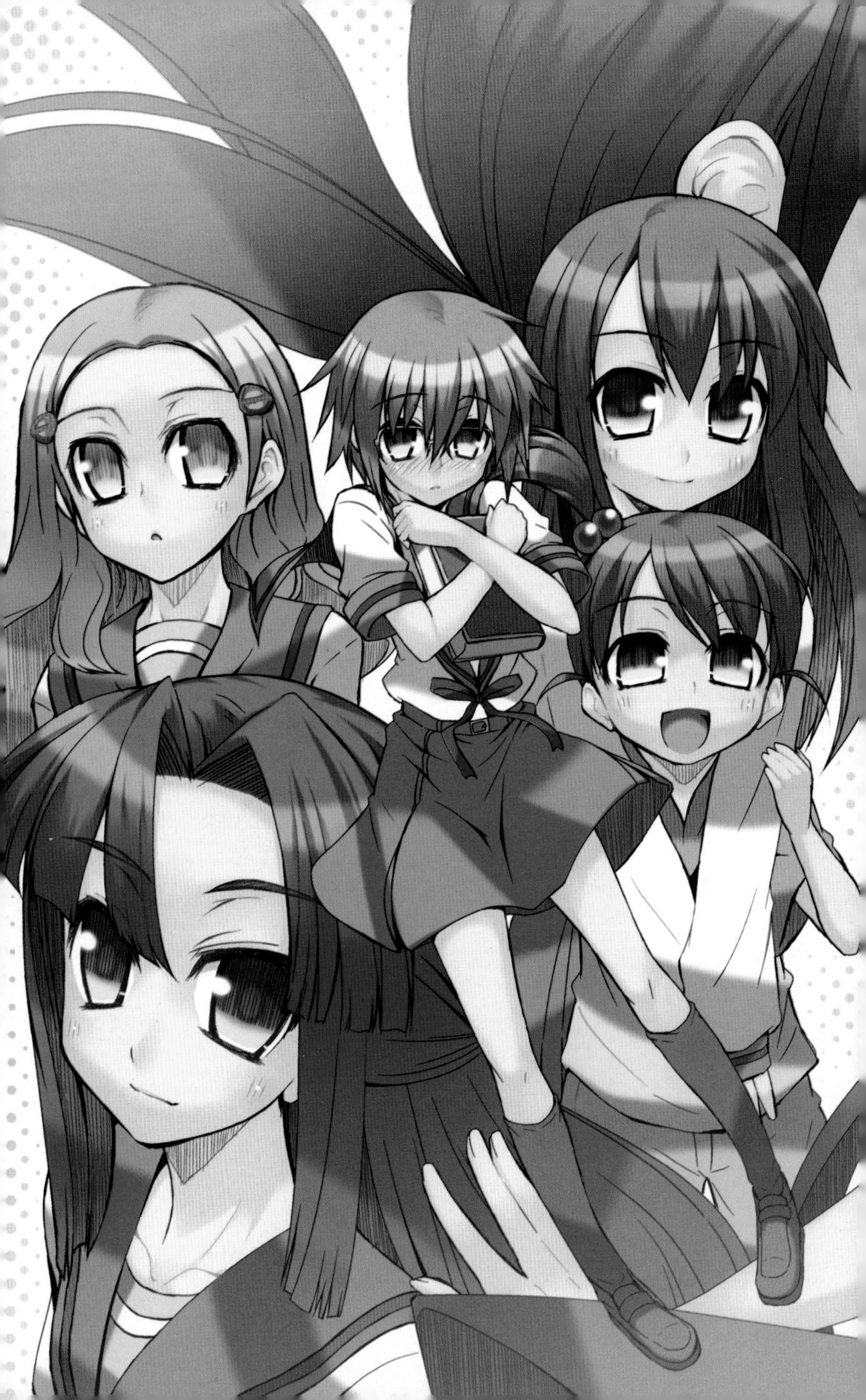

The Melancholy of Suzumiya
Haruhi-chan
02

INDEX

THE MELANCHOLY of SUZUMIYA
HARUHI-CHAN

02

The Untold Adventures of the SOS Brigade

THIS STORY IS **CLASSIFIED INFORMATION.** THERE IS NO **CLASSIFIED INFORMATION** TO ANY REAL **CLASSIFIED INFORMATION, CLASSIFIED INFORMATION,** OR **CLASSIFIED INFORMATION.**

STORY: **NAGARU TANIGAWA** ART: **PUYO** CHARACTERS: NOIZI ITO

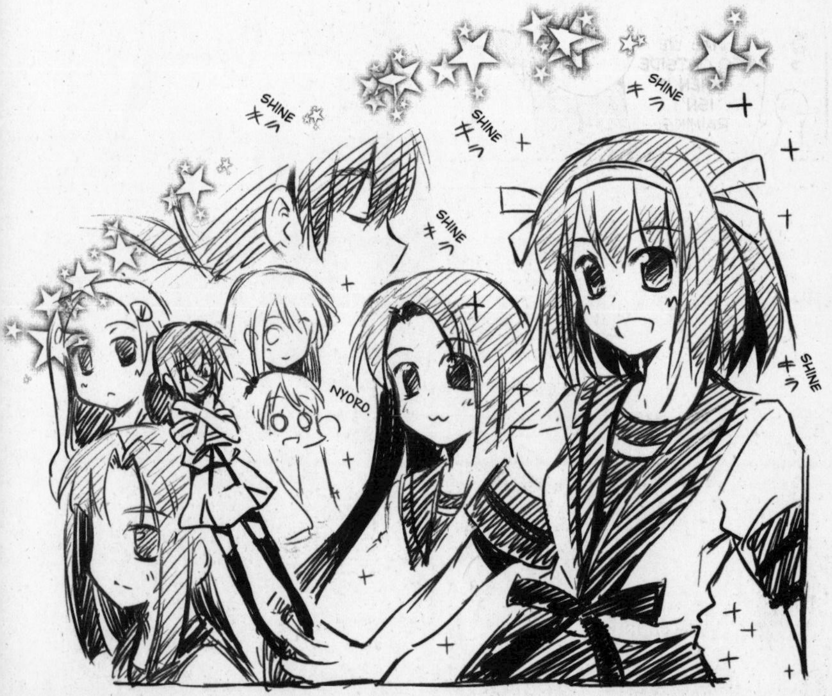
SHINE キラ
SHINE キラ
SHINE キラ
SHINE キラ
SHINE キラ
NYORO.

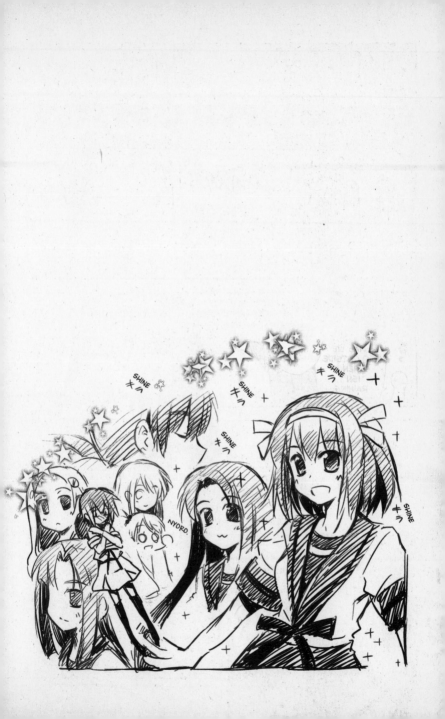

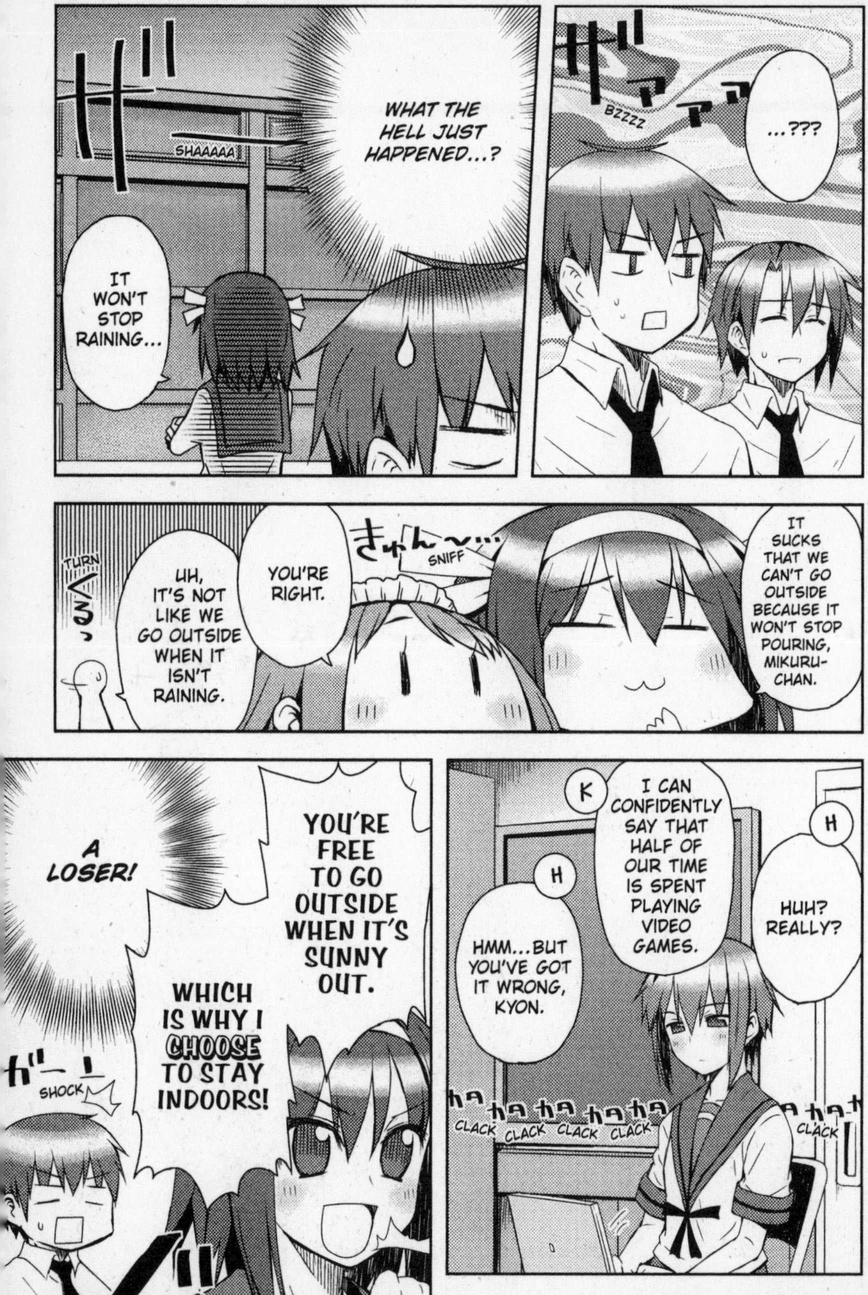

...???
BZZZZ
WHAT THE HELL JUST HAPPENED...?
SHAAAAAA
IT WON'T STOP RAINING...
IT SUCKS THAT WE CAN'T GO OUTSIDE BECAUSE IT WON'T STOP POURING, MIKURU-CHAN.
SNIFF
YOU'RE RIGHT.
UH, IT'S NOT LIKE WE GO OUTSIDE WHEN IT ISN'T RAINING.
TURN
H
HUH? REALLY?
K
I CAN CONFIDENTLY SAY THAT HALF OF OUR TIME IS SPENT PLAYING VIDEO GAMES.
H
HMM...BUT YOU'VE GOT IT WRONG, KYON.
CLACK CLACK CLACK CLACK CLACK
YOU'RE FREE TO GO OUTSIDE WHEN IT'S SUNNY OUT.
A LOSER!
WHICH IS WHY I CHOOSE TO STAY INDOORS!
SHOCK
CLENCH

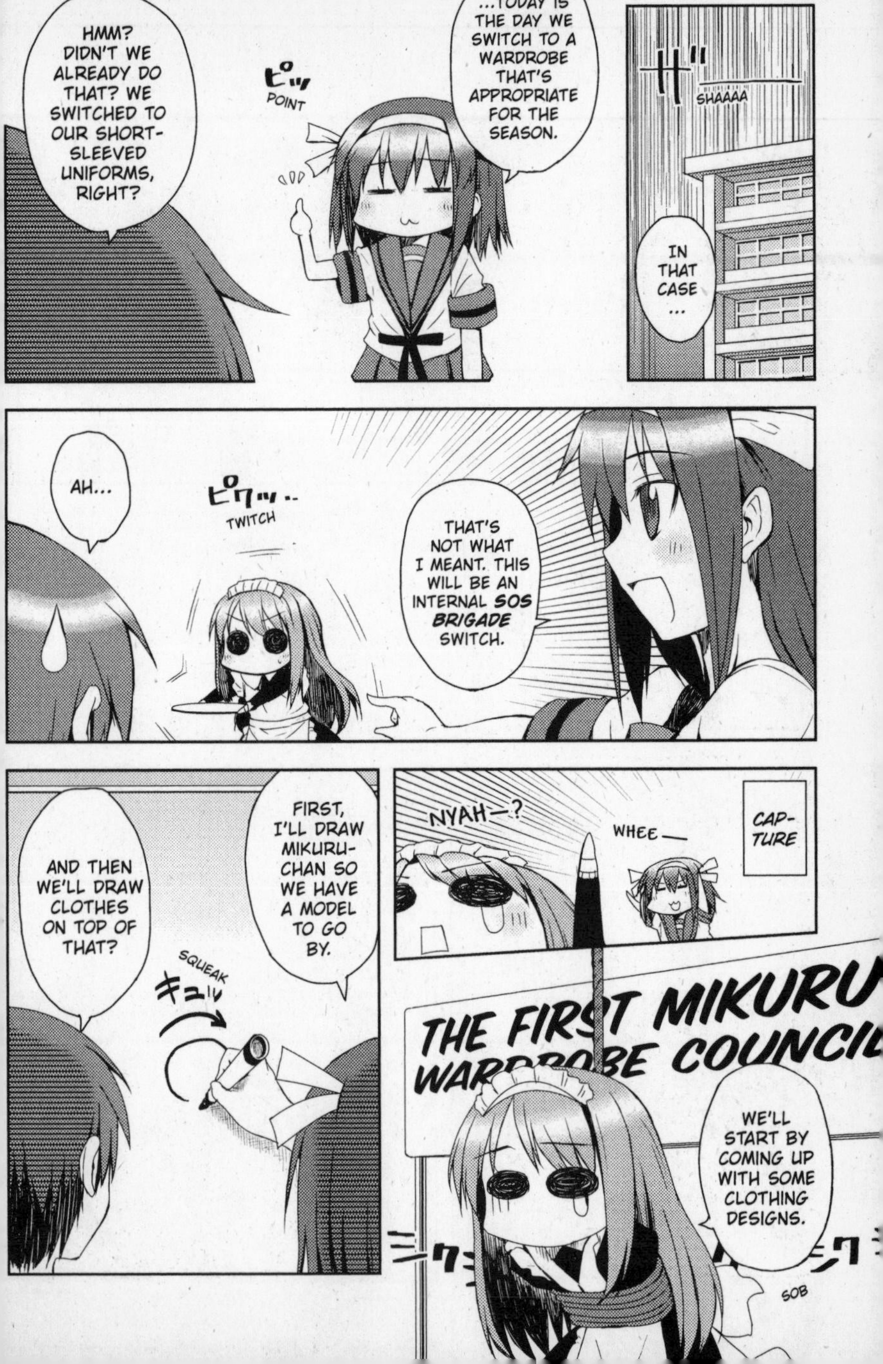
SHAAAA
IN THAT CASE ...
...TODAY IS THE DAY WE SWITCH TO A WARDROBE THAT'S APPROPRIATE FOR THE SEASON.
POINT
HMM? DIDN'T WE ALREADY DO THAT? WE SWITCHED TO OUR SHORT-SLEEVED UNIFORMS, RIGHT?
THAT'S NOT WHAT I MEANT. THIS WILL BE AN INTERNAL SOS BRIGADE SWITCH.
TWITCH
AH...
CAP-TURE
WHEE—
NYAH—?
THE FIRST MIKURU
WARDROBE COUNCI
WE'LL START BY COMING UP WITH SOME CLOTHING DESIGNS.
SOB
FIRST, I'LL DRAW MIKURU-CHAN SO WE HAVE A MODEL TO GO BY.
SQUEAK
AND THEN WE'LL DRAW CLOTHES ON TOP OF THAT?

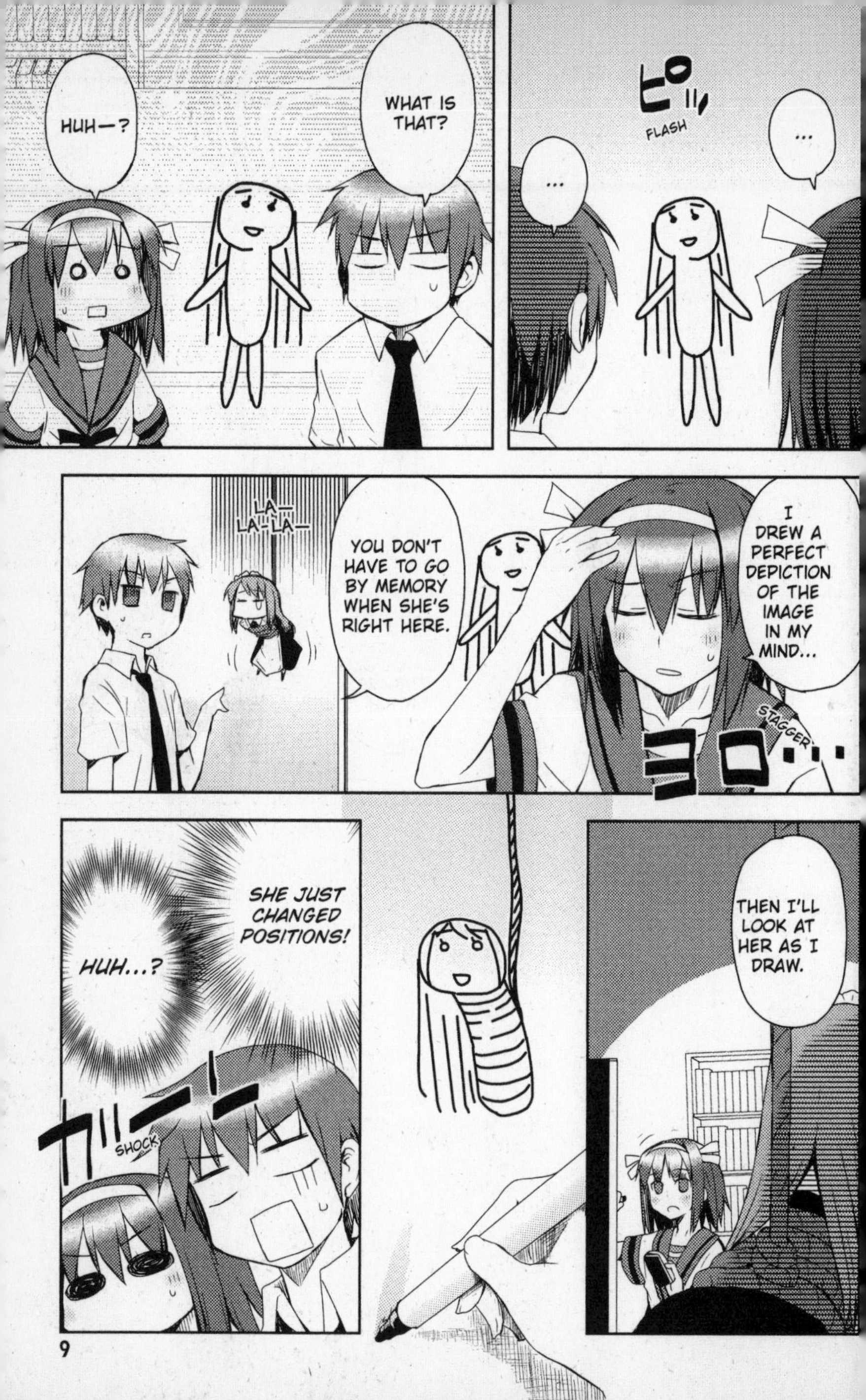
...
FLASH
...
WHAT IS THAT?
HUH—?
I DREW A PERFECT DEPICTION OF THE IMAGE IN MY MIND...
STAGGER
YOU DON'T HAVE TO GO BY MEMORY WHEN SHE'S RIGHT HERE.
LA—LA—LA—
THEN I'LL LOOK AT HER AS I DRAW.
SHE JUST CHANGED POSITIONS!
HUH...?
SHOCK

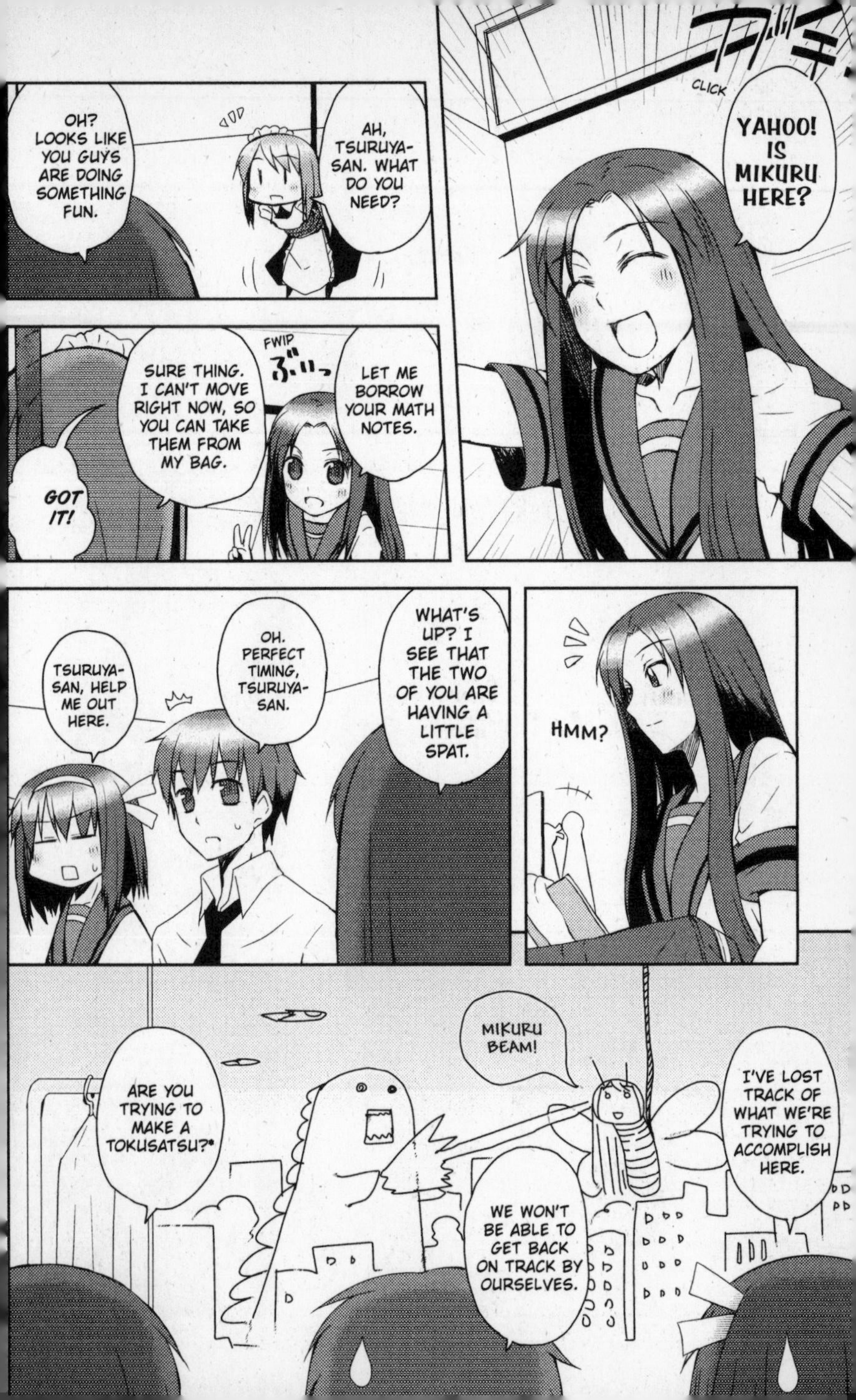
CLICK
YAHOO! IS MIKURU HERE?
AH, TSURUYA-SAN. WHAT DO YOU NEED?
OH? LOOKS LIKE YOU GUYS ARE DOING SOMETHING FUN.
LET ME BORROW YOUR MATH NOTES.
FWIP
SURE THING. I CAN'T MOVE RIGHT NOW, SO YOU CAN TAKE THEM FROM MY BAG.
GOT IT!
HMM?
WHAT'S UP? I SEE THAT THE TWO OF YOU ARE HAVING A LITTLE SPAT.
OH. PERFECT TIMING, TSURUYA-SAN.
TSURUYA-SAN, HELP ME OUT HERE.
I'VE LOST TRACK OF WHAT WE'RE TRYING TO ACCOMPLISH HERE.
MIKURU BEAM!
WE WON'T BE ABLE TO GET BACK ON TRACK BY OURSELVES.
ARE YOU TRYING TO MAKE A TOKUSATSU?*

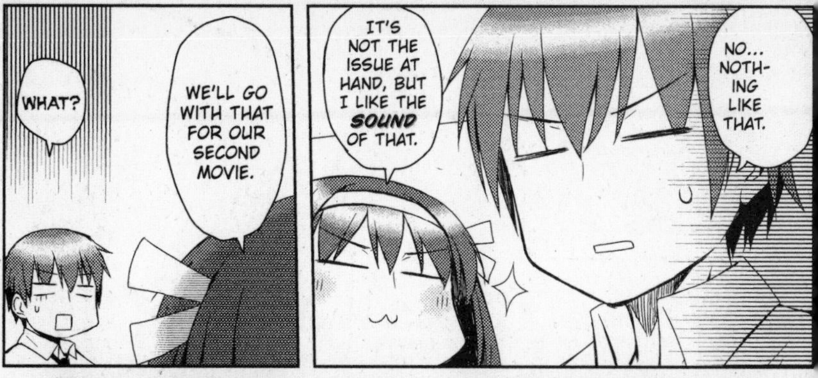
NO... NOTHING LIKE THAT.
IT'S NOT THE ISSUE AT HAND, BUT I LIKE THE ***SOUND*** OF THAT.
WE'LL GO WITH THAT FOR OUR SECOND MOVIE.
WHAT?

EXPLAINING

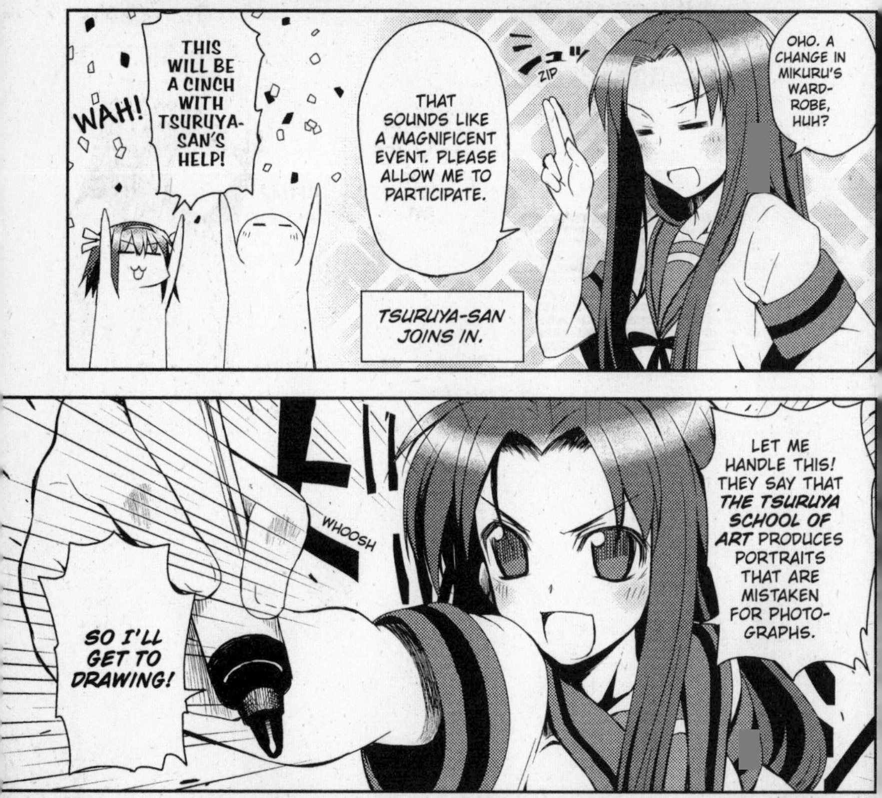
OHO. A CHANGE IN MIKURU'S WARDROBE, HUH?
ZIP
THAT SOUNDS LIKE A MAGNIFICENT EVENT. PLEASE ALLOW ME TO PARTICIPATE.
TSURUYA-SAN JOINS IN.
THIS WILL BE A CINCH WITH TSURUYA-SAN'S HELP!
WAH!
LET ME HANDLE THIS! THEY SAY THAT ***THE TSURUYA SCHOOL OF ART*** PRODUCES PORTRAITS THAT ARE MISTAKEN FOR PHOTOGRAPHS.
WHOOSH
SO I'LL GET TO DRAWING!

**LITERALLY "SFX MOVIE," A TOKUSATSU IS A TYPE OF JAPANESE FILM OR DRAMA THAT USUALLY INCLUDES SUPERHEROES AND/OR COSTUMED MONSTERS AND USES MANY SPECIAL EFFECTS.*

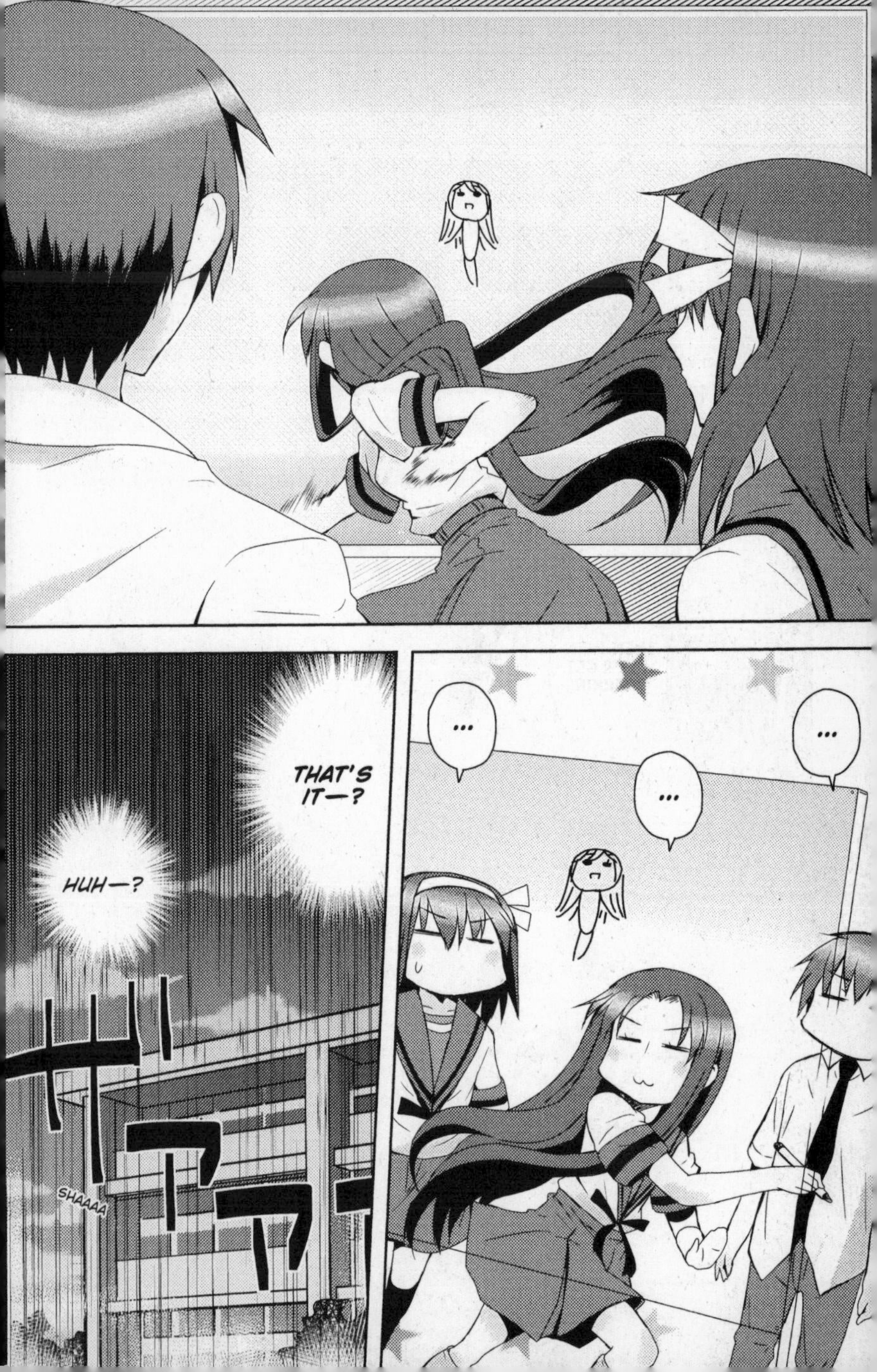
...
...
...
THAT'S IT—?
HUH—?
SHAAAA

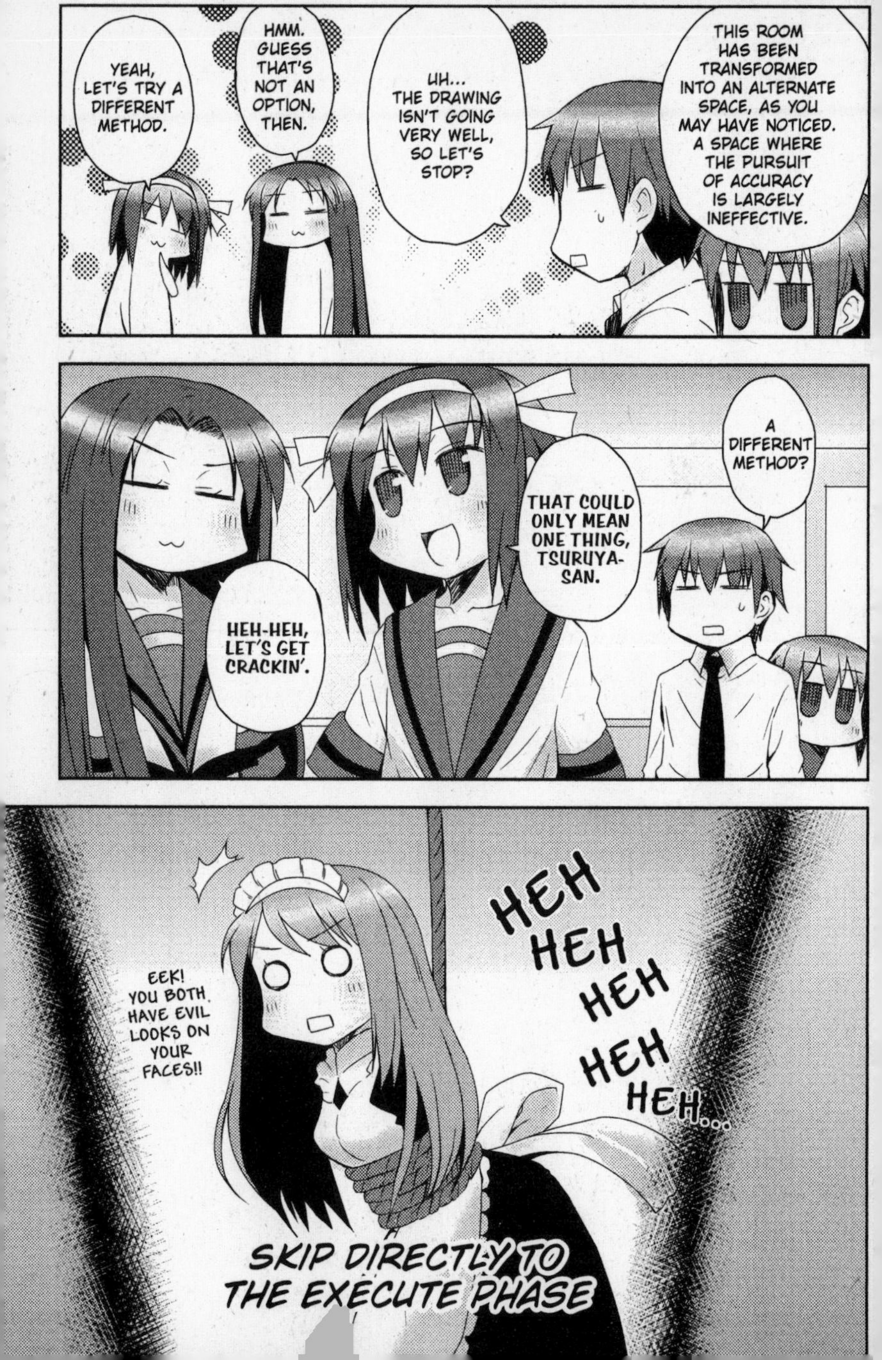
THIS ROOM HAS BEEN TRANSFORMED INTO AN ALTERNATE SPACE, AS YOU MAY HAVE NOTICED. A SPACE WHERE THE PURSUIT OF ACCURACY IS LARGELY INEFFECTIVE.
UH... THE DRAWING ISN'T GOING VERY WELL, SO LET'S STOP?
HMM. GUESS THAT'S NOT AN OPTION, THEN.
YEAH, LET'S TRY A DIFFERENT METHOD.
A DIFFERENT METHOD?
THAT COULD ONLY MEAN ONE THING, TSURUYA-SAN.
HEH-HEH, LET'S GET CRACKIN'.
HEH HEH HEH HEH HEH...
EEK! YOU BOTH HAVE EVIL LOOKS ON YOUR FACES!!
SKIP DIRECTLY TO THE EXECUTE PHASE

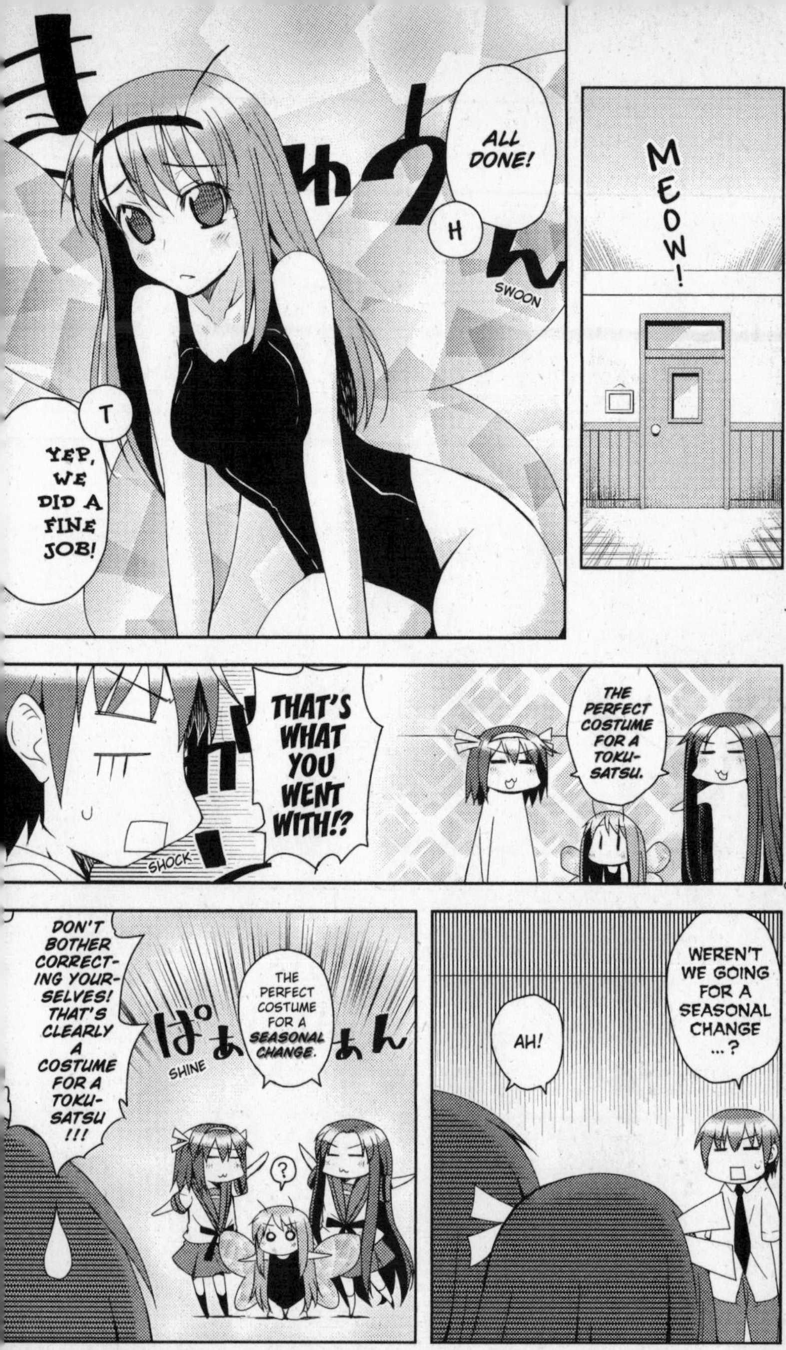
MEOW!
ALL DONE!
H
SWOON
T
YEP, WE DID A FINE JOB!
THE PERFECT COSTUME FOR A TOKU-SATSU.
THAT'S WHAT YOU WENT WITH!?
SHOCK
WEREN'T WE GOING FOR A SEASONAL CHANGE ...?
AH!
THE PERFECT COSTUME FOR A SEASONAL CHANGE.
SHINE
?
DON'T BOTHER CORRECTING YOURSELVES! THAT'S CLEARLY A COSTUME FOR A TOKU-SATSU!!!

•Haruhi-chan •SOS Brigade brigade chief. Occasionally expands on the fundamental ways to fail at life.

•Kyon •Supposed to be the main character in this story. The only person in this story with any common sense and resident straight man.

•Mikuru-chan •Actually from the future. Tends to find herself targeted and captured whenever she has free time.

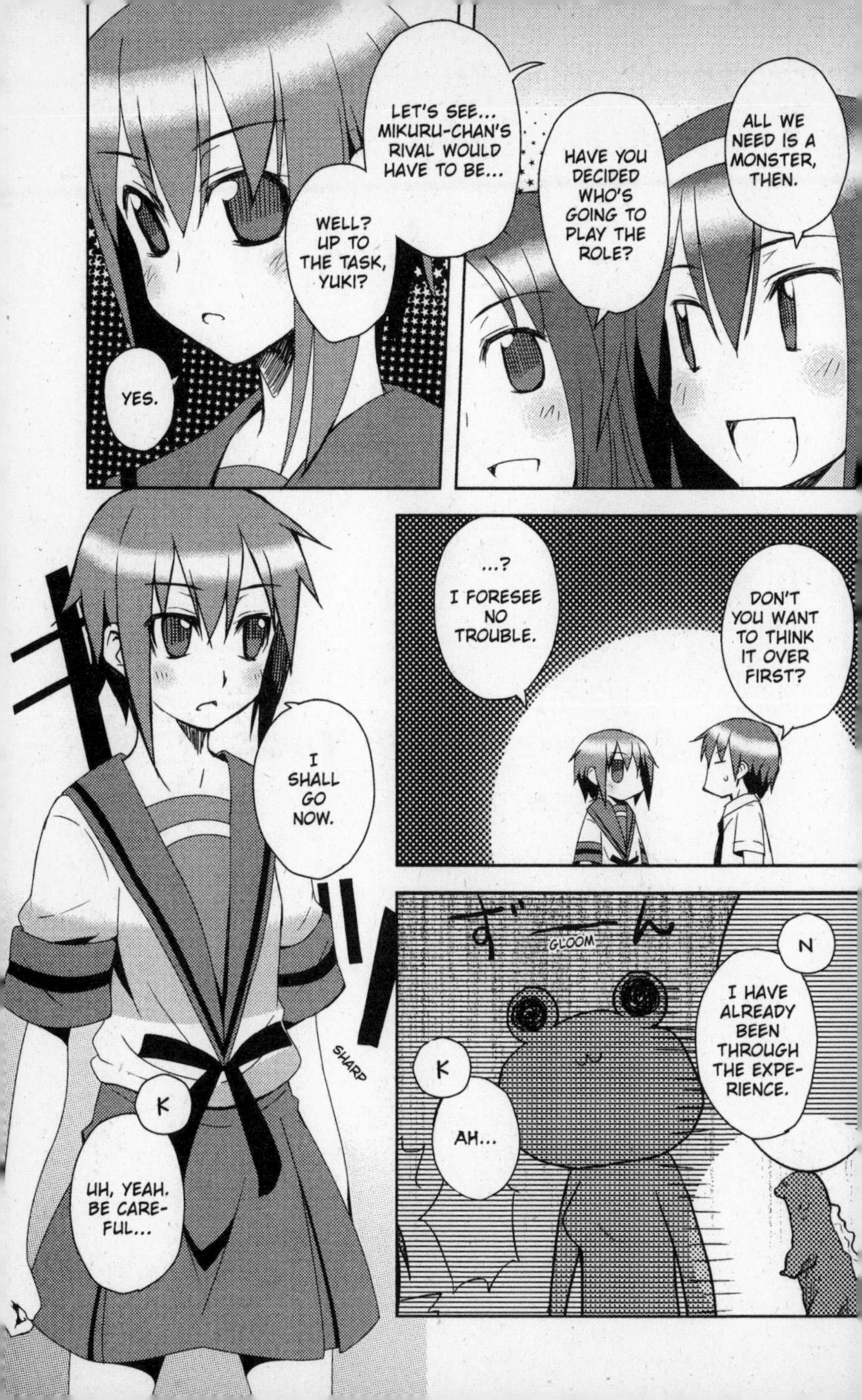
ALL WE NEED IS A MONSTER, THEN.
HAVE YOU DECIDED WHO'S GOING TO PLAY THE ROLE?
LET'S SEE... MIKURU-CHAN'S RIVAL WOULD HAVE TO BE...
WELL? UP TO THE TASK, YUKI?
YES.
DON'T YOU WANT TO THINK IT OVER FIRST?
...? I FORESEE NO TROUBLE.
N
I HAVE ALREADY BEEN THROUGH THE EXPE-RIENCE.
GLOOM
K
AH...
I SHALL GO NOW.
SHARP
K
UH, YEAH. BE CARE-FUL...

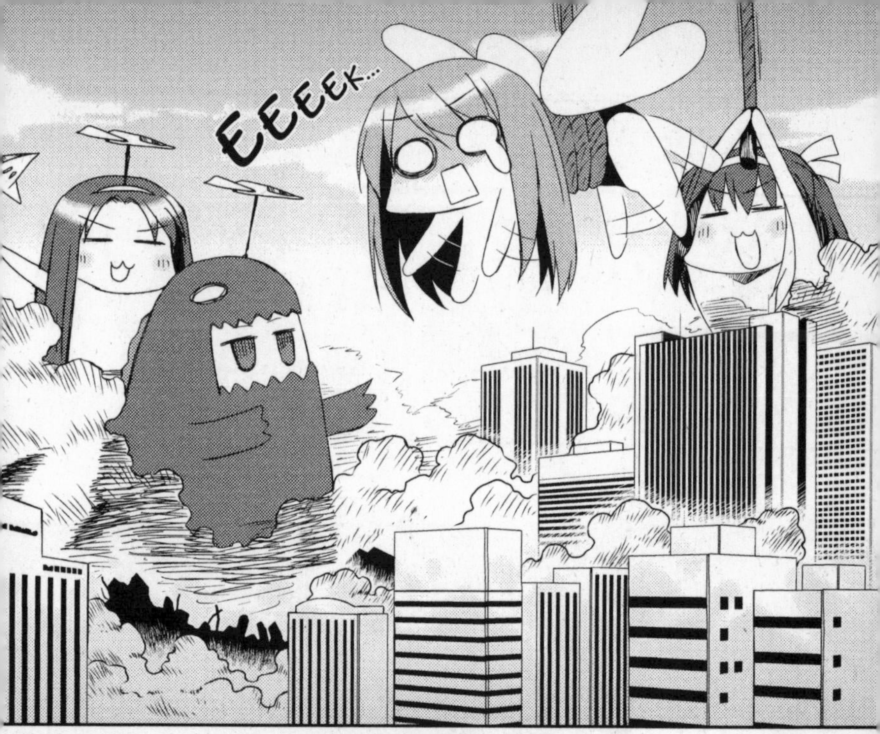
EEEEK...

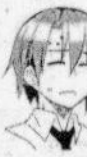

•Koizumi •An enigmatic transfer student who happens to be an esper.
Tends to leave his collar open.

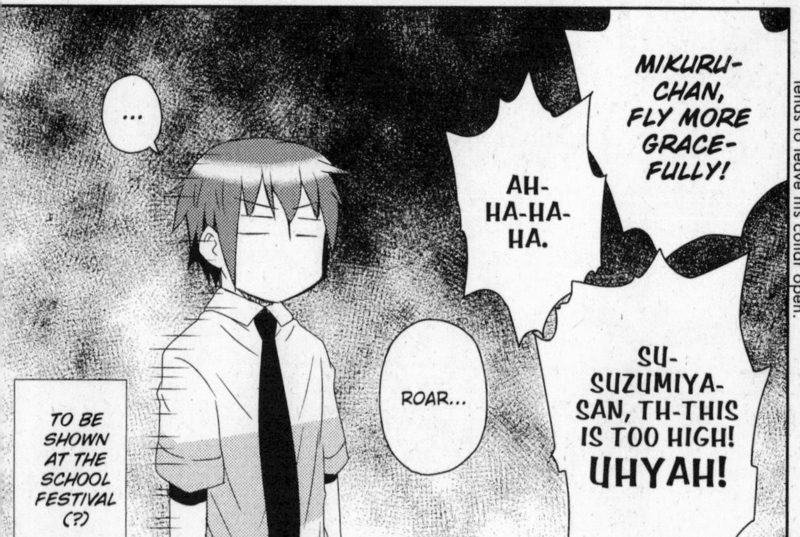
MIKURU-CHAN, FLY MORE GRACE-FULLY!
AH-HA-HA-HA.
SU-SUZUMIYA-SAN, TH-THIS IS TOO HIGH! UHYAH!
ROAR...
...
TO BE SHOWN AT THE SCHOOL FESTIVAL (?)

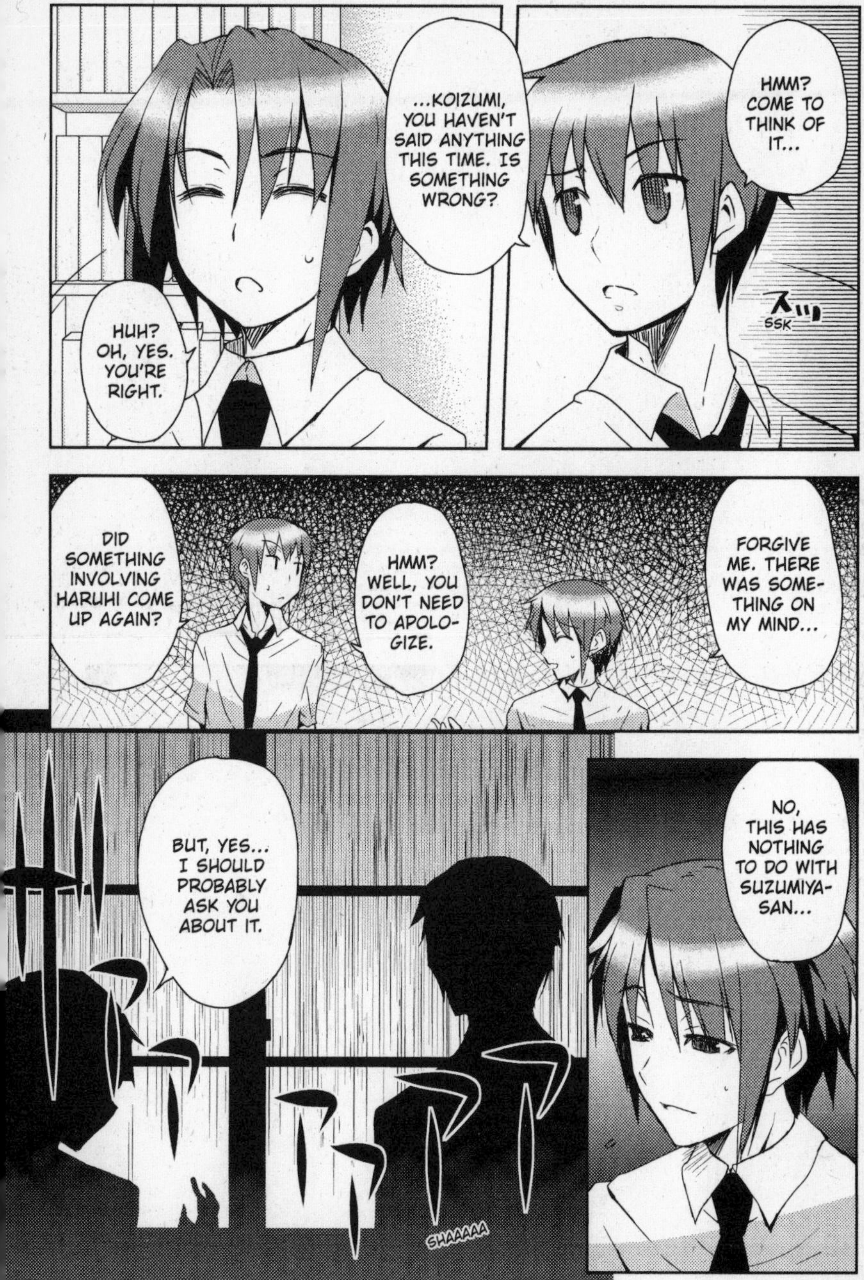
HMM? COME TO THINK OF IT...
SSK
...KOIZUMI, YOU HAVEN'T SAID ANYTHING THIS TIME. IS SOMETHING WRONG?
HUH? OH, YES. YOU'RE RIGHT.
FORGIVE ME. THERE WAS SOME-THING ON MY MIND...
HMM? WELL, YOU DON'T NEED TO APOLO-GIZE.
DID SOMETHING INVOLVING HARUHI COME UP AGAIN?
NO, THIS HAS NOTHING TO DO WITH SUZUMIYA-SAN...
BUT, YES... I SHOULD PROBABLY ASK YOU ABOUT IT.
SHAAAAA

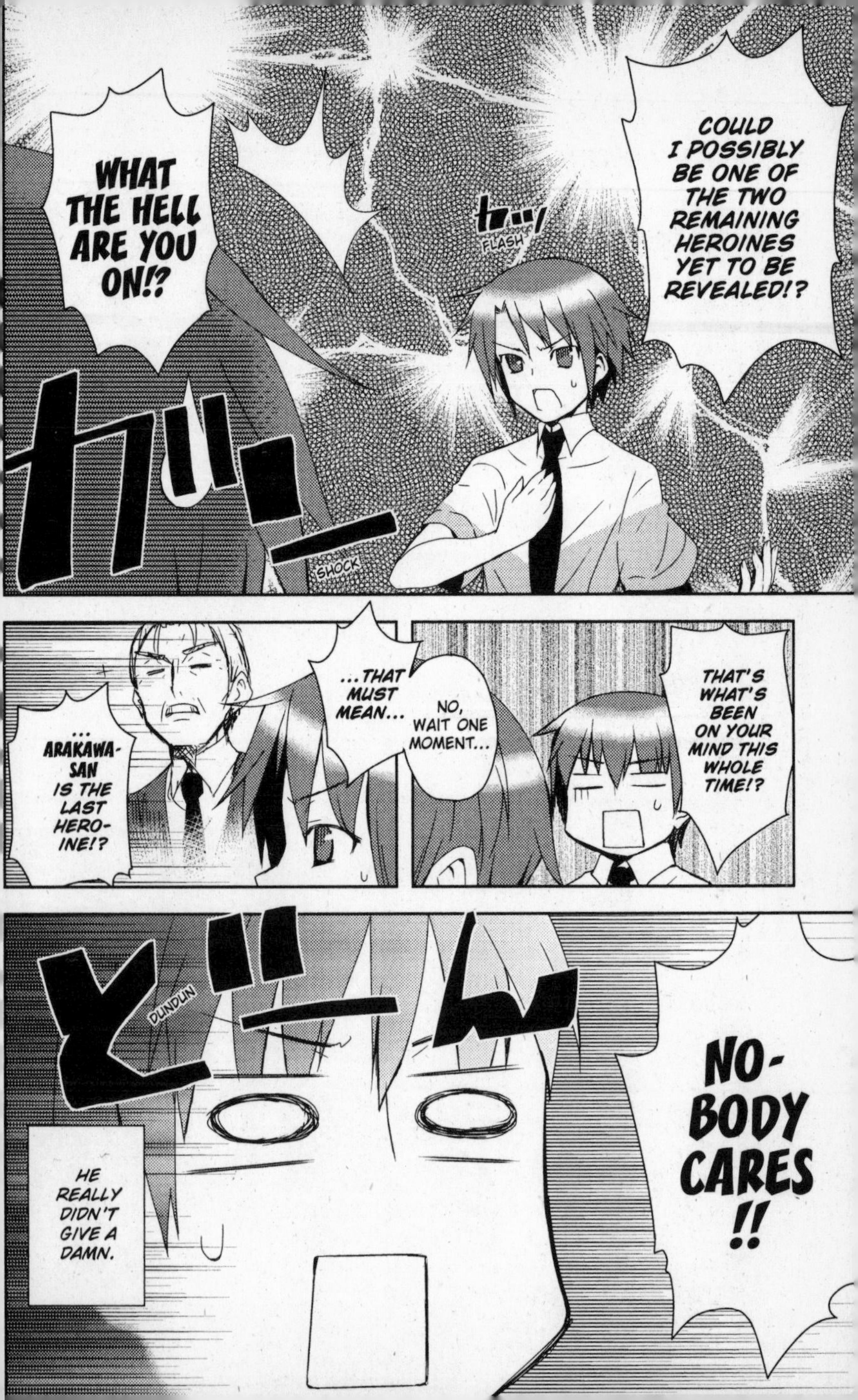
COULD I POSSIBLY BE ONE OF THE TWO REMAINING HEROINES YET TO BE REVEALED!?
FLASH
WHAT THE HELL ARE YOU ON!?
SHOCK
THAT'S WHAT'S BEEN ON YOUR MIND THIS WHOLE TIME!?
NO, WAIT ONE MOMENT...
...THAT MUST MEAN...
...ARAKAWA-SAN IS THE LAST HEROINE!?
NO-BODY CARES!!
DUNDUN
HE REALLY DIDN'T GIVE A DAMN.

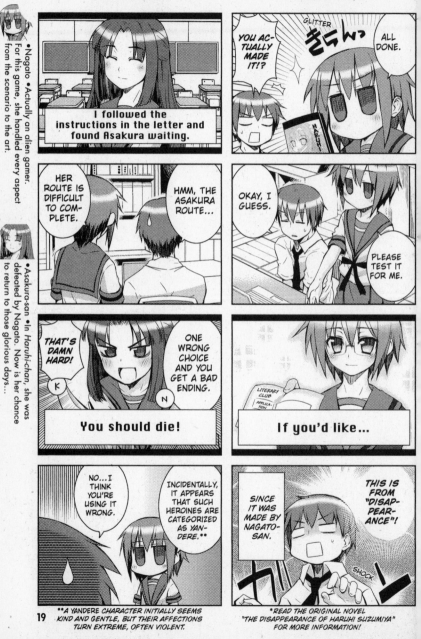

COMPLETE

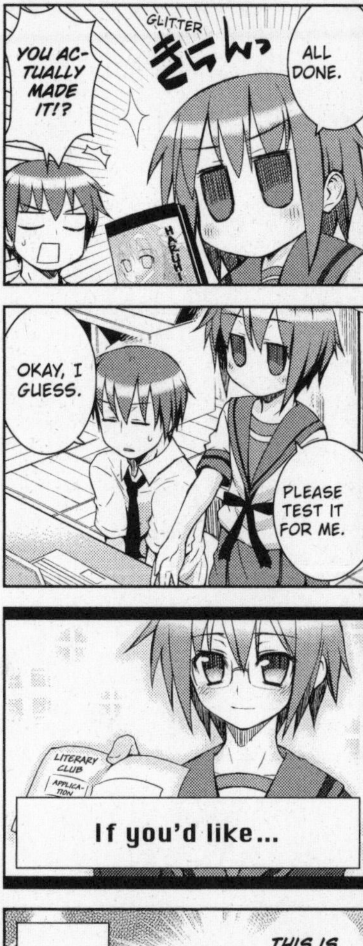
ALL DONE.
GLITTER
きらんっ
YOU ACTUALLY MADE IT!?
PLEASE TEST IT FOR ME.
OKAY, I GUESS.
LITERARY CLUB
APPLICATION
If you'd like...
THIS IS FROM "DISAPPEARANCE"!
SINCE IT WAS MADE BY NAGATO-SAN.
SHOCK

*READ THE ORIGINAL NOVEL "THE DISAPPEARANCE OF HARUHI SUZUMIYA" FOR MORE INFORMATION!

DIFFICULTY

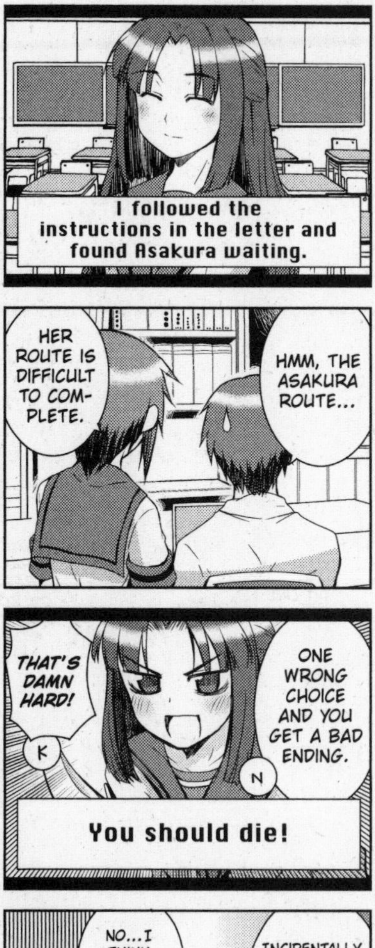
I followed the instructions in the letter and found Asakura waiting.
HMM, THE ASAKURA ROUTE...
HER ROUTE IS DIFFICULT TO COMPLETE.
ONE WRONG CHOICE AND YOU GET A BAD ENDING.
N
THAT'S DAMN HARD!
K
You should die!
INCIDENTALLY, IT APPEARS THAT SUCH HEROINES ARE CATEGORIZED AS YANDERE.**
NO...I THINK YOU'RE USING IT WRONG.

**A YANDERE CHARACTER INITIALLY SEEMS KIND AND GENTLE, BUT THEIR AFFECTIONS TURN EXTREME, OFTEN VIOLENT.

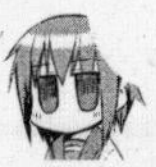

•Nagato •Actually an alien gamer. For this game, she handled every aspect from the scenario to the art.

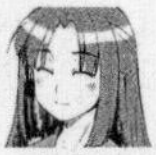

•Asakura-san •In *Haruhi-chan*, she was defeated by Nagato. Now is her chance to return to those glorious days...

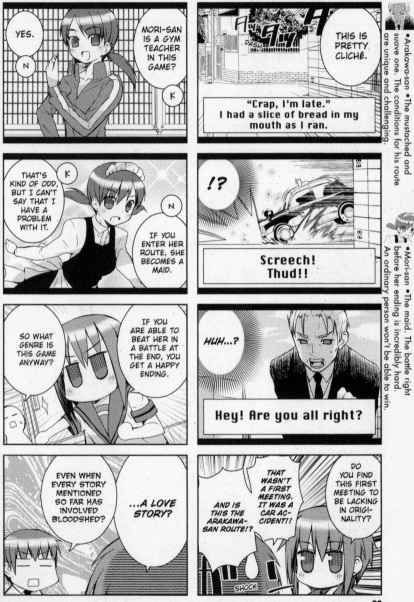

•Arakawa-san •The mustached and suave one. The conditions for his route are unique and challenging.

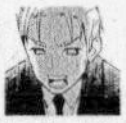

•Mori-san •The maid. The battle right before her ending is incredibly hard. An ordinary person won't be able to win.

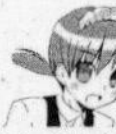

FIRST MEETING

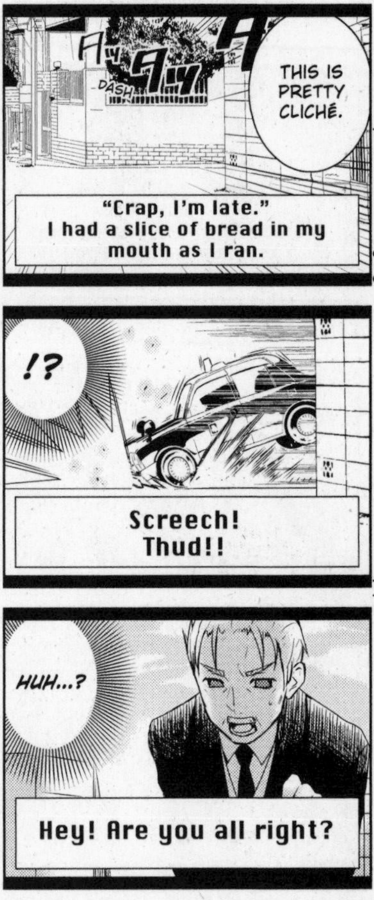
THIS IS PRETTY CLICHÉ.
DASH
"Crap, I'm late." I had a slice of bread in my mouth as I ran.
!?
Screech! Thud!!
HUH...?
Hey! Are you all right?
DO YOU FIND THIS FIRST MEETING TO BE LACKING IN ORIGI-NALITY?
THAT WASN'T A FIRST MEETING. IT WAS A CAR AC-CIDENT!!
AND IS THIS THE ARAKAWA-SAN ROUTE!?
SHOCK

GENRE

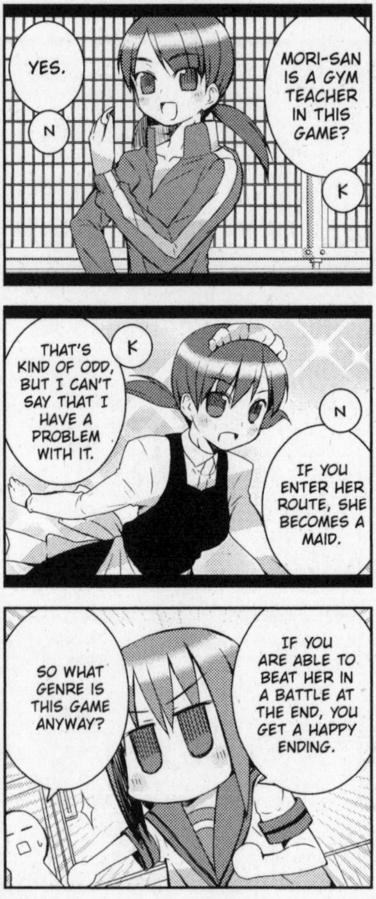
MORI-SAN IS A GYM TEACHER IN THIS GAME?
K
YES.
N
N
IF YOU ENTER HER ROUTE, SHE BECOMES A MAID.
K
THAT'S KIND OF ODD, BUT I CAN'T SAY THAT I HAVE A PROBLEM WITH IT.
IF YOU ARE ABLE TO BEAT HER IN A BATTLE AT THE END, YOU GET A HAPPY ENDING.
SO WHAT GENRE IS THIS GAME ANYWAY?
...A LOVE STORY?
EVEN WHEN EVERY STORY MENTIONED SO FAR HAS INVOLVED BLOODSHED?

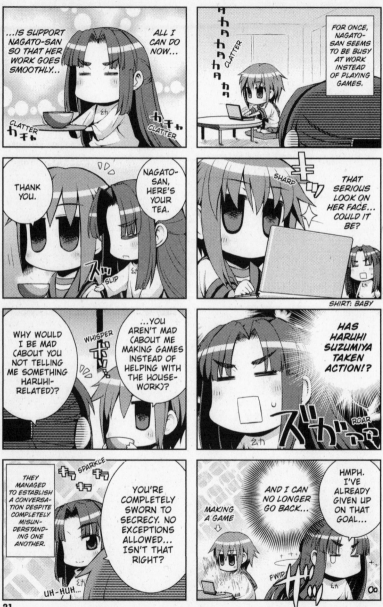

ACTION

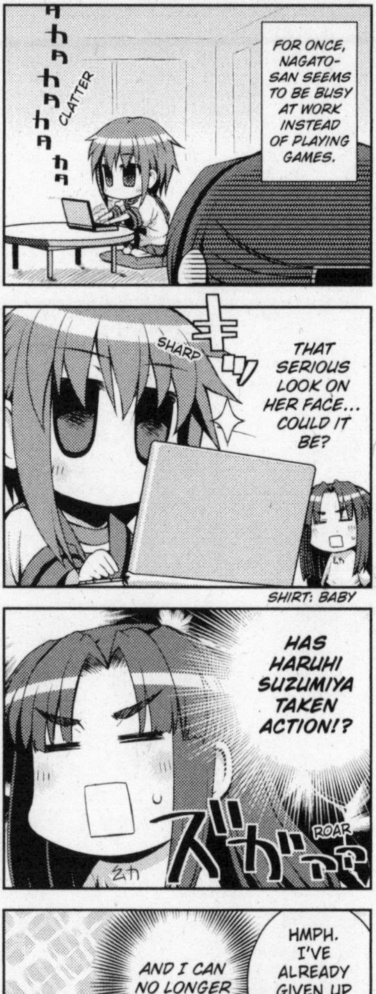

FOR ONCE, NAGATO-SAN SEEMS TO BE BUSY AT WORK INSTEAD OF PLAYING GAMES.
CLATTER
SHARP
THAT SERIOUS LOOK ON HER FACE... COULD IT BE?
SHIRT: BABY
HAS HARUHI SUZUMIYA TAKEN ACTION!?
ROAR
HMPH. I'VE ALREADY GIVEN UP ON THAT GOAL...
AND I CAN NO LONGER GO BACK...
MAKING A GAME
FWIP

SUPPORT

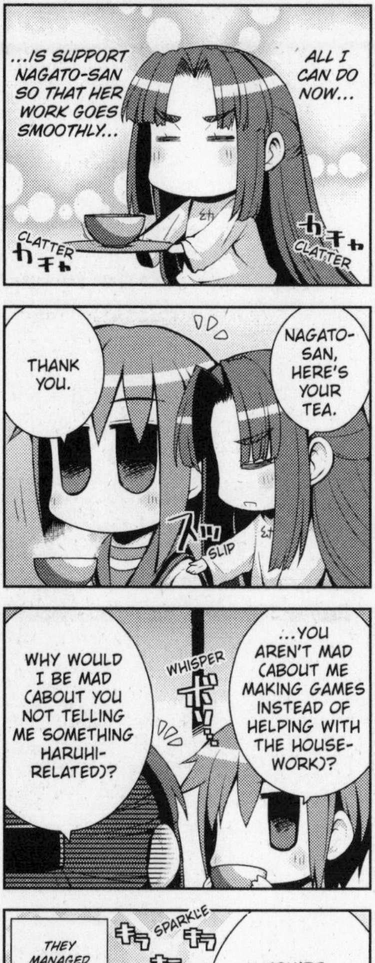

ALL I CAN DO NOW...
...IS SUPPORT NAGATO-SAN SO THAT HER WORK GOES SMOOTHLY...
CLATTER
CLATTER
NAGATO-SAN, HERE'S YOUR TEA.
THANK YOU.
SLIP
...YOU AREN'T MAD (ABOUT ME MAKING GAMES INSTEAD OF HELPING WITH THE HOUSE-WORK)?
WHISPER
WHY WOULD I BE MAD (ABOUT YOU NOT TELLING ME SOMETHING HARUHI-RELATED)?
YOU'RE COMPLETELY SWORN TO SECRECY. NO EXCEPTIONS ALLOWED... ISN'T THAT RIGHT?
SPARKLE
UH-HUH...
THEY MANAGED TO ESTABLISH A CONVERSATION DESPITE COMPLETELY MISUNDERSTANDING ONE ANOTHER.

DOCUMENT

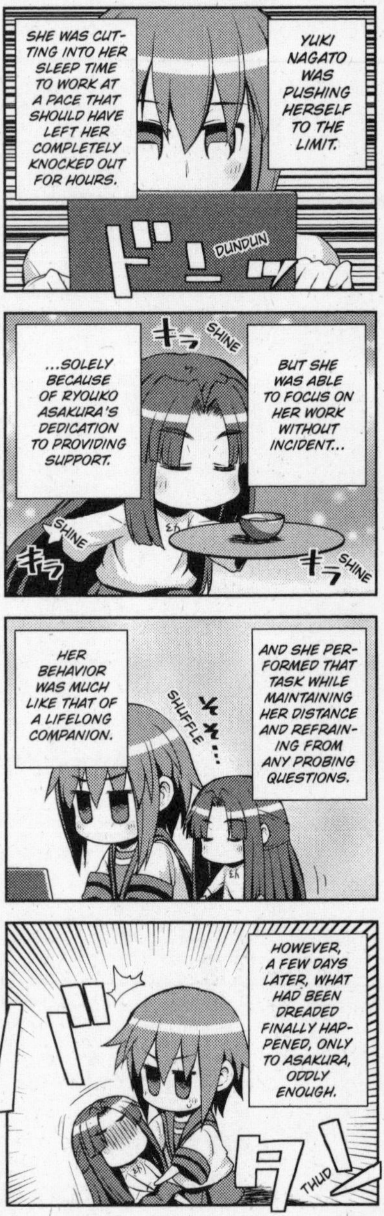
YUKI NAGATO WAS PUSHING HERSELF TO THE LIMIT.
SHE WAS CUTTING INTO HER SLEEP TIME TO WORK AT A PACE THAT SHOULD HAVE LEFT HER COMPLETELY KNOCKED OUT FOR HOURS.
DUNDUN
BUT SHE WAS ABLE TO FOCUS ON HER WORK WITHOUT INCIDENT...
SHINE
...SOLELY BECAUSE OF RYOUKO ASAKURA'S DEDICATION TO PROVIDING SUPPORT.
SHINE
SHINE
AND SHE PERFORMED THAT TASK WHILE MAINTAINING HER DISTANCE AND REFRAINING FROM ANY PROBING QUESTIONS.
SHUFFLE
HER BEHAVIOR WAS MUCH LIKE THAT OF A LIFELONG COMPANION.
HOWEVER, A FEW DAYS LATER, WHAT HAD BEEN DREADED FINALLY HAPPENED, ONLY TO ASAKURA, ODDLY ENOUGH.
THUD

SOMETHING WRONG

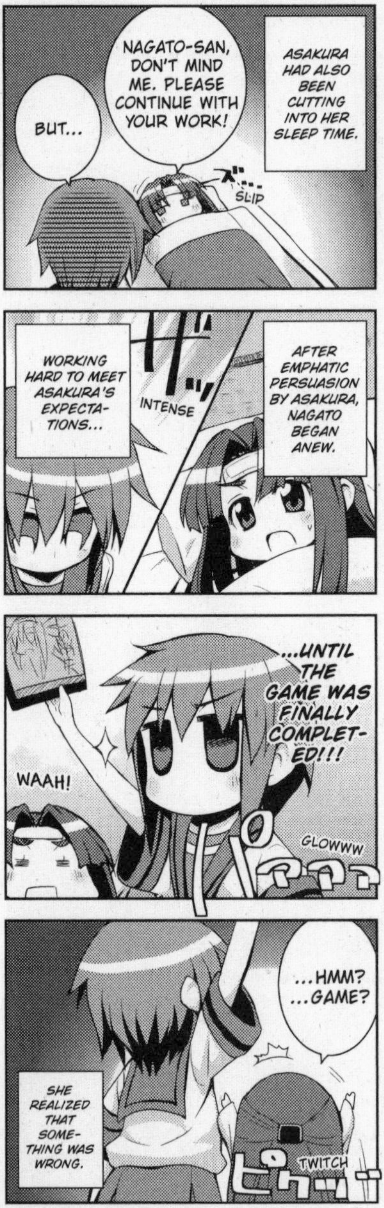
ASAKURA HAD ALSO BEEN CUTTING INTO HER SLEEP TIME.
NAGATO-SAN, DON'T MIND ME. PLEASE CONTINUE WITH YOUR WORK!
SLIP
BUT...
AFTER EMPHATIC PERSUASION BY ASAKURA, NAGATO BEGAN ANEW.
INTENSE
WORKING HARD TO MEET ASAKURA'S EXPECTATIONS...
...UNTIL THE GAME WAS FINALLY COMPLETED!!!
GLOWWW
WAAH!
...HMM? ...GAME?
TWITCH
SHE REALIZED THAT SOMETHING WAS WRONG.

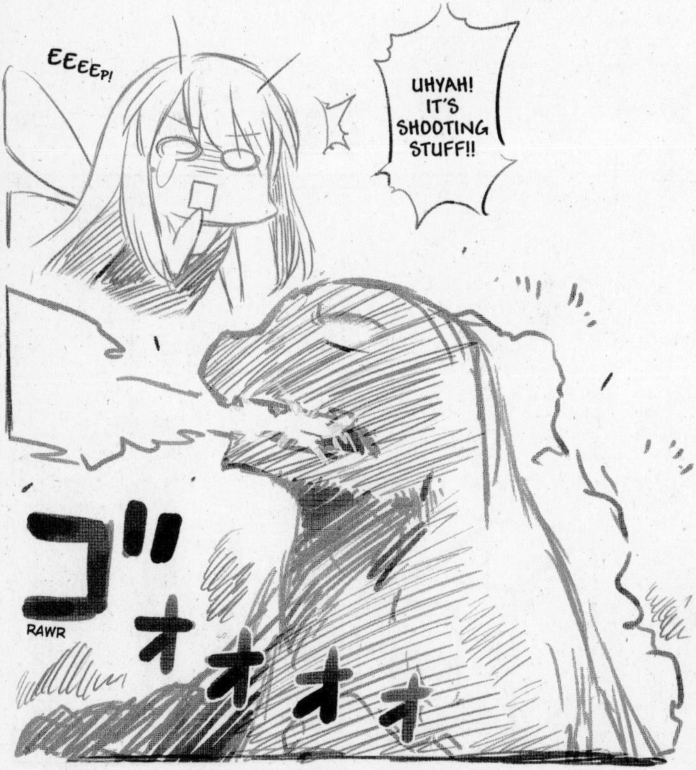
UHYAH! IT'S SHOOTING STUFF!!
EEEEP!
ゴオオオオ
RAWR

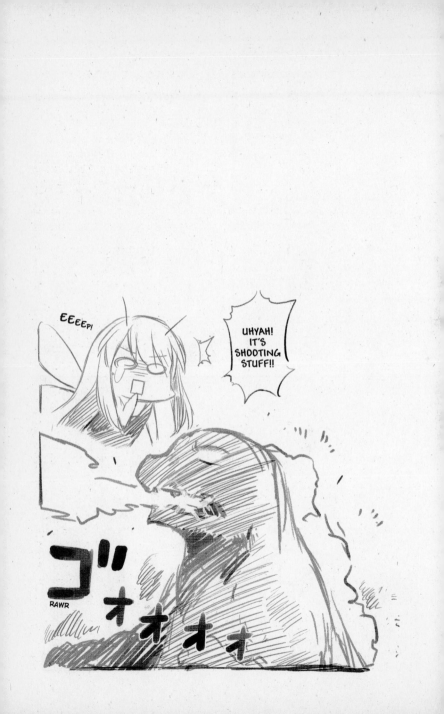

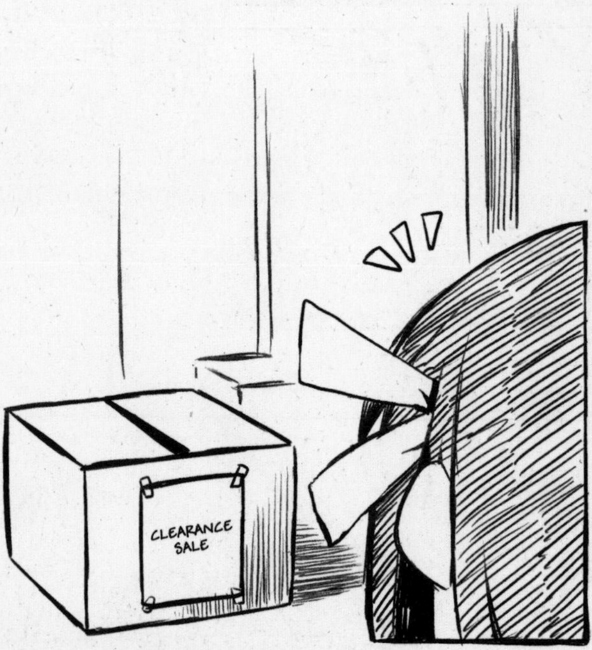
CLEARANCE SALE

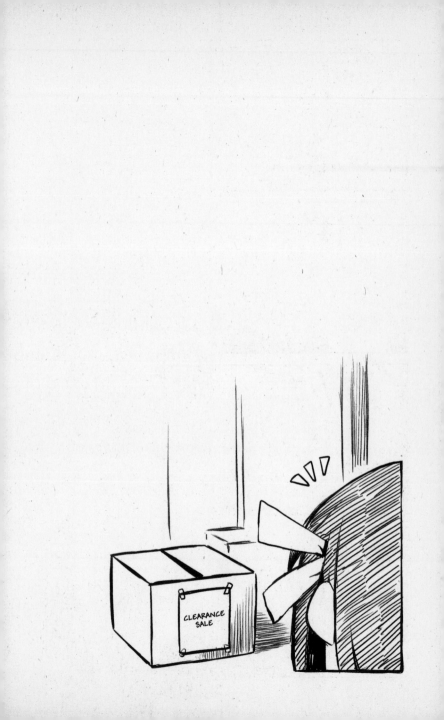

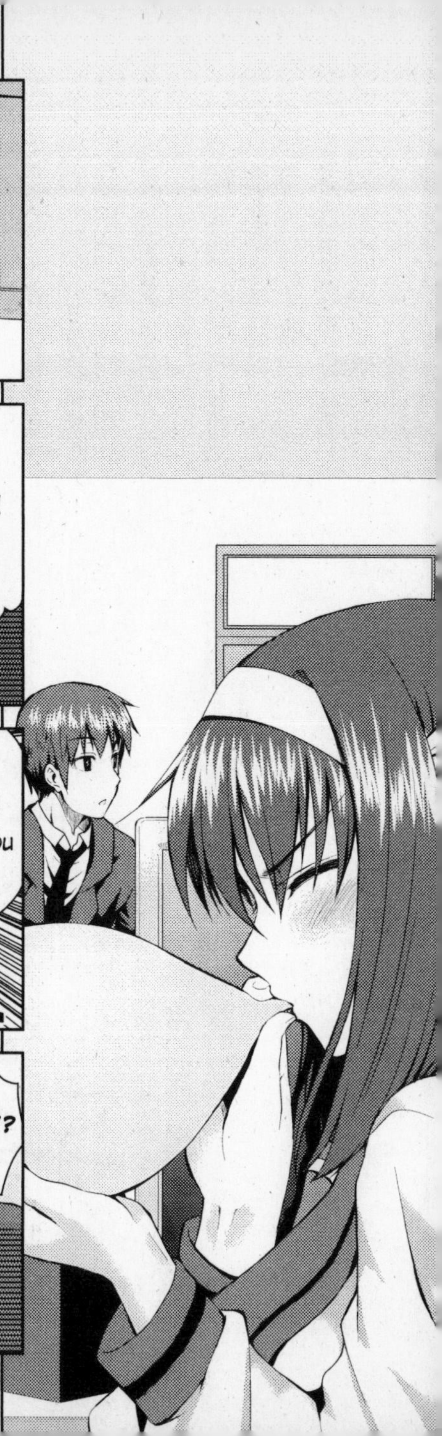

BALLOON

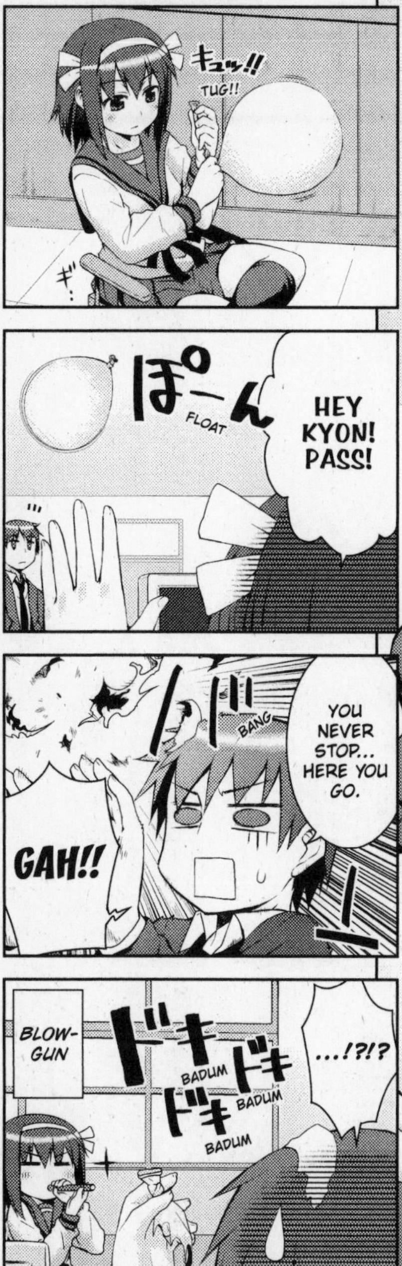

キュッ!!
TUG!!
HEY KYON! PASS!
ぽーん
FLOAT
YOU NEVER STOP... HERE YOU GO.
BANG
GAH!!
...!?!?
ドキ ドキ ドキ
BADUM BADUM BADUM
BLOW-GUN

IN THE FACE

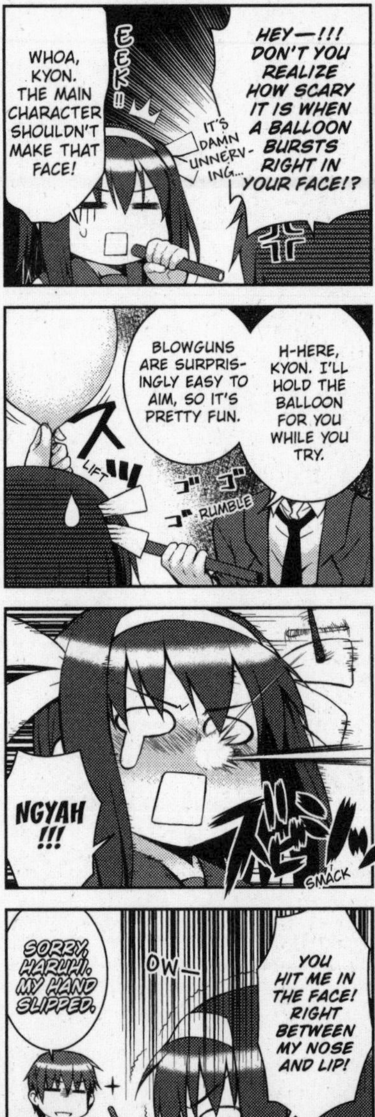
HEY—!!! DON'T YOU REALIZE HOW SCARY IT IS WHEN A BALLOON BURSTS RIGHT IN YOUR FACE!?
IT'S DAMN UNNERVING...
EEK!!
WHOA, KYON. THE MAIN CHARACTER SHOULDN'T MAKE THAT FACE!
H-HERE, KYON. I'LL HOLD THE BALLOON FOR YOU WHILE YOU TRY.
BLOWGUNS ARE SURPRISINGLY EASY TO AIM, SO IT'S PRETTY FUN.
RUMBLE
LIFT
SMACK
NGYAH!!!
YOU HIT ME IN THE FACE! RIGHT BETWEEN MY NOSE AND LIP!
OW—
SORRY, HARUHI. MY HAND SLIPPED.

ORIFICE

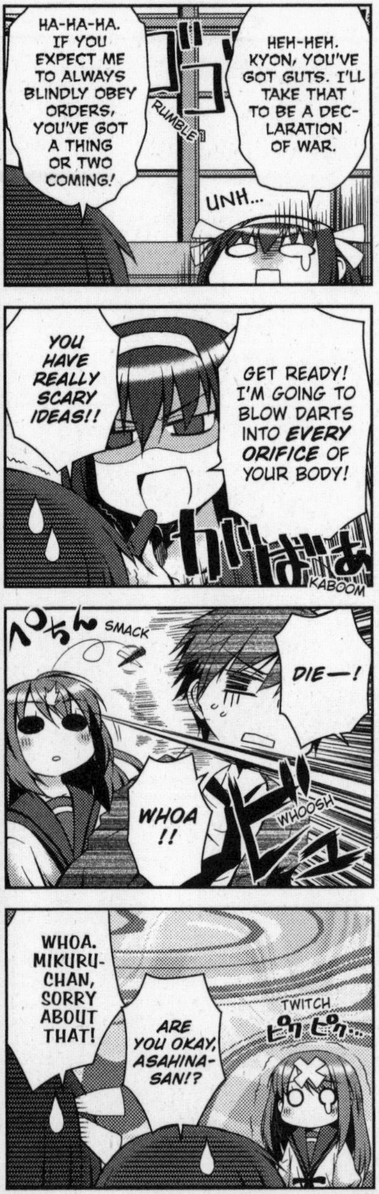
HEH-HEH. KYON, YOU'VE GOT GUTS. I'LL TAKE THAT TO BE A DECLARATION OF WAR.
RUMBLE
UNH...
HA-HA-HA. IF YOU EXPECT ME TO ALWAYS BLINDLY OBEY ORDERS, YOU'VE GOT A THING OR TWO COMING!
GET READY! I'M GOING TO BLOW DARTS INTO EVERY ORIFICE OF YOUR BODY!
KABOOM
YOU HAVE REALLY SCARY IDEAS!!
DIE—!
SMACK
WHOOSH
WHOA!!
TWITCH
ARE YOU OKAY, ASAHINA-SAN!?
WHOA. MIKURU-CHAN, SORRY ABOUT THAT!

•Haruhi-chan •SOS Brigade brigade chief. Enjoys the primitive nature of blowguns.

•Kyon •Supposed to be the main character in this story. Occasionally gets pissed off.

•Mikuru-chan •Actually from the future. Her role is so pitiful that she must have been born under an unlucky star.

*THE CHARACTERS IN THIS MANGA HAVE RECEIVED SPECIAL TRAINING. YOU SHOULD NEVER FIRE A BLOWGUN AT ANOTHER PERSON.

ULTIMATE SACRIFICE

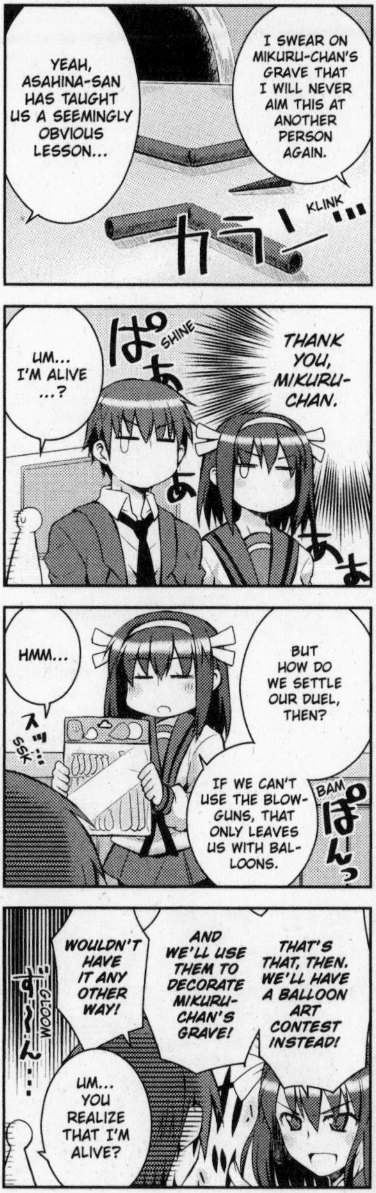
I SWEAR ON MIKURU-CHAN'S GRAVE THAT I WILL NEVER AIM THIS AT ANOTHER PERSON AGAIN.
YEAH, ASAHINA-SAN HAS TAUGHT US A SEEMINGLY OBVIOUS LESSON...
KLINK
カラン
THANK YOU, MIKURU-CHAN.
SHINE
ぱぁぁぁ
UM... I'M ALIVE ...?
BUT HOW DO WE SETTLE OUR DUEL, THEN?
HMM...
BAM
ぽんっ
IF WE CAN'T USE THE BLOW-GUNS, THAT ONLY LEAVES US WITH BALLOONS.
スッ
SSK
THAT'S THAT, THEN. WE'LL HAVE A BALLOON ART CONTEST INSTEAD!
AND WE'LL USE THEM TO DECORATE MIKURU-CHAN'S GRAVE!
WOULDN'T HAVE IT ANY OTHER WAY!
ずーん...
GLOOM
UM... YOU REALIZE THAT I'M ALIVE?

BALLOON FIGHT

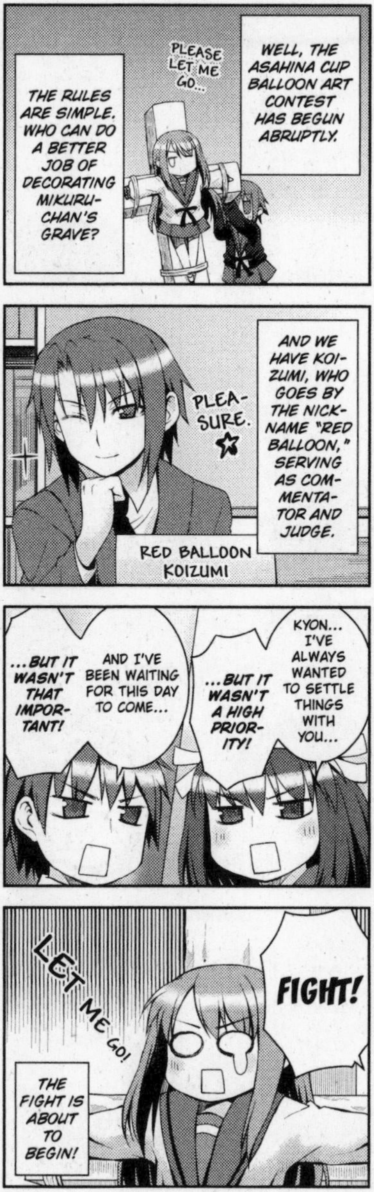
WELL, THE ASAHINA CUP BALLOON ART CONTEST HAS BEGUN ABRUPTLY.
PLEASE LET ME GO...
THE RULES ARE SIMPLE. WHO CAN DO A BETTER JOB OF DECORATING MIKURU-CHAN'S GRAVE?
AND WE HAVE KOIZUMI, WHO GOES BY THE NICKNAME "RED BALLOON," SERVING AS COMMENTATOR AND JUDGE.
PLEASURE.
RED BALLOON KOIZUMI
KYON... I'VE ALWAYS WANTED TO SETTLE THINGS WITH YOU...
...BUT IT WASN'T A HIGH PRIORITY!
AND I'VE BEEN WAITING FOR THIS DAY TO COME...
...BUT IT WASN'T THAT IMPORTANT!
FIGHT!
LET ME GO!
THE FIGHT IS ABOUT TO BEGIN!

10

•Koizumi •An enigmatic transfer student who happens to be an esper. The judge who unabashedly calls himself the Red Balloon.

AMATEUR

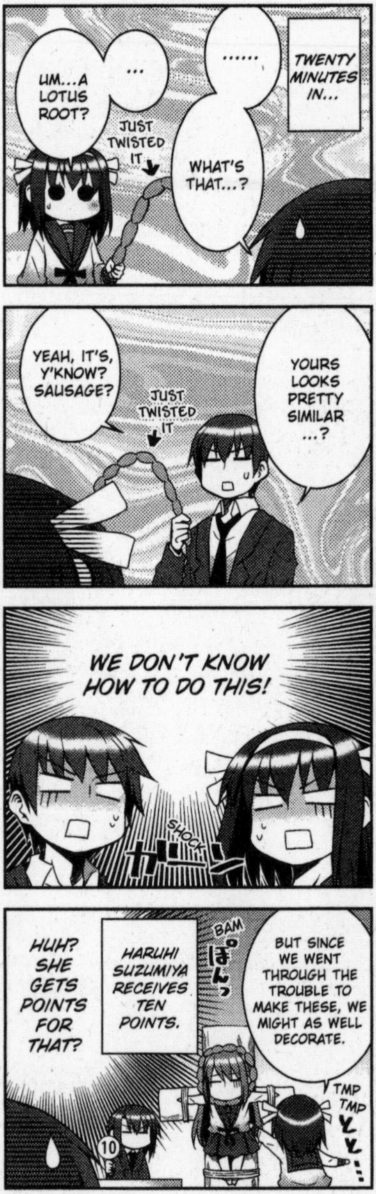
TWENTY MINUTES IN...
......
WHAT'S THAT...?
...
UM...A LOTUS ROOT?
JUST TWISTED IT
YOURS LOOKS PRETTY SIMILAR ...?
JUST TWISTED IT
YEAH, IT'S, Y'KNOW? SAUSAGE?
WE DON'T KNOW HOW TO DO THIS!
SHOCK
BUT SINCE WE WENT THROUGH THE TROUBLE TO MAKE THESE, WE MIGHT AS WELL DECORATE.
BAM
TMP TMP
HARUHI SUZUMIYA RECEIVES TEN POINTS.
HUH? SHE GETS POINTS FOR THAT?
10

RESOLUTION

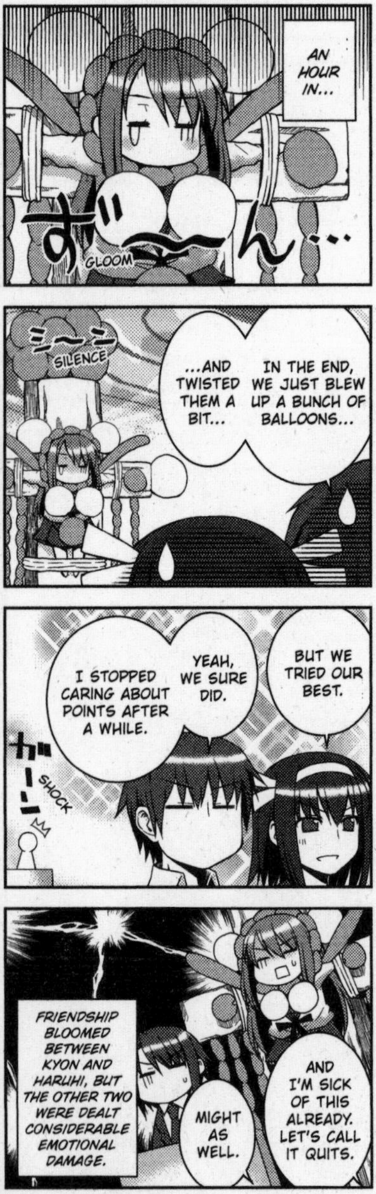
AN HOUR IN...
GLOOM
IN THE END, WE JUST BLEW UP A BUNCH OF BALLOONS...
...AND TWISTED THEM A BIT...
SILENCE
BUT WE TRIED OUR BEST.
YEAH, WE SURE DID.
I STOPPED CARING ABOUT POINTS AFTER A WHILE.
SHOCK
AND I'M SICK OF THIS ALREADY. LET'S CALL IT QUITS.
MIGHT AS WELL.
FRIENDSHIP BLOOMED BETWEEN KYON AND HARUHI, BUT THE OTHER TWO WERE DEALT CONSIDERABLE EMOTIONAL DAMAGE.

Blowguns (*fukiya*) are considered to be a wonderful sport that makes great use of your lungs. They even have a Japan Sports Fukiya Association.

Balloon art comes in many different forms, such as tying many balloons together as a decoration. The art of twisting a thin balloon into a different shape is apparently known as balloon modeling.

HAVING FUN WITH BALLOONS (THE ALIEN WAY)

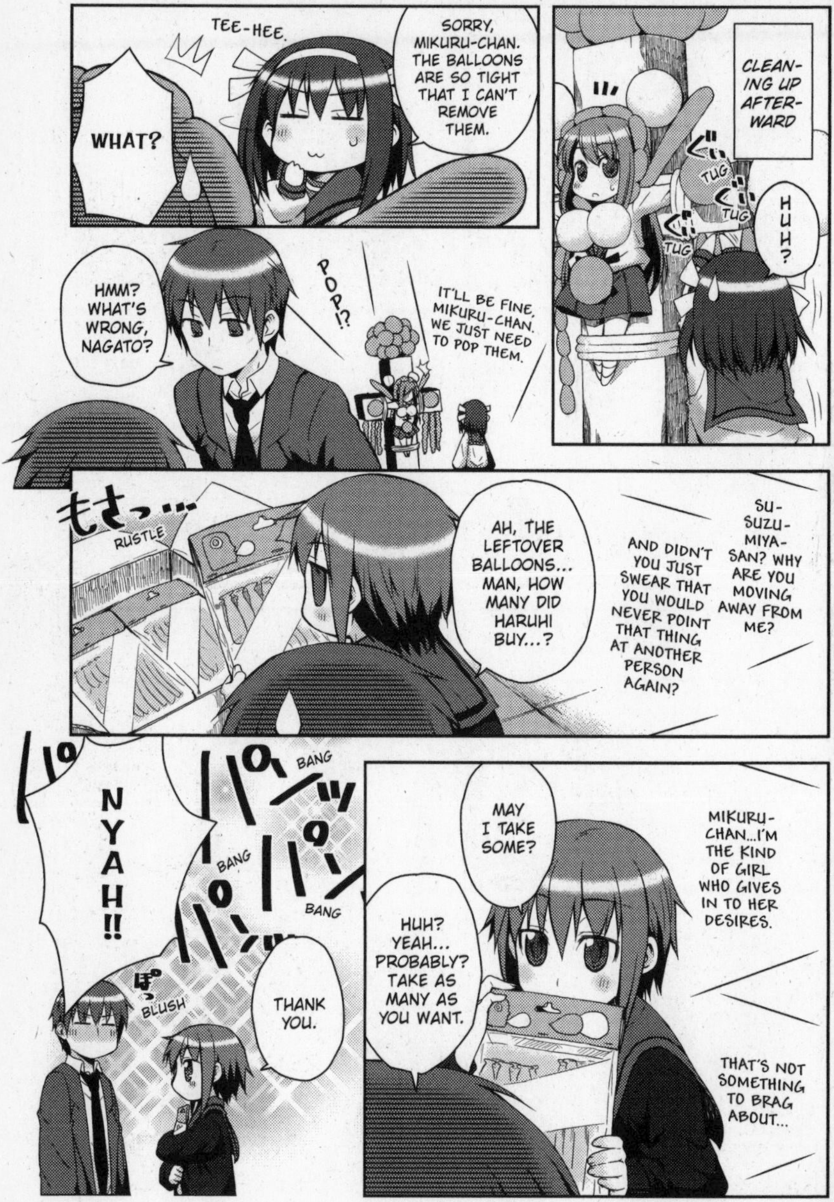
CLEANING UP AFTERWARD
TUG
TUG
TUG
HUH?
SORRY, MIKURU-CHAN. THE BALLOONS ARE SO TIGHT THAT I CAN'T REMOVE THEM.
TEE-HEE.
WHAT?
IT'LL BE FINE, MIKURU-CHAN. WE JUST NEED TO POP THEM.
POP!?
HMM? WHAT'S WRONG, NAGATO?
SU-SUZUMIYA-SAN? WHY ARE YOU MOVING AWAY FROM ME?
AND DIDN'T YOU JUST SWEAR THAT YOU WOULD NEVER POINT THAT THING AT ANOTHER PERSON AGAIN?
AH, THE LEFTOVER BALLOONS... MAN, HOW MANY DID HARUHI BUY...?
もさっ...
RUSTLE
MIKURU-CHAN...I'M THE KIND OF GIRL WHO GIVES IN TO HER DESIRES.
MAY I TAKE SOME?
HUH? YEAH... PROBABLY? TAKE AS MANY AS YOU WANT.
THAT'S NOT SOMETHING TO BRAG ABOUT...
BANG
BANG
BANG
NYAH!!
THANK YOU.
BLUSH

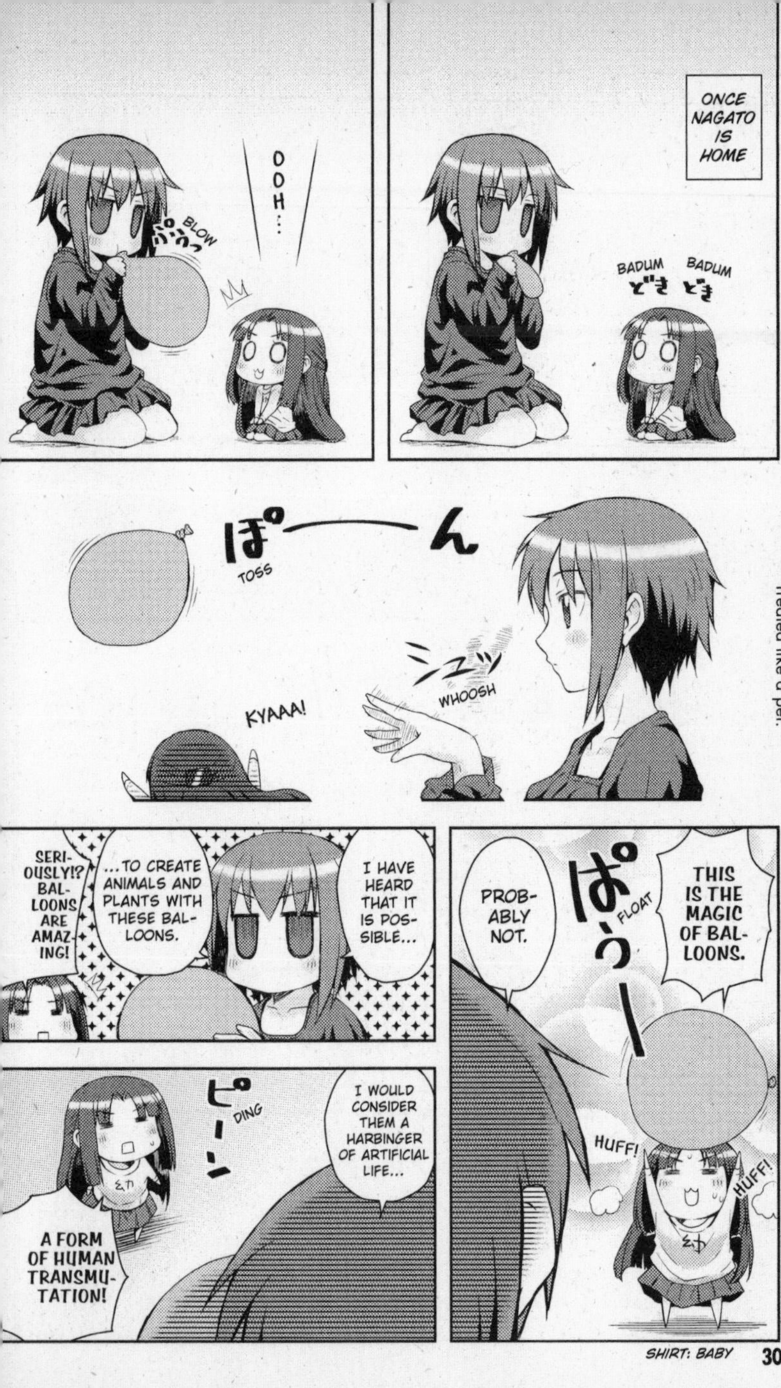
ONCE NAGATO IS HOME
BADUM BADUM
どき どき
BLOW
ぷうっ
OOH...
ぽーーん
TOSS
シュッ
WHOOSH
KYAAA!
THIS IS THE MAGIC OF BALLOONS.
ぱうー
FLOAT
PROBABLY NOT.
HUFF!
HUFF!
I HAVE HEARD THAT IT IS POSSIBLE...
...TO CREATE ANIMALS AND PLANTS WITH THESE BALLOONS.
SERIOUSLY!? BALLOONS ARE AMAZING!
I WOULD CONSIDER THEM A HARBINGER OF ARTIFICIAL LIFE...
ピーン
DING
A FORM OF HUMAN TRANSMUTATION!

•Nagato •Actually an alien gamer. Treats Achakura-san like a pet.

•Achakura-san •Back in miniature action after being destroyed in her battle with Nagato. Treated like a pet.

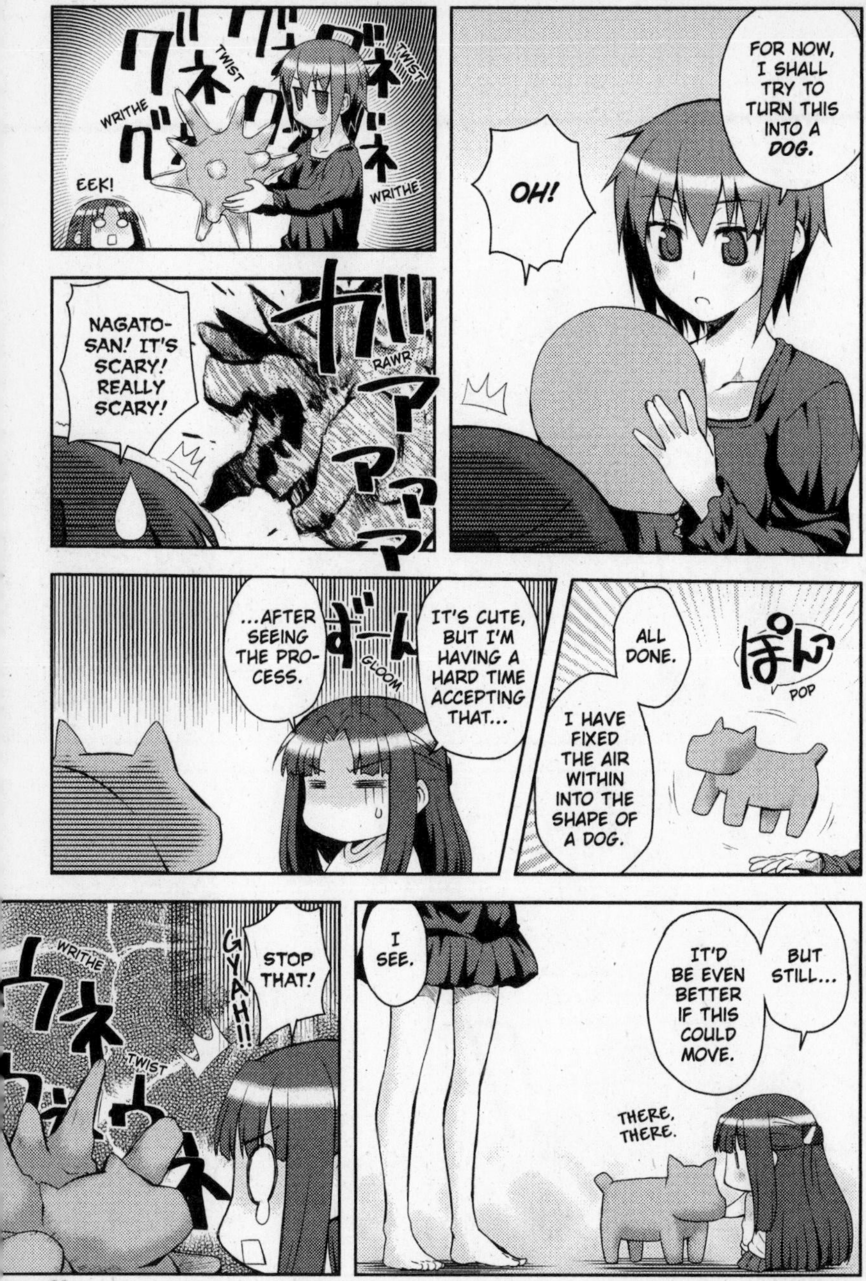

FOR NOW, I SHALL TRY TO TURN THIS INTO A *DOG*.
OH!
TWIST
TWIST
WRITHE
WRITHE
EEK!
RAWR
NAGATO-SAN! IT'S SCARY! REALLY SCARY!
POP
ALL DONE.
I HAVE FIXED THE AIR WITHIN INTO THE SHAPE OF A DOG.
IT'S CUTE, BUT I'M HAVING A HARD TIME ACCEPTING THAT...
GLOOM
...AFTER SEEING THE PRO-CESS.
BUT STILL...
IT'D BE EVEN BETTER IF THIS COULD MOVE.
I SEE.
THERE, THERE.
GYAH!!
STOP THAT!
WRITHE
TWIST

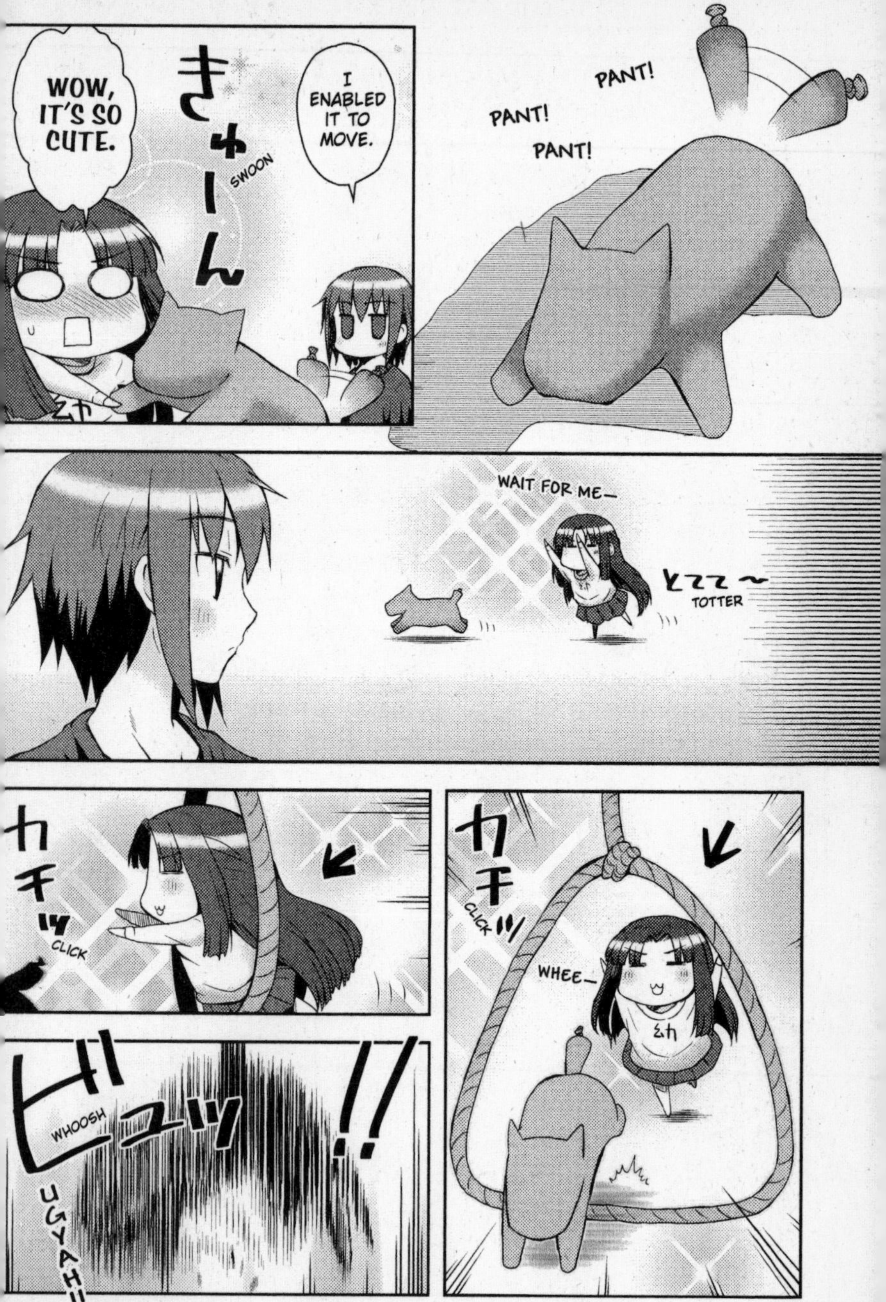
PANT!
PANT!
PANT!
I ENABLED IT TO MOVE.
きゅーん
SWOON
WOW, IT'S SO CUTE.
WAIT FOR ME~
とてて~
TOTTER
カチッ
CLICK
WHEE~
カチッ
CLICK
ビュッ!!
WHOOSH
UGYAH!!

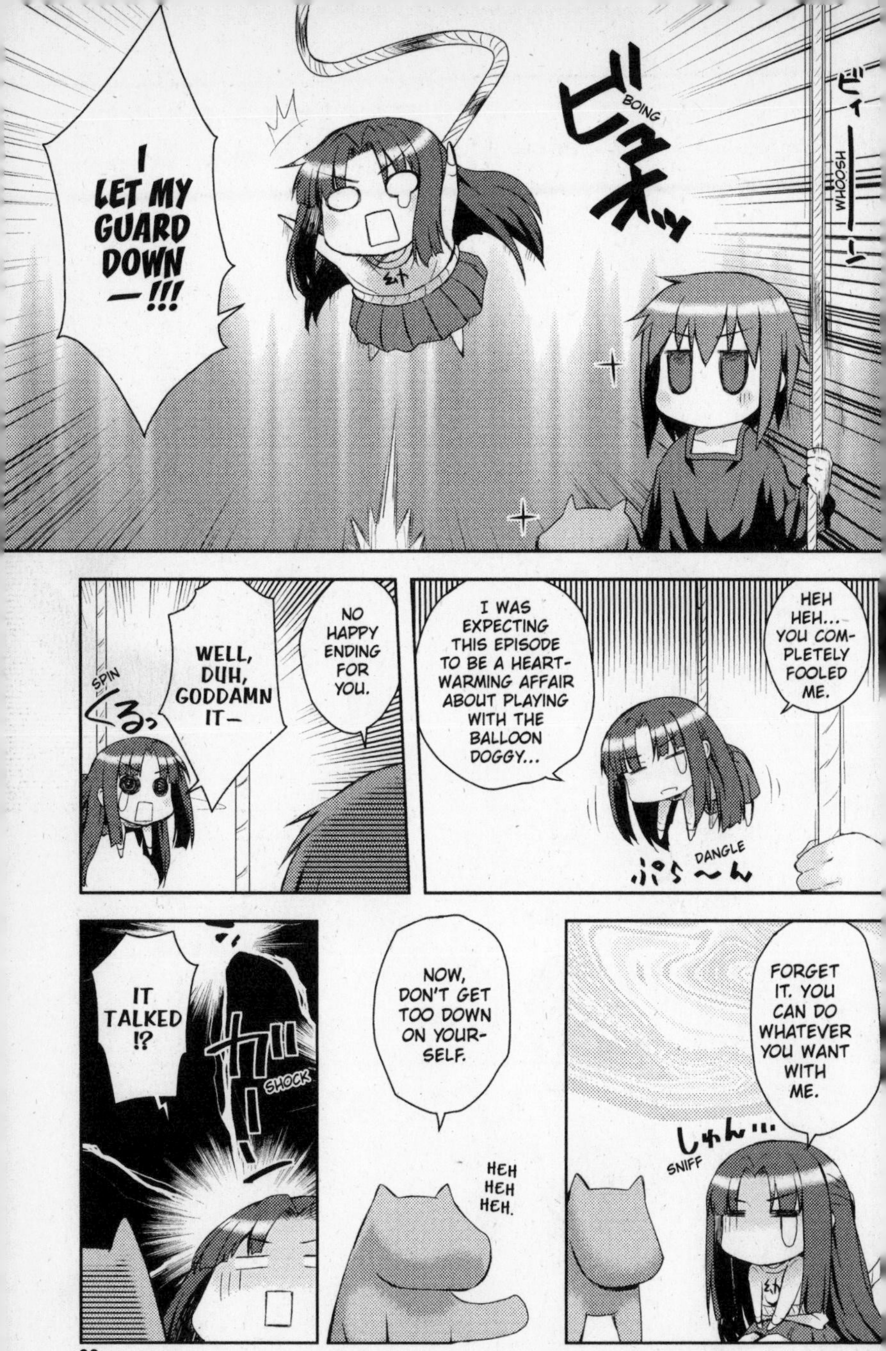
WHOOSH
BOING
I LET MY GUARD DOWN—!!!
HEH HEH... YOU COMPLETELY FOOLED ME.
I WAS EXPECTING THIS EPISODE TO BE A HEART-WARMING AFFAIR ABOUT PLAYING WITH THE BALLOON DOGGY...
ぷら～ん
DANGLE
NO HAPPY ENDING FOR YOU.
WELL, DUH, GODDAMN IT—
くるっ
SPIN
FORGET IT. YOU CAN DO WHATEVER YOU WANT WITH ME.
しゅん…
SNIFF
NOW, DON'T GET TOO DOWN ON YOURSELF.
HEH HEH HEH.
IT TALKED!?
SHOCK

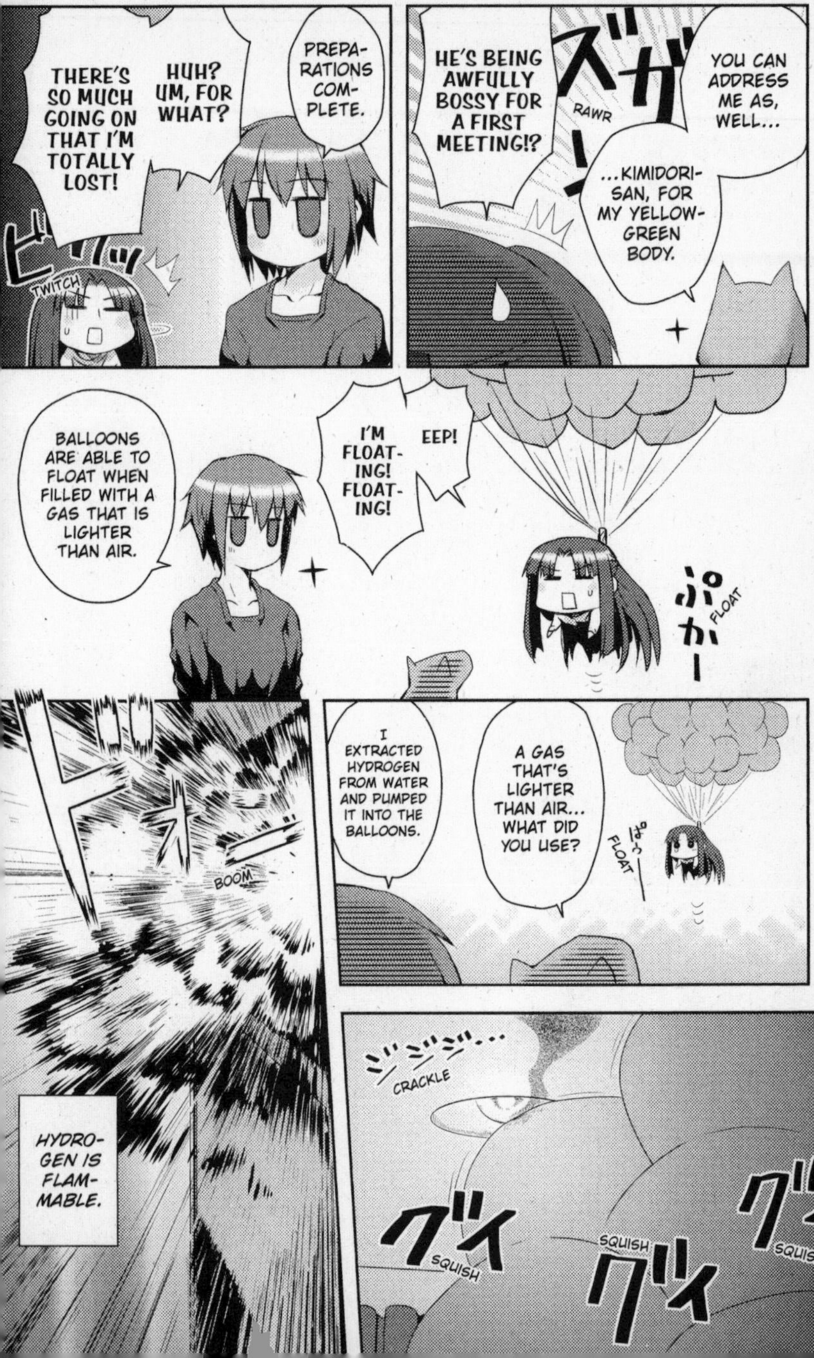
YOU CAN ADDRESS ME AS, WELL...
...KIMIDORI-SAN, FOR MY YELLOW-GREEN BODY.
RAWR
HE'S BEING AWFULLY BOSSY FOR A FIRST MEETING!?
PREPARATIONS COMPLETE.
HUH? UM, FOR WHAT?
THERE'S SO MUCH GOING ON THAT I'M TOTALLY LOST!
TWITCH
EEP! I'M FLOATING! FLOATING!
FLOAT
BALLOONS ARE ABLE TO FLOAT WHEN FILLED WITH A GAS THAT IS LIGHTER THAN AIR.
FLOAT
A GAS THAT'S LIGHTER THAN AIR... WHAT DID YOU USE?
I EXTRACTED HYDROGEN FROM WATER AND PUMPED IT INTO THE BALLOONS.
CRACKLE
SQUISH
SQUISH
SQUISH
BOOM
HYDROGEN IS FLAMMABLE.

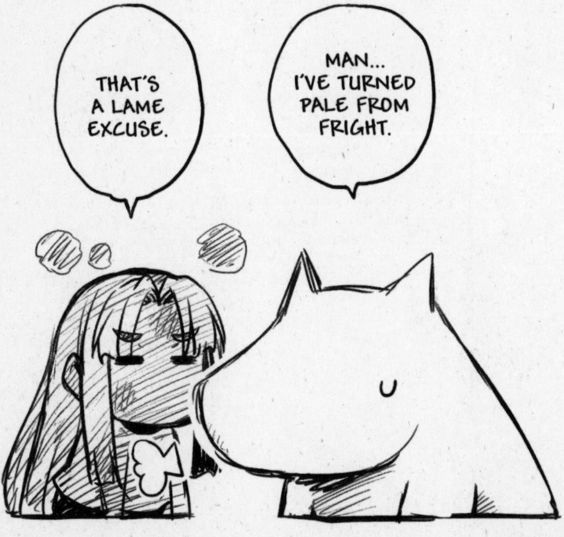
MAN... I'VE TURNED PALE FROM FRIGHT.
THAT'S A LAME EXCUSE.

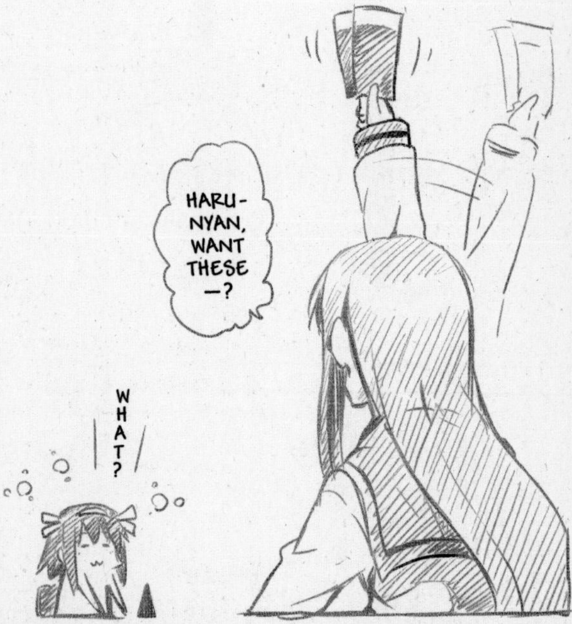
HARU-NYAN, WANT THESE—?
WHAT?

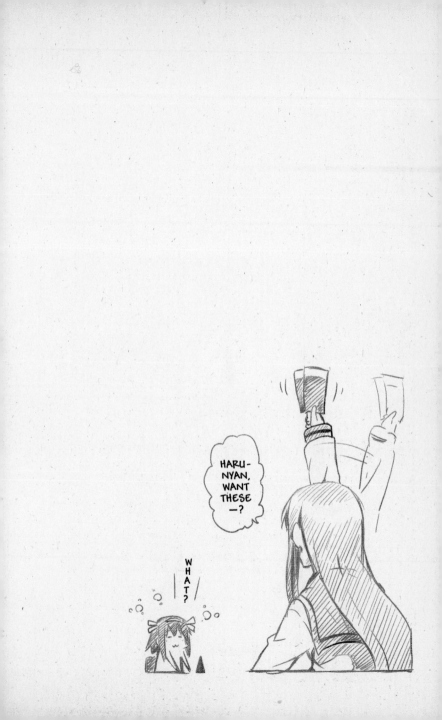

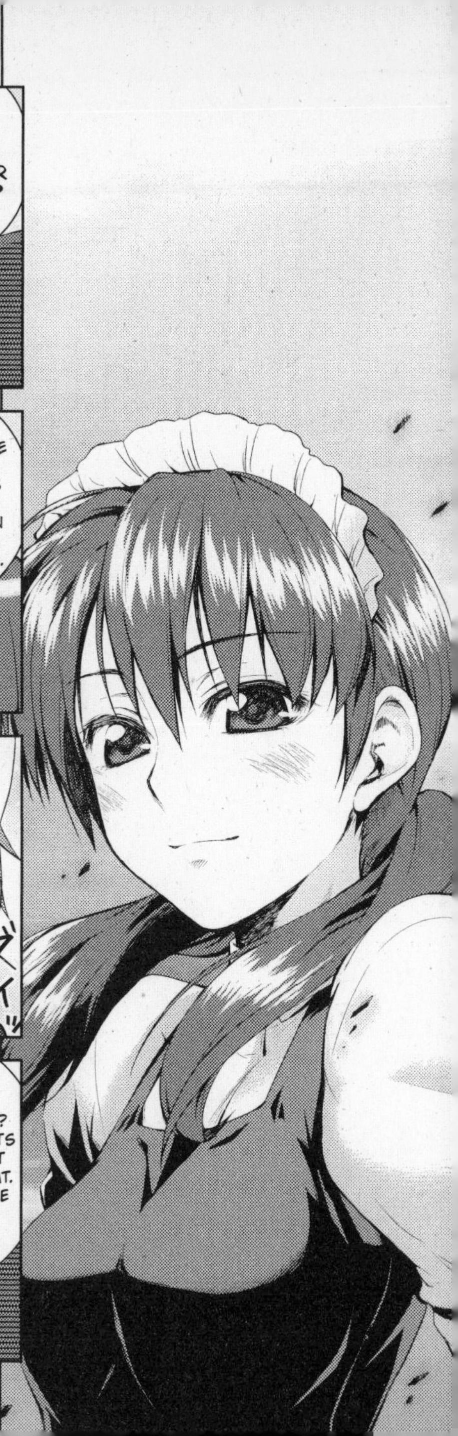

HOBBIES

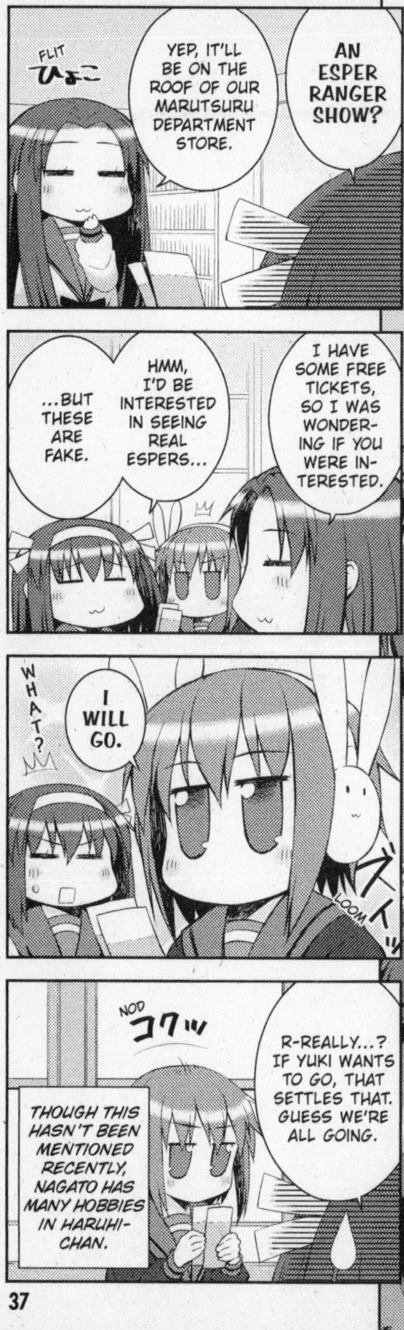

AN ESPER RANGER SHOW?
YEP, IT'LL BE ON THE ROOF OF OUR MARUTSURU DEPARTMENT STORE.
FLIT ひょこ
I HAVE SOME FREE TICKETS, SO I WAS WONDERING IF YOU WERE INTERESTED.
HMM, I'D BE INTERESTED IN SEEING REAL ESPERS...
...BUT THESE ARE FAKE.
I WILL GO.
WHAT?
LOOM ズイッ
R-REALLY...? IF YUKI WANTS TO GO, THAT SETTLES THAT. GUESS WE'RE ALL GOING.
NOD コクッ
THOUGH THIS HASN'T BEEN MENTIONED RECENTLY, NAGATO HAS MANY HOBBIES IN HARUHI-CHAN.

POPULAR

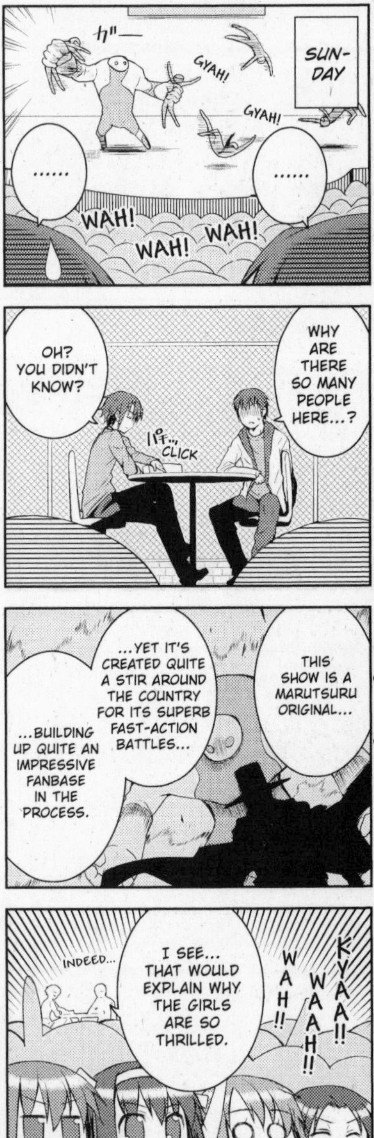
SUN-DAY
GYAH!
GYAH!
......
......
WAH!
WAH!
WAH!
WHY ARE THERE SO MANY PEOPLE HERE...?
OH? YOU DIDN'T KNOW?
CLICK
THIS SHOW IS A MARUTSURU ORIGINAL...
...YET IT'S CREATED QUITE A STIR AROUND THE COUNTRY FOR ITS SUPERB FAST-ACTION BATTLES...
...BUILDING UP QUITE AN IMPRESSIVE FANBASE IN THE PROCESS.
KYAAA!!
WAAAH!!
WAH!!
I SEE... THAT WOULD EXPLAIN WHY THE GIRLS ARE SO THRILLED.
INDEED...

•Haruhi-chan •SOS Brigade brigade chief. Not interested in kiddy shows...?

•Nagato •Actually an alien gamer. We just learned that she loves tokusatsu shows in addition to manga and games.

•Mikuru-chan •Actually from the future. She's very excited since she's never been to one of these shows before.

KILLING TIME

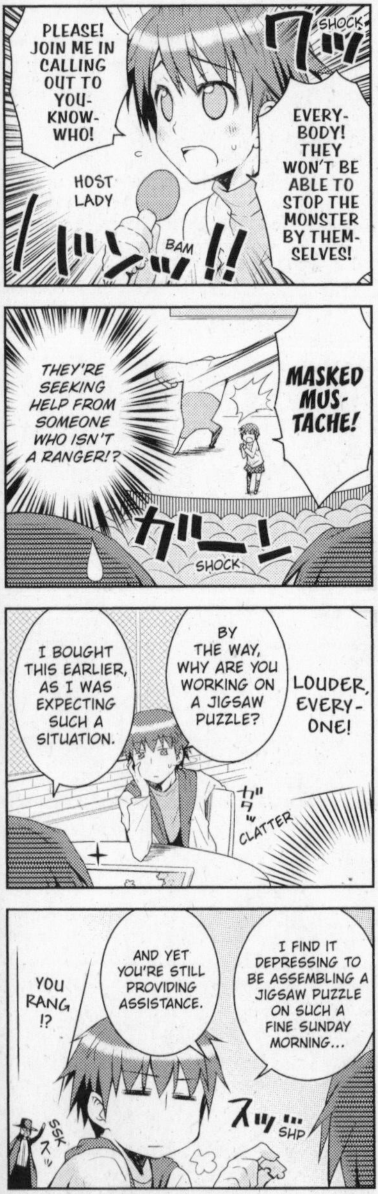
SHOCK
EVERY-BODY! THEY WON'T BE ABLE TO STOP THE MONSTER BY THEM-SELVES!
PLEASE! JOIN ME IN CALLING OUT TO YOU-KNOW-WHO!
HOST LADY
BAM
MASKED MUS-TACHE!
THEY'RE SEEKING HELP FROM SOMEONE WHO ISN'T A RANGER!?
SHOCK
LOUDER, EVERY-ONE!
BY THE WAY, WHY ARE YOU WORKING ON A JIGSAW PUZZLE?
I BOUGHT THIS EARLIER, AS I WAS EXPECTING SUCH A SITUATION.
CLATTER
I FIND IT DEPRESSING TO BE ASSEMBLING A JIGSAW PUZZLE ON SUCH A FINE SUNDAY MORNING...
AND YET YOU'RE STILL PROVIDING ASSISTANCE.
YOU RANG!?
SHP
SSK

PEOPLE WHO CAN DO ANYTHING

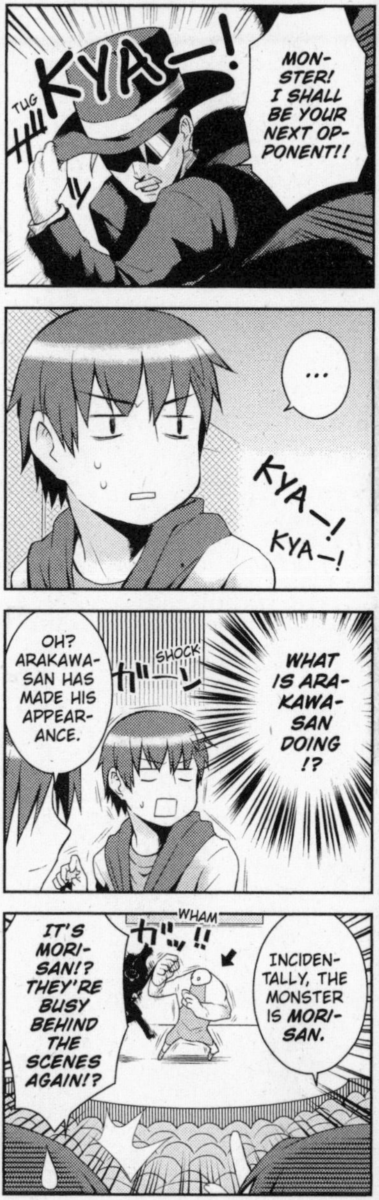
MON-STER! I SHALL BE YOUR NEXT OP-PONENT!!
KYA—!
TUG
...
KYA—!
KYA—!
WHAT IS ARA-KAWA-SAN DOING !?
SHOCK
OH? ARAKAWA-SAN HAS MADE HIS APPEAR-ANCE.
INCIDEN-TALLY, THE MONSTER IS MORI-SAN.
WHAM
IT'S MORI-SAN!? THEY'RE BUSY BEHIND THE SCENES AGAIN!?

AUDIENCE

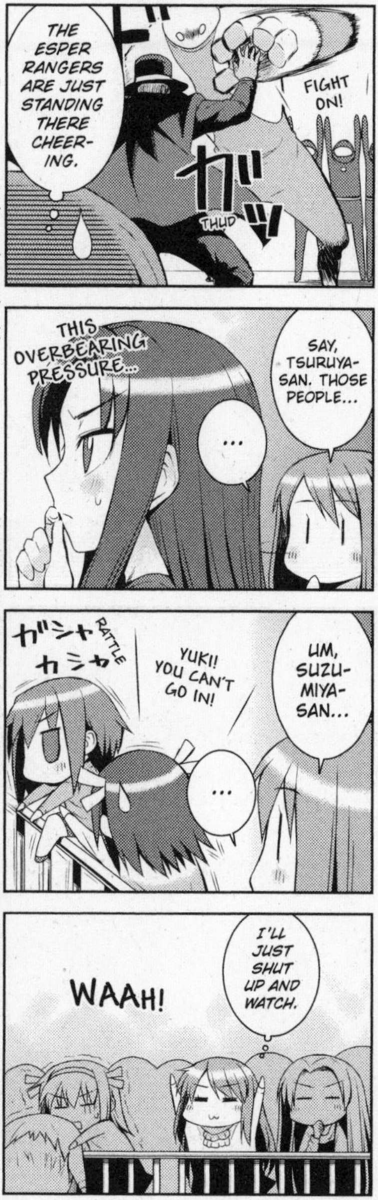
FIGHT ON!
THUD
THE ESPER RANGERS ARE JUST STANDING THERE CHEER-ING.
SAY, TSURUYA-SAN. THOSE PEOPLE...
...
THIS OVERBEARING PRESSURE...
UM, SUZU-MIYA-SAN...
...
YUKI!! YOU CAN'T GO IN!
RATTLE
I'LL JUST SHUT UP AND WATCH.
WAAH!

•Tsuruya-san •Mikuru-chan's buddy. Her grappler instinct has picked up on something.

•Masked Mustache •The hidden hero of the show. His true identity is the mustached and suave one.

•Monster •Displays extraordinary physical prowess, despite the bulky costume. Her true identity is the maid.

AUTOGRAPH

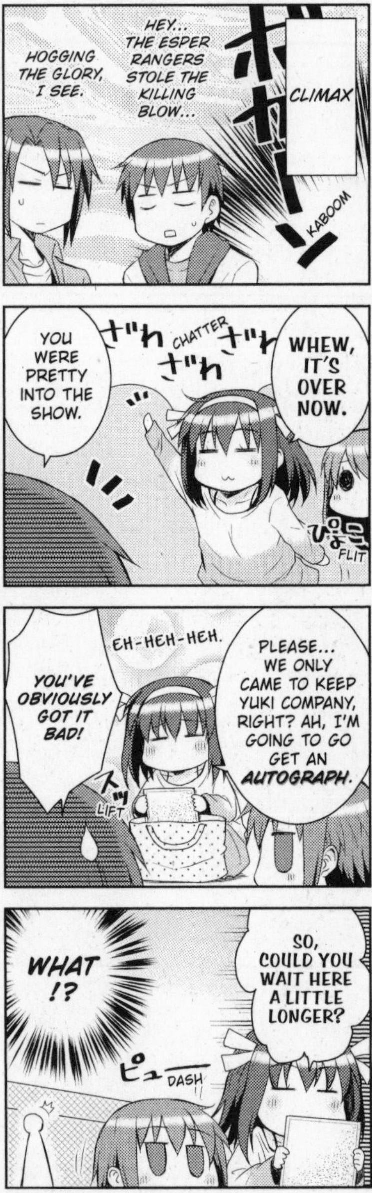
CLIMAX
KABOOM
HEY... THE ESPER RANGERS STOLE THE KILLING BLOW...
HOGGING THE GLORY, I SEE.
WHEW, IT'S OVER NOW.
ざわ ざわ ざわ
CHATTER
YOU WERE PRETTY INTO THE SHOW.
FLIT
PLEASE... WE ONLY CAME TO KEEP YUKI COMPANY, RIGHT? AH, I'M GOING TO GO GET AN AUTOGRAPH.
EH-HEH-HEH.
YOU'VE OBVIOUSLY GOT IT BAD!
LIFT
SO, COULD YOU WAIT HERE A LITTLE LONGER?
WHAT!?
ピュー
DASH

•Kyon •Supposed to be the main character in this story. Ran into a real squad of Esper Rangers when he was in closed space.

•Koizumi •An enigmatic transfer student who happens to be an esper. Not that it matters or anything, but this little snip is all you need to tell that it's Koizumi, yes?

SEPARATE WAYS

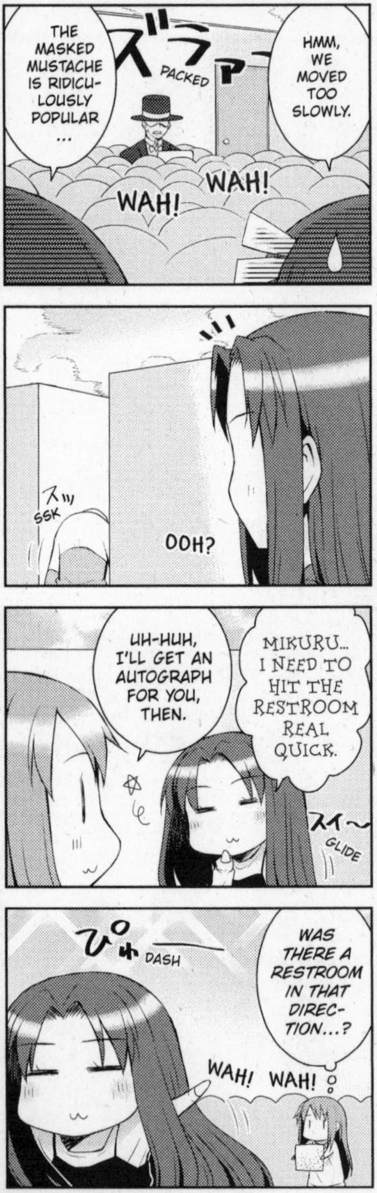
HMM, WE MOVED TOO SLOWLY.
ズラァー
PACKED
THE MASKED MUSTACHE IS RIDICULOUSLY POPULAR...
WAH!
WAH!
OOH?
スッ
SSK
MIKURU... I NEED TO HIT THE RESTROOM REAL QUICK.
UH-HUH, I'LL GET AN AUTOGRAPH FOR YOU, THEN.
スイ〜
GLIDE
WAS THERE A RESTROOM IN THAT DIRECTION...?
ぴゅー
DASH
WAH! WAH!

TSURUYA-SAN VS. MECHA MORI-SAN

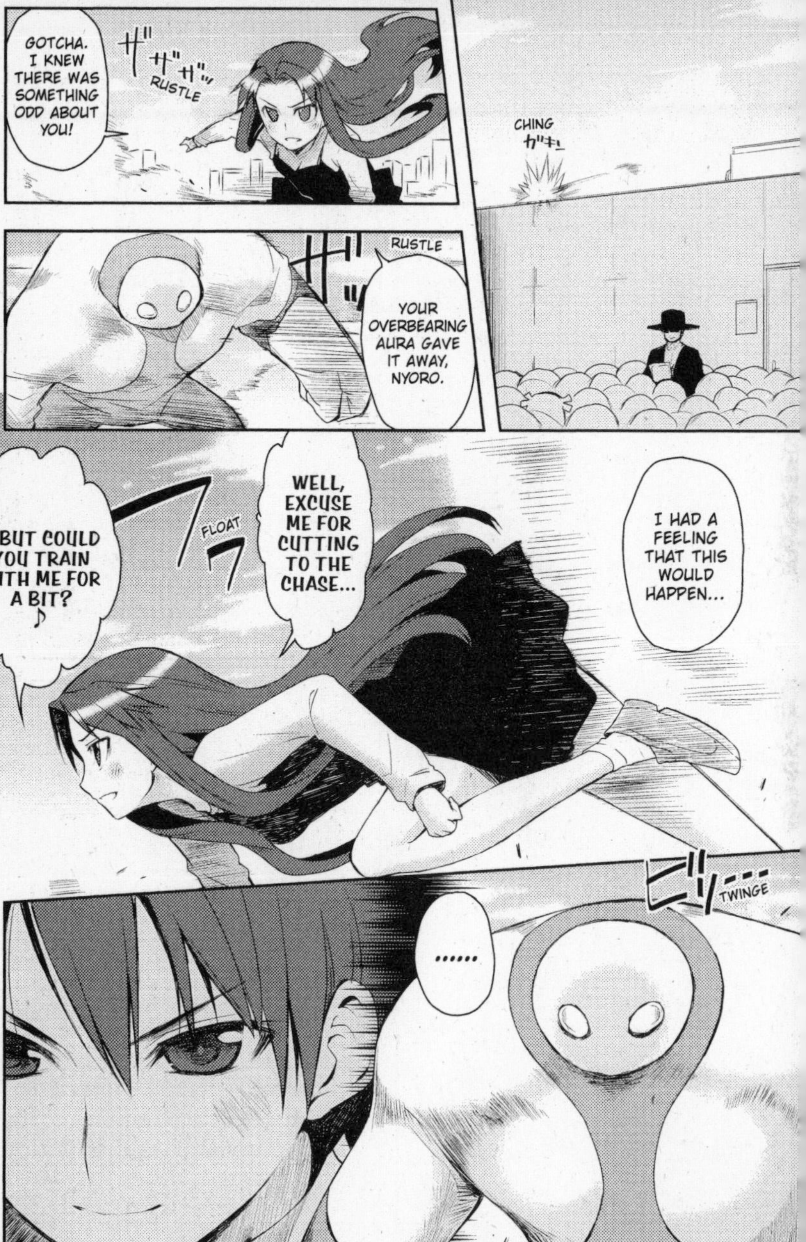
CHING
GOTCHA. I KNEW THERE WAS SOMETHING ODD ABOUT YOU!
RUSTLE
RUSTLE
YOUR OVERBEARING AURA GAVE IT AWAY, NYORO.
I HAD A FEELING THAT THIS WOULD HAPPEN...
WELL, EXCUSE ME FOR CUTTING TO THE CHASE...
FLOAT
...BUT COULD YOU TRAIN WITH ME FOR A BIT? ♪
TWINGE
......

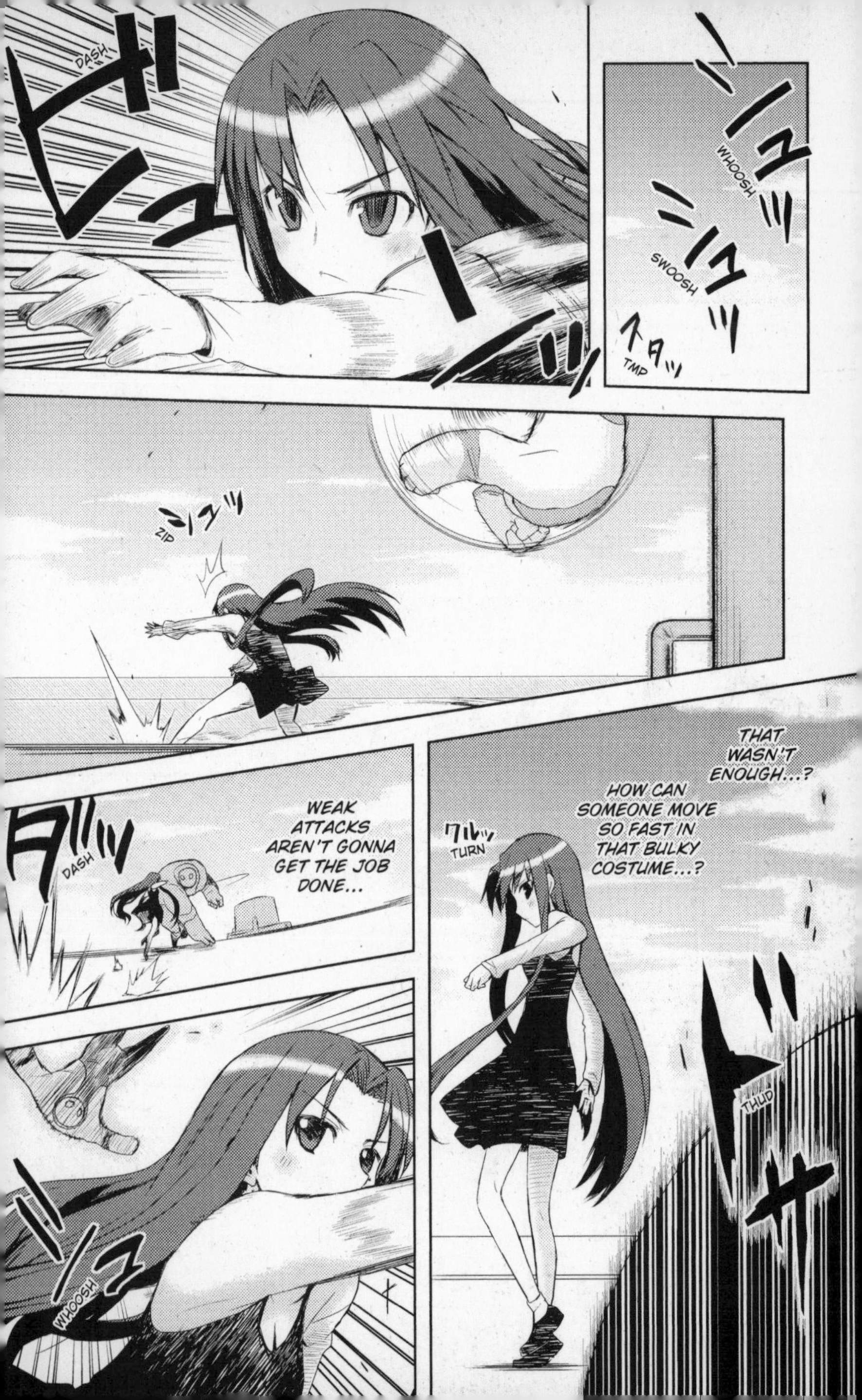
WHOOSH
SWOOSH
TMP
DASH
ZIP
THAT WASN'T ENOUGH...?
HOW CAN SOMEONE MOVE SO FAST IN THAT BULKY COSTUME...?
TURN
THUD
WEAK ATTACKS AREN'T GONNA GET THE JOB DONE...
DASH
WHOOSH

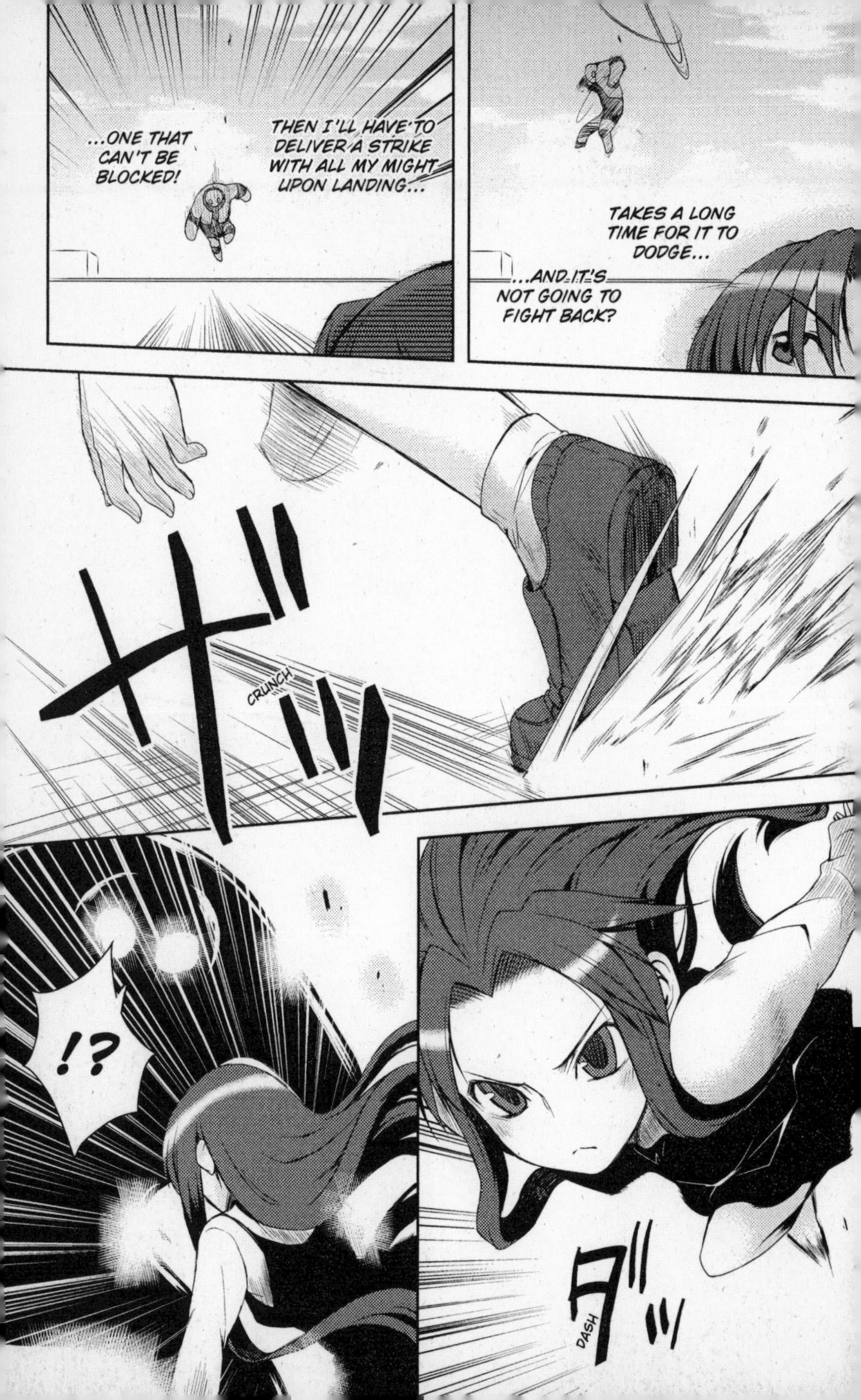
TAKES A LONG TIME FOR IT TO DODGE...
...AND IT'S NOT GOING TO FIGHT BACK?
THEN I'LL HAVE TO DELIVER A STRIKE WITH ALL MY MIGHT UPON LANDING...
...ONE THAT CAN'T BE BLOCKED!
CRUNCH
DASH
!?

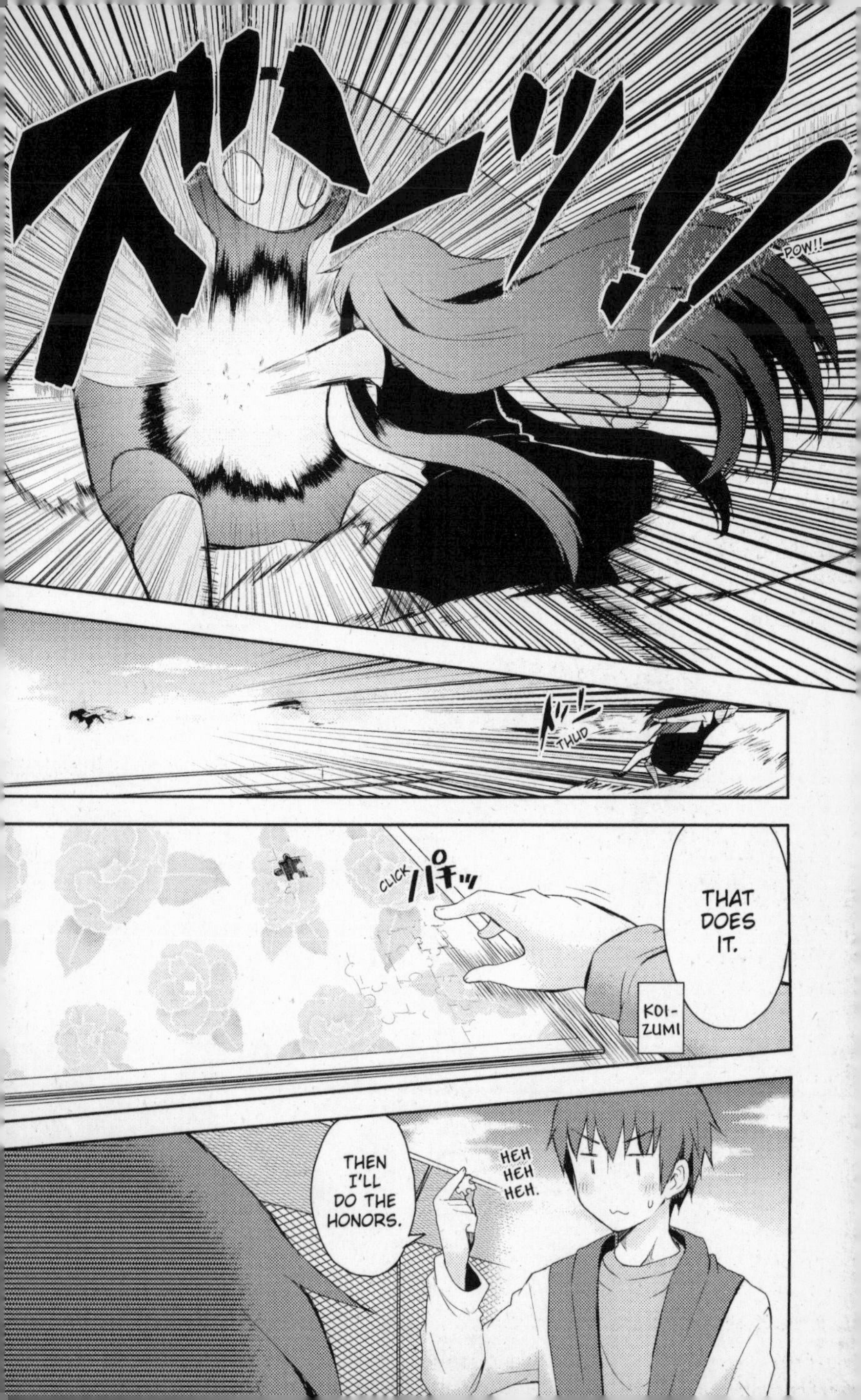
POW!!
THUD
THAT DOES IT.
KOI-ZUMI
CLICK
HEH HEH HEH.
THEN I'LL DO THE HONORS.

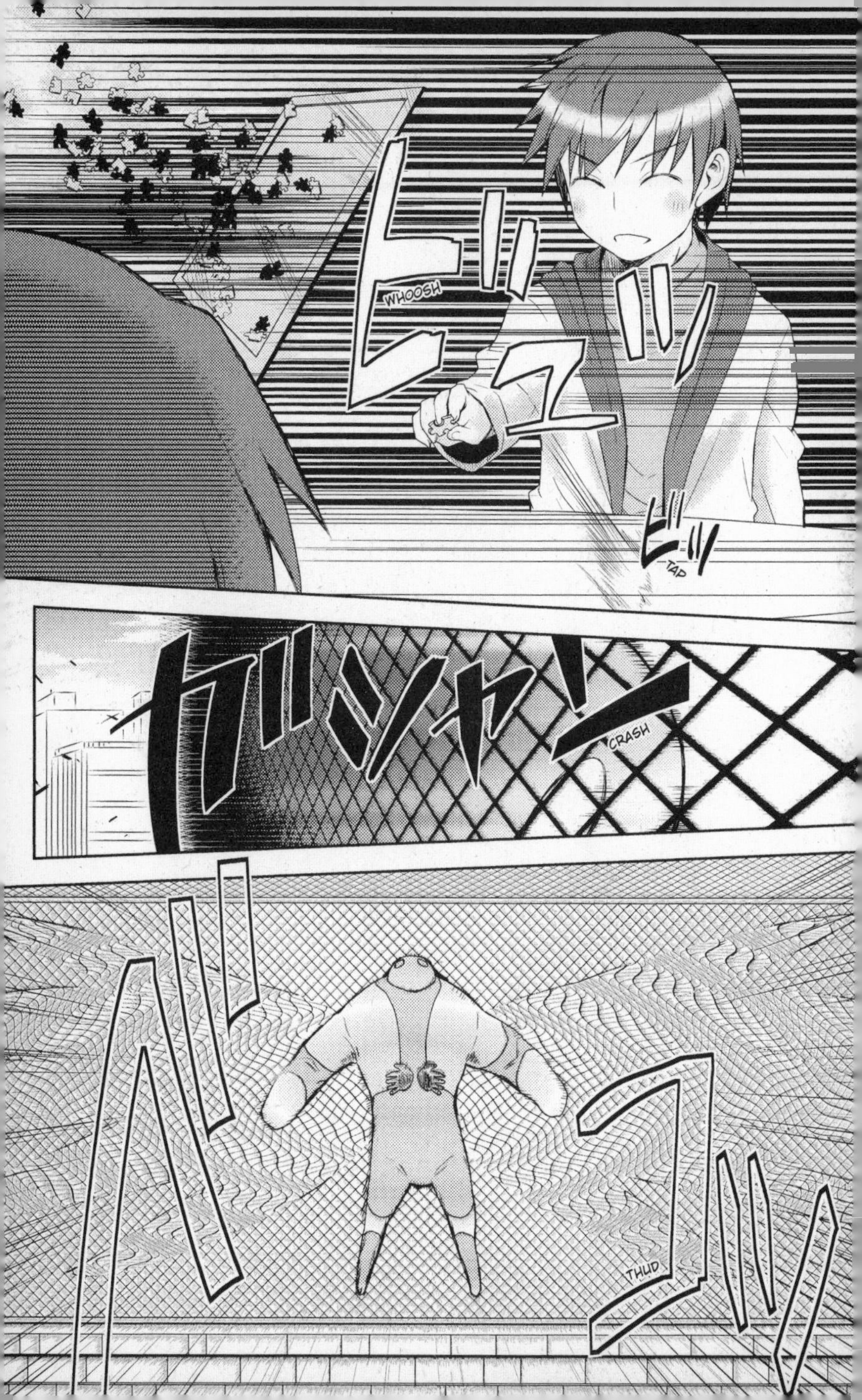
WHOOSH
TAP
CRASH
THUD

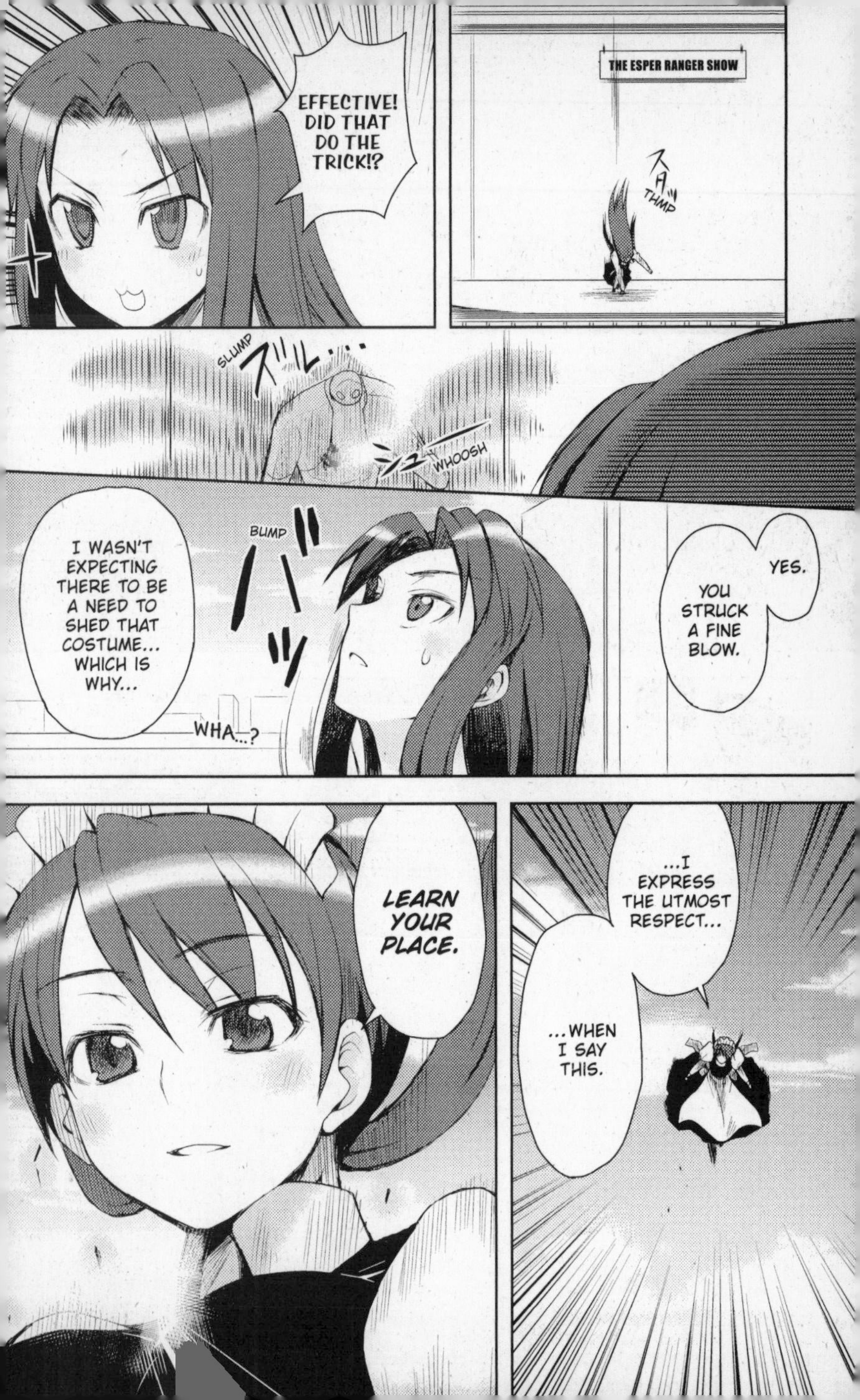
THE ESPER RANGER SHOW
THMP
EFFECTIVE! DID THAT DO THE TRICK!?
SLUMP
WHOOSH
YES.
YOU STRUCK A FINE BLOW.
BUMP
WHA...?
I WASN'T EXPECTING THERE TO BE A NEED TO SHED THAT COSTUME... WHICH IS WHY...
...I EXPRESS THE UTMOST RESPECT...
...WHEN I SAY THIS.
LEARN YOUR PLACE.

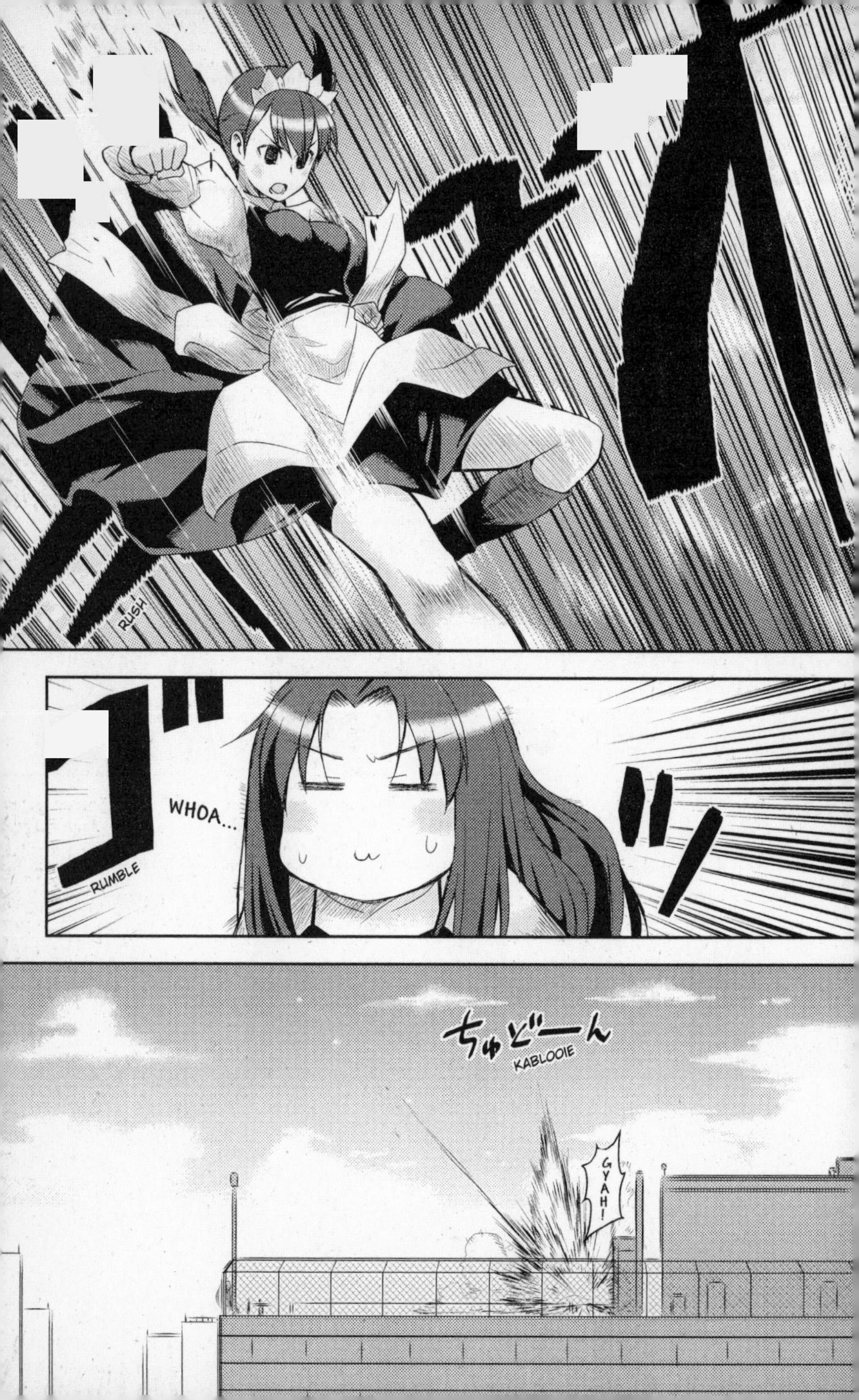
RUSH
WHOA...
RUMBLE
ちゅどーん
KABLOOIE
GYAH!

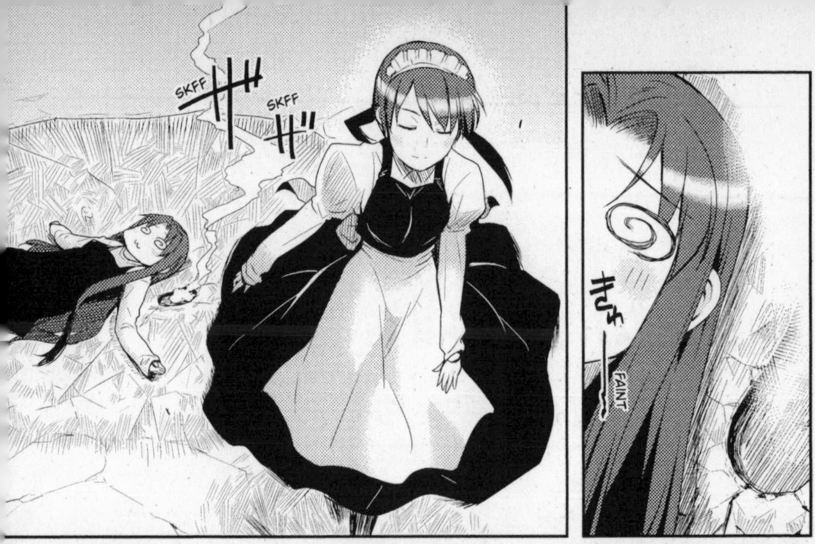
きゅ
FAINT
SKFF
ザ
SKFF
ザ

THANK YOU SO MUCH!

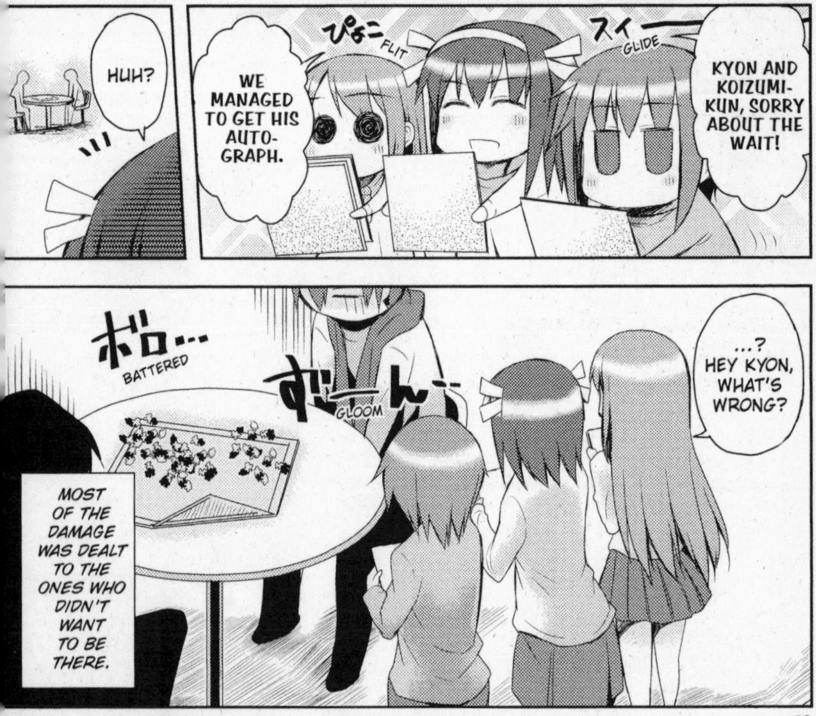
KYON AND KOIZUMI-KUN, SORRY ABOUT THE WAIT!
スイー
GLIDE
ぴよこ
FLIT
WE MANAGED TO GET HIS AUTO-GRAPH.
HUH?
...? HEY KYON, WHAT'S WRONG?
ずーん
GLOOM
ボロ...
BATTERED
MOST OF THE DAMAGE WAS DEALT TO THE ONES WHO DIDN'T WANT TO BE THERE.

CONFERENCE

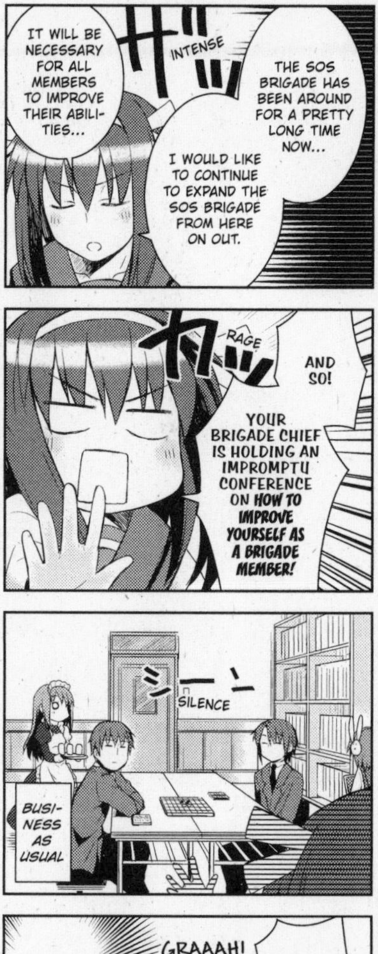
THE SOS BRIGADE HAS BEEN AROUND FOR A PRETTY LONG TIME NOW...
INTENSE
I WOULD LIKE TO CONTINUE TO EXPAND THE SOS BRIGADE FROM HERE ON OUT.
IT WILL BE NECESSARY FOR ALL MEMBERS TO IMPROVE THEIR ABILITIES...
AND SO!
RAGE
YOUR BRIGADE CHIEF IS HOLDING AN IMPROMPTU CONFERENCE ON HOW TO IMPROVE YOURSELF AS A BRIGADE MEMBER!
SILENCE
BUSINESS AS USUAL
GET READY!
GRAAAH!
FOR WHAT—!?

TIME TRAVELER

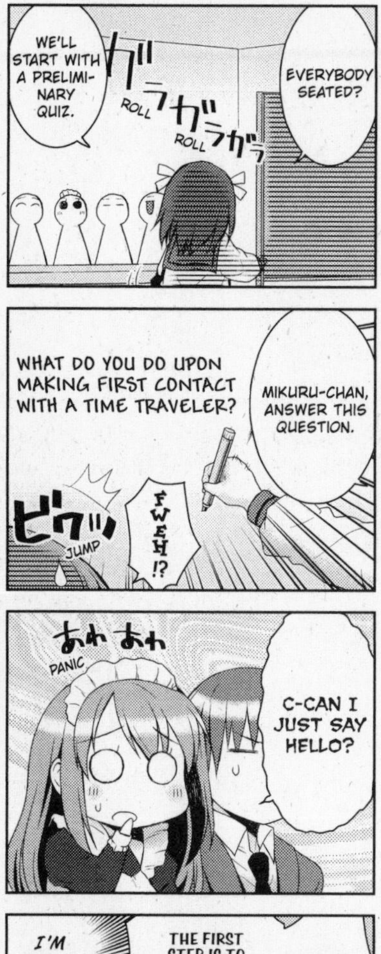
EVERYBODY SEATED?
ROLL
ROLL
WE'LL START WITH A PRELIMINARY QUIZ.
MIKURU-CHAN, ANSWER THIS QUESTION.
WHAT DO YOU DO UPON MAKING FIRST CONTACT WITH A TIME TRAVELER?
FWEH!?
JUMP
C-CAN I JUST SAY HELLO?
PANIC
BZZT. WRONG ANSWER.
THE FIRST STEP IS TO CAPTURE THEM! THE EARLIER YOU GRAB A TIME TRAVELER, THE MORE USEFUL HIS INFORMATION ON THE FUTURE WILL BE!
BAM
I'M GOING TO BE CAPTURED!?
TIME TRAVELER
SHOCK

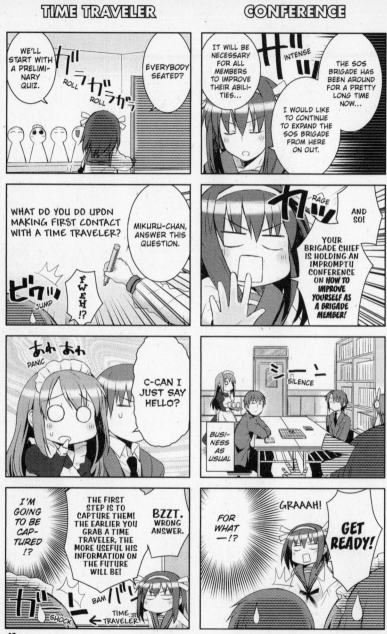

ESPER

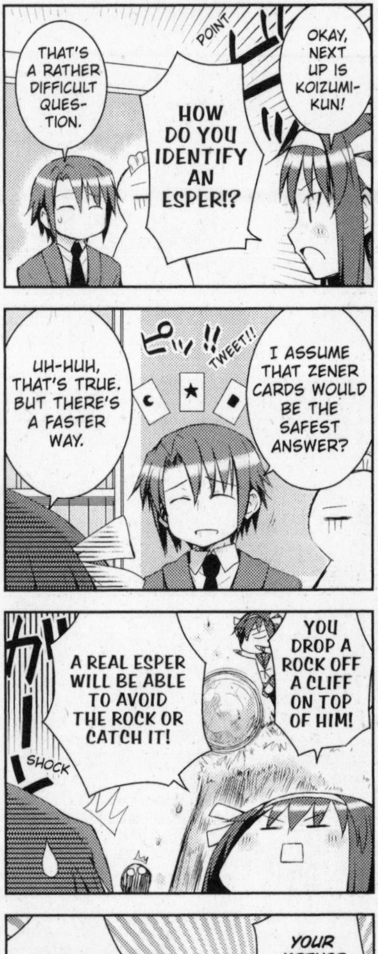
OKAY, NEXT UP IS KOIZUMI-KUN!
POINT
HOW DO YOU IDENTIFY AN ESPER!?
THAT'S A RATHER DIFFICULT QUES-TION.
I ASSUME THAT ZENER CARDS WOULD BE THE SAFEST ANSWER?
TWEET!!
UH-HUH, THAT'S TRUE. BUT THERE'S A FASTER WAY.
YOU DROP A ROCK OFF A CLIFF ON TOP OF HIM!
A REAL ESPER WILL BE ABLE TO AVOID THE ROCK OR CATCH IT!
SHOCK
YOUR METHOD MEANS HE'LL EITHER BE AN ESPER OR DEAD!
HUMANS ARE FORCED TO DO CRUEL THINGS AT TIMES!

ALIEN

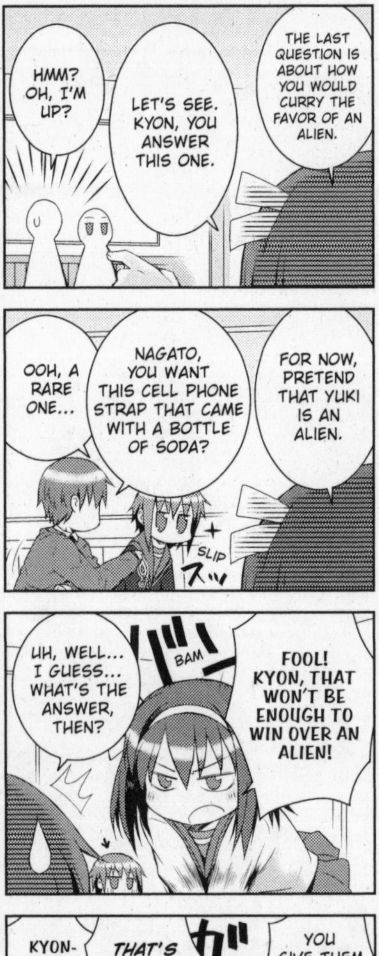
THE LAST QUESTION IS ABOUT HOW YOU WOULD CURRY THE FAVOR OF AN ALIEN.
LET'S SEE. KYON, YOU ANSWER THIS ONE.
HMM? OH, I'M UP?
FOR NOW, PRETEND THAT YUKI IS AN ALIEN.
NAGATO, YOU WANT THIS CELL PHONE STRAP THAT CAME WITH A BOTTLE OF SODA?
SLIP
OOH, A RARE ONE...
FOOL! KYON, THAT WON'T BE ENOUGH TO WIN OVER AN ALIEN!
BAM
UH, WELL... I GUESS... WHAT'S THE ANSWER, THEN?
YOU GIVE THEM MIKURU-CHAN. BECAUSE SHE'S CUTE!
CLENCH
THAT'S THE SAME THING I WAS TRYING TO DO!
KYON-KUN, I THINK YOU'RE MISS-ING THE POINT!

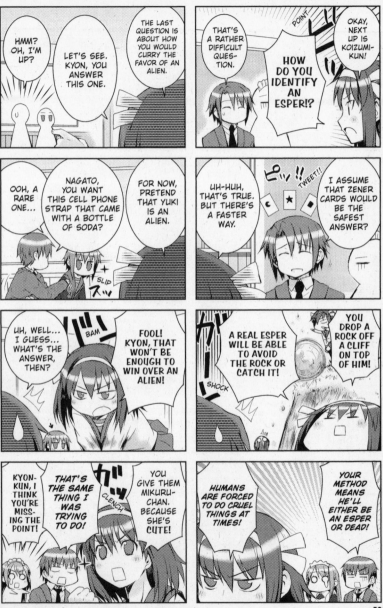

ACTING

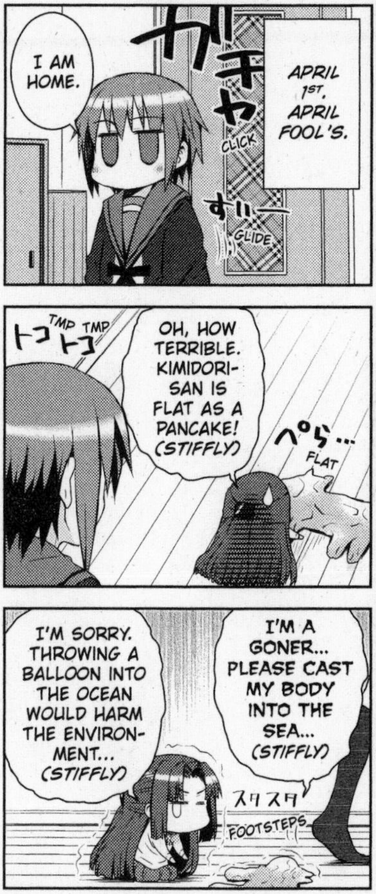
APRIL 1st, APRIL FOOL'S.
ガチャ
CLICK
I AM HOME.
すぃー
GLIDE
TMP TMP
OH, HOW TERRIBLE. KIMIDORI-SAN IS FLAT AS A PANCAKE! (STIFFLY)
FLAT
I'M A GONER... PLEASE CAST MY BODY INTO THE SEA... (STIFFLY)
I'M SORRY. THROWING A BALLOON INTO THE OCEAN WOULD HARM THE ENVIRONMENT... (STIFFLY)
FOOTSTEPS
NAGATO-SAN'S A SHARP ONE. COMPLETELY IGNORED US...
WELL, CONSIDERING THE SHODDY PERFORMANCE WE PUT ON...
CLICK
IN ANY CASE, COULD YOU REINFLATE ME?
YES...
SHAKE

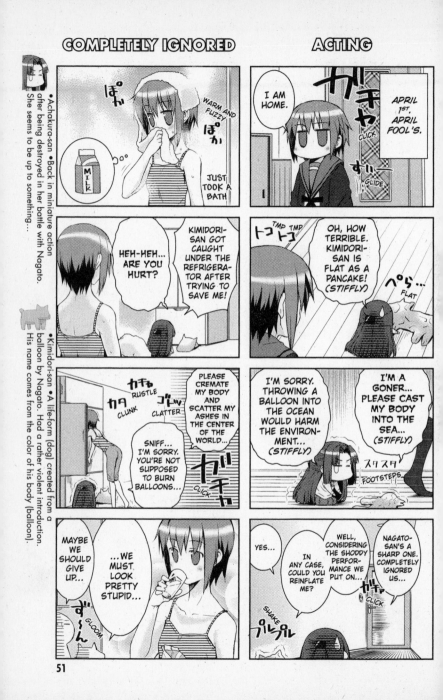

COMPLETELY IGNORED

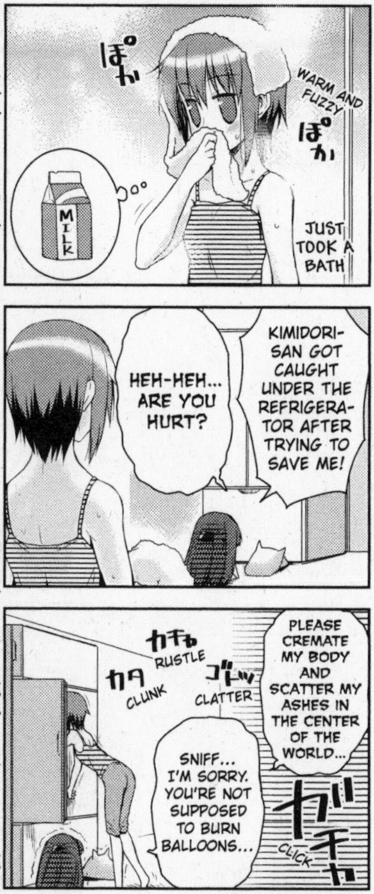
WARM AND FUZZY
JUST TOOK A BATH
MILK
KIMIDORI-SAN GOT CAUGHT UNDER THE REFRIGERATOR AFTER TRYING TO SAVE ME!
HEH-HEH... ARE YOU HURT?
PLEASE CREMATE MY BODY AND SCATTER MY ASHES IN THE CENTER OF THE WORLD...
CLATTER
RUSTLE
CLUNK
SNIFF... I'M SORRY. YOU'RE NOT SUPPOSED TO BURN BALLOONS...
CLICK
...WE MUST LOOK PRETTY STUPID...
MAYBE WE SHOULD GIVE UP...
GLOOM

•Achakura-san •Back in miniature action after being destroyed in her battle with Nagato. She seems to be up to something...

•Kimidori-san •A life-form (dog) created from a balloon by Nagato. Had a rather violent introduction. His name comes from the color of his body (balloon).

RESCUE DRAMA

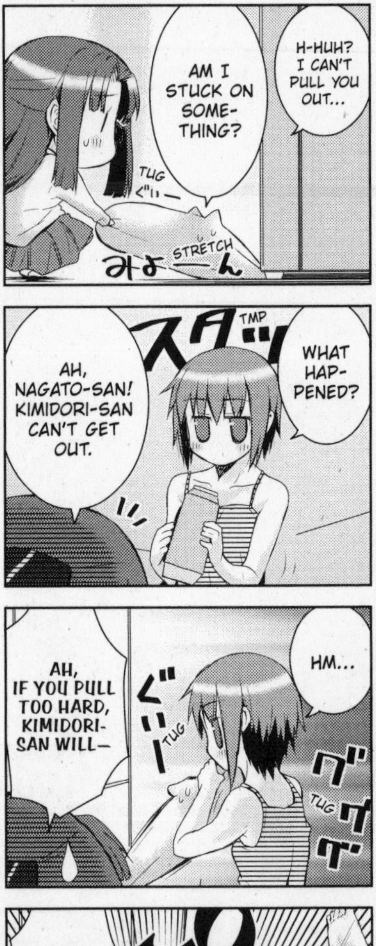
H-HUH? I CAN'T PULL YOU OUT...
AM I STUCK ON SOME-THING?
TUG ぐぃー
STRETCH みよーん
TMP スタッ
WHAT HAP-PENED?
AH, NAGATO-SAN! KIMIDORI-SAN CAN'T GET OUT.
HM...
グググ
TUG
ぐいー
TUG
AH, IF YOU PULL TOO HARD, KIMIDORI-SAN WILL—
パ!
BANG
EEEEK !?

REGRET

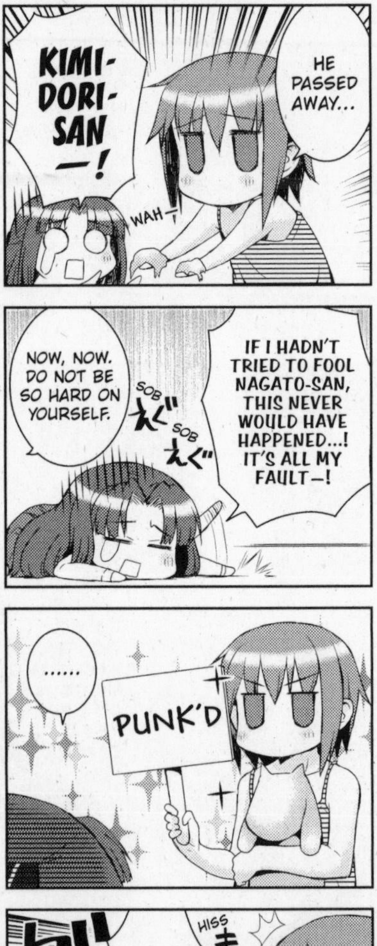
HE PASSED AWAY...
KIMI-DORI-SAN—!
WAH—
IF I HADN'T TRIED TO FOOL NAGATO-SAN, THIS NEVER WOULD HAVE HAPPENED...! IT'S ALL MY FAULT—!
SOB えぐ
SOB えぐ
NOW, NOW. DO NOT BE SO HARD ON YOURSELF.
......
PUNK'D
HISS キシャー
YOU TRICKED ME—!!!
ROAR がー
POT, MEET KETTLE.

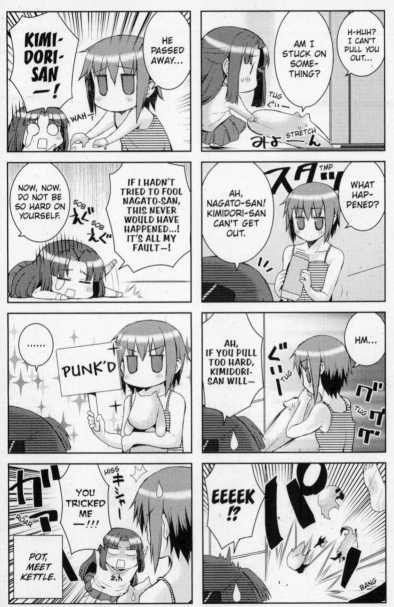

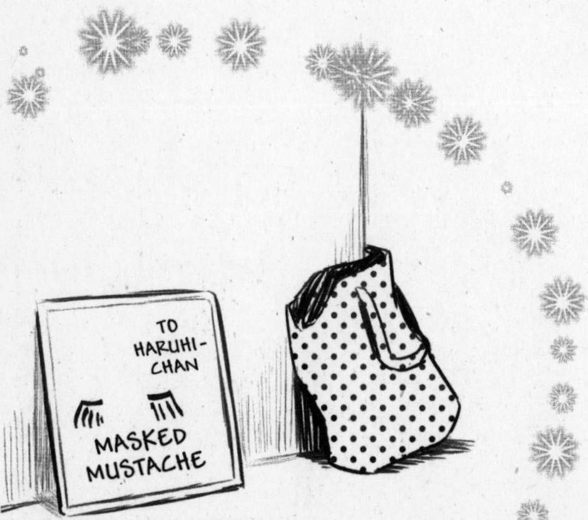
TO HARUHI-CHAN
MASKED MUSTACHE

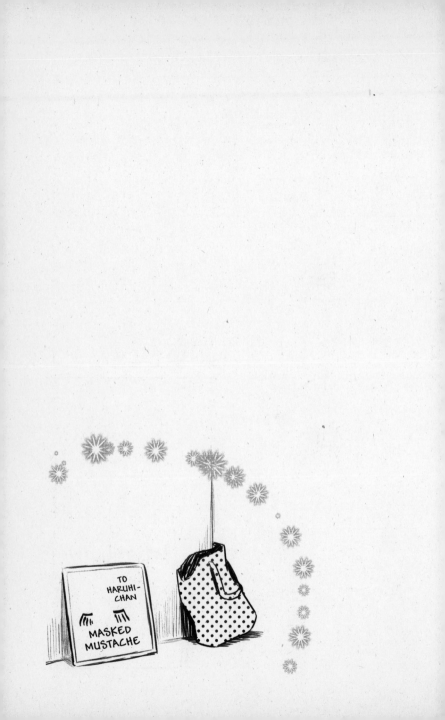

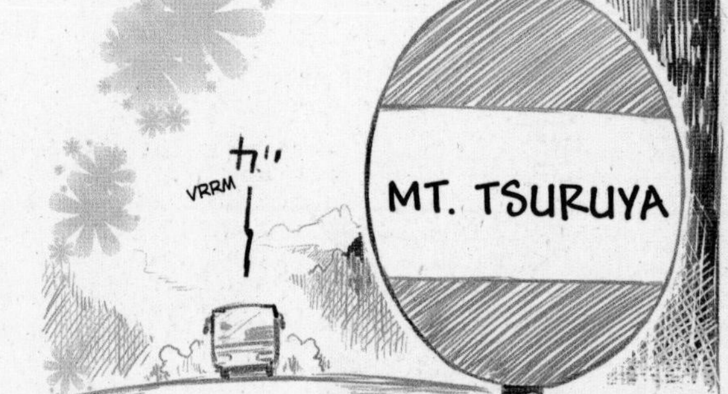
MT. TSURUYA
ガ
VRRM

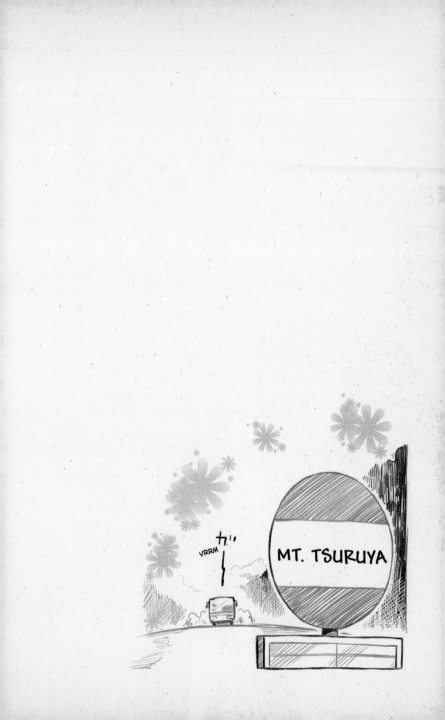

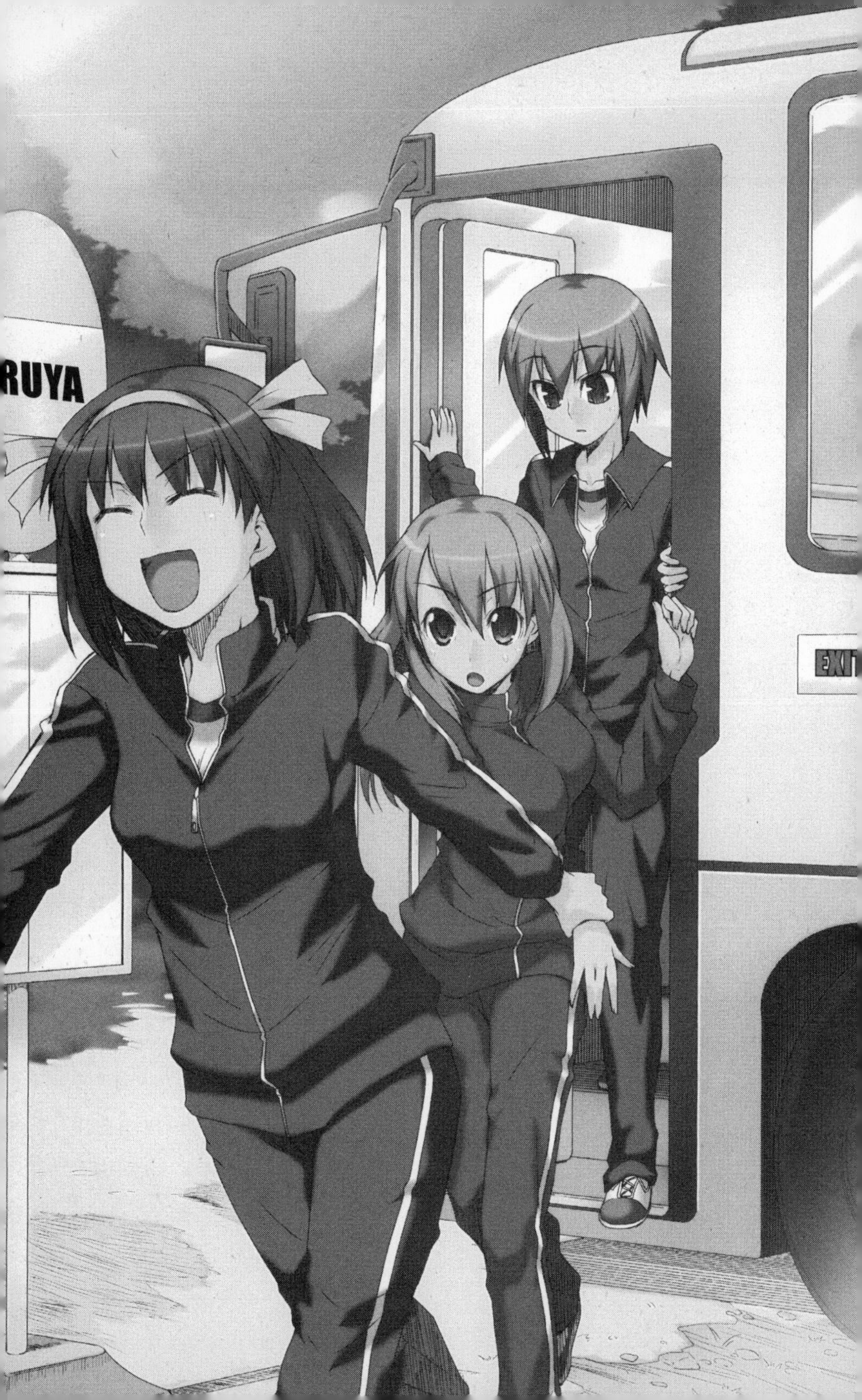
RUYA

INTRODUCTORY ROAR

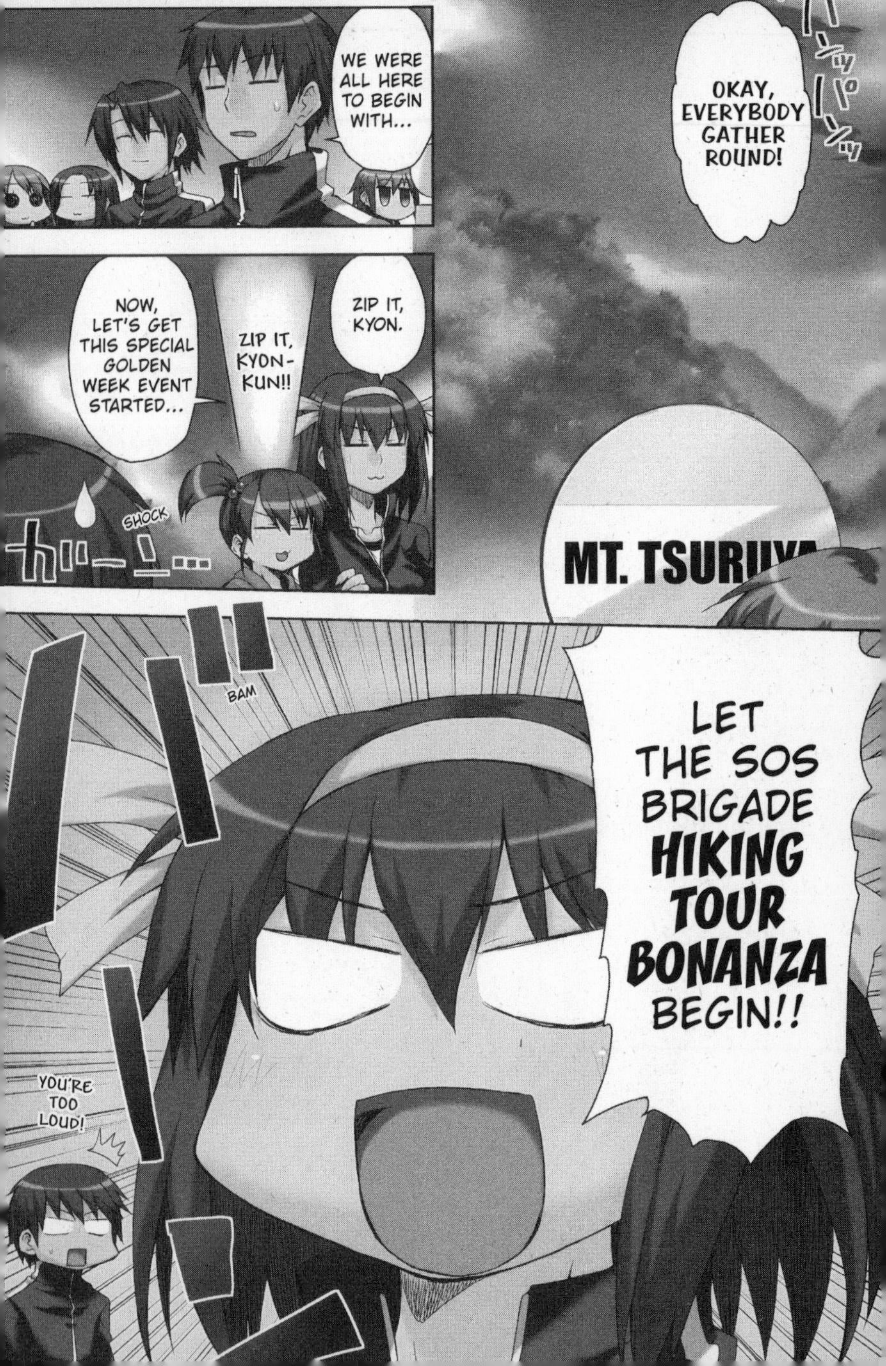

CLAP
OKAY, EVERYBODY GATHER ROUND!
MT. TSURU
WE WERE ALL HERE TO BEGIN WITH...
NOW, LET'S GET THIS SPECIAL GOLDEN WEEK EVENT STARTED...
ZIP IT, KYON.
ZIP IT, KYON-KUN!!
SHOCK
LET THE SOS BRIGADE **HIKING TOUR BONANZA** BEGIN!!
BAM
YOU'RE TOO LOUD!

TODAY'S SCHEDULE

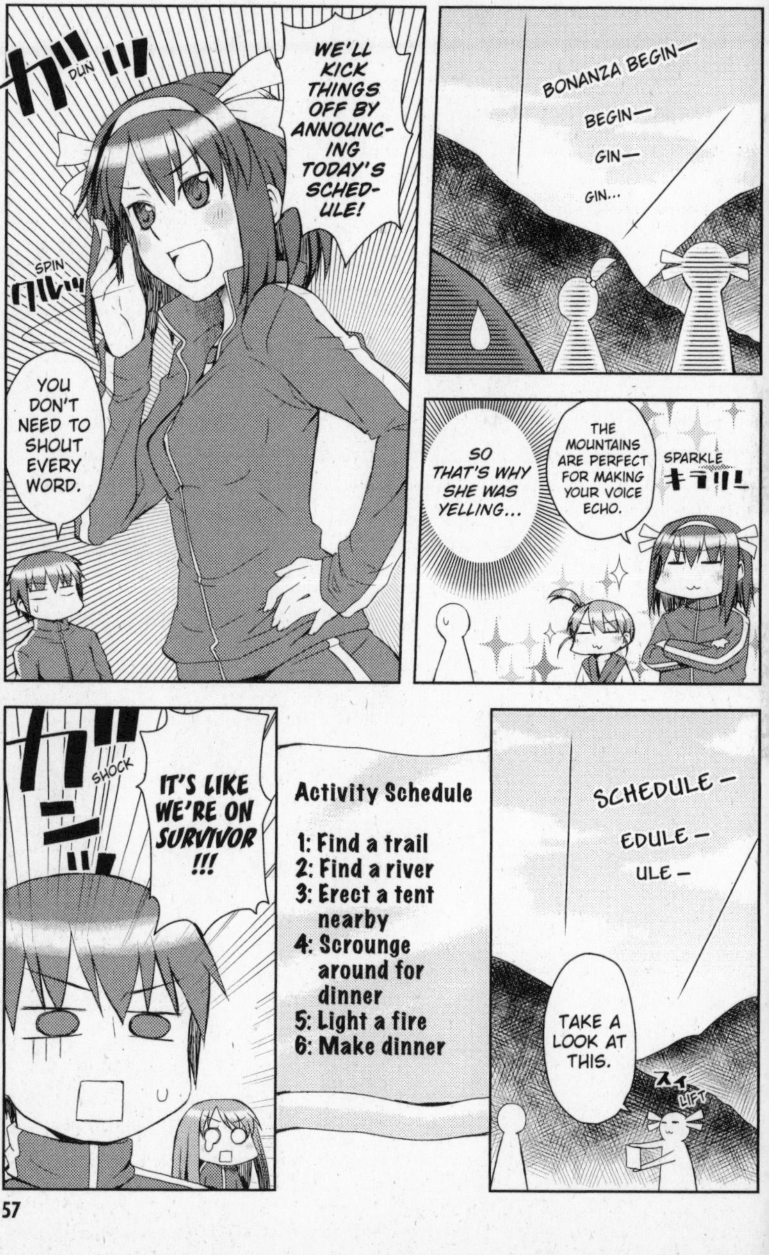
BONANZA BEGIN—
BEGIN—
GIN—
GIN...
THE MOUNTAINS ARE PERFECT FOR MAKING YOUR VOICE ECHO.
SPARKLE
キラリーン
SO THAT'S WHY SHE WAS YELLING...
ガッ
DUN
WE'LL KICK THINGS OFF BY ANNOUNCING TODAY'S SCHEDULE!
SPIN
クルッ
YOU DON'T NEED TO SHOUT EVERY WORD.
SCHEDULE—
EDULE—
ULE—
TAKE A LOOK AT THIS.
スイ
LIFT
Activity Schedule
1: Find a trail
2: Find a river
3: Erect a tent nearby
4: Scrounge around for dinner
5: Light a fire
6: Make dinner
ガーン
SHOCK
IT'S LIKE WE'RE ON SURVIVOR!!!

•Haruhi-chan •SOS Brigade brigade chief. At an age where mountains feel romantic.

•Kyon's sister •Hasn't appeared for quite some time. She seems to get along well with Haruhi. And she's cute.

•Mikuru-chan •Actually from the future. Is she having difficulty surviving in the wilderness because she's from the future?

TRAIL

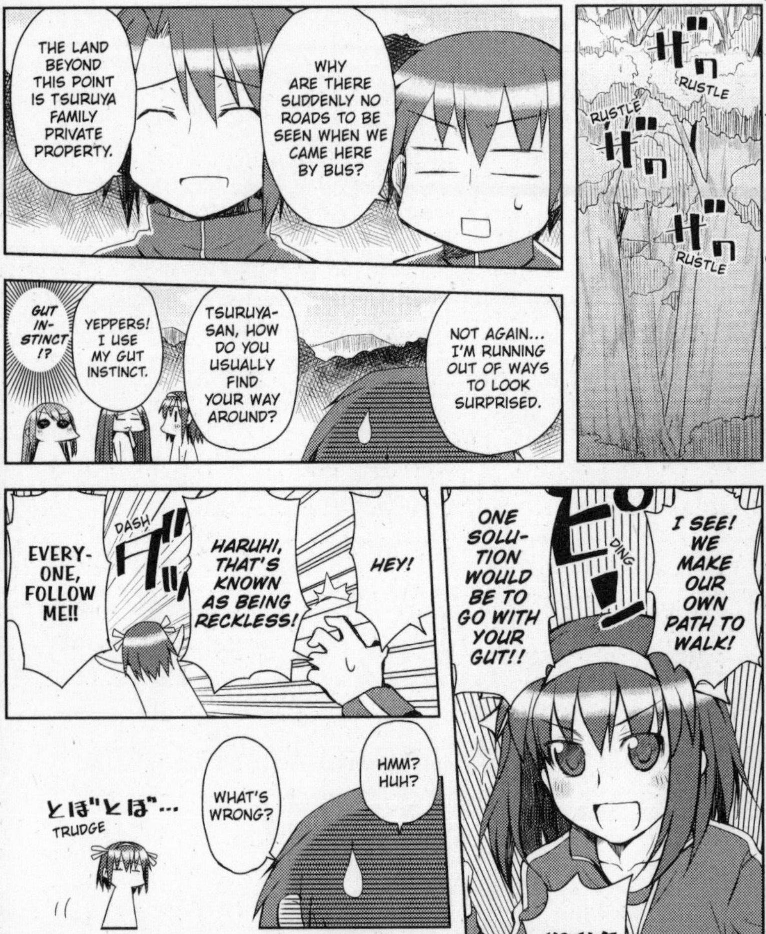
ザワ
RUSTLE
ザワ
RUSTLE
ザワ
RUSTLE
WHY ARE THERE SUDDENLY NO ROADS TO BE SEEN WHEN WE CAME HERE BY BUS?
THE LAND BEYOND THIS POINT IS TSURUYA FAMILY PRIVATE PROPERTY.
NOT AGAIN... I'M RUNNING OUT OF WAYS TO LOOK SURPRISED.
TSURUYA-SAN, HOW DO YOU USUALLY FIND YOUR WAY AROUND?
YEPPERS! I USE MY GUT INSTINCT.
GUT INSTINCT!?
I SEE! WE MAKE OUR OWN PATH TO WALK!
ピーン
DING
ONE SOLUTION WOULD BE TO GO WITH YOUR GUT!!
YOU'VE GOT IT TOTALLY WRONG!
HEY!
HARUHI, THAT'S KNOWN AS BEING RECKLESS!
ダッ
DASH
EVERY-ONE, FOLLOW ME!!
HMM? HUH?
WHAT'S WRONG?
とぼ"とぼ"...
TRUDGE
しゅん
DEJECTED
THERE WAS AN ANIMAL TRAIL BY THE EN-TRANCE.
HARUHI-SAN'S POWER HAS KICKED IN.
I SEE...

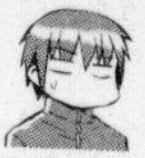

•Kyon •Supposed to be the main character in this story. He's looking to expand on his repertoire as a straight man.

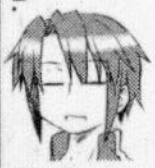

•Koizumi •An enigmatic transfer student who happens to be an esper. Of late, the reviews for each volume are tied to how many sexy shots of him there are.

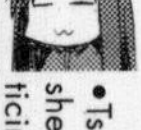

•Tsuruya-san •Mikuru-chan's buddy. Does she often train in the mountains when prac-ticing the Tsuruya School of Martial Arts?

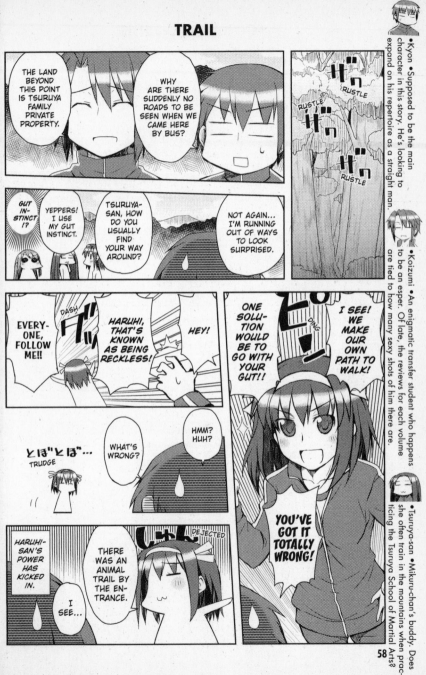

ANIMALS

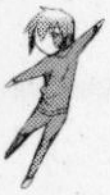

•Nagato •Actually an alien gamer. She prefers to stay indoors, but she's not bad enough to play games on a hiking trip.

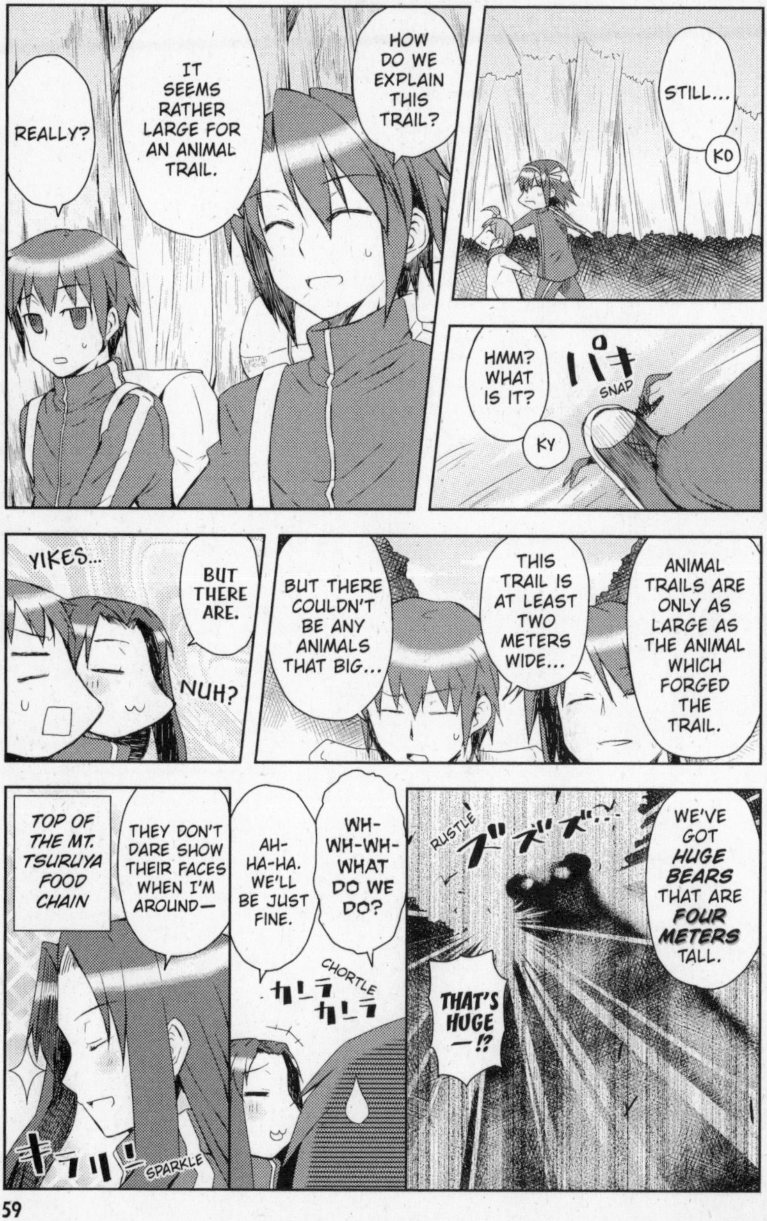
STILL...
KO
HMM? WHAT IS IT?
KY
SNAP
HOW DO WE EXPLAIN THIS TRAIL?
IT SEEMS RATHER LARGE FOR AN ANIMAL TRAIL.
REALLY?
ANIMAL TRAILS ARE ONLY AS LARGE AS THE ANIMAL WHICH FORGED THE TRAIL.
THIS TRAIL IS AT LEAST TWO METERS WIDE...
BUT THERE COULDN'T BE ANY ANIMALS THAT BIG...
BUT THERE ARE.
NUH?
YIKES...
WE'VE GOT HUGE BEARS THAT ARE FOUR METERS TALL.
RUSTLE
THAT'S HUGE—!?
WH-WH-WH-WHAT DO WE DO?
AH-HA-HA. WE'LL BE JUST FINE.
CHORTLE
THEY DON'T DARE SHOW THEIR FACES WHEN I'M AROUND—
TOP OF THE MT. TSURUYA FOOD CHAIN
SPARKLE

RIVER SEARCH

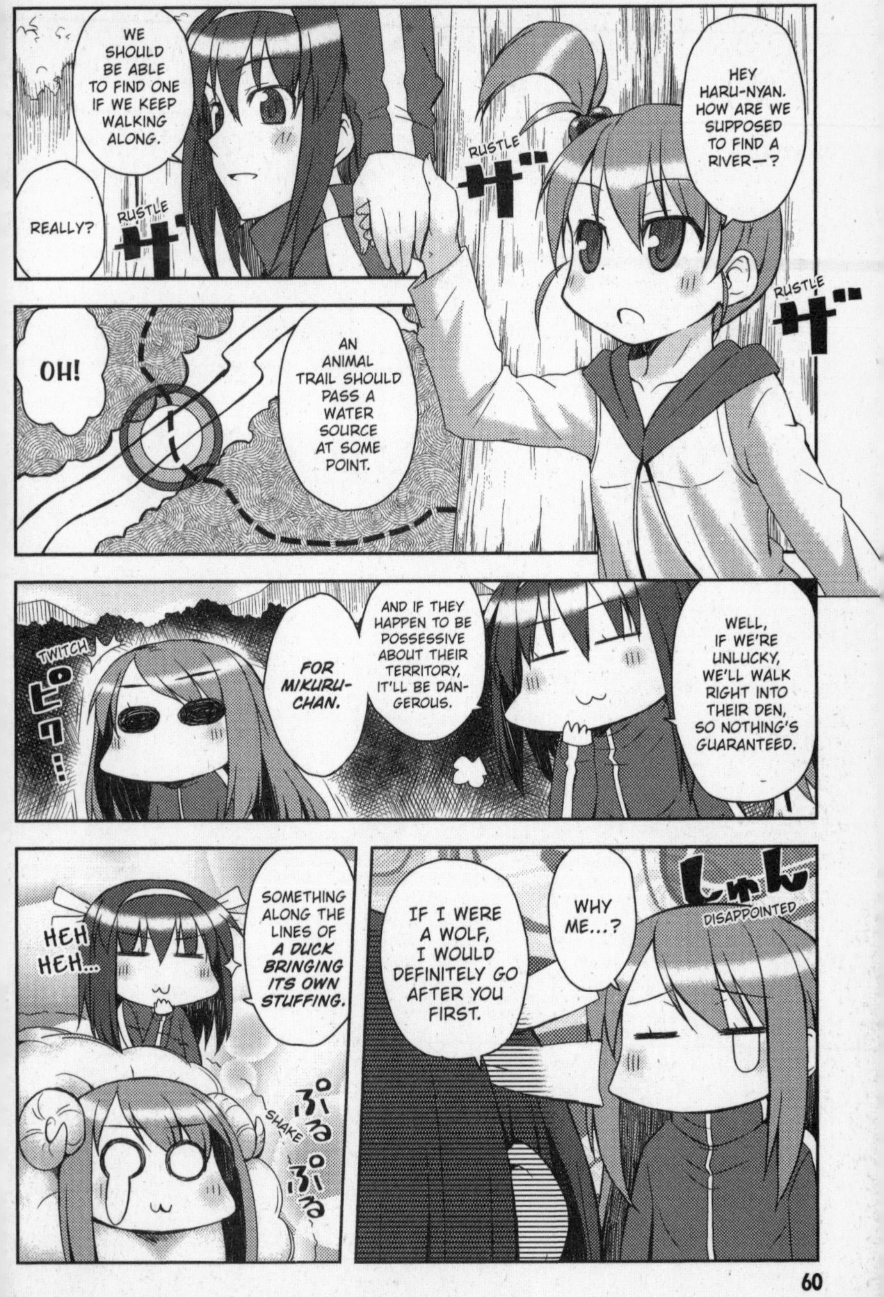

HEY HARU-NYAN. HOW ARE WE SUPPOSED TO FIND A RIVER—?
RUSTLE
WE SHOULD BE ABLE TO FIND ONE IF WE KEEP WALKING ALONG.
RUSTLE
REALLY?
RUSTLE
AN ANIMAL TRAIL SHOULD PASS A WATER SOURCE AT SOME POINT.
OH!
WELL, IF WE'RE UNLUCKY, WE'LL WALK RIGHT INTO THEIR DEN, SO NOTHING'S GUARANTEED.
AND IF THEY HAPPEN TO BE POSSESSIVE ABOUT THEIR TERRITORY, IT'LL BE DANGEROUS.
FOR MIKURU-CHAN.
TWITCH
しゅん
DISAPPOINTED
WHY ME...?
IF I WERE A WOLF, I WOULD DEFINITELY GO AFTER YOU FIRST.
SOMETHING ALONG THE LINES OF A DUCK BRINGING ITS OWN STUFFING.
HEH HEH...
ぷるぷる
SHAKE

CONVENTION

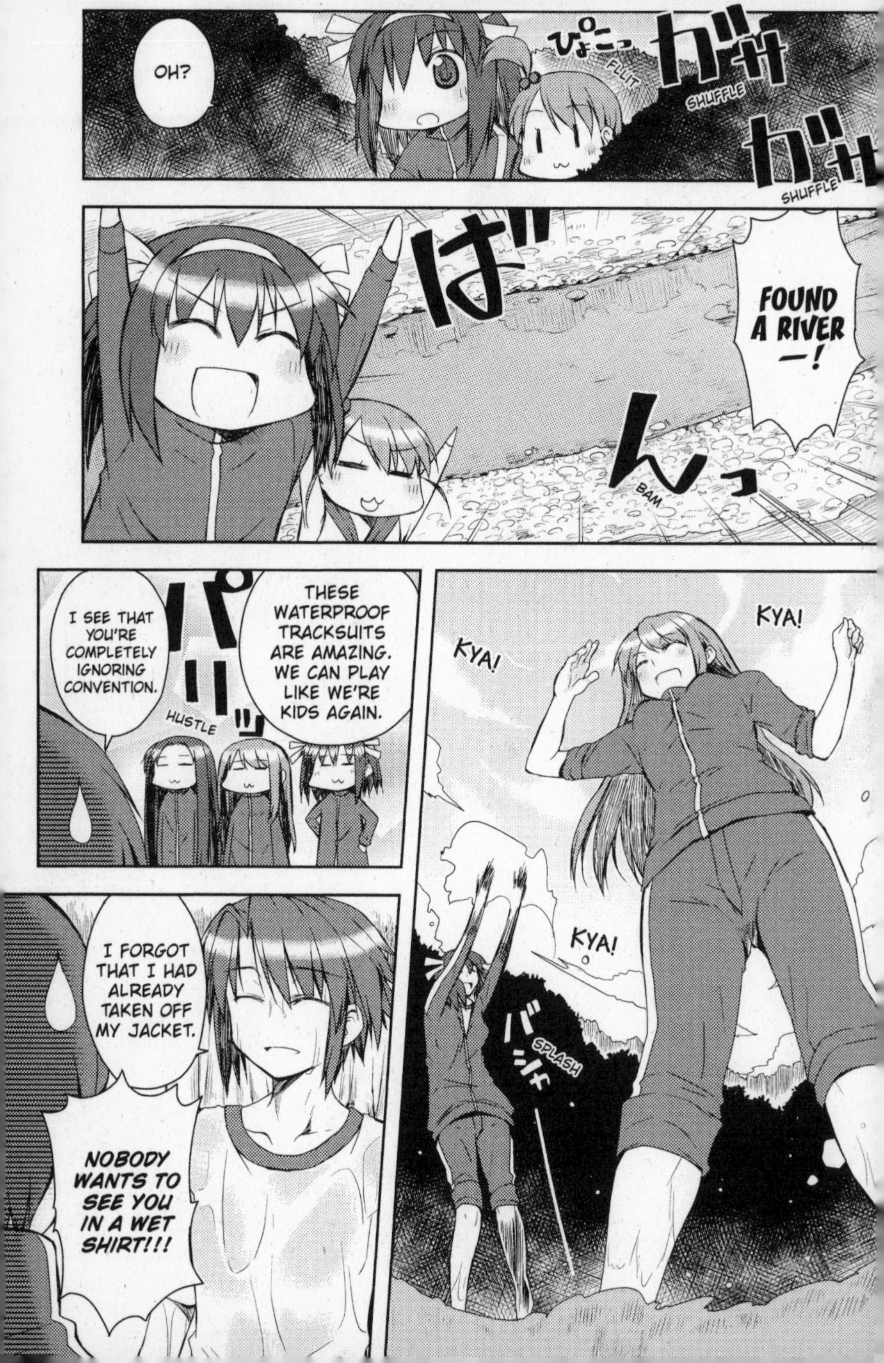
OH?
ぴょこっ
FLLIT
がさ
SHUFFLE
がさ
SHUFFLE
FOUND A RIVER—!
ばーんっ
BAM
KYA!
KYA!
KYA!
バシャ
SPLASH
THESE WATERPROOF TRACKSUITS ARE AMAZING. WE CAN PLAY LIKE WE'RE KIDS AGAIN.
パーッ
HUSTLE
I SEE THAT YOU'RE COMPLETELY IGNORING CONVENTION.
I FORGOT THAT I HAD ALREADY TAKEN OFF MY JACKET.
NOBODY WANTS TO SEE YOU IN A WET SHIRT!!!

DELEGATING RESPONSIBILITY

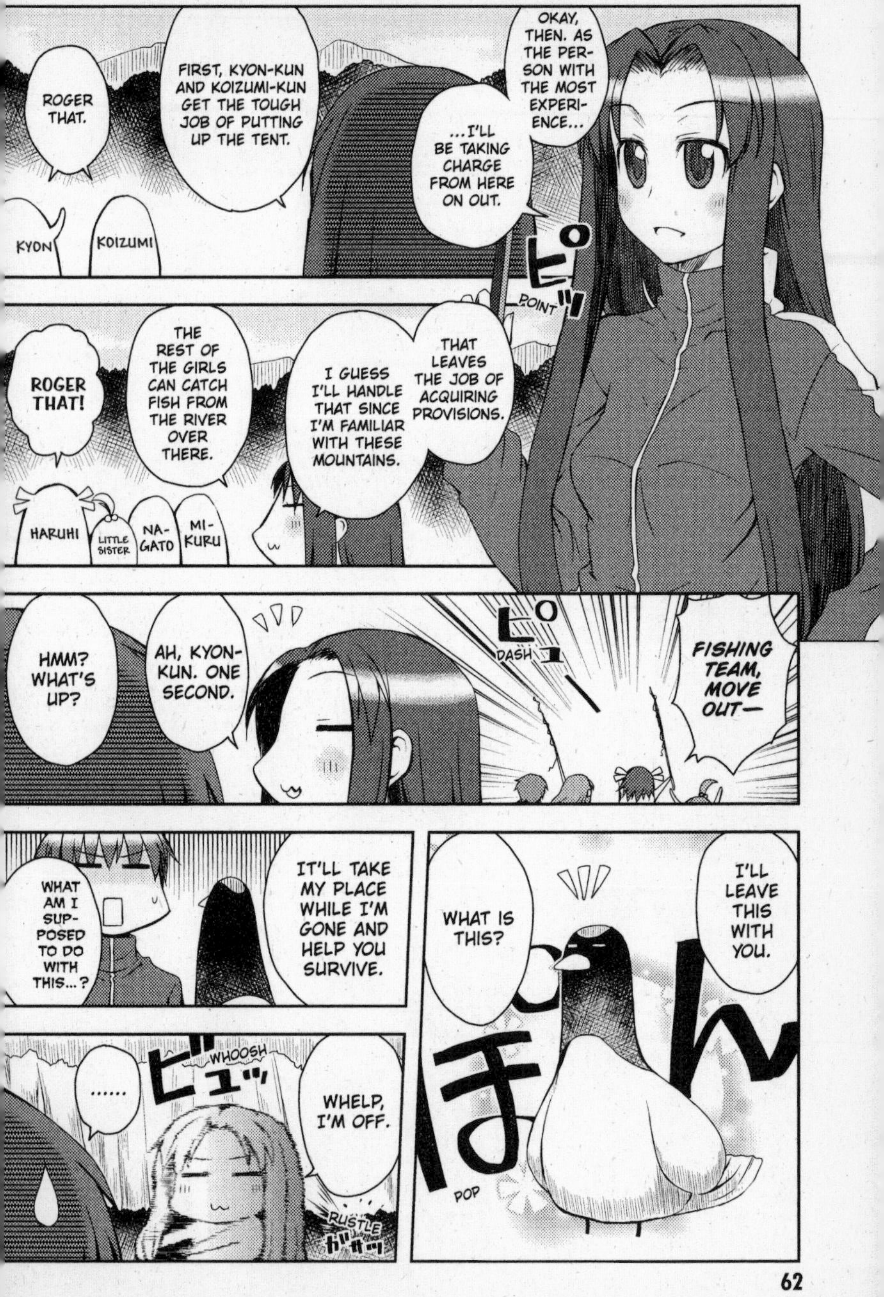
OKAY, THEN. AS THE PERSON WITH THE MOST EXPERIENCE...
...I'LL BE TAKING CHARGE FROM HERE ON OUT.
POINT
FIRST, KYON-KUN AND KOIZUMI-KUN GET THE TOUGH JOB OF PUTTING UP THE TENT.
ROGER THAT.
KOIZUMI
KYON
THAT LEAVES THE JOB OF ACQUIRING PROVISIONS.
I GUESS I'LL HANDLE THAT SINCE I'M FAMILIAR WITH THESE MOUNTAINS.
THE REST OF THE GIRLS CAN CATCH FISH FROM THE RIVER OVER THERE.
ROGER THAT!
MI-KURU
NA-GATO
LITTLE SISTER
HARUHI
FISHING TEAM, MOVE OUT—
DASH
AH, KYON-KUN. ONE SECOND.
HMM? WHAT'S UP?
I'LL LEAVE THIS WITH YOU.
WHAT IS THIS?
POP
IT'LL TAKE MY PLACE WHILE I'M GONE AND HELP YOU SURVIVE.
WHAT AM I SUPPOSED TO DO WITH THIS...?
WHELP, I'M OFF.
WHOOSH
......
RUSTLE

EFFECT OF THE DOLL LEFT BEHIND

•Crane Doll •An object infused with Tsuruya-san's presence. Able to chase away bears with the fighting spirit within.

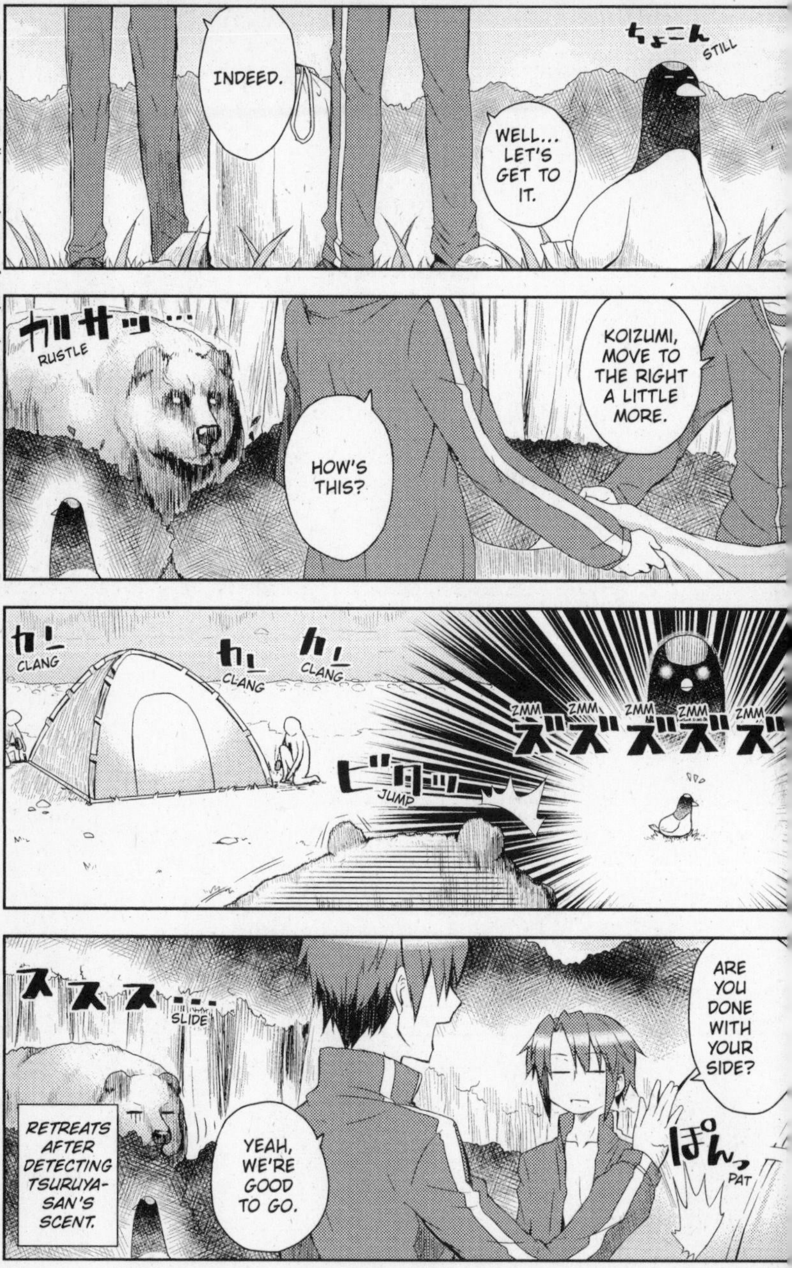
ちょこん
STILL
WELL... LET'S GET TO IT.
INDEED.
KOIZUMI, MOVE TO THE RIGHT A LITTLE MORE.
HOW'S THIS?
カサッ…
RUSTLE
ZMM ZMM ZMM ZMM ZMM
ズズズズズ
ビクッ
JUMP
カン
CLANG
カン
CLANG
カン
CLANG
ARE YOU DONE WITH YOUR SIDE?
ぽんっ
PAT
YEAH, WE'RE GOOD TO GO.
ススス…
SLIDE
RETREATS AFTER DETECTING TSURUYA-SAN'S SCENT.

FISHING

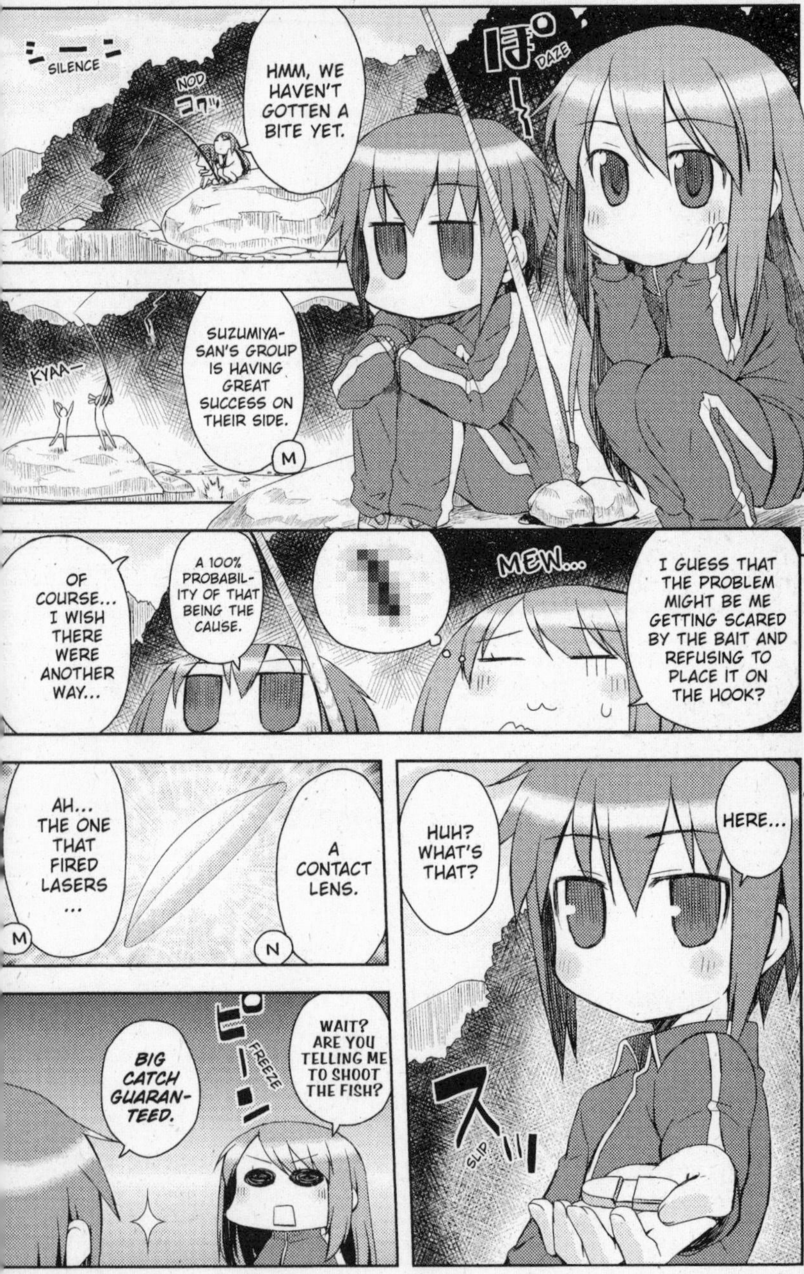

DAZE
HMM, WE HAVEN'T GOTTEN A BITE YET.
SILENCE
NOD
SUZUMIYA-SAN'S GROUP IS HAVING GREAT SUCCESS ON THEIR SIDE.
M
KYAA—
I GUESS THAT THE PROBLEM MIGHT BE ME GETTING SCARED BY THE BAIT AND REFUSING TO PLACE IT ON THE HOOK?
MEW...
A 100% PROBABILITY OF THAT BEING THE CAUSE.
OF COURSE... I WISH THERE WERE ANOTHER WAY...
HERE...
HUH? WHAT'S THAT?
SLIP
A CONTACT LENS.
N
AH... THE ONE THAT FIRED LASERS ...
M
WAIT? ARE YOU TELLING ME TO SHOOT THE FISH?
FREEZE
BIG CATCH GUARANTEED.

•Color contact •The contact lenses used during the filming of the movie "The Adventures of Mikuru Asahina." Nagato confiscated them after an invisible coherent light (laser) was emitted.

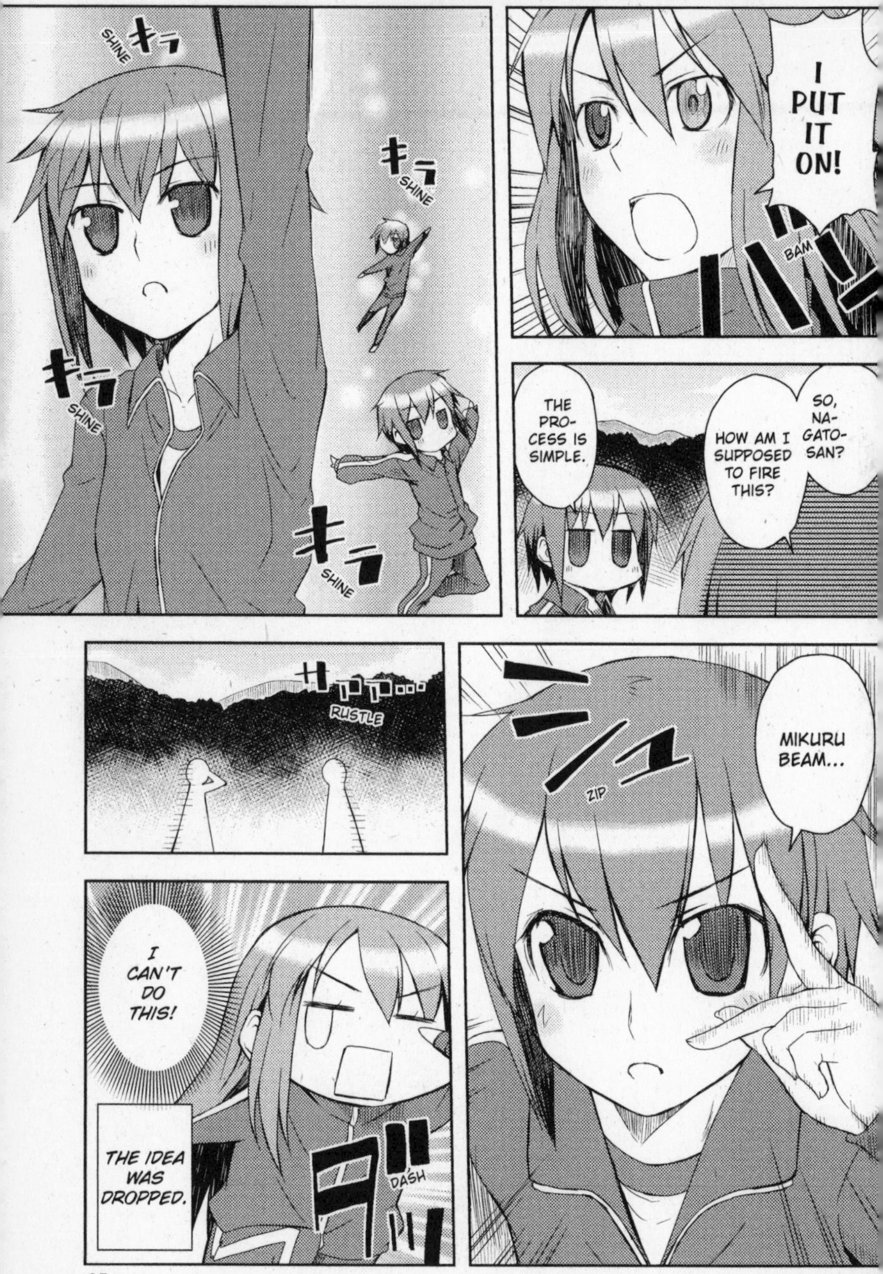
I PUT IT ON!
BAM
SO, NAGATO-SAN?
HOW AM I SUPPOSED TO FIRE THIS?
THE PROCESS IS SIMPLE.
SHINE
SHINE
SHINE
SHINE
MIKURU BEAM...
ZIP
RUSTLE
I CAN'T DO THIS!
DASH
THE IDEA WAS DROPPED.

BIG CATCH

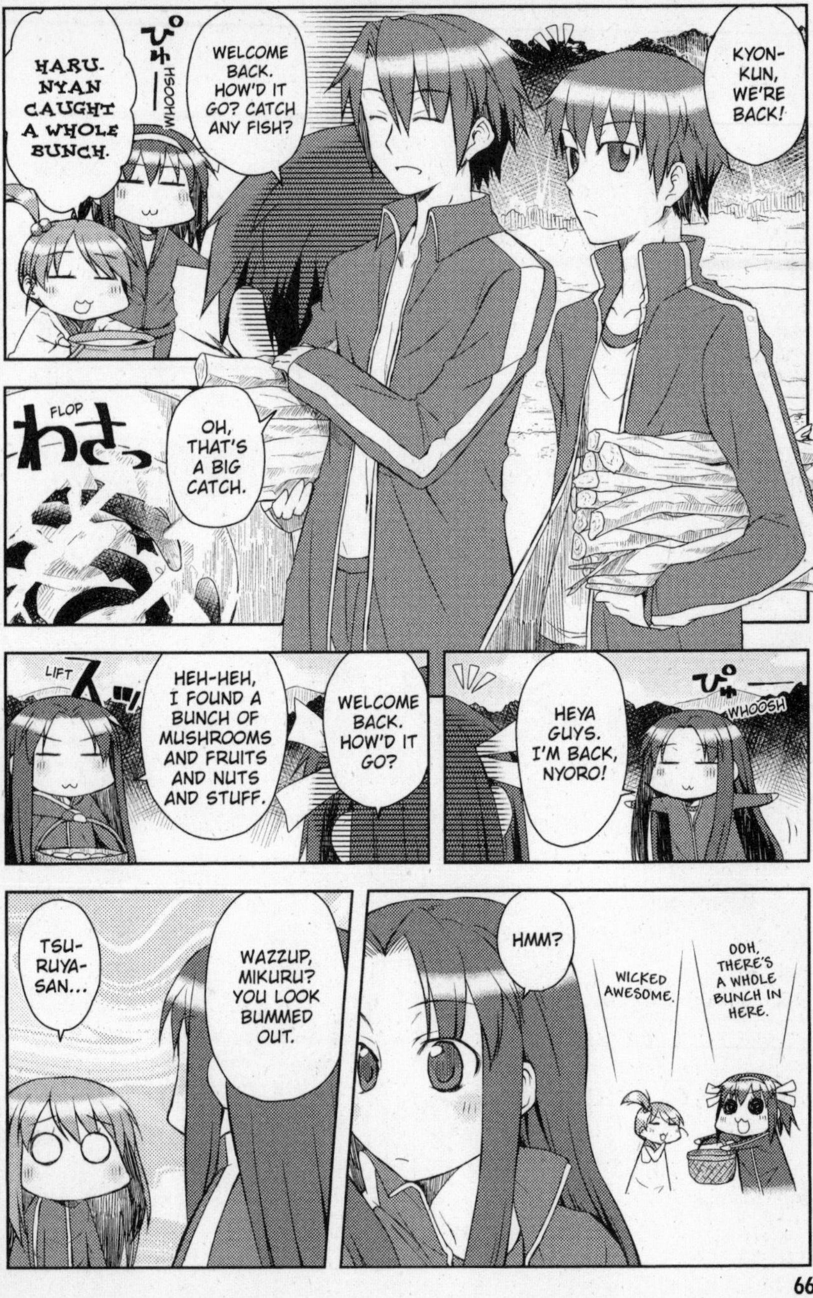
KYON-KUN, WE'RE BACK!
WELCOME BACK. HOW'D IT GO? CATCH ANY FISH?
ぴゅー
WHOOSH
HARU-NYAN CAUGHT A WHOLE BUNCH.
わさっ
FLOP
OH, THAT'S A BIG CATCH.
ぴゅー
WHOOSH
HEYA GUYS. I'M BACK, NYORO!
WELCOME BACK. HOW'D IT GO?
HEH-HEH, I FOUND A BUNCH OF MUSHROOMS AND FRUITS AND NUTS AND STUFF.
ん
LIFT
OOH, THERE'S A WHOLE BUNCH IN HERE.
WICKED AWESOME.
HMM?
WAZZUP, MIKURU? YOU LOOK BUMMED OUT.
TSU-RUYA-SAN...

REDEMPTION

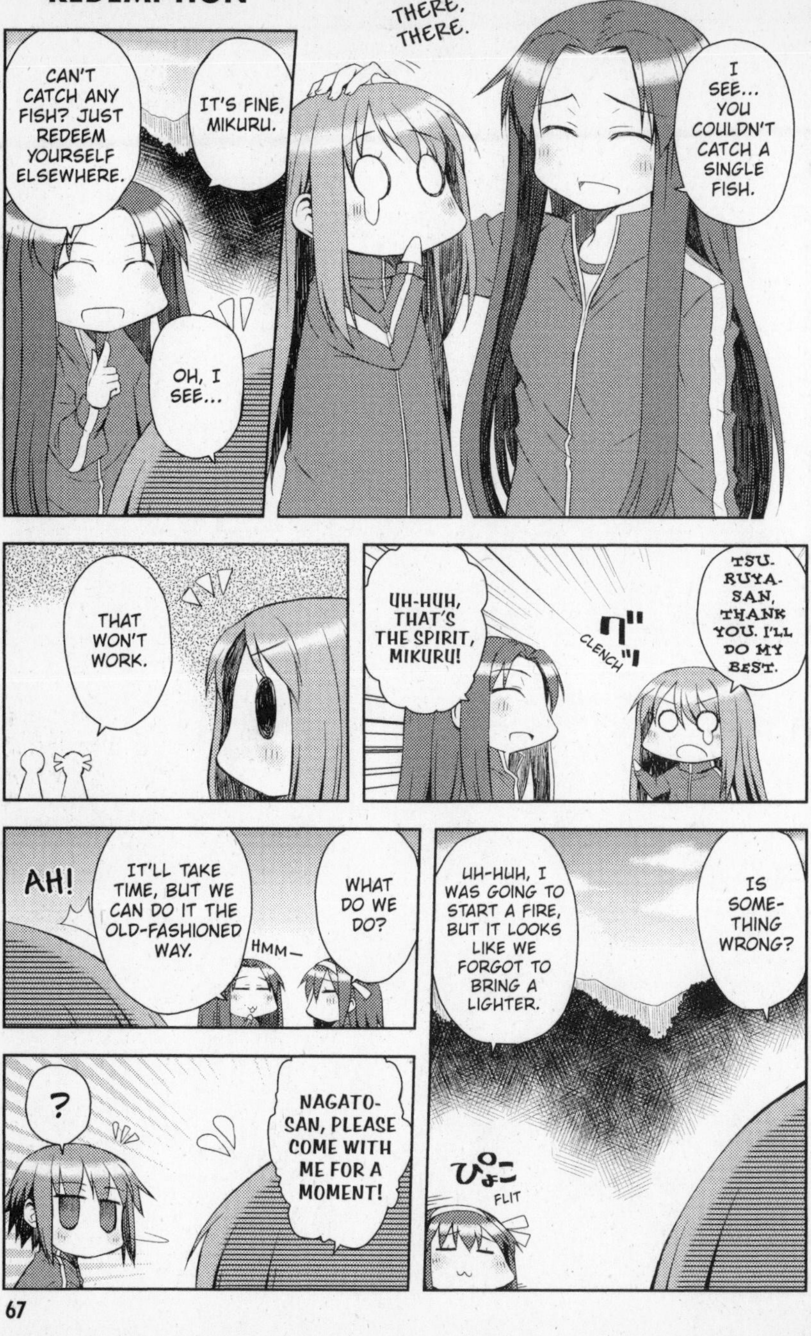
I SEE... YOU COULDN'T CATCH A SINGLE FISH.
THERE, THERE.
IT'S FINE, MIKURU.
CAN'T CATCH ANY FISH? JUST REDEEM YOURSELF ELSEWHERE.
OH, I SEE...
TSU-RUYA-SAN, THANK YOU. I'LL DO MY BEST.
CLENCH
UH-HUH, THAT'S THE SPIRIT, MIKURU!
THAT WON'T WORK.
IS SOMETHING WRONG?
UH-HUH, I WAS GOING TO START A FIRE, BUT IT LOOKS LIKE WE FORGOT TO BRING A LIGHTER.
ぴょこ
FLIT
WHAT DO WE DO?
IT'LL TAKE TIME, BUT WE CAN DO IT THE OLD-FASHIONED WAY.
HMM—
AH!
NAGATO-SAN, PLEASE COME WITH ME FOR A MOMENT!
?

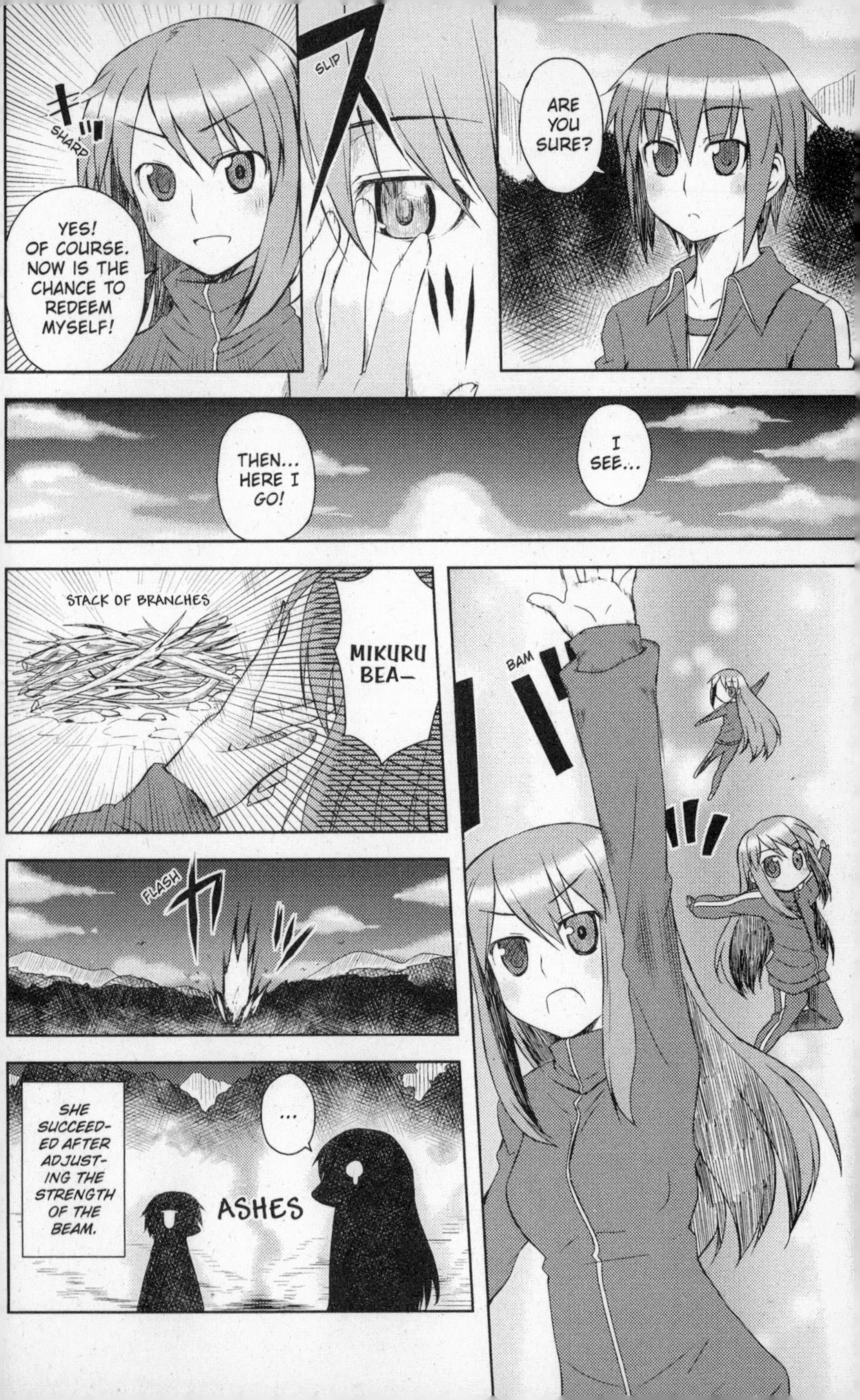
ARE YOU SURE?
SLIP
SHARP
YES! OF COURSE. NOW IS THE CHANCE TO REDEEM MYSELF!
I SEE...
THEN... HERE I GO!
BAM
STACK OF BRANCHES
MIKURU BEA—
FLASH
...
SHE SUCCEEDED AFTER ADJUSTING THE STRENGTH OF THE BEAM.
ASHES

MAY SICKNESS

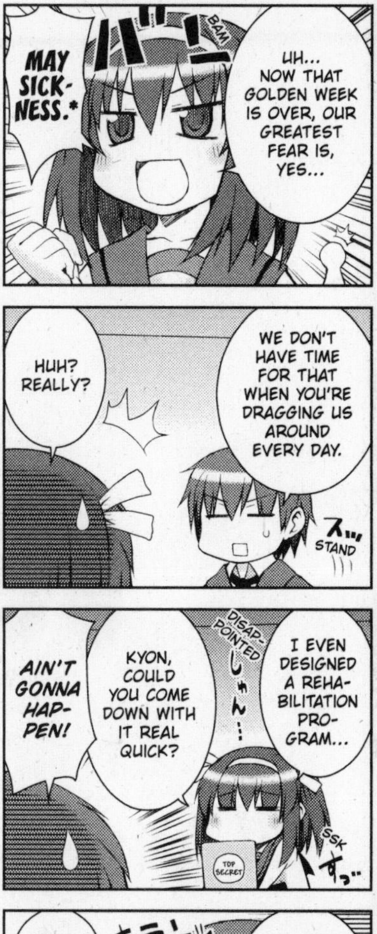
BAM
UH... NOW THAT GOLDEN WEEK IS OVER, OUR GREATEST FEAR IS, YES...
MAY SICKNESS.*
WE DON'T HAVE TIME FOR THAT WHEN YOU'RE DRAGGING US AROUND EVERY DAY.
HUH? REALLY?
STAND
I EVEN DESIGNED A REHABILITATION PROGRAM...
DISAPPOINTED
KYON, COULD YOU COME DOWN WITH IT REAL QUICK?
AIN'T GONNA HAPPEN!
TOP SECRET
SSK
HOWEVER, I HAPPEN TO KNOW SOMEONE WHO'S GOT IT BAD.
SPARKLE
NICE ONE, KYON.
YAY!
TURN

TEST SUBJECT

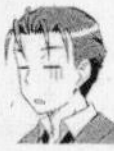

•Taniguchi •Kyon's unlucky friend.
The person most susceptible to May sickness.

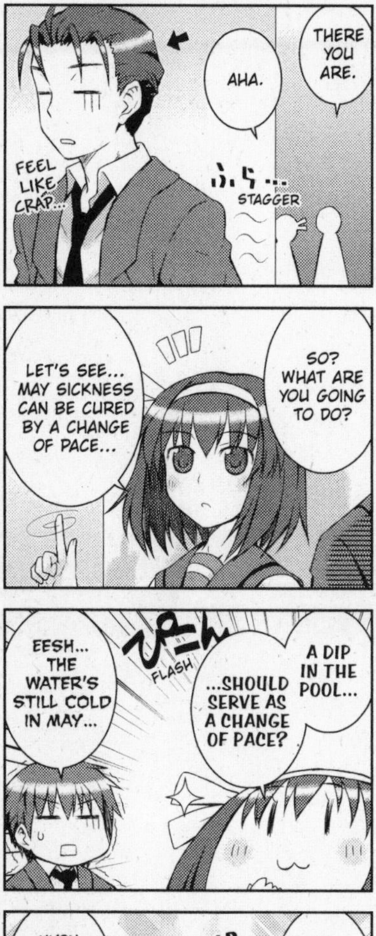
THERE YOU ARE.
AHA.
STAGGER
FEEL LIKE CRAP...
SO? WHAT ARE YOU GOING TO DO?
LET'S SEE... MAY SICKNESS CAN BE CURED BY A CHANGE OF PACE...
A DIP IN THE POOL...
...SHOULD SERVE AS A CHANGE OF PACE?
FLASH
EESH... THE WATER'S STILL COLD IN MAY...
BUT I GUESS THAT MAKES SENSE.
SHINE
EH HEH HEH HEH.
KYON, YOU'RE AWFULLY UNDERSTANDING TODAY.

*BECAUSE THE JAPANESE SCHOOL YEAR STARTS IN APRIL, "MAY SICKNESS" IS WHEN NEW STUDENTS STRUGGLE TO GET BACK TO THEIR ROUTINE AFTER THE BREAK.

BAIT

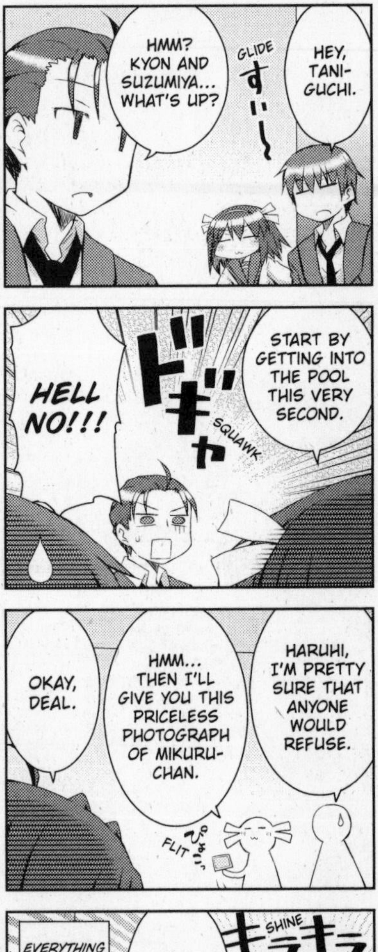
HEY, TANI-GUCHI.
GLIDE
すぃ~
HMM? KYON AND SUZUMIYA... WHAT'S UP?
START BY GETTING INTO THE POOL THIS VERY SECOND.
ドギャ
SQUAWK
HELL NO!!!
HARUHI, I'M PRETTY SURE THAT ANYONE WOULD REFUSE.
HMM... THEN I'LL GIVE YOU THIS PRICELESS PHOTOGRAPH OF MIKURU-CHAN.
OKAY, DEAL.
FLIT
キラキラ
SHINE
LET'S DO THIS.
EVERYTHING WENT AS PLANNED, AND THEY WERE STILL PISSED FOR SOME REASON.
THUMBS UP
SNAP

COMPLETELY CURED

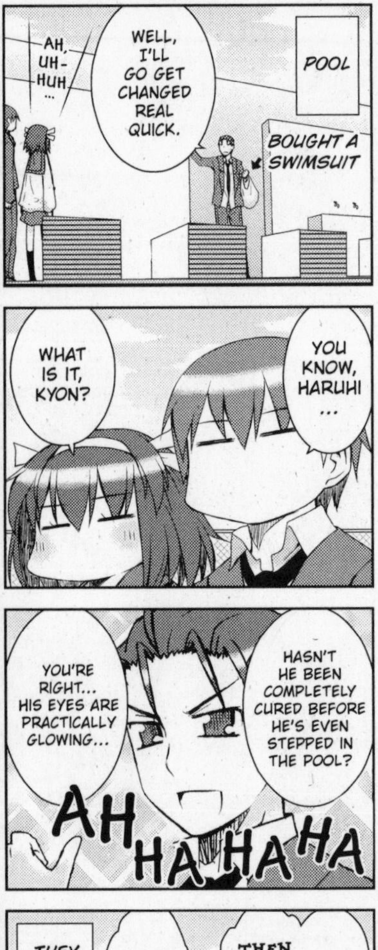
POOL
WELL, I'LL GO GET CHANGED REAL QUICK.
AH, UH-HUH...
BOUGHT A SWIMSUIT
YOU KNOW, HARUHI...
WHAT IS IT, KYON?
HASN'T HE BEEN COMPLETELY CURED BEFORE HE'S EVEN STEPPED IN THE POOL?
YOU'RE RIGHT... HIS EYES ARE PRACTICALLY GLOWING...
AH HA HA HA HA
OKAY...
THEN LET'S GET OUTTA HERE!
YEP!
THEY LEFT IN A HURRY.
SHOOM

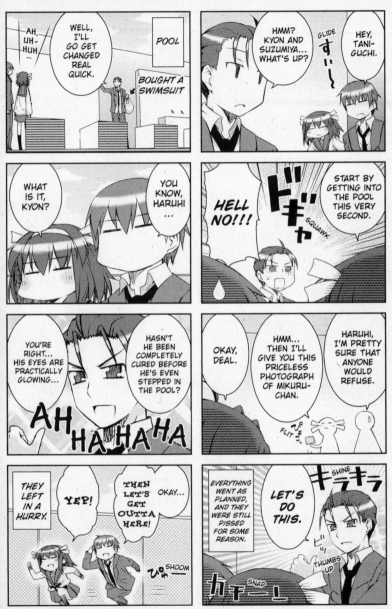

CHILDREN'S DAY

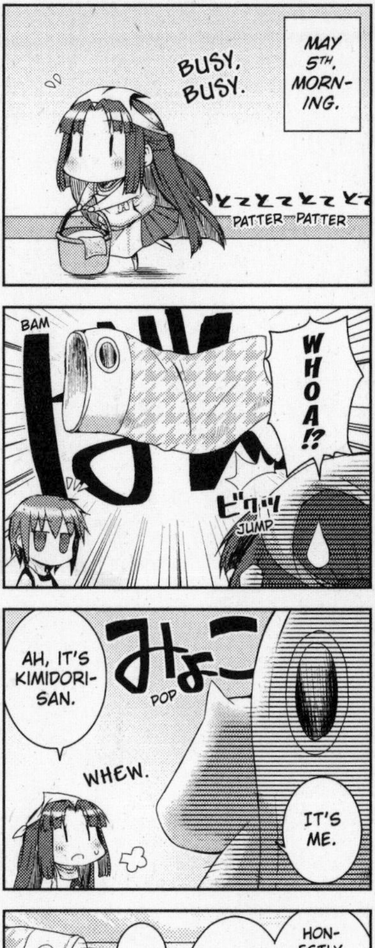
MAY 5TH, MORNING.
BUSY, BUSY.
PATTER PATTER
BAM
WHOA!?
ビクッ
JUMP
AH, IT'S KIMIDORI-SAN.
みょこ
POP
WHEW.
IT'S ME.
HONESTLY, WHAT ARE YOU DOING...?
IF YOU'RE BORED, YOU CAN HELP ME CLEAN.
...
ACHAKURA-SAN IS TOO BUSY IN THE MORNING TO ENTERTAIN THEM.
プンスカ
SCOWL

HOUSEKEEPER MODE

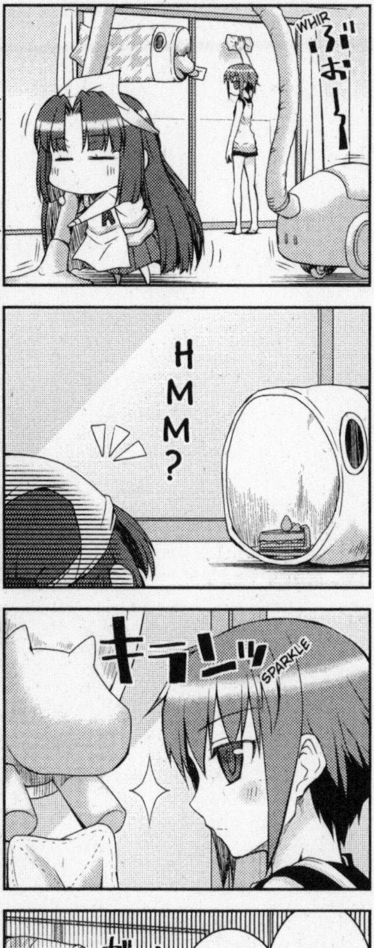
WHIR
HMM?
SPARKLE
NAGATO-SAN IS SO HOPELESS...
SHE ALWAYS LEAVES HER TOYS LYING AROUND.
SHOCK
たたみっ
PAT
ACHAKURA-SAN IN HOUSEKEEPER MODE IS A TOUGH NUT TO CRACK.

•Achakura-san •Back in miniature action after being destroyed in her battle with Nagato. Seems to enjoy doing housework.

•Kimidori-san •A life form (dog) created from a balloon by Nagato. Has a rather playful nature.

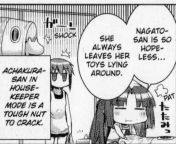

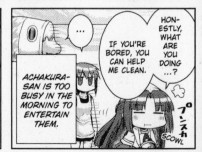

POSITIVE REINFORCEMENT

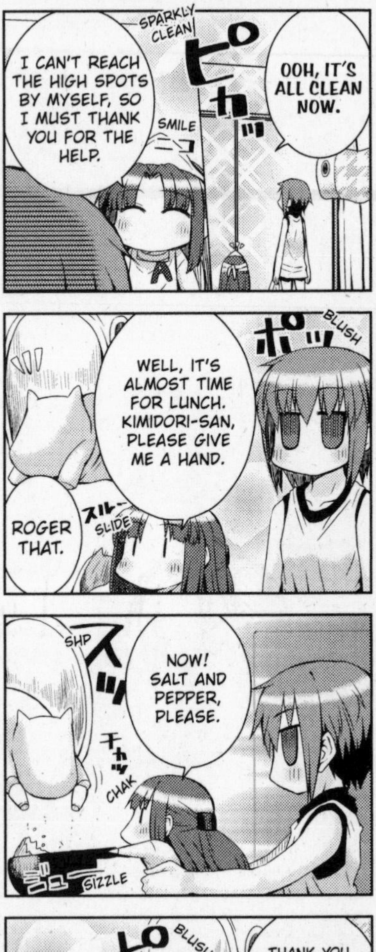
OOH, IT'S ALL CLEAN NOW.
ピカッ
SPARKLY CLEAN
ニコ
SMILE
I CAN'T REACH THE HIGH SPOTS BY MYSELF, SO I MUST THANK YOU FOR THE HELP.
ポッ
BLUSH
WELL, IT'S ALMOST TIME FOR LUNCH. KIMIDORI-SAN, PLEASE GIVE ME A HAND.
スルー
SLIDE
ROGER THAT.
NOW! SALT AND PEPPER, PLEASE.
スッ
SHP
チャッ
CHAK
SIZZLE
THANK YOU VERY MUCH, KIMIDORI-SAN. IT'S SO MUCH EASIER WITH YOUR HELP.
ポッ
BLUSH
IT FEELS LIKE THEY'RE BEING TAMED BY ACHAKURA-SAN.

BUT IN THE END

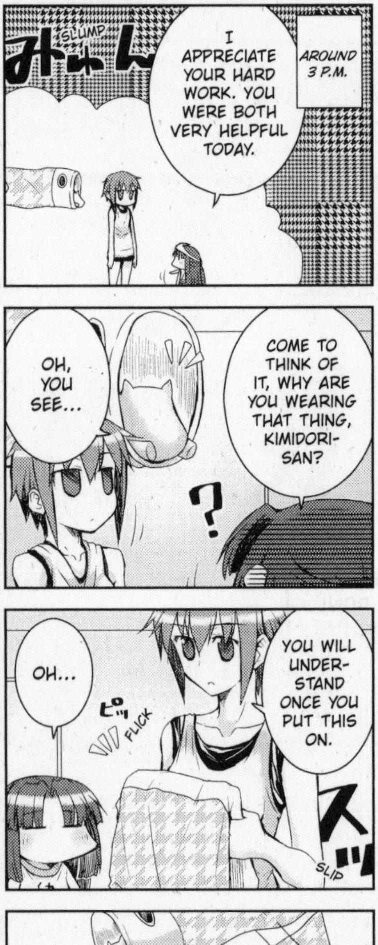
AROUND 3 P.M.
I APPRECIATE YOUR HARD WORK. YOU WERE BOTH VERY HELPFUL TODAY.
みょん
SLUMP
COME TO THINK OF IT, WHY ARE YOU WEARING THAT THING, KIMIDORI-SAN?
?
OH, YOU SEE...
YOU WILL UNDER-STAND ONCE YOU PUT THIS ON.
スッ
SLIP
ピッ
FLICK
OH...
AH—
STILL ENDS UP AS NAGATO'S PLAY-THING.

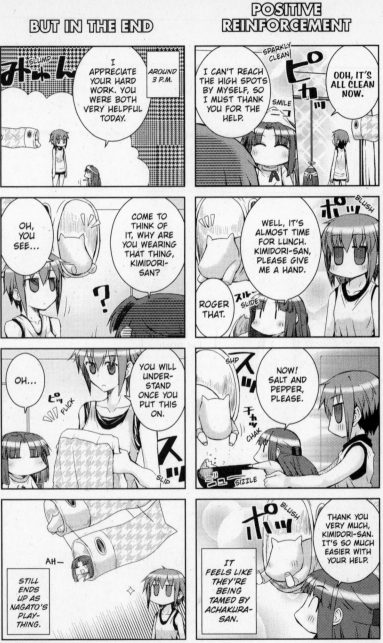

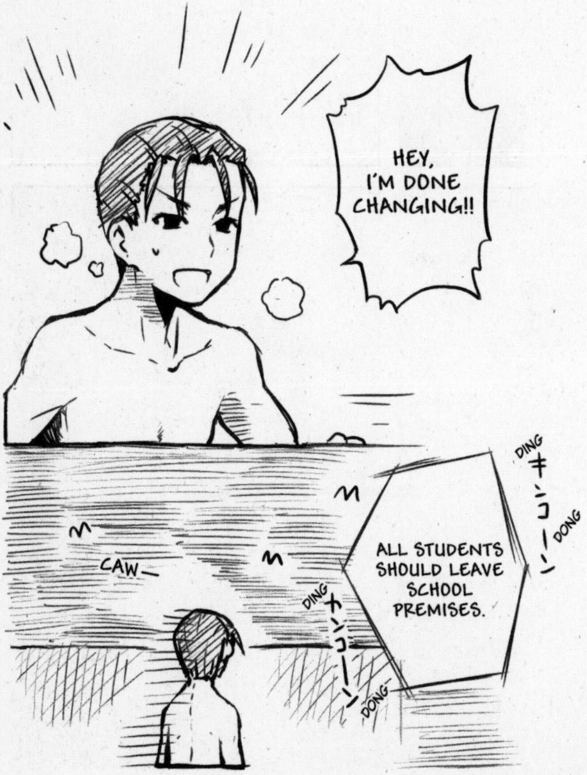
HEY, I'M DONE CHANGING!!
DING キンコーン DONG
ALL STUDENTS SHOULD LEAVE SCHOOL PREMISES.
DING キンコーン DONG
CAW—

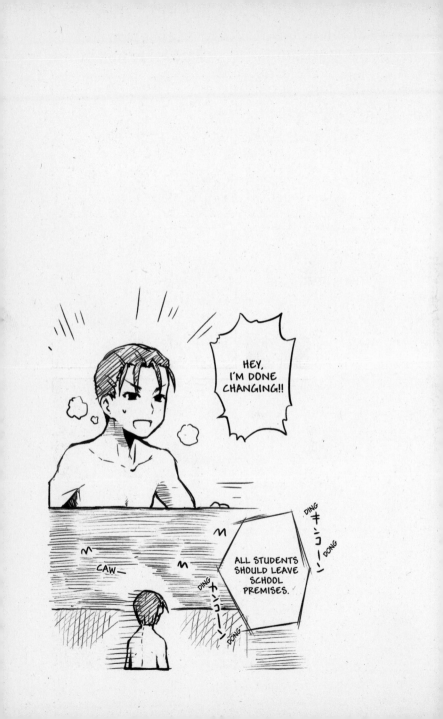

BAMBOO IN TRANSIT

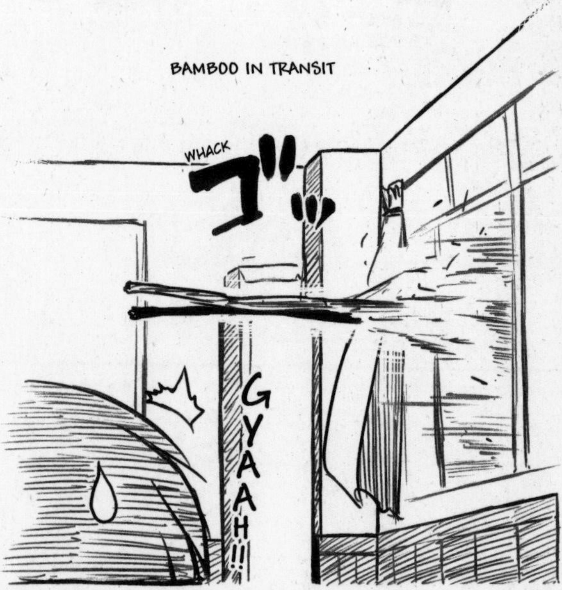
WHACK
ゴッ
GYAAH!!

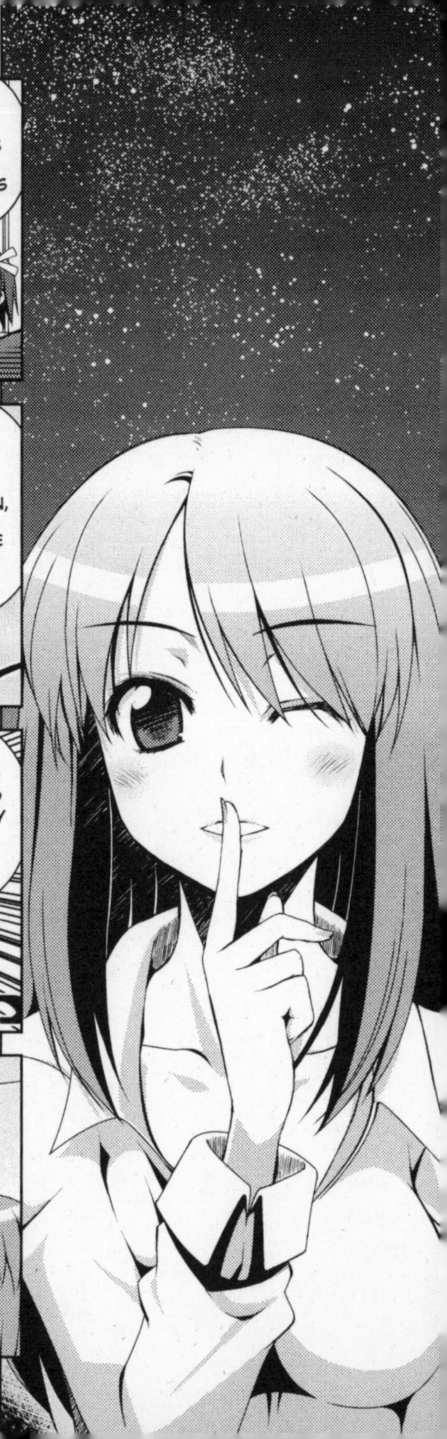

JULY 7TH

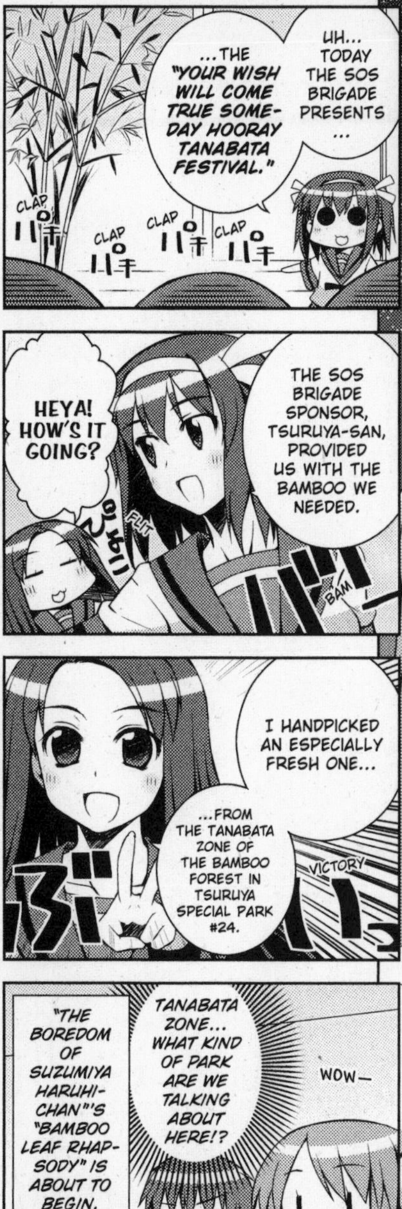

UH... TODAY THE SOS BRIGADE PRESENTS ...
...THE "YOUR WISH WILL COME TRUE SOME-DAY HOORAY TANABATA FESTIVAL."
CLAP
CLAP
CLAP
CLAP
THE SOS BRIGADE SPONSOR, TSURUYA-SAN, PROVIDED US WITH THE BAMBOO WE NEEDED.
HEYA! HOW'S IT GOING?
FLIT
BAM
I HANDPICKED AN ESPECIALLY FRESH ONE...
...FROM THE TANABATA ZONE OF THE BAMBOO FOREST IN TSURUYA SPECIAL PARK #24.
VICTORY
WOW—
TANABATA ZONE... WHAT KIND OF PARK ARE WE TALKING ABOUT HERE!?
"THE BOREDOM OF SUZUMIYA HARUHI-CHAN"*'S "BAMBOO LEAF RHAPSODY" IS ABOUT TO BEGIN.
SHOCK

*READ THE STORY "BAMBOO LEAF RHAPSODY" FOUND IN THE ORIGINAL NOVEL "THE BOREDOM OF HARUHI SUZUMIYA" FOR MORE INFORMATION!

REMEDY

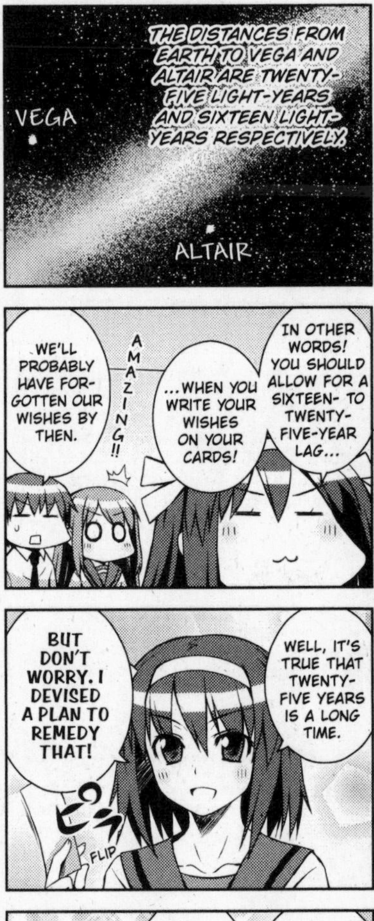
THE DISTANCES FROM EARTH TO VEGA AND ALTAIR ARE TWENTY-FIVE LIGHT-YEARS AND SIXTEEN LIGHT-YEARS RESPECTIVELY.
VEGA
ALTAIR
IN OTHER WORDS! YOU SHOULD ALLOW FOR A SIXTEEN- TO TWENTY-FIVE-YEAR LAG...
...WHEN YOU WRITE YOUR WISHES ON YOUR CARDS!
AMAZING!!
WE'LL PROBABLY HAVE FORGOTTEN OUR WISHES BY THEN.
WELL, IT'S TRUE THAT TWENTY-FIVE YEARS IS A LONG TIME.
BUT DON'T WORRY. I DEVISED A PLAN TO REMEDY THAT!
FLIP
SEE? I WROTE EXPRESS ON THE CARDS.
I'M GUESSING THAT IT'LL ONLY TAKE HALF THE TIME THIS WAY.
I SEE.
THAT'S ALL IT TAKES?
FWP
EXPRESS

MOTIVATION

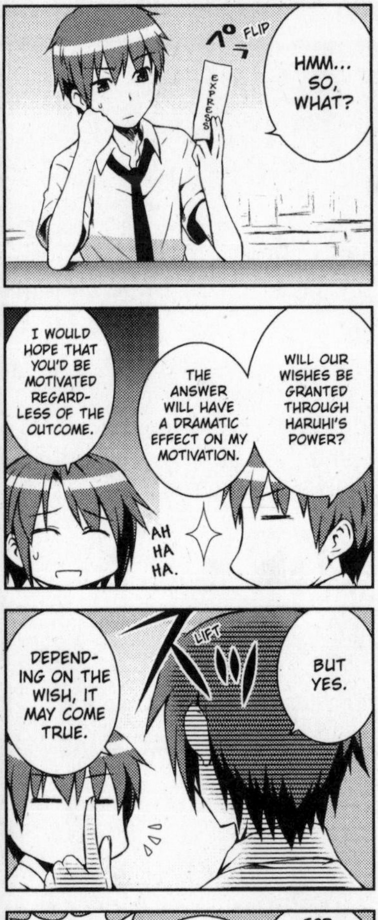
HMM... SO, WHAT?
FLIP
EXPRESS
WILL OUR WISHES BE GRANTED THROUGH HARUHI'S POWER?
THE ANSWER WILL HAVE A DRAMATIC EFFECT ON MY MOTIVATION.
I WOULD HOPE THAT YOU'D BE MOTIVATED REGARDLESS OF THE OUTCOME.
AH HA HA.
BUT YES.
LIFT
DEPENDING ON THE WISH, IT MAY COME TRUE.
FOR EXAMPLE, SOMETHING ALONG THE LINES OF "YOU AND SUZUMIYA WILL OOOO."
THAT SHOULD SERVE TO LESSEN MY WORKLOAD WITH THE AGENCY. MIND IF I WRITE THAT DOWN?
WHEN DID TANABATA TURN INTO A PARTY GAME!?
EXPRE

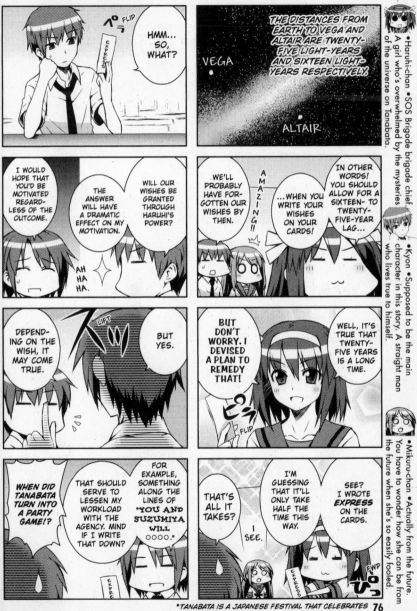

•Haruhi-chan •SOS Brigade brigade chief. A girl who's overwhelmed by the mysteries of the universe on Tanabata.

•Kyon •Supposed to be the main character in this story. A straight man who lives true to himself.

•Mikuru-chan •Actually from the future. You have to wonder how she can be from the future when she's so easily fooled.

*TANABATA IS A JAPANESE FESTIVAL THAT CELEBRATES THE ANNUAL REUNION OF LOVERS ORIHIME (THE STAR VEGA) AND HIKOBOSHI (THE STAR ALTAIR).

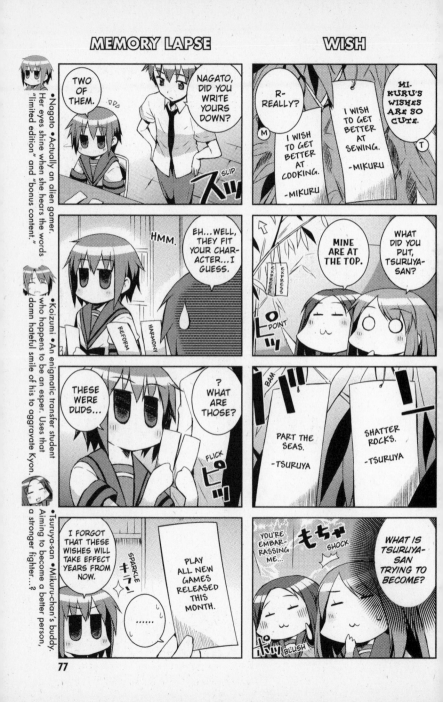

WISH

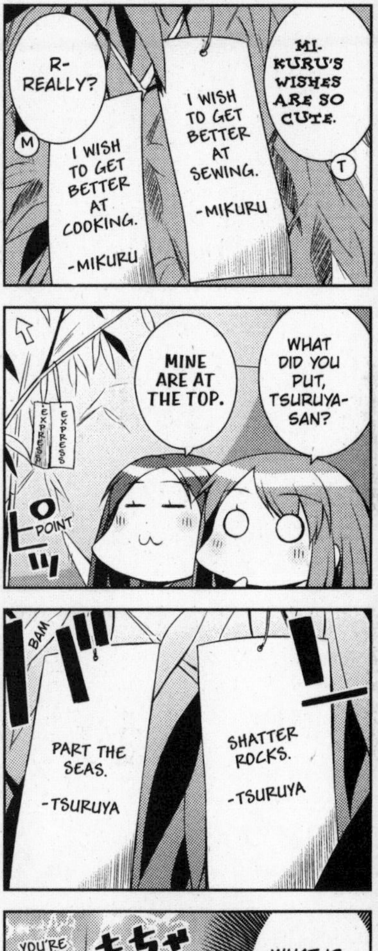

MI-KURU'S WISHES ARE SO CUTE.
T
I WISH TO GET BETTER AT SEWING. -MIKURU
R- REALLY?
M
I WISH TO GET BETTER AT COOKING. -MIKURU
WHAT DID YOU PUT, TSURUYA-SAN?
MINE ARE AT THE TOP.
EXPRESS
EXPRESS
POINT
SHATTER ROCKS. -TSURUYA
BAM
PART THE SEAS. -TSURUYA
WHAT IS TSURUYA-SAN TRYING TO BECOME?
SHOCK
YOU'RE EMBARRASSING ME...
BLUSH

MEMORY LAPSE

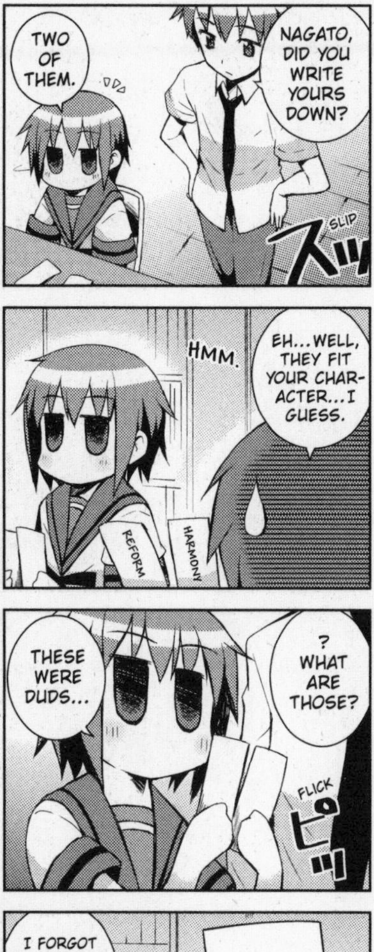

NAGATO, DID YOU WRITE YOURS DOWN?
SLIP
TWO OF THEM.
EH...WELL, THEY FIT YOUR CHARACTER...I GUESS.
HMM.
HARMONY
REFORM
? WHAT ARE THOSE?
FLICK
THESE WERE DUDS...
PLAY ALL NEW GAMES RELEASED THIS MONTH.
......
SPARKLE
I FORGOT THAT THESE WISHES WILL TAKE EFFECT YEARS FROM NOW.

•Nagato •Actually an alien gamer. Her eyes shine when she hears the words "limited edition" and "bonus content."

•Koizumi •An enigmatic transfer student who happens to be an esper. Uses that damn hateful smile of his to aggravate Kyon.

•Tsuruya-san •Mikuru-chan's buddy. Aiming to become a better person, a stronger fighter...?

MISSION

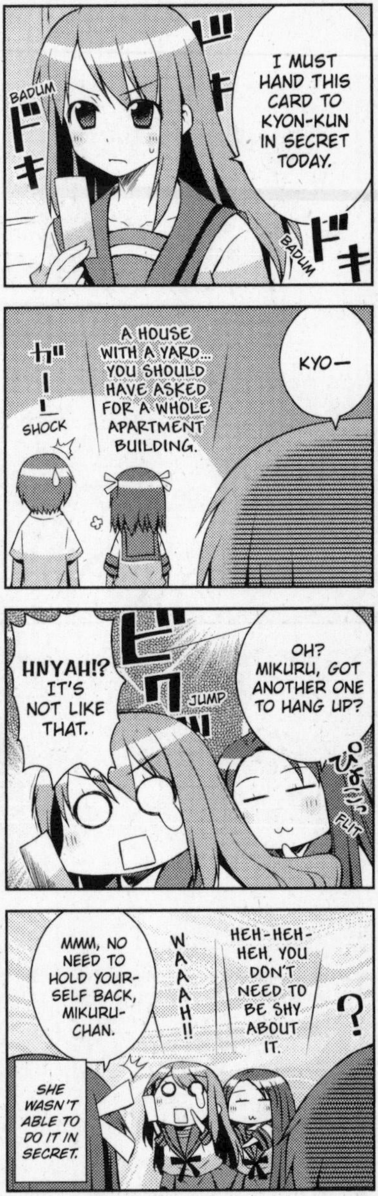
BADUM
I MUST HAND THIS CARD TO KYON-KUN IN SECRET TODAY.
BADUM
KYO—
A HOUSE WITH A YARD... YOU SHOULD HAVE ASKED FOR A WHOLE APARTMENT BUILDING.
SHOCK
OH? MIKURU, GOT ANOTHER ONE TO HANG UP?
HNYAH!? IT'S NOT LIKE THAT.
JUMP
FLIT
HEH-HEH-HEH, YOU DON'T NEED TO BE SHY ABOUT IT.
?
WAAAH!!
MMM, NO NEED TO HOLD YOURSELF BACK, MIKURU-CHAN.
SHE WASN'T ABLE TO DO IT IN SECRET.

RECYCLE

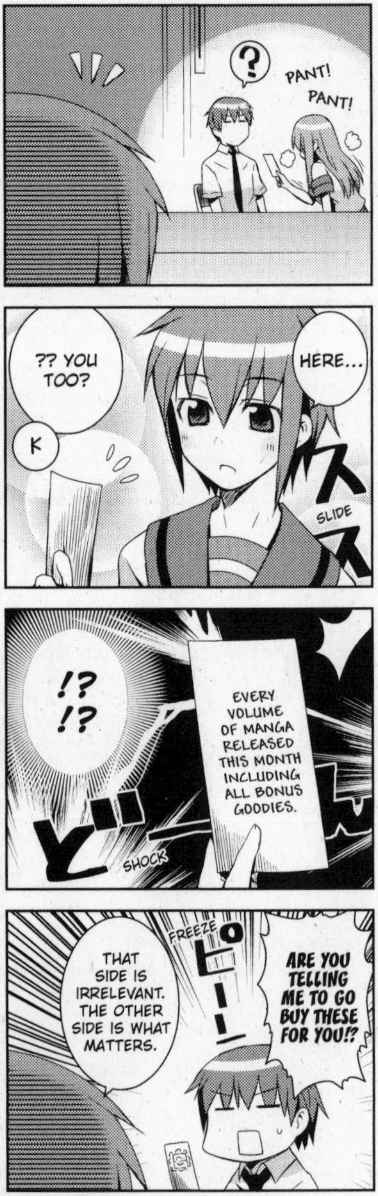
?
PANT!
PANT!
HERE...
SLIDE
?? YOU TOO?
K
!? !?
EVERY VOLUME OF MANGA RELEASED THIS MONTH INCLUDING ALL BONUS GOODIES.
SHOCK
FREEZE
ARE YOU TELLING ME TO GO BUY THESE FOR YOU!?
THAT SIDE IS IRRELEVANT. THE OTHER SIDE IS WHAT MATTERS.

•Mikuru's Card •It says, "Please wait in the clubroom after we're done."

•Nagato's Card •Decorated by an odd symbol. Actually an important item.

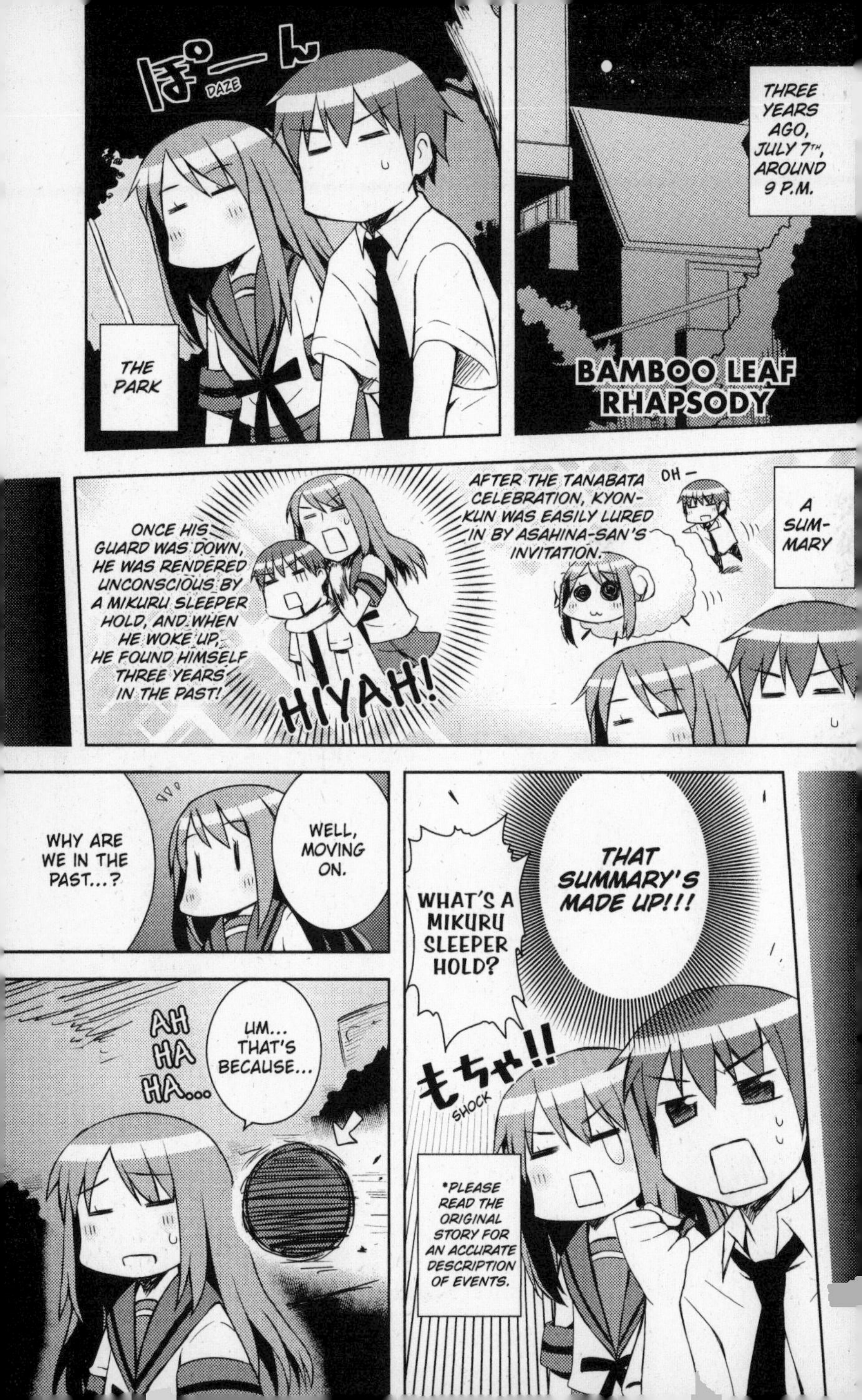
THREE YEARS AGO, JULY 7TH, AROUND 9 P.M.
BAMBOO LEAF RHAPSODY
ぽーん
DAZE
THE PARK
A SUMMARY
OH—
AFTER THE TANABATA CELEBRATION, KYON-KUN WAS EASILY LURED IN BY ASAHINA-SAN'S INVITATION.
ONCE HIS GUARD WAS DOWN, HE WAS RENDERED UNCONSCIOUS BY A MIKURU SLEEPER HOLD, AND WHEN HE WOKE UP, HE FOUND HIMSELF THREE YEARS IN THE PAST!
HIYAH!
THAT SUMMARY'S MADE UP!!!
WHAT'S A MIKURU SLEEPER HOLD?
もちゃ!!
SHOCK
*PLEASE READ THE ORIGINAL STORY FOR AN ACCURATE DESCRIPTION OF EVENTS.
WELL, MOVING ON.
WHY ARE WE IN THE PAST...?
UM... THAT'S BECAUSE...
AH HA HA...

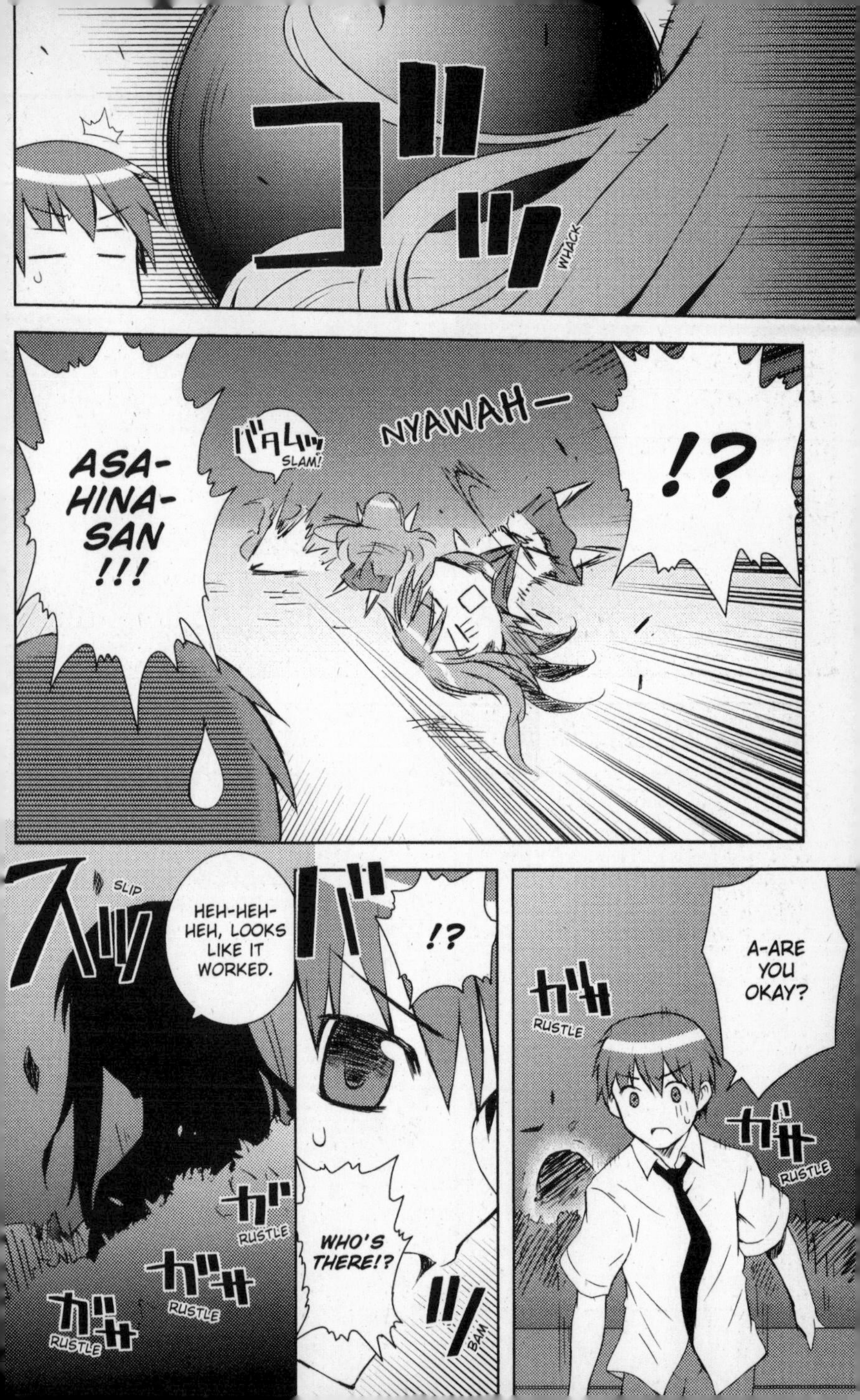
ゴッ
WHACK
NYAWAH—
!?
バタムッ
SLAM!
ASA-HINA-SAN!!!
A-ARE YOU OKAY?
ガサ
RUSTLE
ガサ
RUSTLE
バ
!?
WHO'S THERE!?
ッ
BAM
スッ
SLIP
HEH-HEH-HEH, LOOKS LIKE IT WORKED.
ガ
RUSTLE
ガサ
RUSTLE
ガサ
RUSTLE

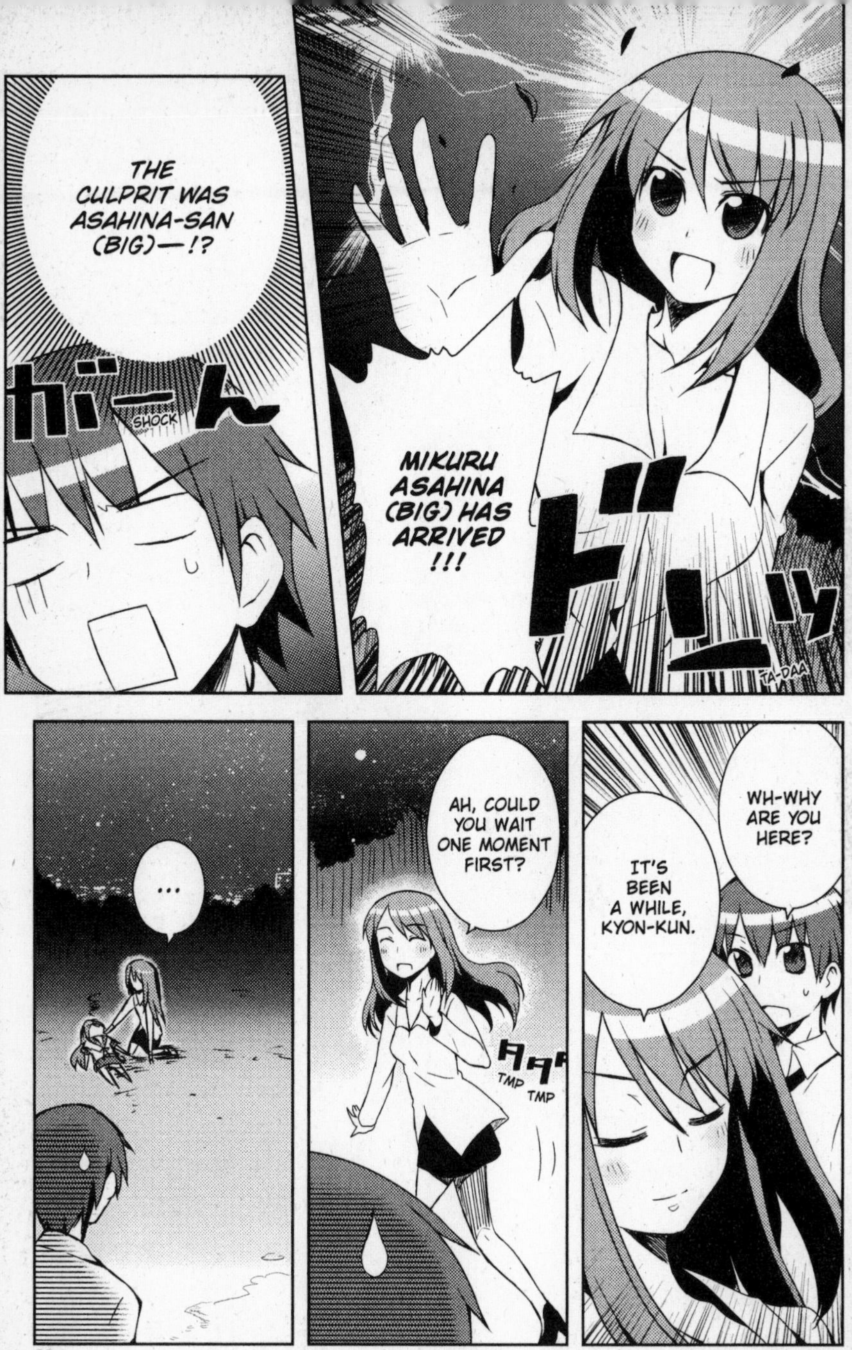
MIKURU ASAHINA (BIG) HAS ARRIVED!!!
TA-DAA
THE CULPRIT WAS ASAHINA-SAN (BIG)—!?
がーん
SHOCK
WH-WHY ARE YOU HERE?
IT'S BEEN A WHILE, KYON-KUN.
AH, COULD YOU WAIT ONE MOMENT FIRST?
タタ
TMP TMP
...

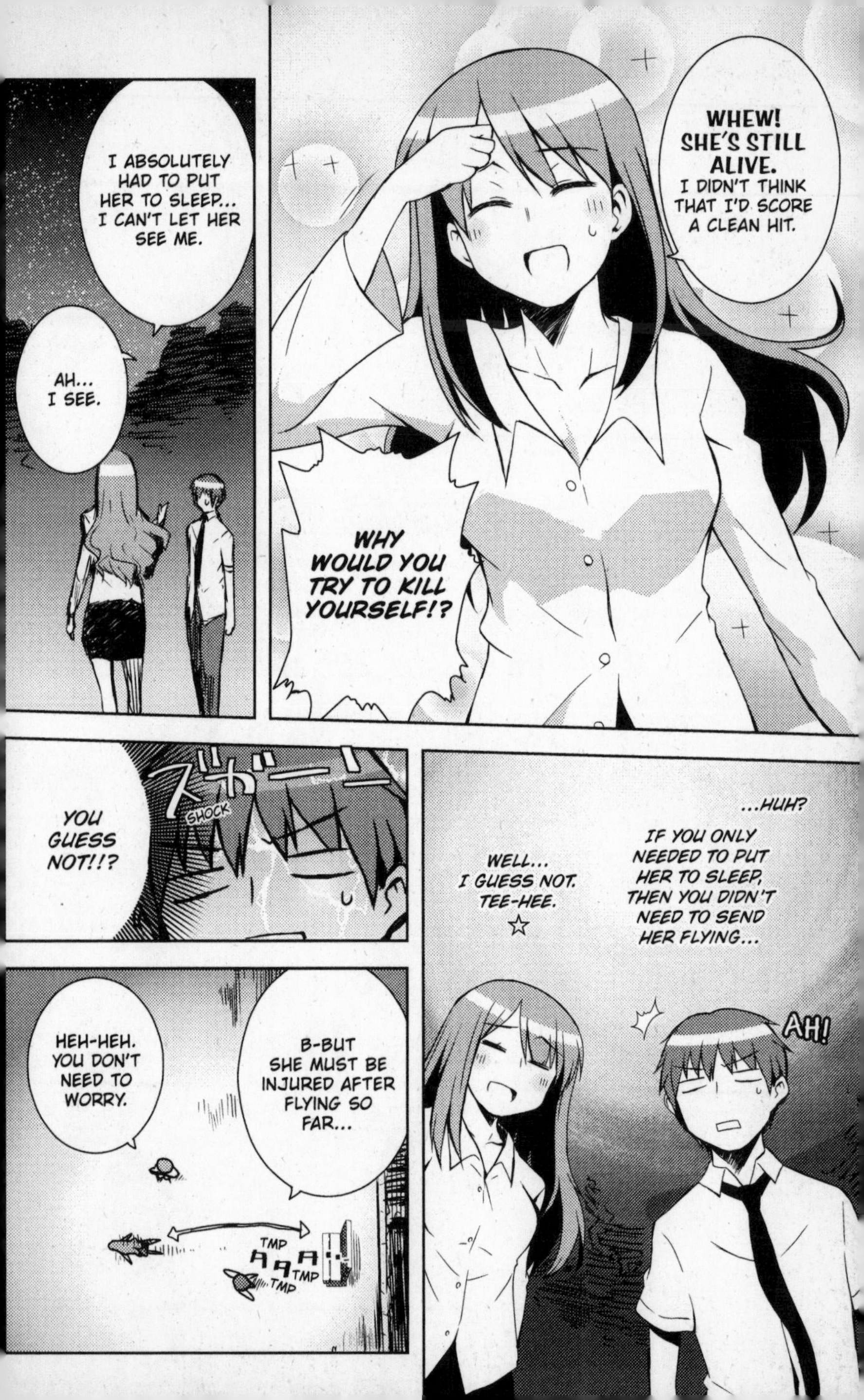
WHEW! SHE'S STILL ALIVE. I DIDN'T THINK THAT I'D SCORE A CLEAN HIT.
WHY WOULD YOU TRY TO KILL YOURSELF!?
I ABSOLUTELY HAD TO PUT HER TO SLEEP... I CAN'T LET HER SEE ME.
AH... I SEE.
...HUH?
IF YOU ONLY NEEDED TO PUT HER TO SLEEP, THEN YOU DIDN'T NEED TO SEND HER FLYING...
WELL... I GUESS NOT. TEE-HEE. ☆
AH!
SHOCK
YOU GUESS NOT!!?
B-BUT SHE MUST BE INJURED AFTER FLYING SO FAR...
HEH-HEH. YOU DON'T NEED TO WORRY.
TMP
TMP
TMP

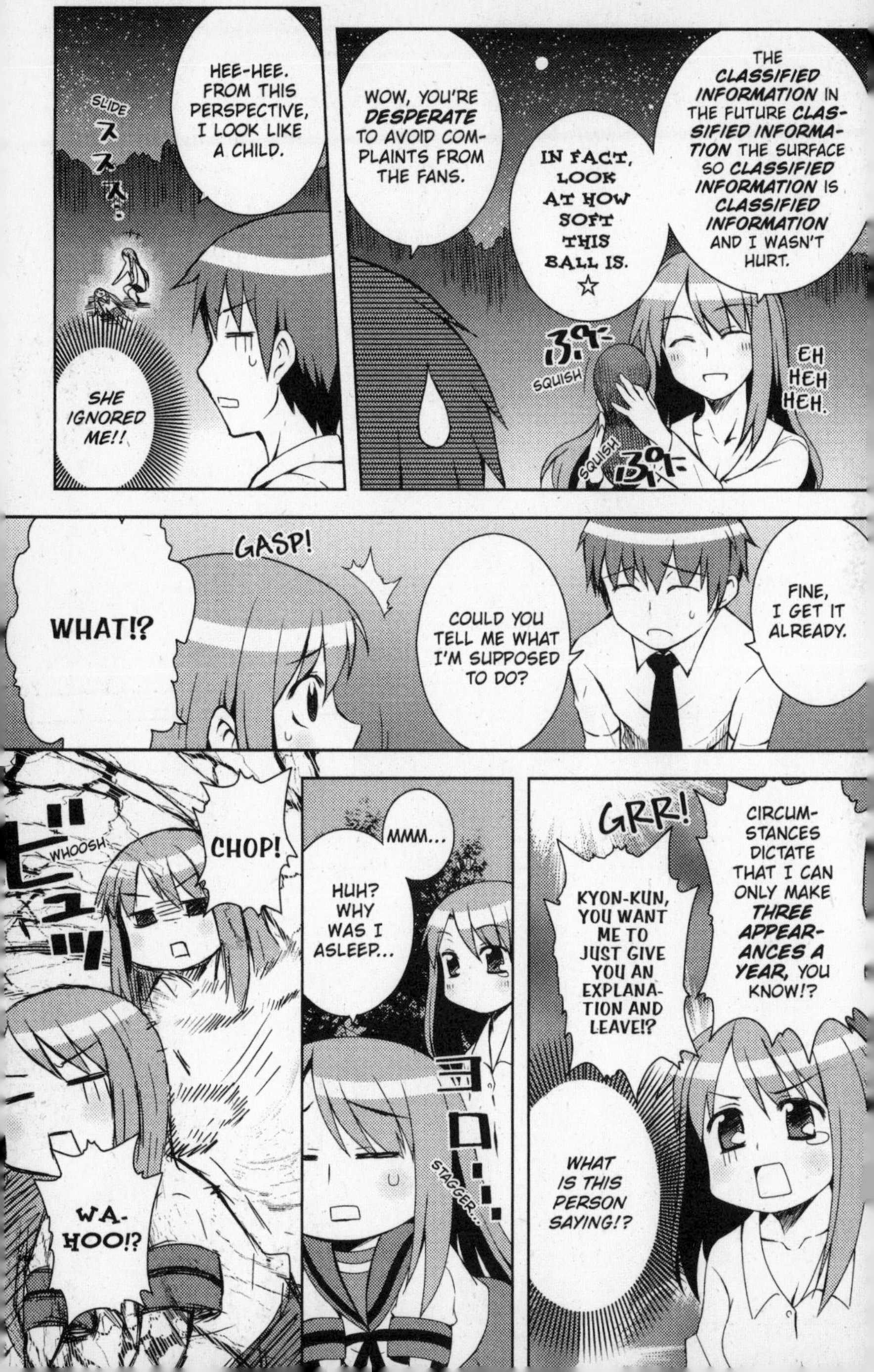

THE CLASSIFIED INFORMATION IN THE FUTURE CLASSIFIED INFORMATION THE SURFACE SO CLASSIFIED INFORMATION IS CLASSIFIED INFORMATION AND I WASN'T HURT.
IN FACT, LOOK AT HOW SOFT THIS BALL IS. ☆
WOW, YOU'RE DESPERATE TO AVOID COMPLAINTS FROM THE FANS.
EH HEH HEH.
SQUISH
SQUISH
HEE-HEE. FROM THIS PERSPECTIVE, I LOOK LIKE A CHILD.
SLIDE
SHE IGNORED ME!!
FINE, I GET IT ALREADY.
COULD YOU TELL ME WHAT I'M SUPPOSED TO DO?
GASP!
WHAT!?
CIRCUMSTANCES DICTATE THAT I CAN ONLY MAKE THREE APPEARANCES A YEAR, YOU KNOW!?
GRR!
KYON-KUN, YOU WANT ME TO JUST GIVE YOU AN EXPLANATION AND LEAVE!?
WHAT IS THIS PERSON SAYING!?
MMM...
HUH? WHY WAS I ASLEEP...
STAGGER...
CHOP!
WHOOSH
WA-HOO!?

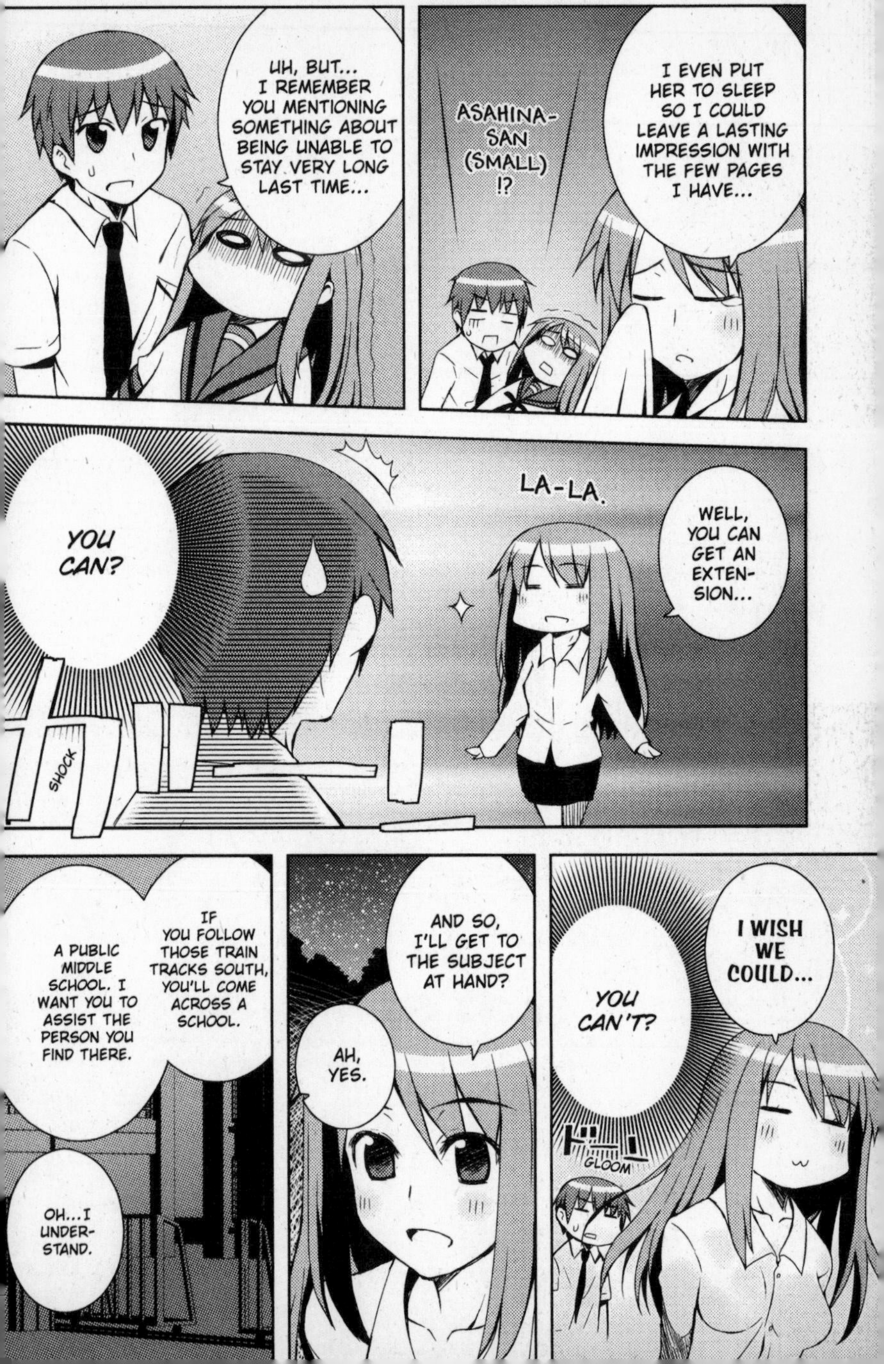
I EVEN PUT HER TO SLEEP SO I COULD LEAVE A LASTING IMPRESSION WITH THE FEW PAGES I HAVE...
ASAHINA-SAN (SMALL) !?
UH, BUT... I REMEMBER YOU MENTIONING SOMETHING ABOUT BEING UNABLE TO STAY VERY LONG LAST TIME...
LA-LA.
WELL, YOU CAN GET AN EXTENSION...
YOU CAN?
SHOCK
I WISH WE COULD...
YOU CAN'T?
GLOOM
AND SO, I'LL GET TO THE SUBJECT AT HAND?
AH, YES.
IF YOU FOLLOW THOSE TRAIN TRACKS SOUTH, YOU'LL COME ACROSS A SCHOOL.
A PUBLIC MIDDLE SCHOOL. I WANT YOU TO ASSIST THE PERSON YOU FIND THERE.
OH...I UNDERSTAND.

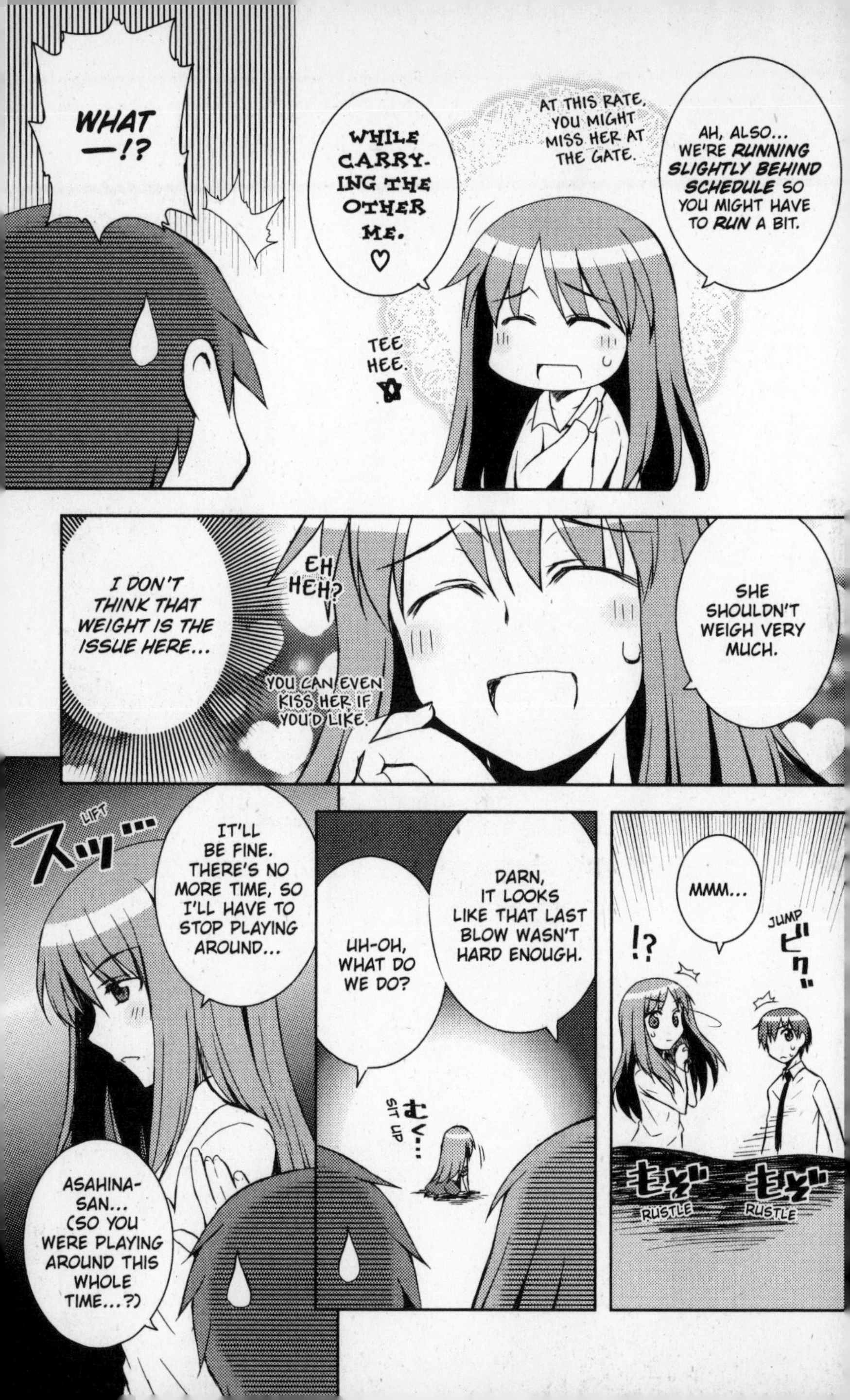
AH, ALSO... WE'RE RUNNING SLIGHTLY BEHIND SCHEDULE SO YOU MIGHT HAVE TO RUN A BIT.
AT THIS RATE, YOU MIGHT MISS HER AT THE GATE.
WHILE CARRYING THE OTHER ME. ♡
TEE HEE.
WHAT —!?
SHE SHOULDN'T WEIGH VERY MUCH.
EH HEH?
YOU CAN EVEN KISS HER IF YOU'D LIKE.
I DON'T THINK THAT WEIGHT IS THE ISSUE HERE...
MMM...
ビクッ
JUMP
!?
もぞ
RUSTLE
もぞ
RUSTLE
DARN, IT LOOKS LIKE THAT LAST BLOW WASN'T HARD ENOUGH.
UH-OH, WHAT DO WE DO?
むく…
SIT UP
スッ…
LIFT
IT'LL BE FINE. THERE'S NO MORE TIME, SO I'LL HAVE TO STOP PLAYING AROUND...
ASAHINA-SAN... (SO YOU WERE PLAYING AROUND THIS WHOLE TIME...?)

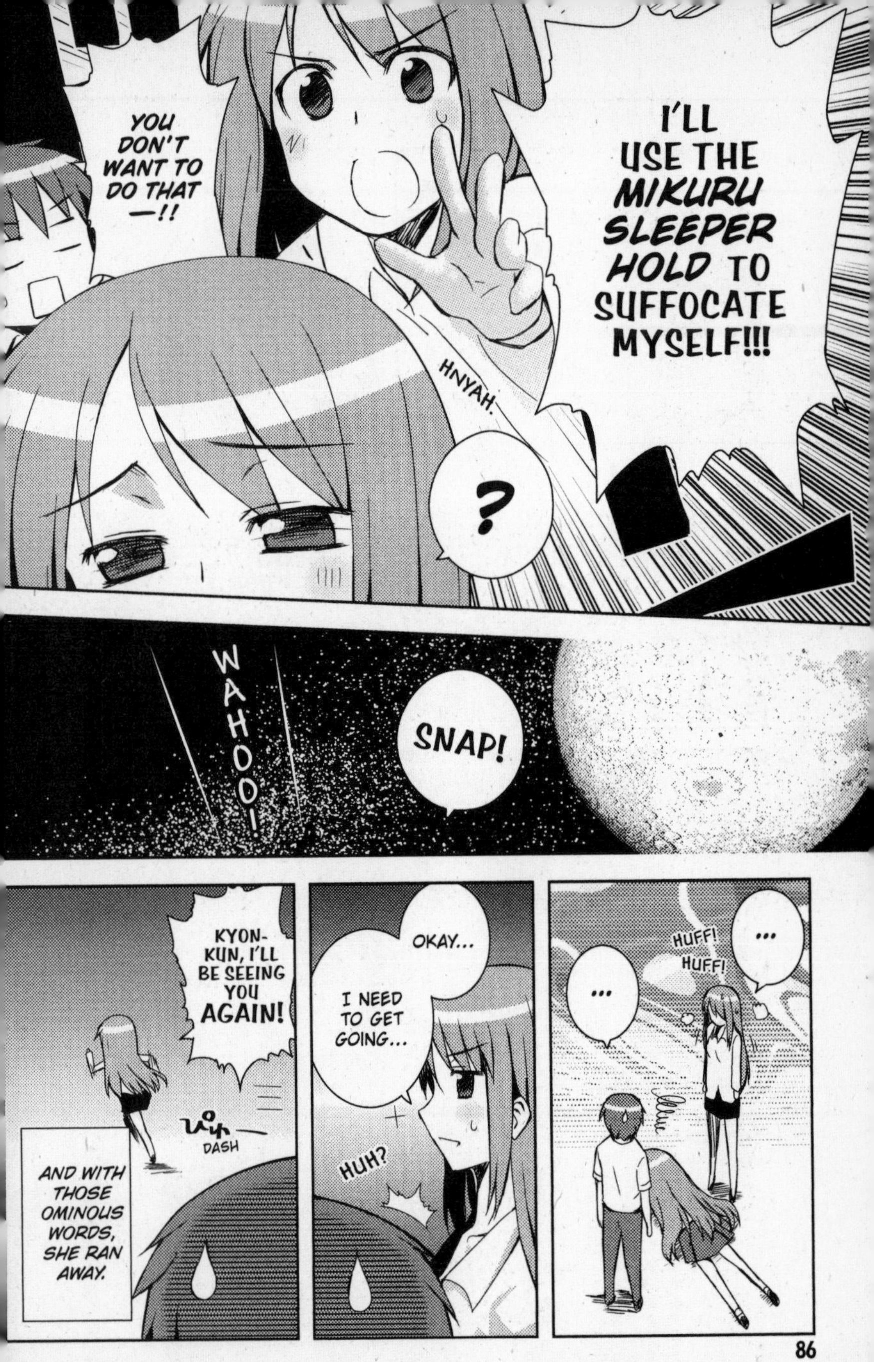
I'LL USE THE MIKURU SLEEPER HOLD TO SUFFOCATE MYSELF!!!
YOU DON'T WANT TO DO THAT—!!
HNYAH.
?
SNAP!
WAHOO!
...
HUFF! HUFF!
...
OKAY...
I NEED TO GET GOING...
HUH?
KYON-KUN, I'LL BE SEEING YOU AGAIN!
ぴゅ— DASH
AND WITH THOSE OMINOUS WORDS, SHE RAN AWAY.

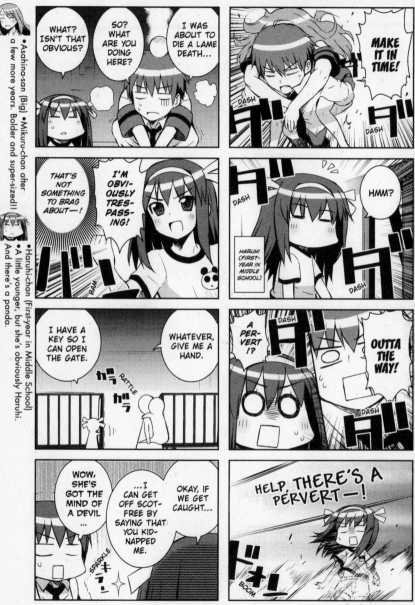

PERVERT

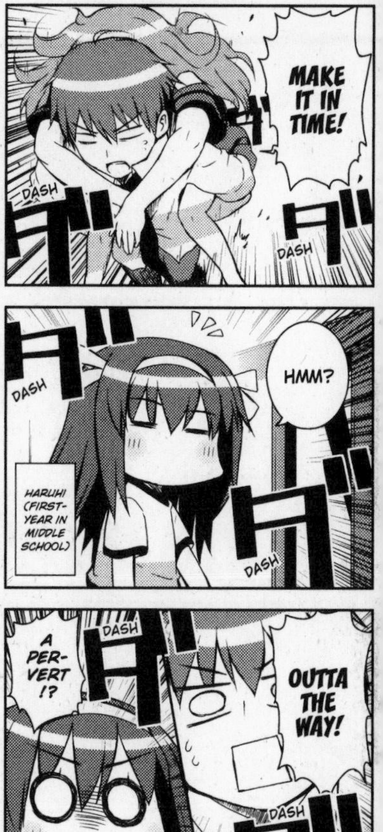
MAKE IT IN TIME!
DASH
DASH
HMM?
DASH
HARUHI (FIRST-YEAR IN MIDDLE SCHOOL)
DASH
OUTTA THE WAY!
DASH
A PERVERT!?
DASH
HELP, THERE'S A PERVERT—!
BOOM

TRESPASSING

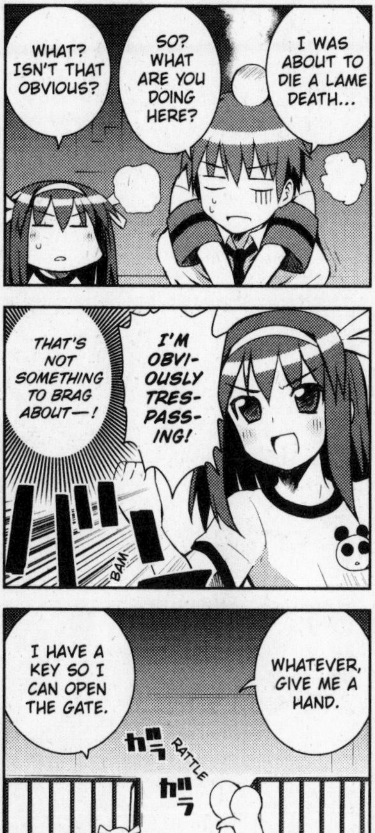
I WAS ABOUT TO DIE A LAME DEATH...
SO? WHAT ARE YOU DOING HERE?
WHAT? ISN'T THAT OBVIOUS?
I'M OBVIOUSLY TRESPASSING!
THAT'S NOT SOMETHING TO BRAG ABOUT—!
BAM
WHATEVER, GIVE ME A HAND.
I HAVE A KEY SO I CAN OPEN THE GATE.
RATTLE
OKAY, IF WE GET CAUGHT...
...I CAN GET OFF SCOT-FREE BY SAYING THAT YOU KIDNAPPED ME.
WOW, SHE'S GOT THE MIND OF A DEVIL...
SPARKLE

•Asahina-san (Big) •Mikuru-chan after a few more years. Bolder and super-sized!!

•Haruhi-chan (First-year in Middle School) •A little younger, but she's obviously Haruhi. And there's a panda.

GEOGLYPH

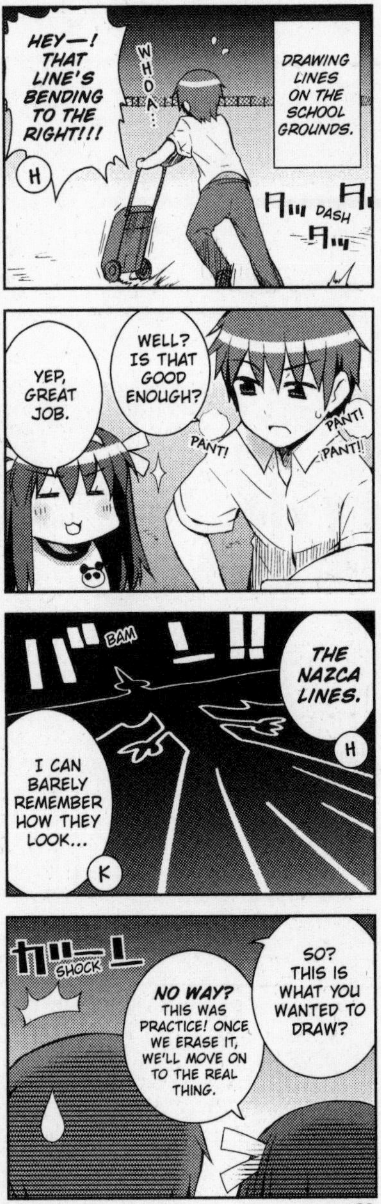
DRAWING LINES ON THE SCHOOL GROUNDS.
WHOA...
HEY—! THAT LINE'S BENDING TO THE RIGHT!!!
H
DASH
WELL? IS THAT GOOD ENOUGH?
PANT!
PANT!
PANT!
YEP, GREAT JOB.
THE NAZCA LINES.
H
BAM
I CAN BARELY REMEMBER HOW THEY LOOK...
K
SO? THIS IS WHAT YOU WANTED TO DRAW?
SHOCK
NO WAY? THIS WAS PRACTICE! ONCE WE ERASE IT, WE'LL MOVE ON TO THE REAL THING.

AWAKENING

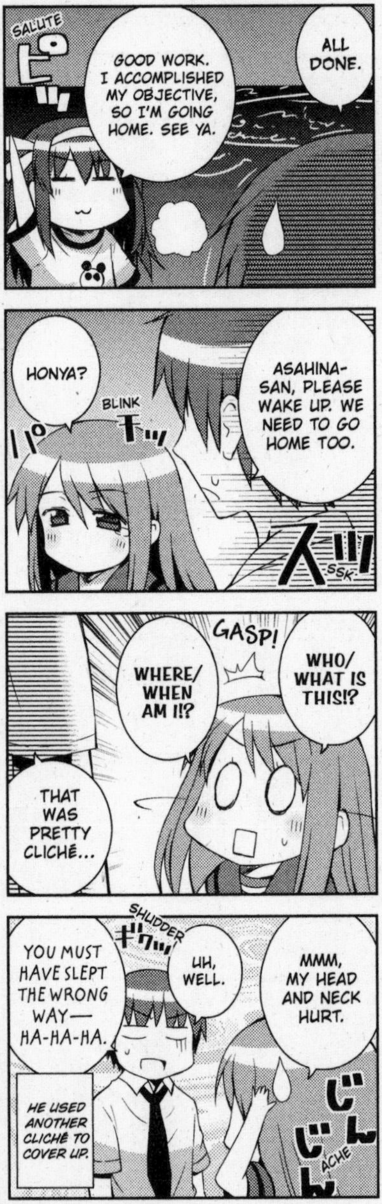
ALL DONE.
GOOD WORK. I ACCOMPLISHED MY OBJECTIVE, SO I'M GOING HOME. SEE YA.
SALUTE
ASAHINA-SAN, PLEASE WAKE UP. WE NEED TO GO HOME TOO.
BLINK
HONYA?
SSK
WHO/ WHAT IS THIS!?
GASP!
WHERE/ WHEN AM I!?
THAT WAS PRETTY CLICHÉ...
MMM, MY HEAD AND NECK HURT.
UH, WELL.
SHUDDER
YOU MUST HAVE SLEPT THE WRONG WAY— HA-HA-HA.
ACHE
HE USED ANOTHER CLICHÉ TO COVER UP.

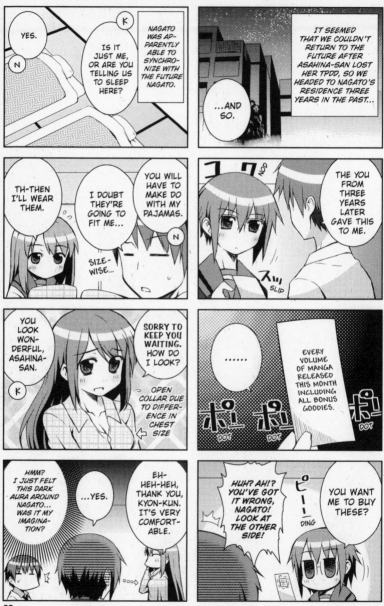

ERRAND

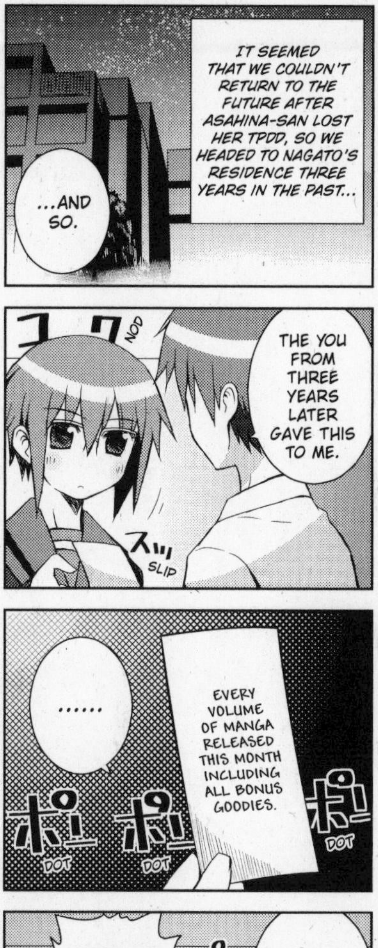
IT SEEMED THAT WE COULDN'T RETURN TO THE FUTURE AFTER ASAHINA-SAN LOST HER TPDD, SO WE HEADED TO NAGATO'S RESIDENCE THREE YEARS IN THE PAST...
...AND SO.
THE YOU FROM THREE YEARS LATER GAVE THIS TO ME.
コク NOD
スッ SLIP
EVERY VOLUME OF MANGA RELEASED THIS MONTH INCLUDING ALL BONUS GOODIES.
......
DOT
DOT
DOT
YOU WANT ME TO BUY THESE?
DING
HUH? AH!? YOU'VE GOT IT WRONG, NAGATO! LOOK AT THE OTHER SIDE!

PAJAMAS

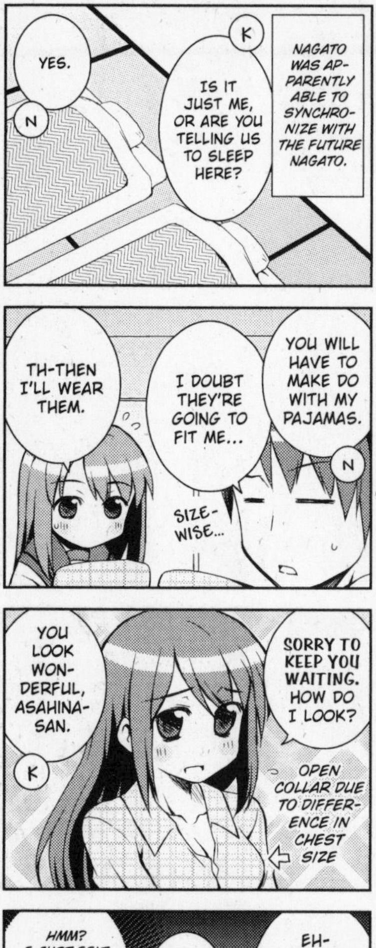
NAGATO WAS APPARENTLY ABLE TO SYNCHRONIZE WITH THE FUTURE NAGATO.
K
IS IT JUST ME, OR ARE YOU TELLING US TO SLEEP HERE?
YES.
N
YOU WILL HAVE TO MAKE DO WITH MY PAJAMAS.
N
I DOUBT THEY'RE GOING TO FIT ME...
SIZE-WISE...
TH-THEN I'LL WEAR THEM.
SORRY TO KEEP YOU WAITING. HOW DO I LOOK?
OPEN COLLAR DUE TO DIFFERENCE IN CHEST SIZE
YOU LOOK WONDERFUL, ASAHINA-SAN.
K
EH-HEH-HEH, THANK YOU, KYON-KUN. IT'S VERY COMFORTABLE.
...YES.
HMM? I JUST FELT THIS DARK AURA AROUND NAGATO... WAS IT MY IMAGINATION?

DECIPHER

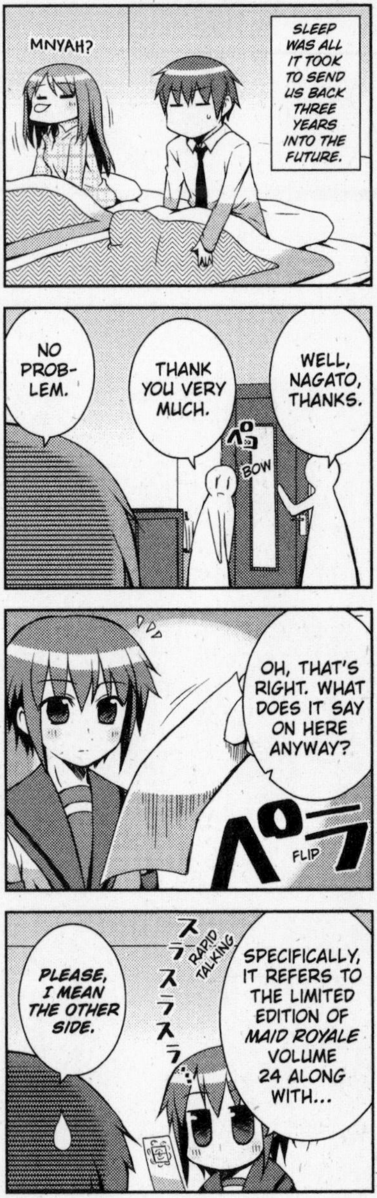
SLEEP WAS ALL IT TOOK TO SEND US BACK THREE YEARS INTO THE FUTURE.
MNYAH?
WELL, NAGATO, THANKS.
THANK YOU VERY MUCH.
ペコ
BOW
NO PROB-LEM.
OH, THAT'S RIGHT. WHAT DOES IT SAY ON HERE ANYWAY?
ペラ
FLIP
SPECIFICALLY, IT REFERS TO THE LIMITED EDITION OF MAID ROYALE VOLUME 24 ALONG WITH...
スラスラスラ
RAPID TALKING
PLEASE, I MEAN THE OTHER SIDE.

NEAR MISS

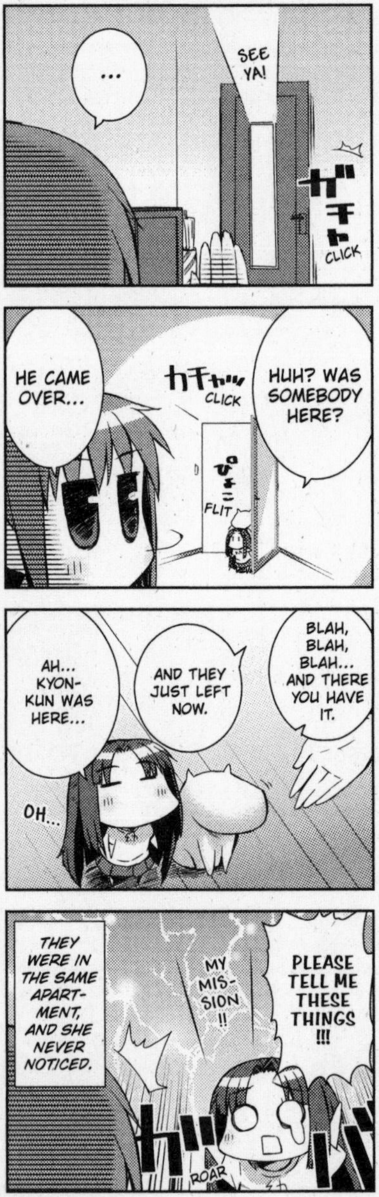
ガチャ
CLICK
SEE YA!
...
HUH? WAS SOMEBODY HERE?
カチャッ
CLICK
ぴょこ
FLIT
HE CAME OVER...
BLAH, BLAH, BLAH... AND THERE YOU HAVE IT.
AND THEY JUST LEFT NOW.
AH... KYON-KUN WAS HERE...
OH...
PLEASE TELL ME THESE THINGS!!!
MY MIS-SION!!
THEY WERE IN THE SAME APART-MENT, AND SHE NEVER NOTICED.
ROAR

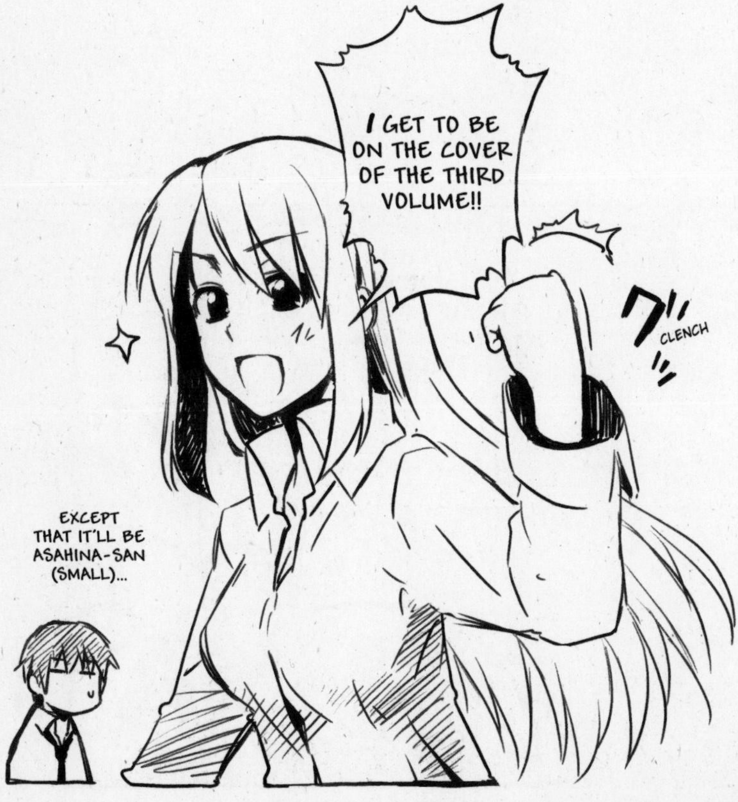
I GET TO BE ON THE COVER OF THE THIRD VOLUME!!
CLENCH
EXCEPT THAT IT'LL BE ASAHINA-SAN (SMALL)...

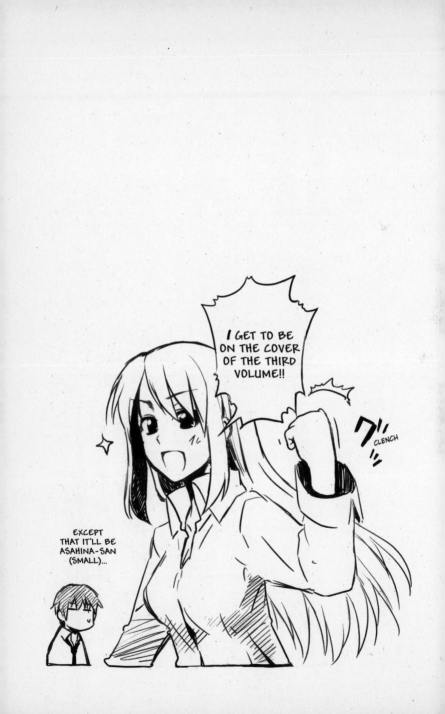

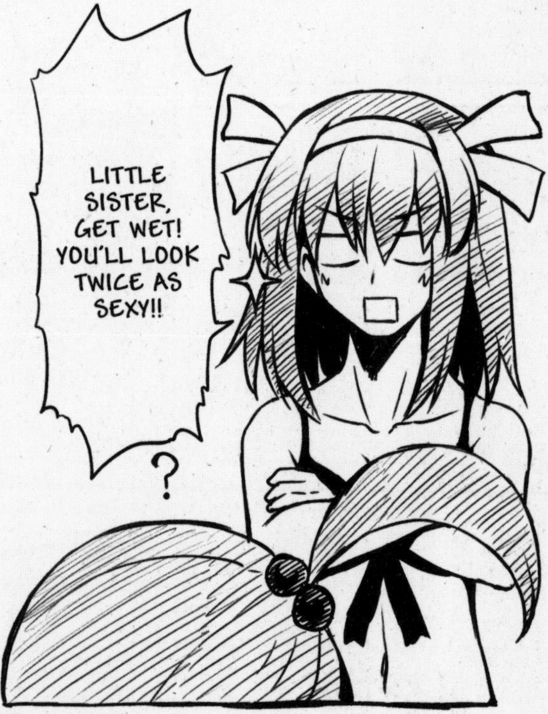
LITTLE SISTER, GET WET! YOU'LL LOOK TWICE AS SEXY!!
?

MEMORY

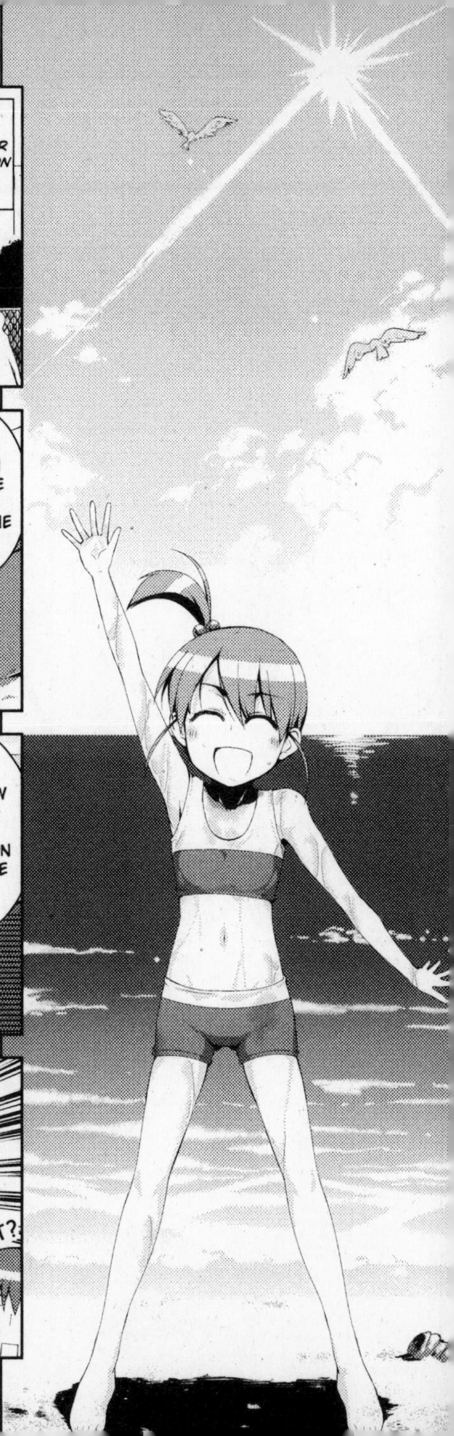

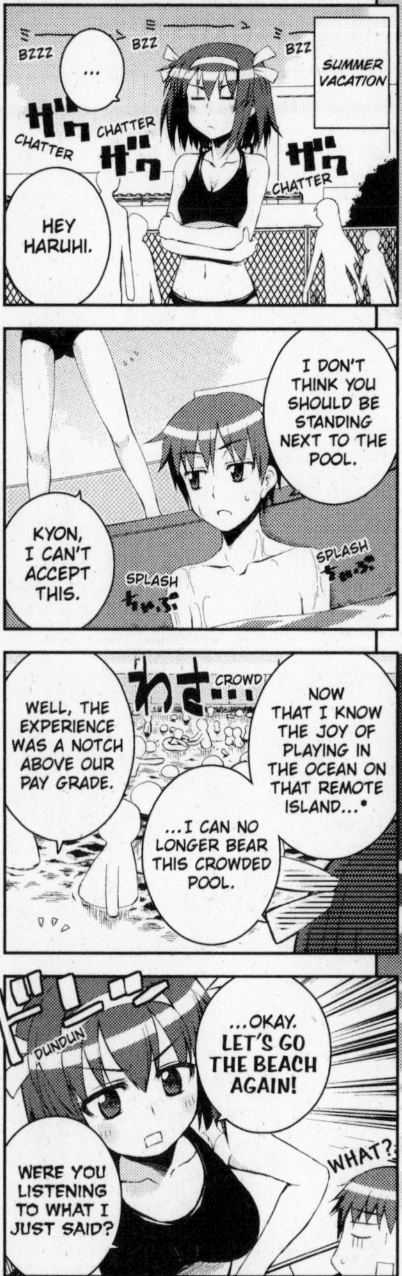
SUMMER VACATION
BZZ
BZZ
...
BZZZ
ザワ
CHATTER
ザワ
CHATTER
ザワ
CHATTER
HEY HARUHI.
I DON'T THINK YOU SHOULD BE STANDING NEXT TO THE POOL.
SPLASH
ちゃぷ
KYON, I CAN'T ACCEPT THIS.
SPLASH
ちゃぷ
NOW THAT I KNOW THE JOY OF PLAYING IN THE OCEAN ON THAT REMOTE ISLAND...*
CROWD
...I CAN NO LONGER BEAR THIS CROWDED POOL.
WELL, THE EXPERIENCE WAS A NOTCH ABOVE OUR PAY GRADE.
...OKAY. LET'S GO THE BEACH AGAIN!
DUNDUN
WHAT?
WERE YOU LISTENING TO WHAT I JUST SAID?

*REFERRING TO "REMOTE ISLAND SYNDROME" FROM THE ORIGINAL NOVEL "THE BOREDOM OF HARUHI SUZUMIYA."

•Haruhi-chan •SOS Brigade brigade chief. She has realized that the pool cannot satisfy her inner desires.

•Kyon •Supposed to be the main character in this story. Feeling a little lonely since he keeps getting ignored.

•Tsuruya-san •Did someone call for, did someone call for Tsuruya-san—?

THE USUAL

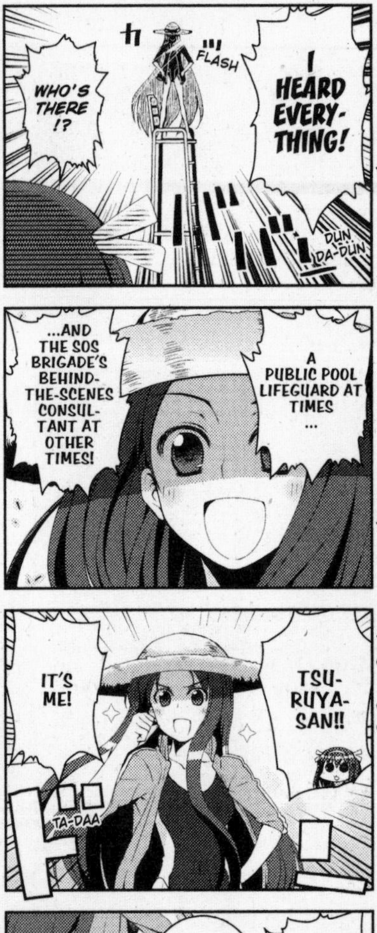
I HEARD EVERY-THING!
FLASH
WHO'S THERE !?
DUN DA-DUN
A PUBLIC POOL LIFEGUARD AT TIMES ...
...AND THE SOS BRIGADE'S BEHIND-THE-SCENES CONSUL-TANT AT OTHER TIMES!
TSU-RUYA-SAN!!
IT'S ME!
TA-DAA
WHY ARE YOU HERE!?
HEH-HEH-HEH. MY FAMILY OWNS THE PLACE.

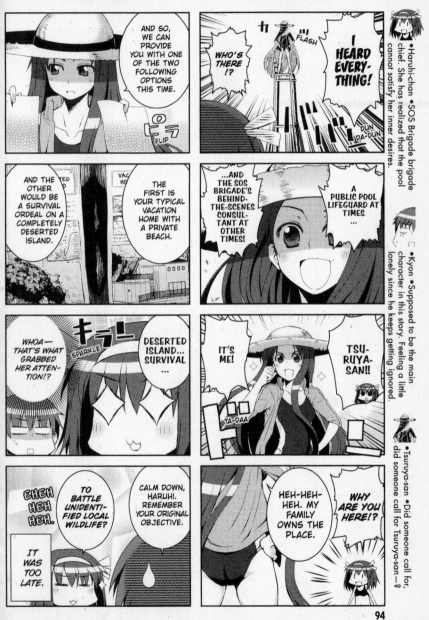

PROVIDE

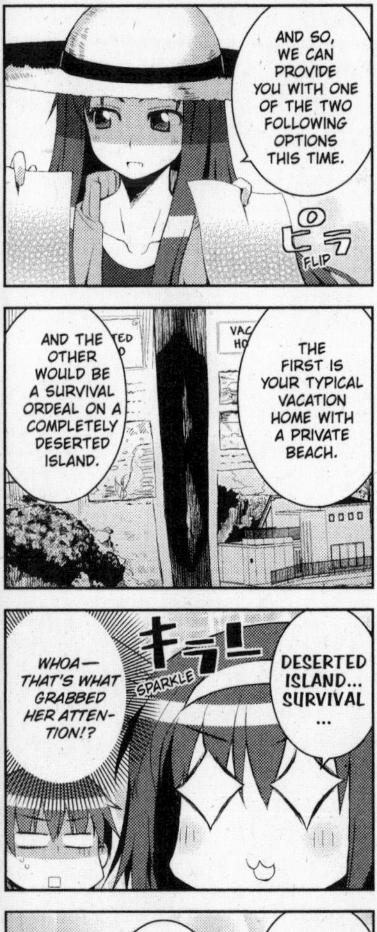
AND SO, WE CAN PROVIDE YOU WITH ONE OF THE TWO FOLLOWING OPTIONS THIS TIME.
FLIP
THE FIRST IS YOUR TYPICAL VACATION HOME WITH A PRIVATE BEACH.
AND THE OTHER WOULD BE A SURVIVAL ORDEAL ON A COMPLETELY DESERTED ISLAND.
DESERTED ISLAND... SURVIVAL ...
SPARKLE
WHOA— THAT'S WHAT GRABBED HER ATTEN-TION!?
CALM DOWN, HARUHI. REMEMBER YOUR ORIGINAL OBJECTIVE.
TO BATTLE UNIDENTI-FIED LOCAL WILDLIFE?
EHEH HEH HEH.
IT WAS TOO LATE.

UNEXPECTED DEVELOPMENT

AS AN ADULT

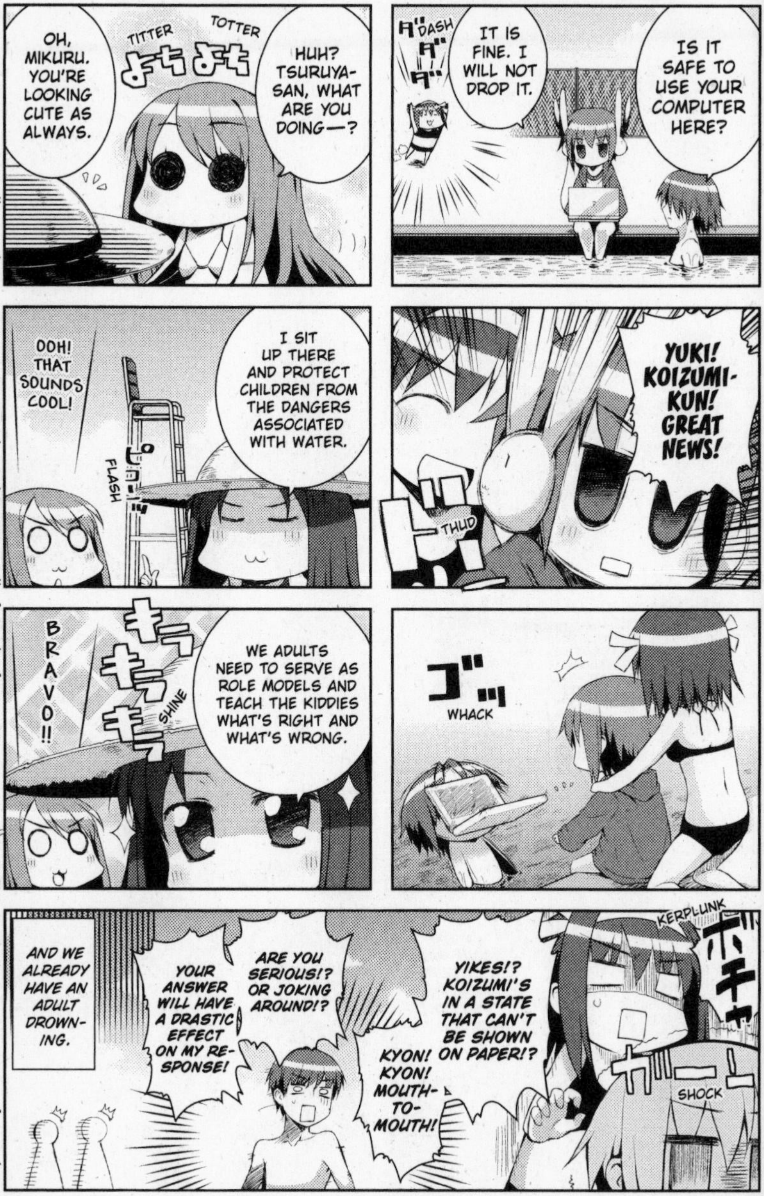
IS IT SAFE TO USE YOUR COMPUTER HERE?
IT IS FINE. I WILL NOT DROP IT.
DASH
YUKI! KOIZUMI-KUN! GREAT NEWS!
THUD
WHACK
KERPLUNK
SHOCK
YIKES!? KOIZUMI'S IN A STATE THAT CAN'T BE SHOWN ON PAPER!?
KYON! KYON! MOUTH-TO-MOUTH!
HUH? TSURUYA-SAN, WHAT ARE YOU DOING—?
TITTER TOTTER
OH, MIKURU. YOU'RE LOOKING CUTE AS ALWAYS.
I SIT UP THERE AND PROTECT CHILDREN FROM THE DANGERS ASSOCIATED WITH WATER.
FLASH
OOH! THAT SOUNDS COOL!
WE ADULTS NEED TO SERVE AS ROLE MODELS AND TEACH THE KIDDIES WHAT'S RIGHT AND WHAT'S WRONG.
SHINE
BRAVO!!
ARE YOU SERIOUS!? OR JOKING AROUND!?
YOUR ANSWER WILL HAVE A DRASTIC EFFECT ON MY RE-SPONSE!
AND WE ALREADY HAVE AN ADULT DROWN-ING.

•Nagato •Actually an alien gamer. An indoor person who brings her computer to the pool.

•Mikuru-chan •Actually from the future. Very happy when she hears someone say something reasonable, given the people she associates with.

•Koizumi •An enigmatic transfer student who happens to be an esper. Left in a state that cannot be shown to the fans…

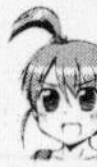
•Kyon's sister •Kyon's sister.
A dreadful girl who's willing to sacrifice herself in the name of having fun.

DAY BEFORE THE TRIP

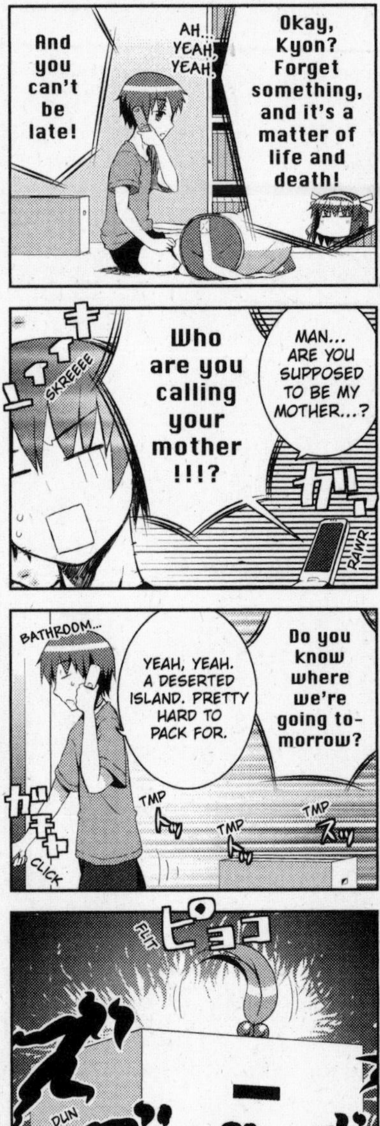
Okay, Kyon? Forget something, and it's a matter of life and death!
AH... YEAH, YEAH.
And you can't be late!
MAN... ARE YOU SUPPOSED TO BE MY MOTHER...?
Who are you calling your mother!!!?
SKREEEE
RAWR
Do you know where we're going tomorrow?
YEAH, YEAH. A DESERTED ISLAND. PRETTY HARD TO PACK FOR.
BATHROOM...
TMP
TMP
TMP
CLICK
FLIT
DUN
DUN
DUN
DUN

DAY OF THE TRIP

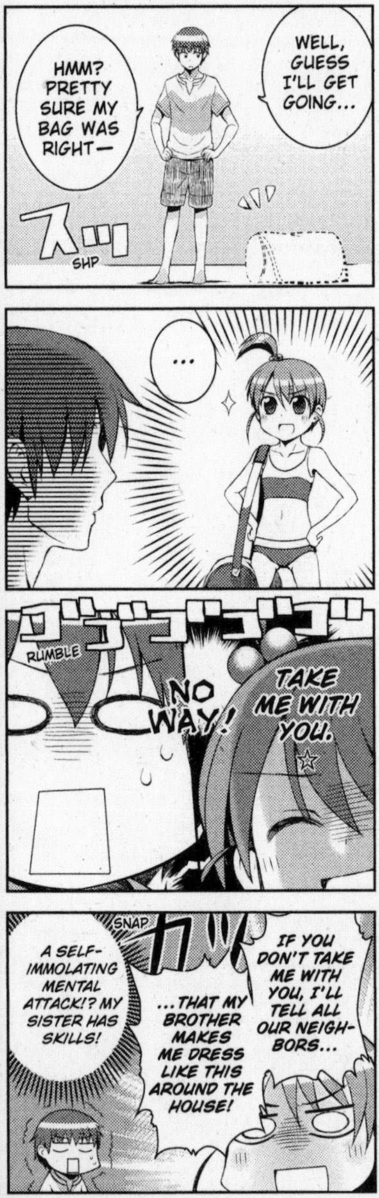
WELL, GUESS I'LL GET GOING...
HMM? PRETTY SURE MY BAG WAS RIGHT—
SHP
...
RUMBLE
TAKE ME WITH YOU.☆
NO WAY!
IF YOU DON'T TAKE ME WITH YOU, I'LL TELL ALL OUR NEIGHBORS...
...THAT MY BROTHER MAKES ME DRESS LIKE THIS AROUND THE HOUSE!
SNAP
A SELF-IMMOLATING MENTAL ATTACK!? MY SISTER HAS SKILLS!

DESERTED ISLAND CRUISE

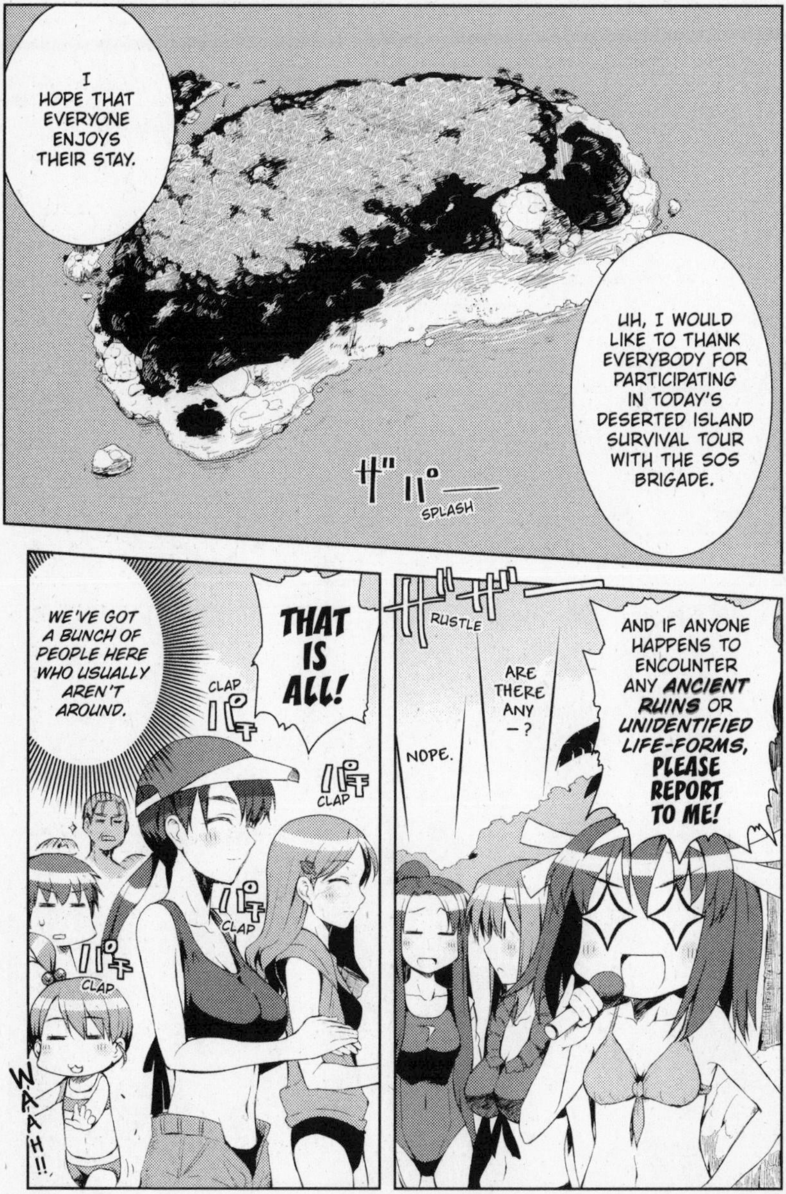
UH, I WOULD LIKE TO THANK EVERYBODY FOR PARTICIPATING IN TODAY'S DESERTED ISLAND SURVIVAL TOUR WITH THE SOS BRIGADE.
I HOPE THAT EVERYONE ENJOYS THEIR STAY.
ザパー
SPLASH
ザザー
RUSTLE
AND IF ANYONE HAPPENS TO ENCOUNTER ANY ANCIENT RUINS OR UNIDENTIFIED LIFE-FORMS, PLEASE REPORT TO ME!
ARE THERE ANY—?
NOPE.
THAT IS ALL!
パチ
CLAP
パチ
CLAP
WE'VE GOT A BUNCH OF PEOPLE HERE WHO USUALLY AREN'T AROUND.
パチ
CLAP
パチ
CLAP
WAAAH!!

SOMETHING MISSING

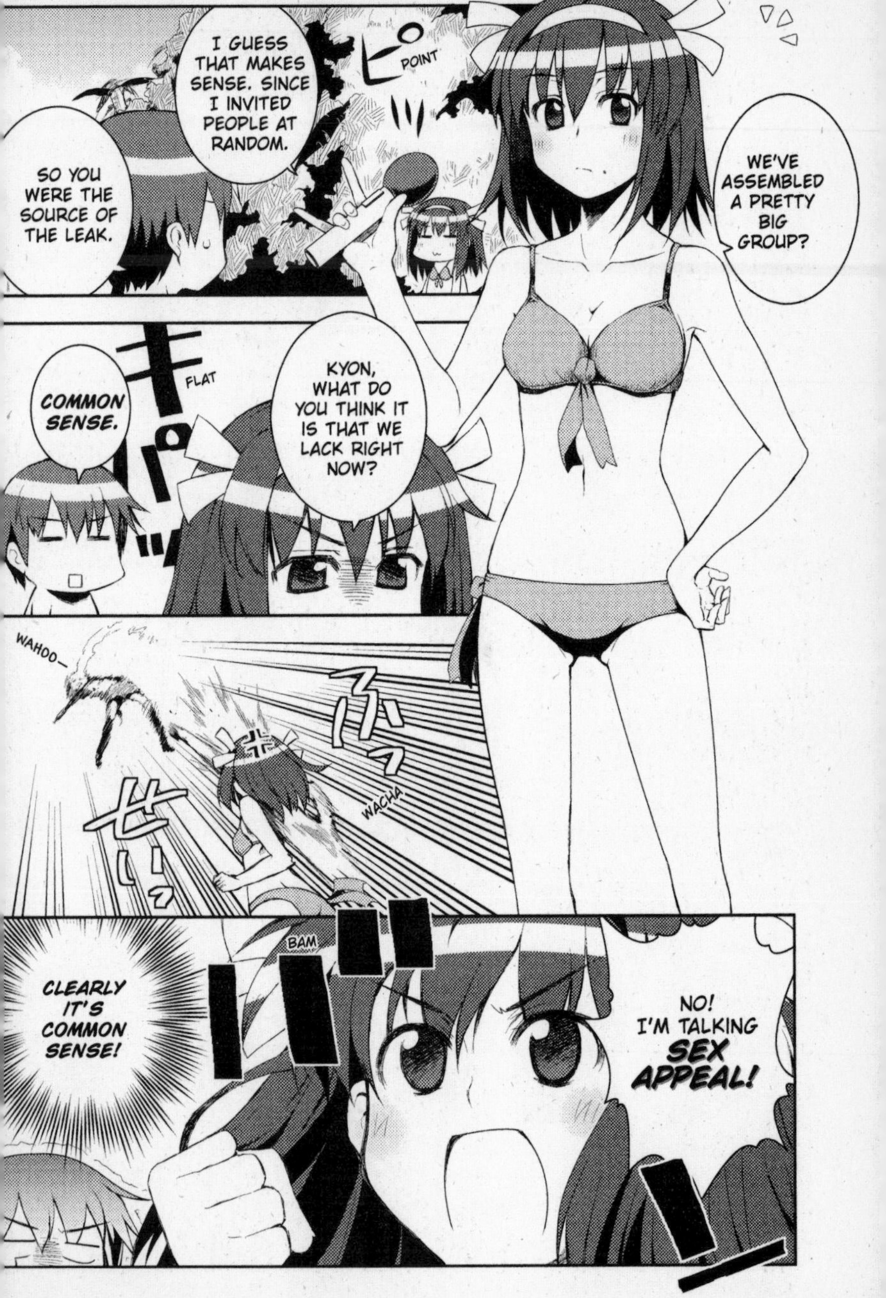
WE'VE ASSEMBLED A PRETTY BIG GROUP?
I GUESS THAT MAKES SENSE. SINCE I INVITED PEOPLE AT RANDOM.
POINT
SO YOU WERE THE SOURCE OF THE LEAK.
KYON, WHAT DO YOU THINK IT IS THAT WE LACK RIGHT NOW?
FLAT
COMMON SENSE.
WACHA
WAHOO–
NO! I'M TALKING **SEX APPEAL!**
BAM
CLEARLY IT'S COMMON SENSE!

SEX APPEAL

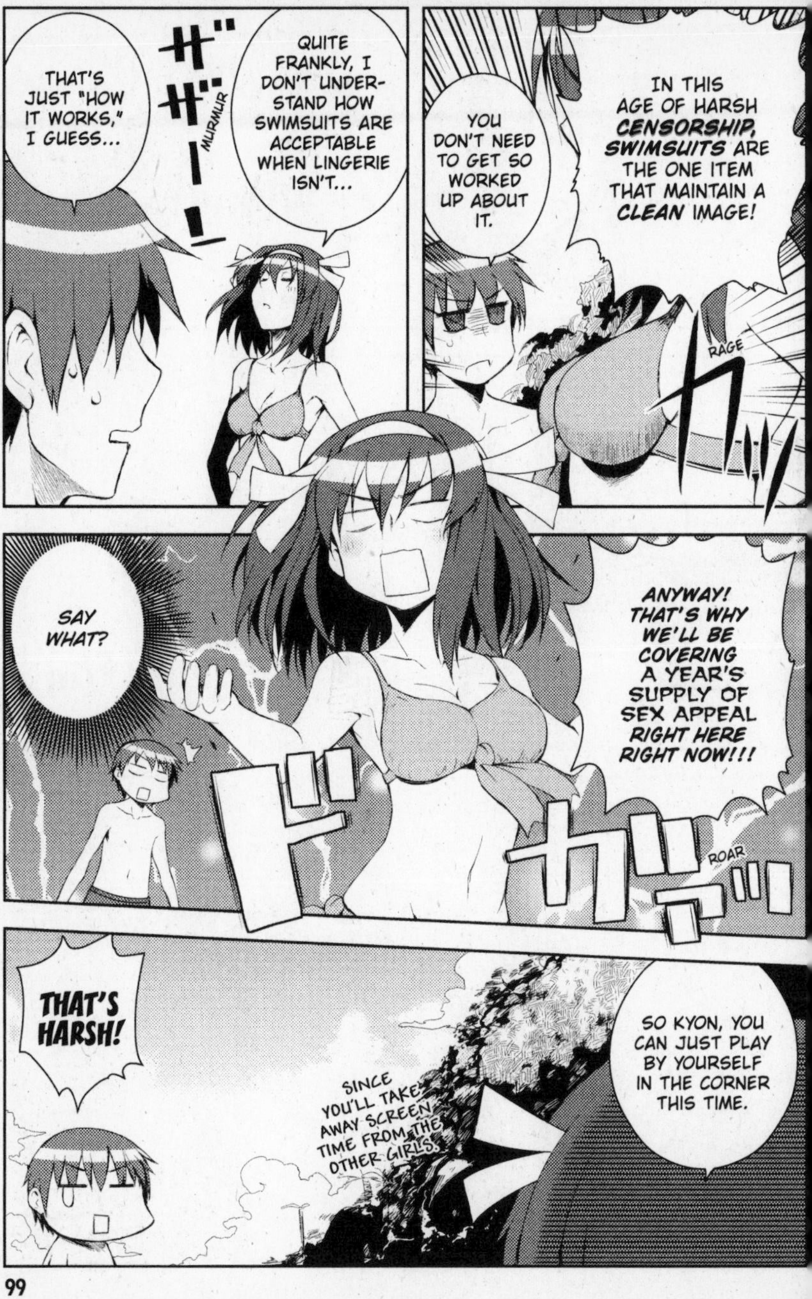
IN THIS AGE OF HARSH CENSORSHIP, SWIMSUITS ARE THE ONE ITEM THAT MAINTAIN A CLEAN IMAGE!
YOU DON'T NEED TO GET SO WORKED UP ABOUT IT.
RAGE
QUITE FRANKLY, I DON'T UNDERSTAND HOW SWIMSUITS ARE ACCEPTABLE WHEN LINGERIE ISN'T...
MURMUR
THAT'S JUST "HOW IT WORKS," I GUESS...
ANYWAY! THAT'S WHY WE'LL BE COVERING A YEAR'S SUPPLY OF SEX APPEAL RIGHT HERE RIGHT NOW!!!
SAY WHAT?
ROAR
SO KYON, YOU CAN JUST PLAY BY YOURSELF IN THE CORNER THIS TIME.
SINCE YOU'LL TAKE AWAY SCREEN TIME FROM THE OTHER GIRLS.
THAT'S HARSH!

PLAY

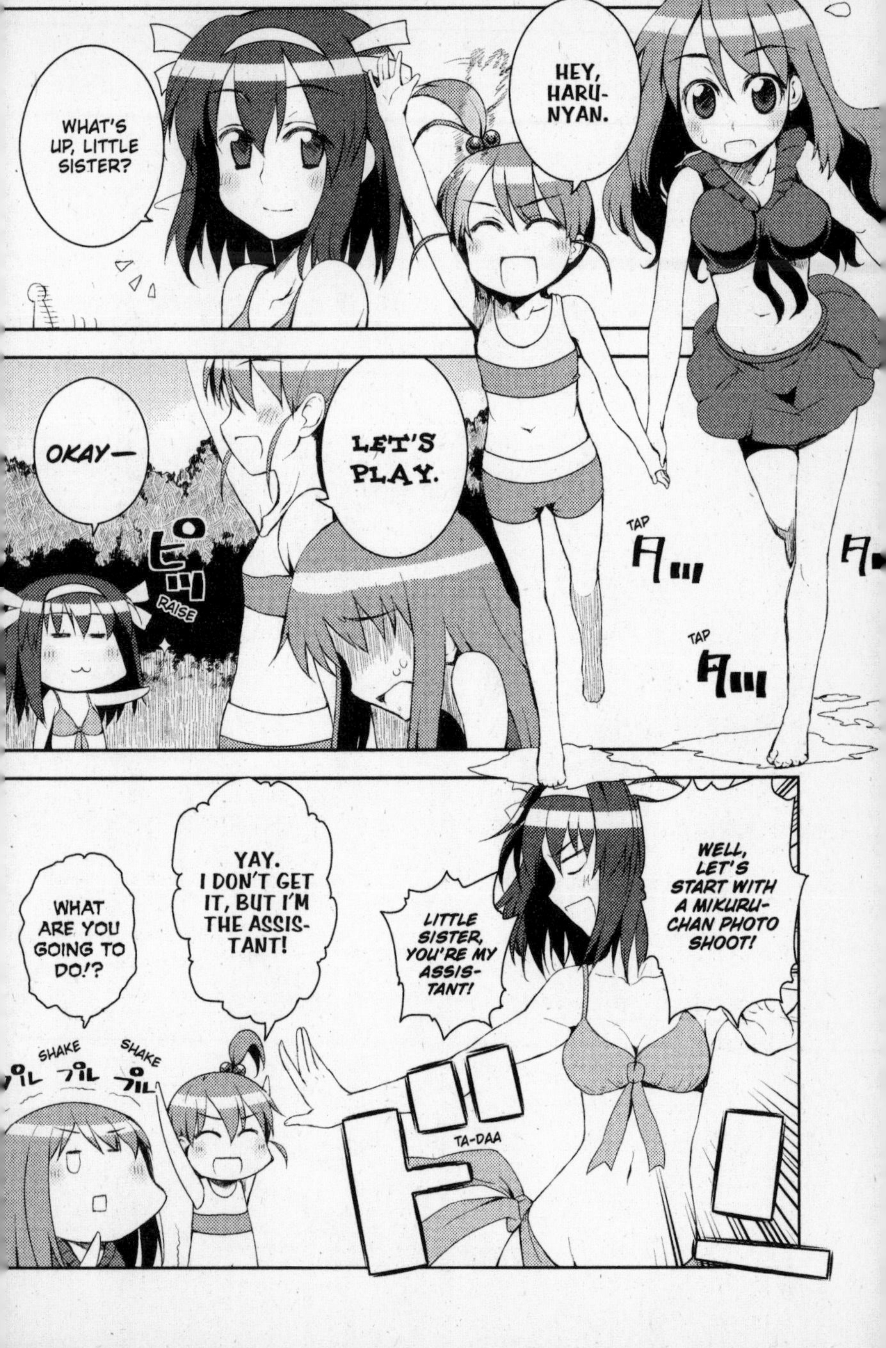
HEY, HARU-NYAN.
WHAT'S UP, LITTLE SISTER?
LET'S PLAY.
TAP
OKAY—
RAISE
TAP
WELL, LET'S START WITH A MIKURU-CHAN PHOTO SHOOT!
LITTLE SISTER, YOU'RE MY ASSISTANT!
TA-DAA
YAY. I DON'T GET IT, BUT I'M THE ASSISTANT!
WHAT ARE YOU GOING TO DO!?
SHAKE
SHAKE

PHOTO SHOOT

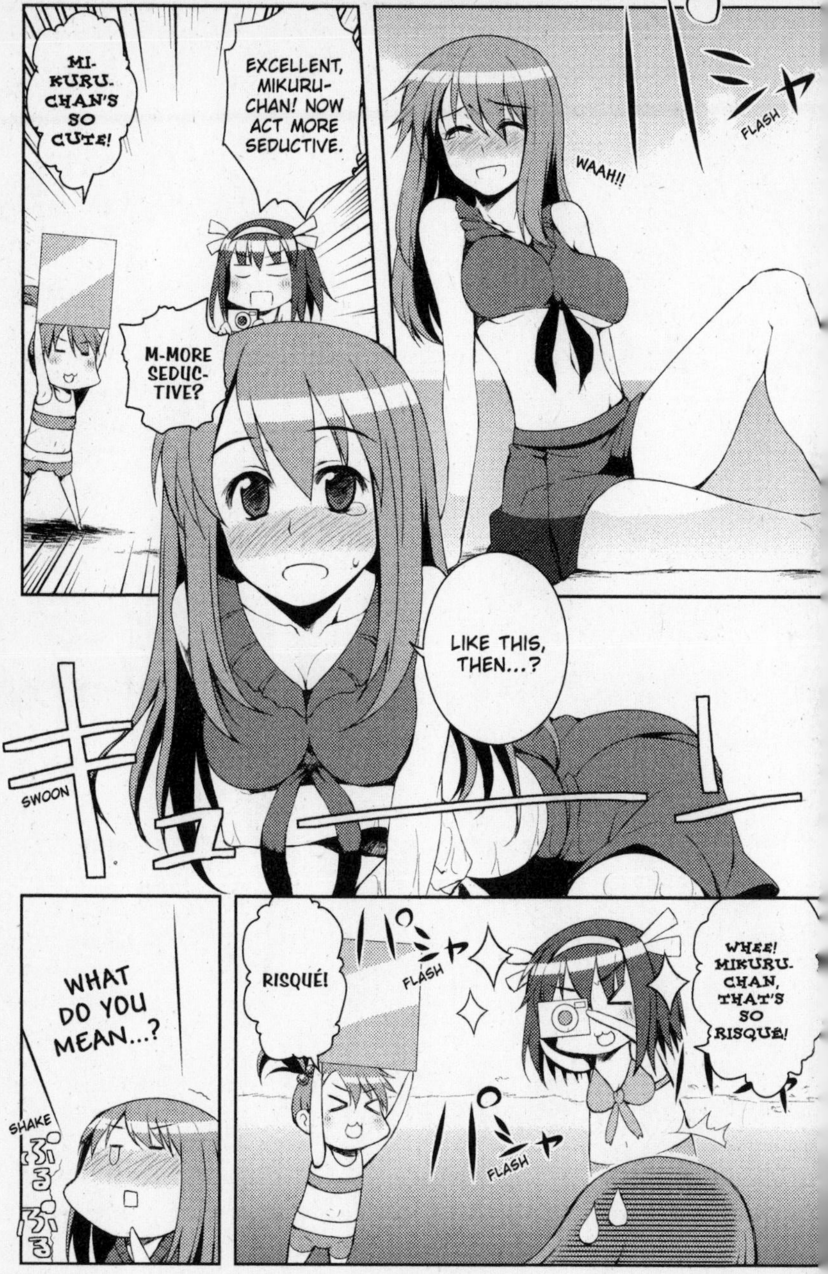

FLASH
WAAH!!
EXCELLENT, MIKURU-CHAN! NOW ACT MORE SEDUCTIVE.
MI-KURU-CHAN'S SO CUTE!
M-MORE SEDUC-TIVE?
LIKE THIS, THEN...?
SWOON
WHEE! MIKURU-CHAN, THAT'S SO RISQUÉ!
FLASH
RISQUÉ!
FLASH
WHAT DO YOU MEAN...?
SHAKE

A LITTLE TASTE

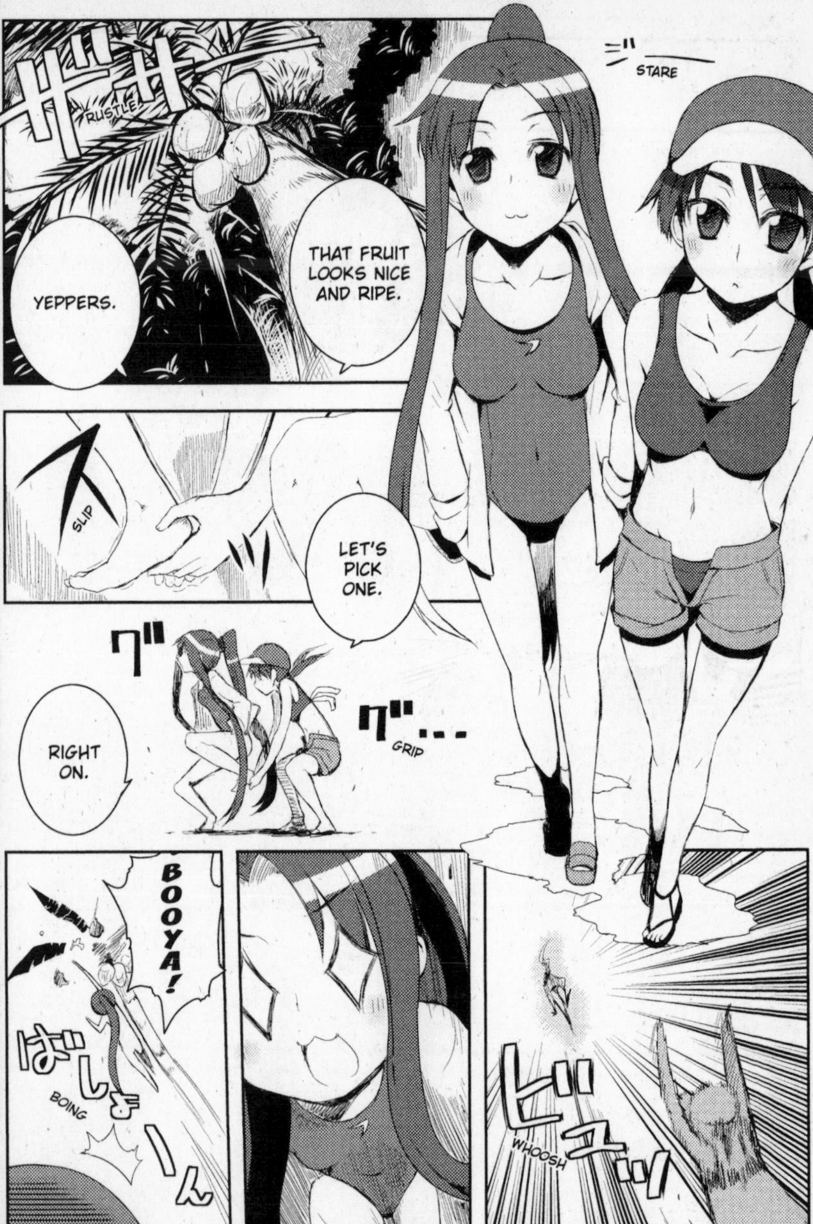
STARE
RUSTLE
THAT FRUIT LOOKS NICE AND RIPE.
YEPPERS.
SLIP
LET'S PICK ONE.
RIGHT ON.
GRIP
WHOOSH
BOOYA!
BOING

BIRDS OF A FEATHER

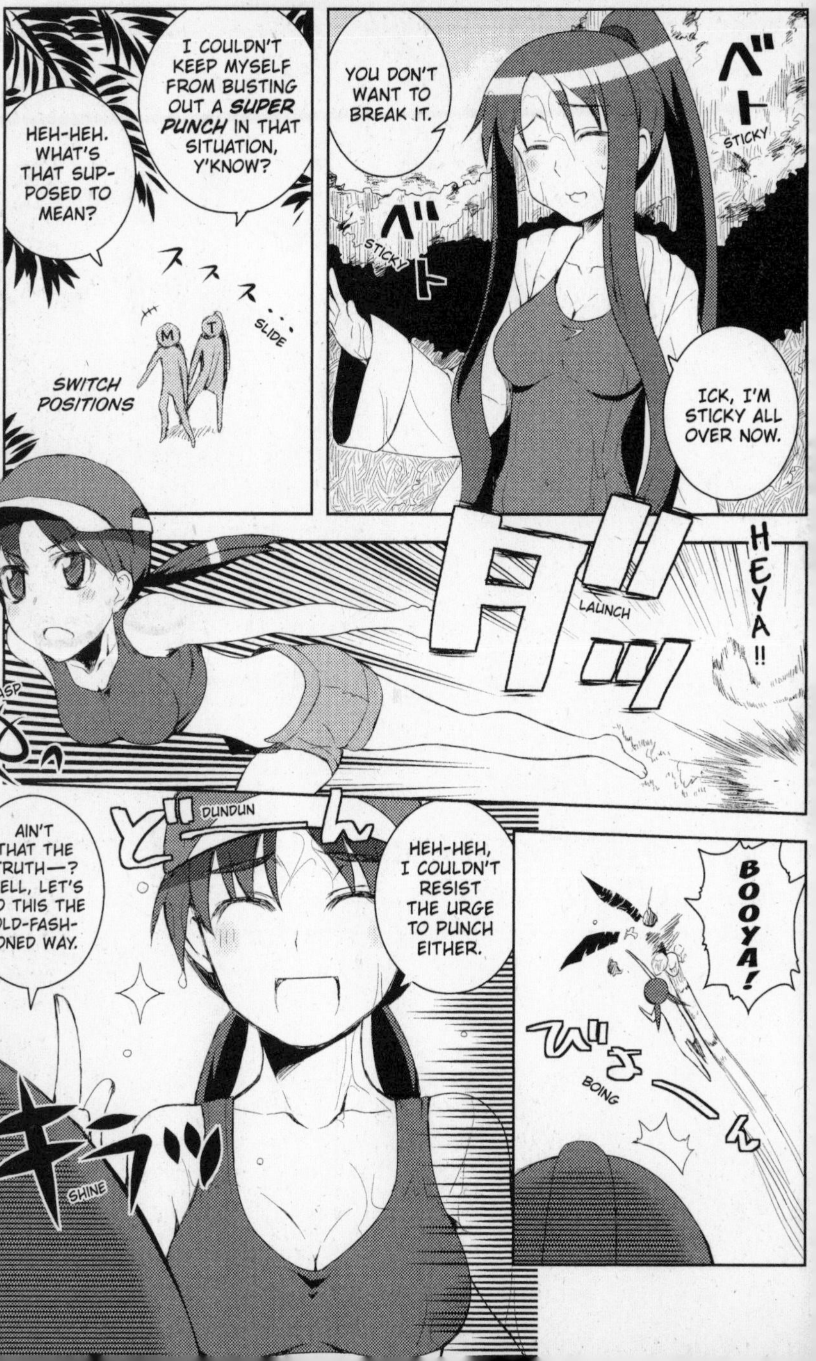
STICKY
YOU DON'T WANT TO BREAK IT.
STICKY
ICK, I'M STICKY ALL OVER NOW.
I COULDN'T KEEP MYSELF FROM BUSTING OUT A ***SUPER PUNCH*** IN THAT SITUATION, Y'KNOW?
HEH-HEH. WHAT'S THAT SUP-POSED TO MEAN?
SLIDE
SWITCH POSITIONS
HEYA!!
LAUNCH
GASP
BOOYA!
BOING
DUNDUN
HEH-HEH, I COULDN'T RESIST THE URGE TO PUNCH EITHER.
AIN'T THAT THE TRUTH—? WELL, LET'S DO THIS THE OLD-FASH-IONED WAY.
SHINE

MEAT

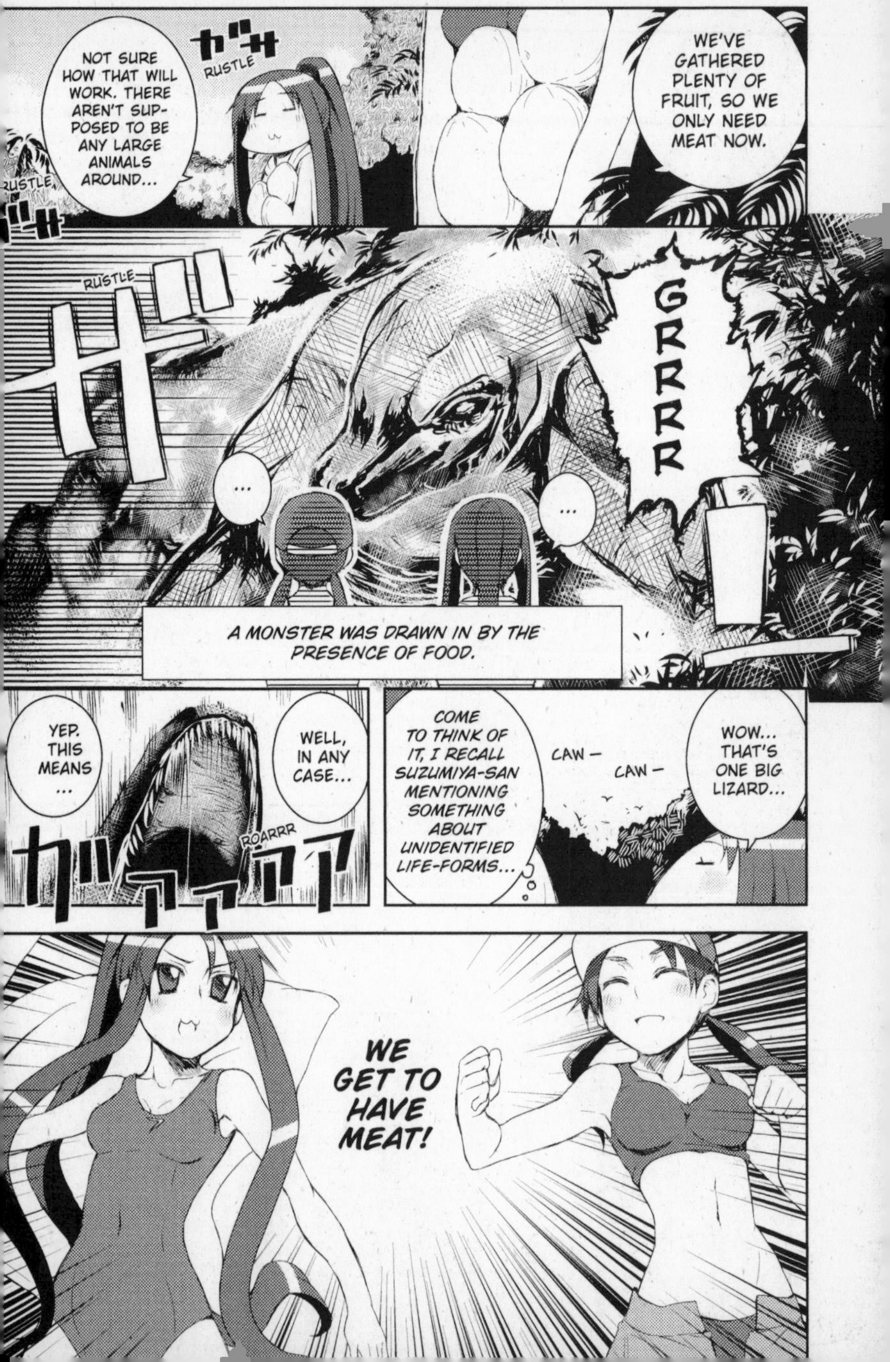

WE'VE GATHERED PLENTY OF FRUIT, SO WE ONLY NEED MEAT NOW.
RUSTLE
NOT SURE HOW THAT WILL WORK. THERE AREN'T SUPPOSED TO BE ANY LARGE ANIMALS AROUND...
RUSTLE
RUSTLE
GRRRR
...
...
A MONSTER WAS DRAWN IN BY THE PRESENCE OF FOOD.
WOW... THAT'S ONE BIG LIZARD...
CAW —
CAW —
COME TO THINK OF IT, I RECALL SUZUMIYA-SAN MENTIONING SOMETHING ABOUT UNIDENTIFIED LIFE-FORMS...
WELL, IN ANY CASE...
YEP. THIS MEANS...
ROARRR
WE GET TO HAVE MEAT!

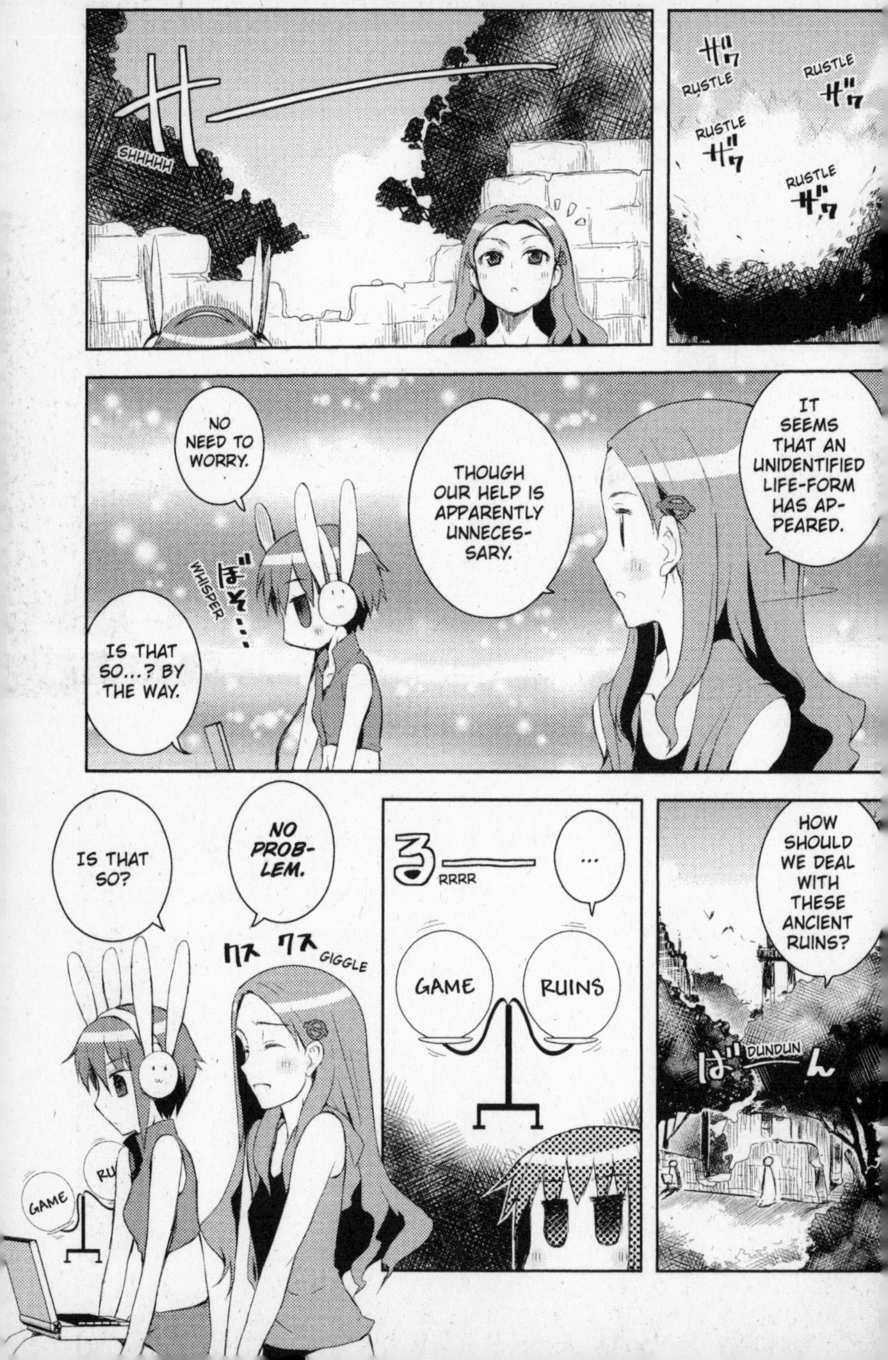
ザワ RUSTLE
RUSTLE ザワ
RUSTLE ザワ
RUSTLE ザワ
SHHHHH
IT SEEMS THAT AN UNIDENTIFIED LIFE-FORM HAS APPEARED.
THOUGH OUR HELP IS APPARENTLY UNNECESSARY.
NO NEED TO WORRY.
ぼそ… WHISPER
IS THAT SO…? BY THE WAY.
HOW SHOULD WE DEAL WITH THESE ANCIENT RUINS?
ば ん DUNDUN
…
る— RRRR
GAME
RUINS
NO PROBLEM.
クス クス GIGGLE
IS THAT SO?
RU
GAME

THE CHARACTERS NOBODY WANTED TO SEE THIS TIME

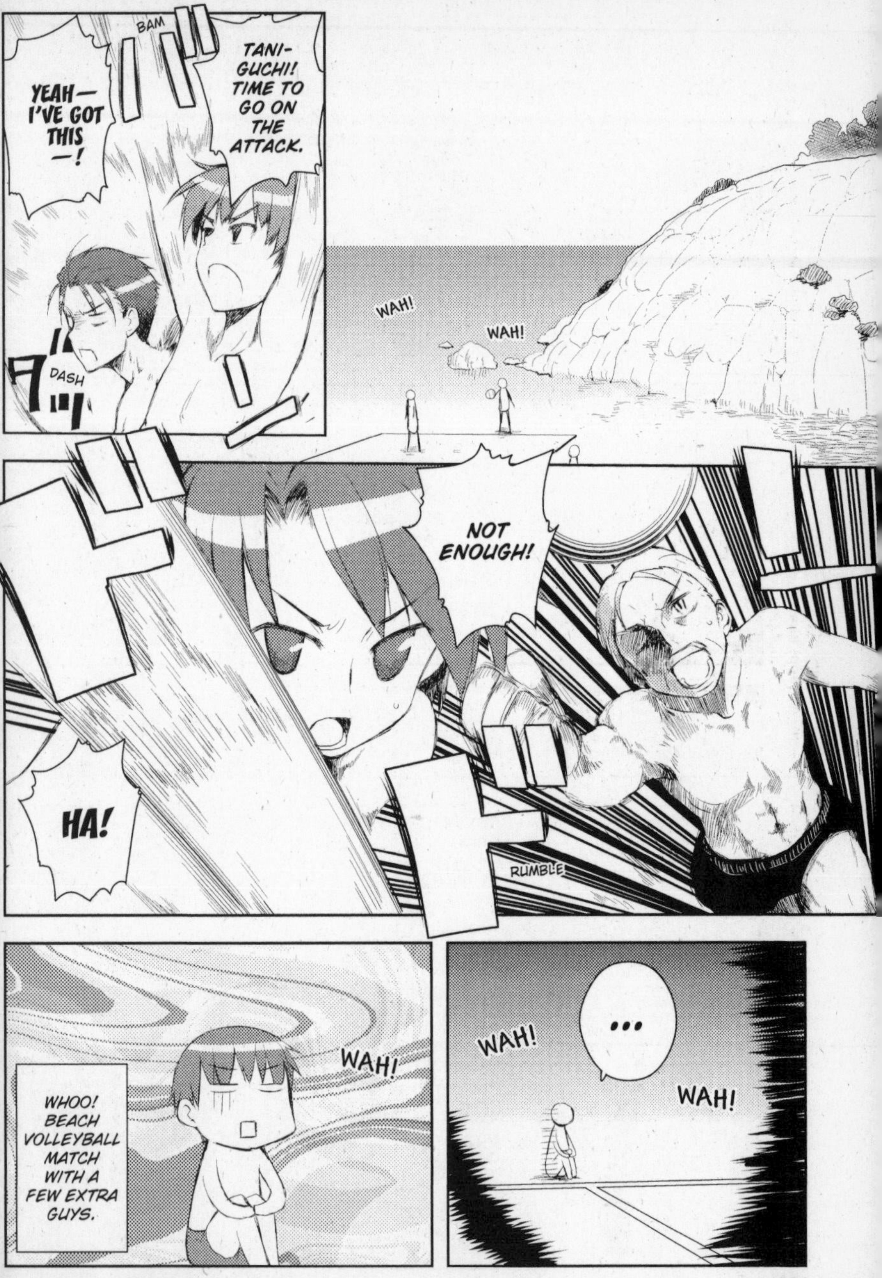
WAH!
WAH!
BAM
TANI-GUCHI! TIME TO GO ON THE ATTACK.
YEAH— I'VE GOT THIS —!
DASH
NOT ENOUGH!
HA!
RUMBLE
WAH!
...
WAH!
WAH!
WHOO! BEACH VOLLEYBALL MATCH WITH A FEW EXTRA GUYS.

MODEST ENTERTAINMENT

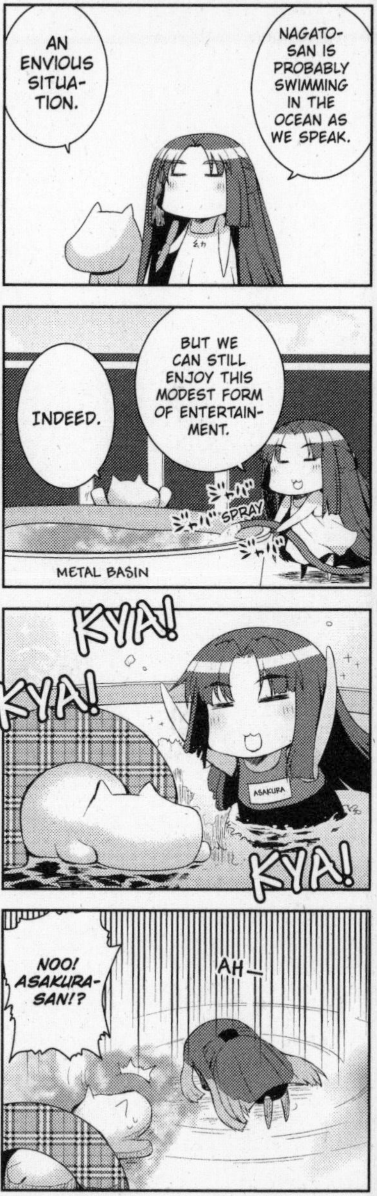
NAGATO-SAN IS PROBABLY SWIMMING IN THE OCEAN AS WE SPEAK.
AN ENVIOUS SITUATION.
BUT WE CAN STILL ENJOY THIS MODEST FORM OF ENTERTAINMENT.
INDEED.
SPRAY
METAL BASIN
KYA!
KYA!
ASAKURA
KYA!
AH—
NOO! ASAKURA-SAN!?

ON A WHIM

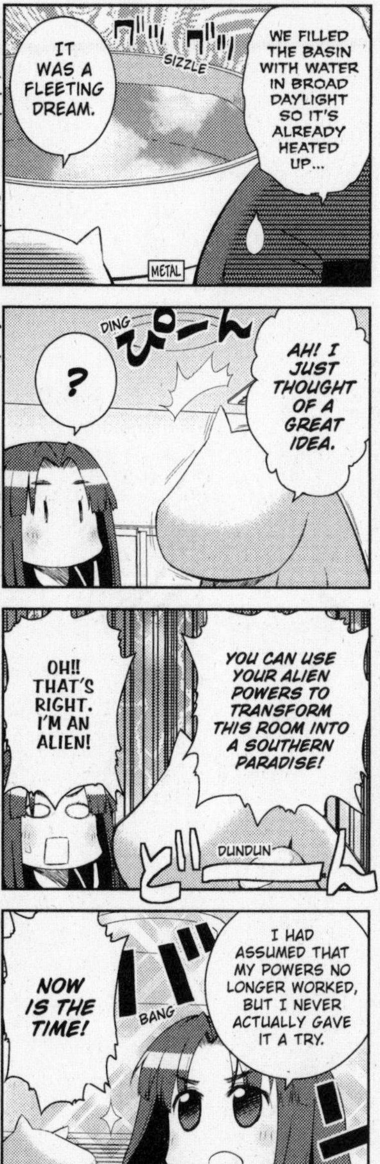
WE FILLED THE BASIN WITH WATER IN BROAD DAYLIGHT SO IT'S ALREADY HEATED UP...
SIZZLE
IT WAS A FLEETING DREAM.
METAL
AH! I JUST THOUGHT OF A GREAT IDEA.
DING
?
YOU CAN USE YOUR ALIEN POWERS TO TRANSFORM THIS ROOM INTO A SOUTHERN PARADISE!
OH!! THAT'S RIGHT. I'M AN ALIEN!
DUNDUN
I HAD ASSUMED THAT MY POWERS NO LONGER WORKED, BUT I NEVER ACTUALLY GAVE IT A TRY.
BANG
NOW IS THE TIME!

•Achakura-san •Back in action after being destroyed and crashing at Nagato's place. No trace remains of her former glory.

•Kimidori-san •A life-form (dog) created from a balloon by Nagato. Unrelated to Kimidori-san the human?

ALIEN POWER

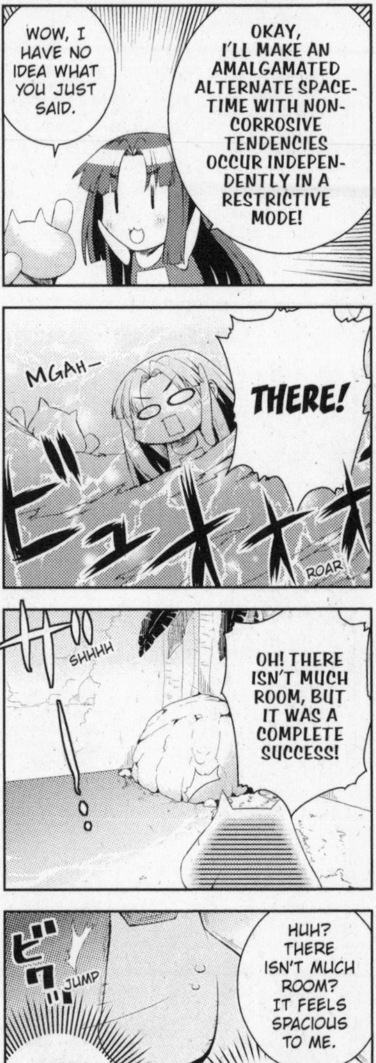
OKAY, I'LL MAKE AN AMALGAMATED ALTERNATE SPACE-TIME WITH NON-CORROSIVE TENDENCIES OCCUR INDEPENDENTLY IN A RESTRICTIVE MODE!
WOW, I HAVE NO IDEA WHAT YOU JUST SAID.
THERE!
MGAH—
ROAR
OH! THERE ISN'T MUCH ROOM, BUT IT WAS A COMPLETE SUCCESS!
SHHHH
HUH? THERE ISN'T MUCH ROOM? IT FEELS SPACIOUS TO ME.
JUMP
NOO! SHE SHRUNK EVEN MORE!?

SACRIFICE THE BODY

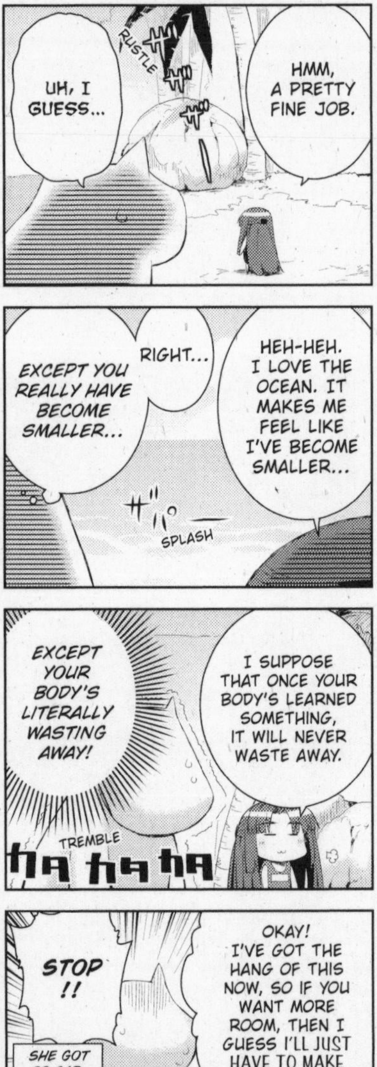
HMM, A PRETTY FINE JOB.
RUSTLE
UH, I GUESS...
HEH-HEH. I LOVE THE OCEAN. IT MAKES ME FEEL LIKE I'VE BECOME SMALLER...
RIGHT...
EXCEPT YOU REALLY HAVE BECOME SMALLER...
SPLASH
I SUPPOSE THAT ONCE YOUR BODY'S LEARNED SOMETHING, IT WILL NEVER WASTE AWAY.
EXCEPT YOUR BODY'S LITERALLY WASTING AWAY!
TREMBLE
OKAY! I'VE GOT THE HANG OF THIS NOW, SO IF YOU WANT MORE ROOM, THEN I GUESS I'LL JUST HAVE TO MAKE MORE ROOM.
STOP!!
SHE GOT SO CARRIED AWAY THAT SHE ALMOST OBLITERATED HERSELF.
SHOCK

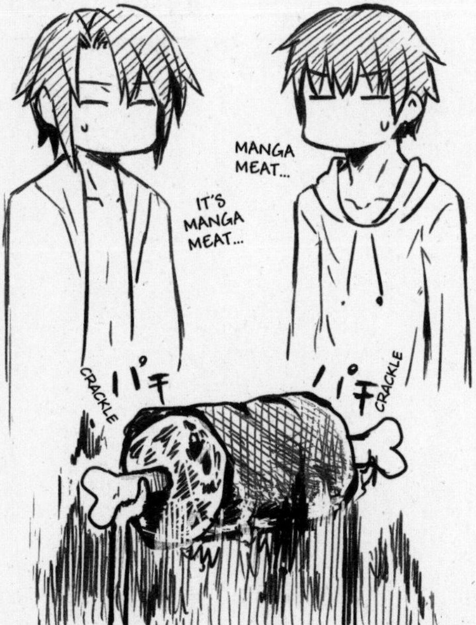
MANGA MEAT...
IT'S MANGA MEAT...
パチ
CRACKLE
パチ
CRACKLE

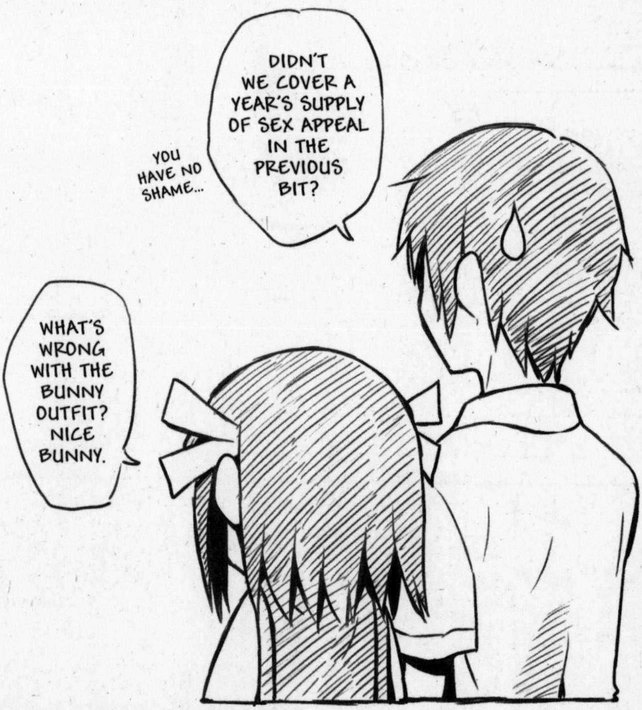
DIDN'T WE COVER A YEAR'S SUPPLY OF SEX APPEAL IN THE PREVIOUS BIT?
YOU HAVE NO SHAME...
WHAT'S WRONG WITH THE BUNNY OUTFIT? NICE BUNNY.

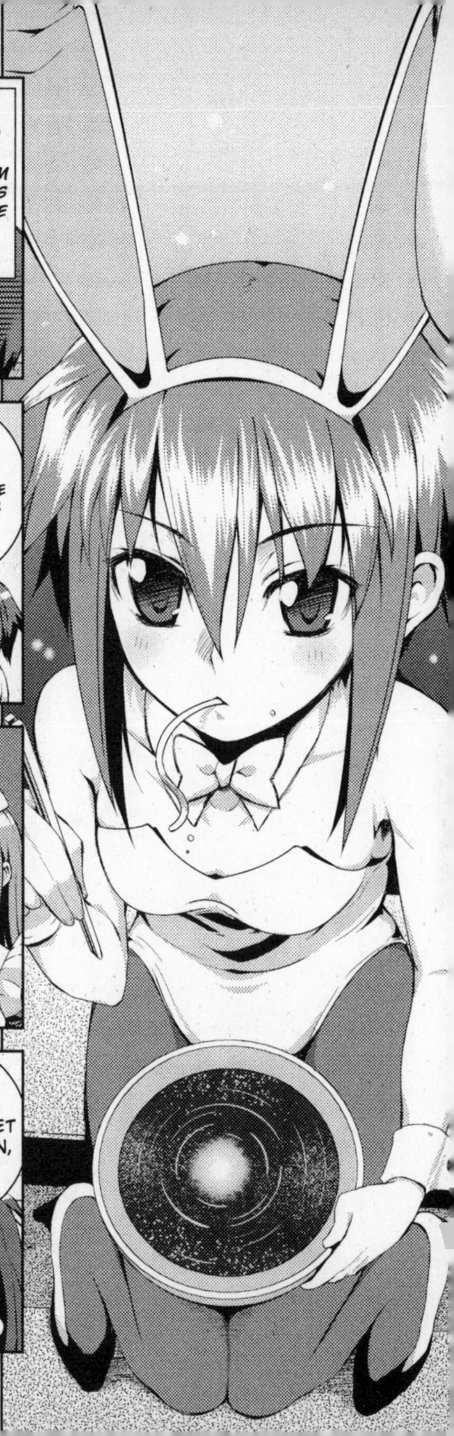

MOONGAZING

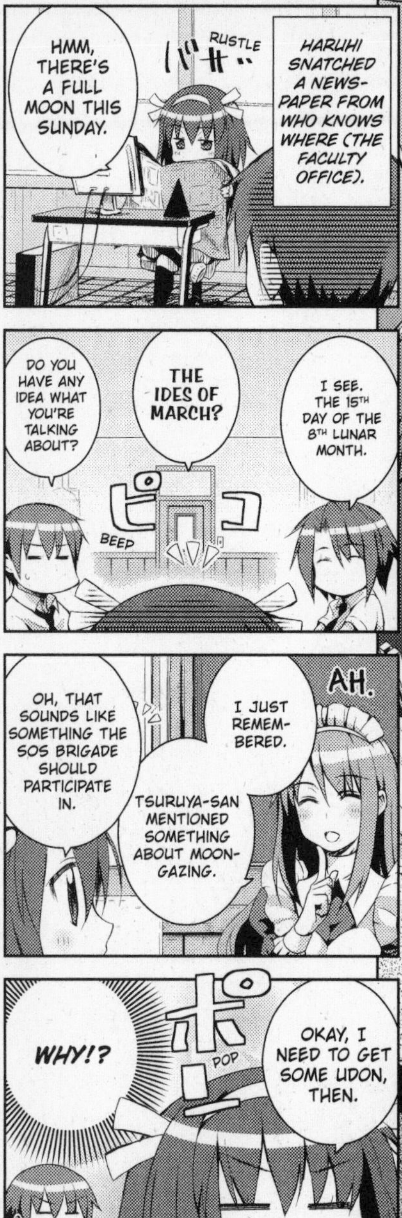

HARUHI SNATCHED A NEWSPAPER FROM WHO KNOWS WHERE (THE FACULTY OFFICE).
RUSTLE
HMM, THERE'S A FULL MOON THIS SUNDAY.
I SEE. THE 15TH DAY OF THE 8TH LUNAR MONTH.
THE IDES OF MARCH?
DO YOU HAVE ANY IDEA WHAT YOU'RE TALKING ABOUT?
BEEP
AH.
I JUST REMEMBERED.
TSURUYA-SAN MENTIONED SOMETHING ABOUT MOONGAZING.
OH, THAT SOUNDS LIKE SOMETHING THE SOS BRIGADE SHOULD PARTICIPATE IN.
OKAY, I NEED TO GET SOME UDON, THEN.
POP
WHY!?

•Haruhi-chan •SOS Brigade brigade chief. Her blood starts to boil when she's moongazing.

•Kyon •Supposed to be the main character in this story. Verbal riposting has become his life's work.

•Mikuru-chan •Actually from the future. Still wearing her maid outfit in the summer, this is key.

TOP SECRET

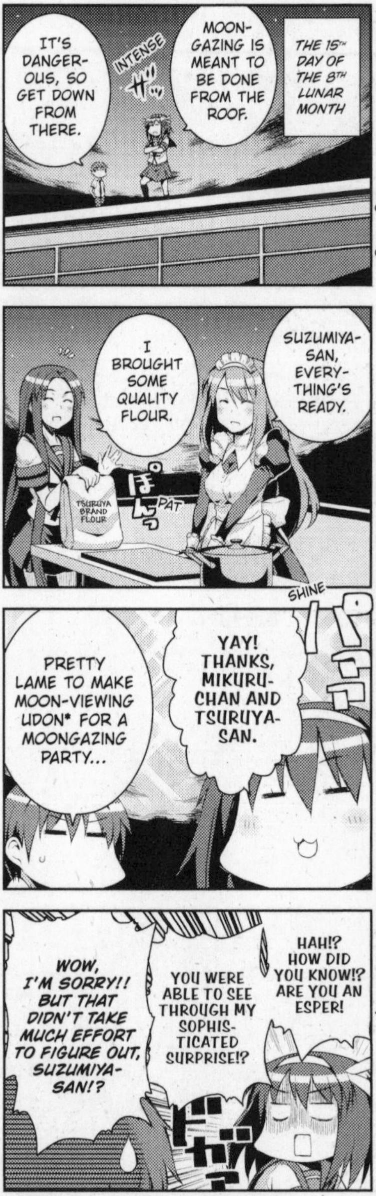
THE 15TH DAY OF THE 8TH LUNAR MONTH
MOON-GAZING IS MEANT TO BE DONE FROM THE ROOF.
INTENSE
IT'S DANGER-OUS, SO GET DOWN FROM THERE.
SUZUMIYA-SAN, EVERY-THING'S READY.
I BROUGHT SOME QUALITY FLOUR.
PAT
TSURUYA BRAND FLOUR
SHINE
YAY! THANKS, MIKURU-CHAN AND TSURUYA-SAN.
PRETTY LAME TO MAKE MOON-VIEWING UDON* FOR A MOONGAZING PARTY...
HAH!? HOW DID YOU KNOW!? ARE YOU AN ESPER!
YOU WERE ABLE TO SEE THROUGH MY SOPHIS-TICATED SURPRISE!?
WOW, I'M SORRY!! BUT THAT DIDN'T TAKE MUCH EFFORT TO FIGURE OUT, SUZUMIYA-SAN!?

ROME

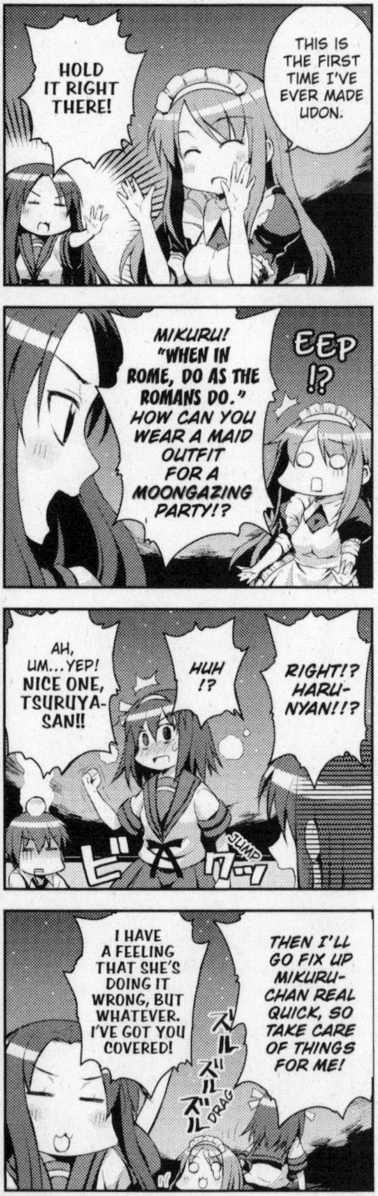
THIS IS THE FIRST TIME I'VE EVER MADE UDON.
HOLD IT RIGHT THERE!
EEP !?
MIKURU! "WHEN IN ROME, DO AS THE ROMANS DO." HOW CAN YOU WEAR A MAID OUTFIT FOR A MOONGAZING PARTY!?
RIGHT!? HARU-NYAN!!?
HUH !?
AH, UM...YEP! NICE ONE, TSURUYA-SAN!!
JUMP
THEN I'LL GO FIX UP MIKURU-CHAN REAL QUICK, SO TAKE CARE OF THINGS FOR ME!
I HAVE A FEELING THAT SHE'S DOING IT WRONG, BUT WHATEVER. I'VE GOT YOU COVERED!
DRAG

*TSUKIMI UDON ("MOON-VIEWING UDON") IS AN UDON NOODLE SOUP TOPPED WITH A RAW EGG, WHICH POACHES IN THE HOT BROTH.

GENIUS

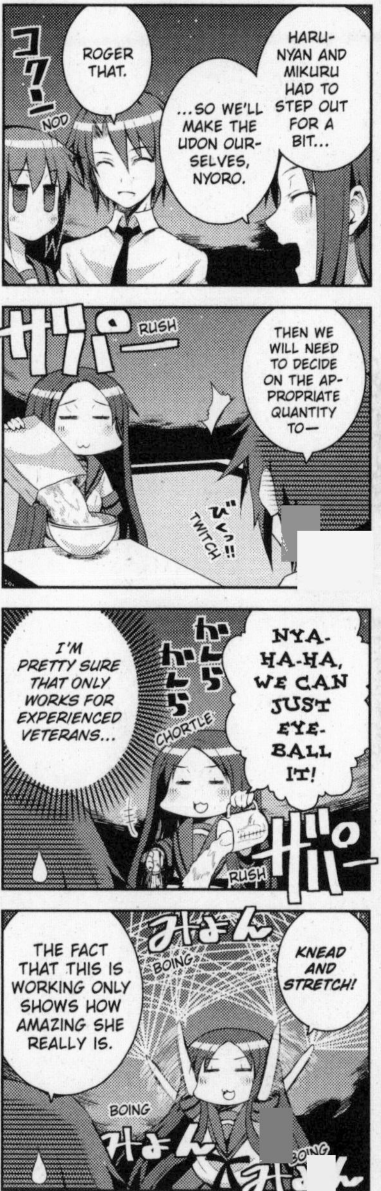

HARU-NYAN AND MIKURU HAD TO STEP OUT FOR A BIT...
...SO WE'LL MAKE THE UDON OURSELVES, NYORO.
ROGER THAT.
NOD
RUSH
THEN WE WILL NEED TO DECIDE ON THE APPROPRIATE QUANTITY TO—
TWITCH
NYA-HA-HA, WE CAN JUST EYEBALL IT!
CHORTLE
I'M PRETTY SURE THAT ONLY WORKS FOR EXPERIENCED VETERANS...
RUSH
KNEAD AND STRETCH!
BOING
THE FACT THAT THIS IS WORKING ONLY SHOWS HOW AMAZING SHE REALLY IS.
BOING
BOING

EMULATION

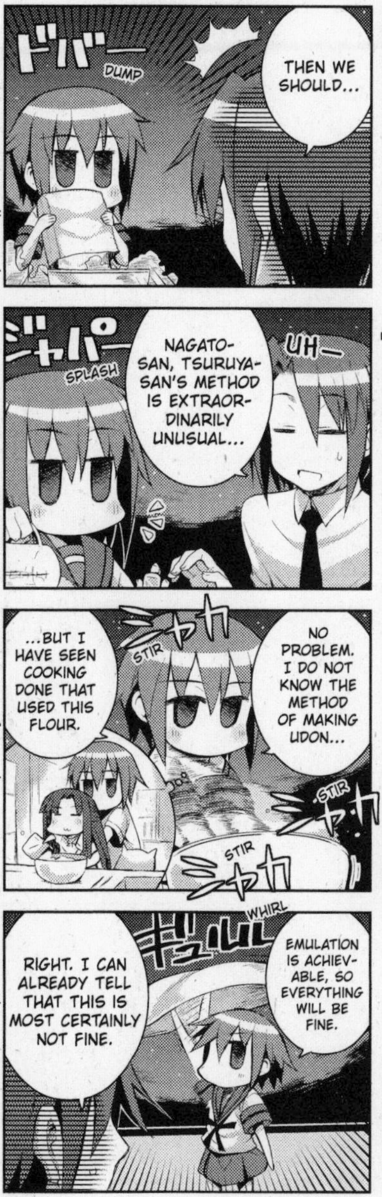

THEN WE SHOULD...
DUMP
UH—
NAGATO-SAN, TSURUYA-SAN'S METHOD IS EXTRAORDINARILY UNUSUAL...
SPLASH
NO PROBLEM. I DO NOT KNOW THE METHOD OF MAKING UDON...
STIR
...BUT I HAVE SEEN COOKING DONE THAT USED THIS FLOUR.
STIR
STIR
EMULATION IS ACHIEVABLE, SO EVERYTHING WILL BE FINE.
WHIRL
RIGHT. I CAN ALREADY TELL THAT THIS IS MOST CERTAINLY NOT FINE.

•Nagato •Actually an alien gamer. The SOS Brigade member who loves food the most?

•Koizumi •An enigmatic transfer student who happens to be an esper. Specializes in analysis while dabbling in verbal riposte.

•Tsuruya-san •The superwoman everybody should be familiar with. But is that really how you make udon...?

EGGS

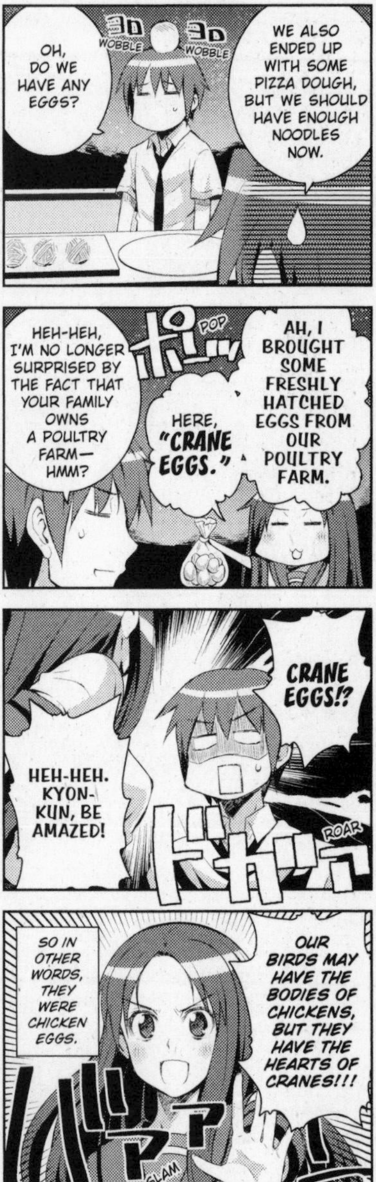

WE ALSO ENDED UP WITH SOME PIZZA DOUGH, BUT WE SHOULD HAVE ENOUGH NOODLES NOW.
WOBBLE
WOBBLE
OH, DO WE HAVE ANY EGGS?
AH, I BROUGHT SOME FRESHLY HATCHED EGGS FROM OUR POULTRY FARM.
POP
HERE, "CRANE EGGS."
HEH-HEH, I'M NO LONGER SURPRISED BY THE FACT THAT YOUR FAMILY OWNS A POULTRY FARM—HMM?
CRANE EGGS!?
ROAR
HEH-HEH. KYON-KUN, BE AMAZED!
OUR BIRDS MAY HAVE THE BODIES OF CHICKENS, BUT THEY HAVE THE HEARTS OF CRANES!!!
SLAM
SO IN OTHER WORDS, THEY WERE CHICKEN EGGS.

FIX UP

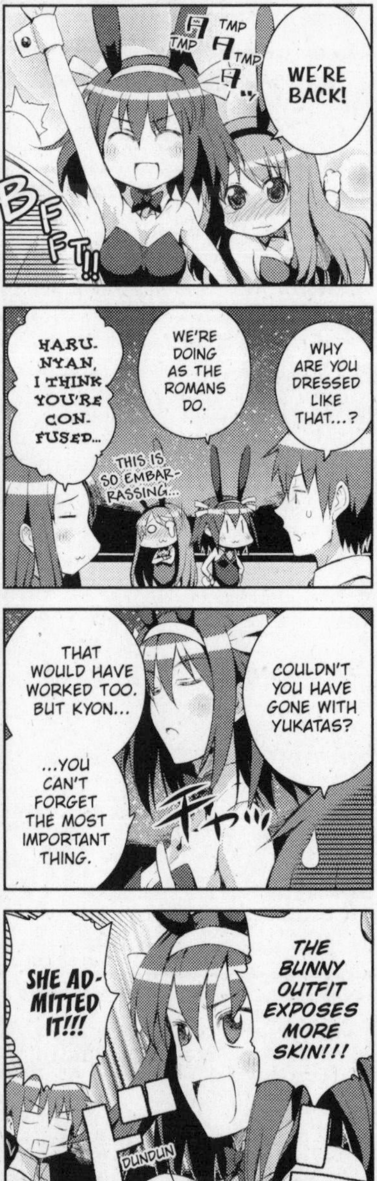

WE'RE BACK!
TMP
TMP
TMP
BFFT!!
WHY ARE YOU DRESSED LIKE THAT...?
WE'RE DOING AS THE ROMANS DO.
HARU-NYAN, I THINK YOU'RE CON-FUSED...
THIS IS SO EMBAR-RASSING...
COULDN'T YOU HAVE GONE WITH YUKATAS?
THAT WOULD HAVE WORKED TOO. BUT KYON...
...YOU CAN'T FORGET THE MOST IMPORTANT THING.
THE BUNNY OUTFIT EXPOSES MORE SKIN!!!
SHE AD-MITTED IT!!!
DUNDUN

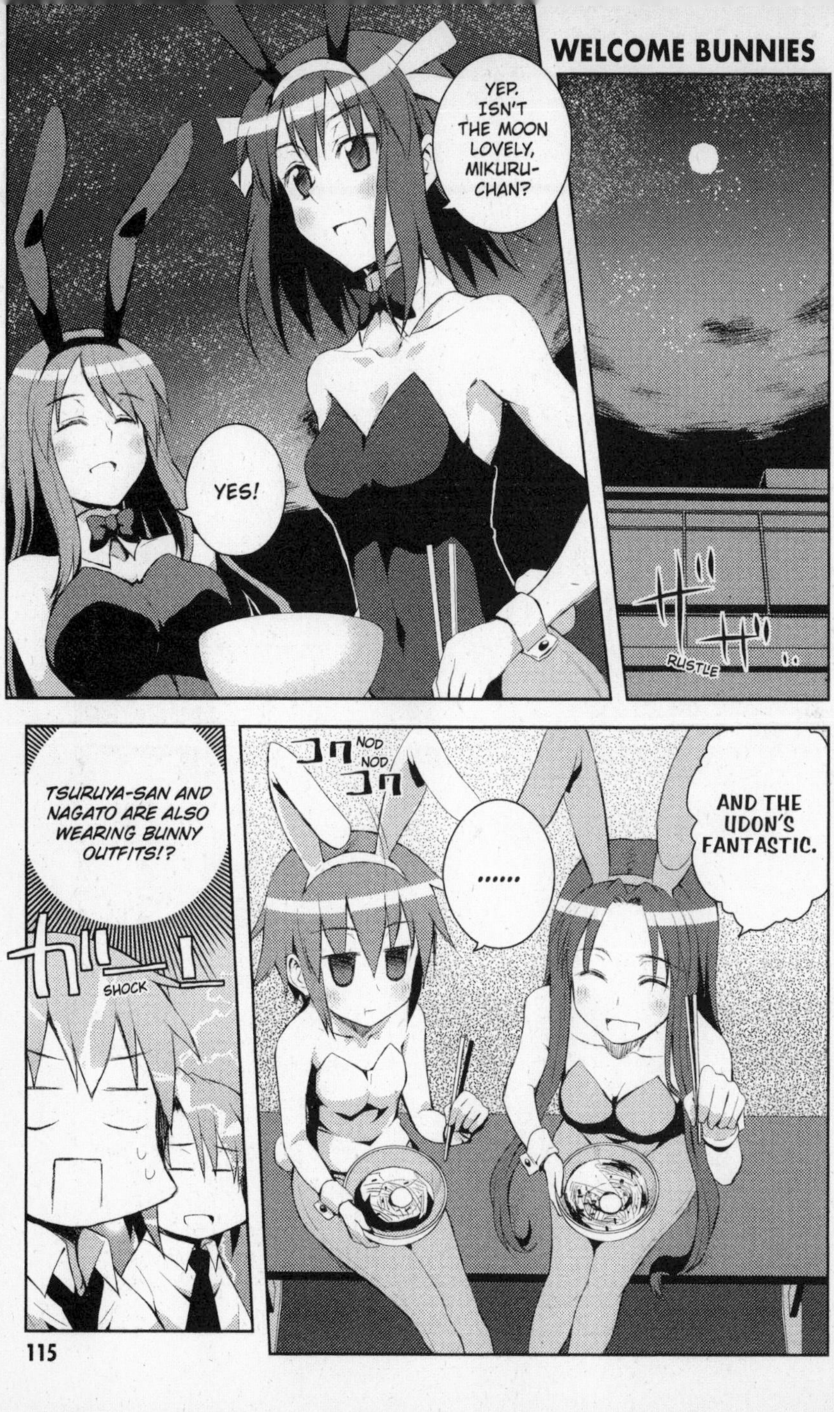
RUSTLE
YEP. ISN'T THE MOON LOVELY, MIKURU-CHAN?
YES!
AND THE UDON'S FANTASTIC.
NOD NOD
......
TSURUYA-SAN AND NAGATO ARE ALSO WEARING BUNNY OUTFITS!?
SHOCK

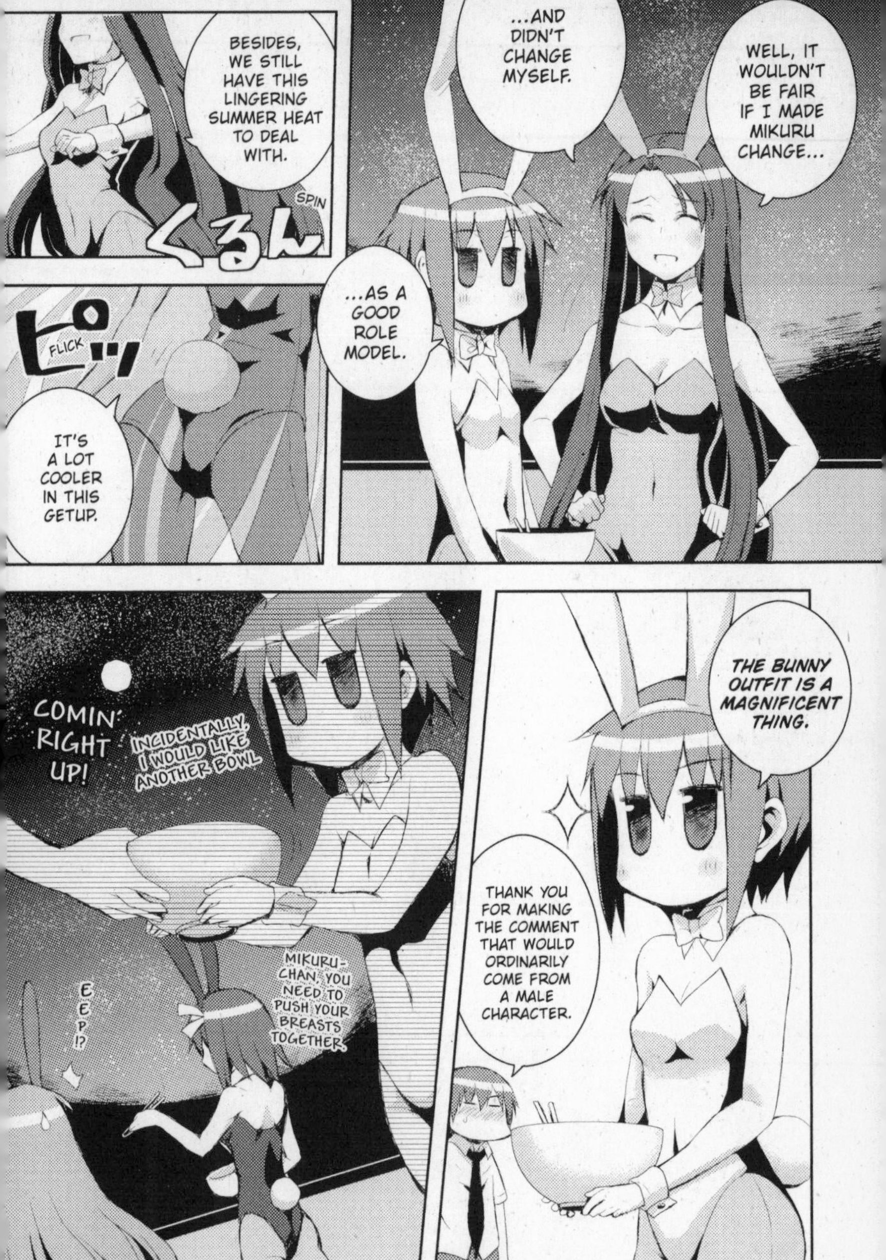
WELL, IT WOULDN'T BE FAIR IF I MADE MIKURU CHANGE...
...AND DIDN'T CHANGE MYSELF.
...AS A GOOD ROLE MODEL.
BESIDES, WE STILL HAVE THIS LINGERING SUMMER HEAT TO DEAL WITH.
くるん
SPIN
ピッ
FLICK
IT'S A LOT COOLER IN THIS GETUP.
THE BUNNY OUTFIT IS A MAGNIFICENT THING.
THANK YOU FOR MAKING THE COMMENT THAT WOULD ORDINARILY COME FROM A MALE CHARACTER.
INCIDENTALLY, I WOULD LIKE ANOTHER BOWL
COMIN' RIGHT UP!
MIKURU-CHAN, YOU NEED TO PUSH YOUR BREASTS TOGETHER.
EEP!?

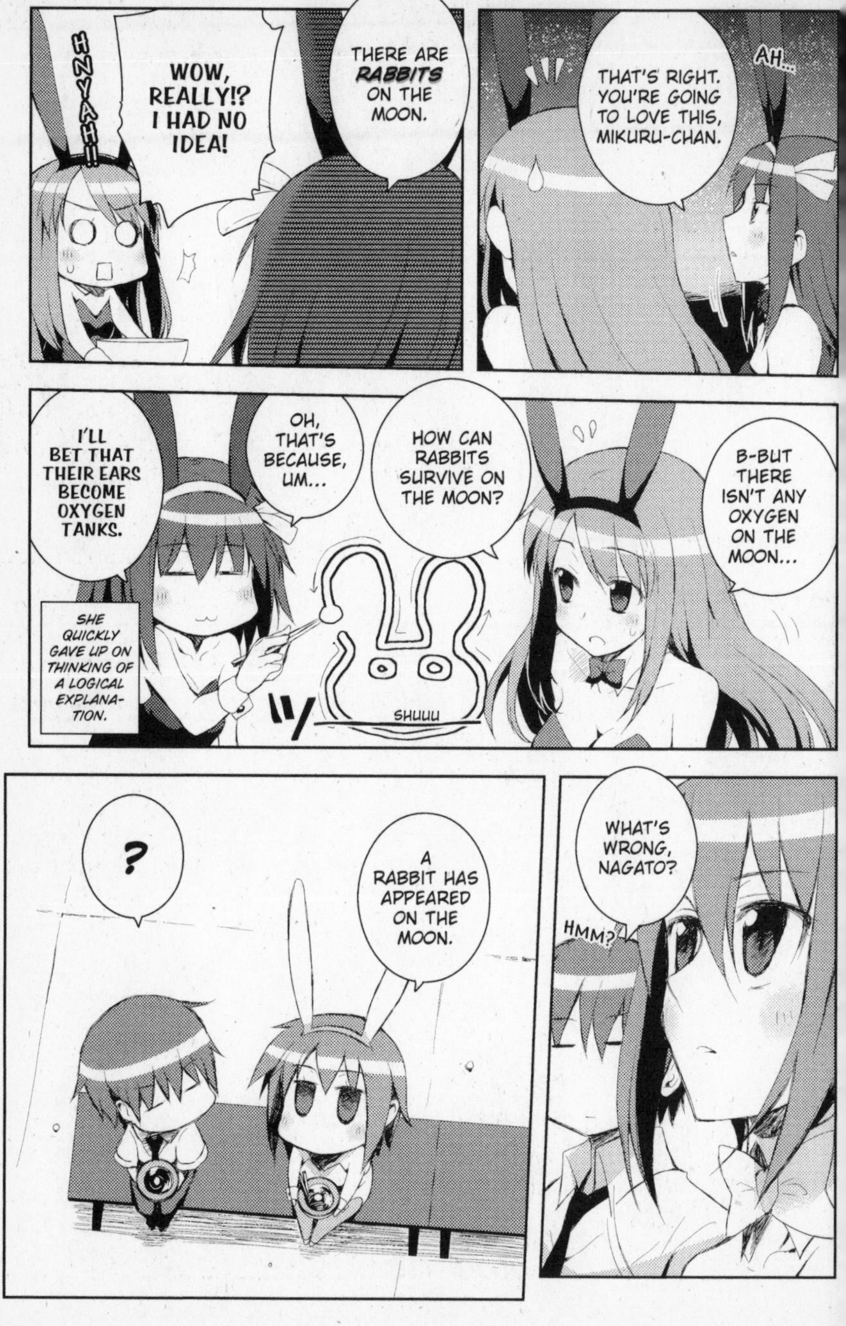
AH...
THAT'S RIGHT. YOU'RE GOING TO LOVE THIS, MIKURU-CHAN.
THERE ARE RABBITS ON THE MOON.
WOW, REALLY!? I HAD NO IDEA!
HNYAH!!
B-BUT THERE ISN'T ANY OXYGEN ON THE MOON...
HOW CAN RABBITS SURVIVE ON THE MOON?
OH, THAT'S BECAUSE, UM...
I'LL BET THAT THEIR EARS BECOME OXYGEN TANKS.
SHE QUICKLY GAVE UP ON THINKING OF A LOGICAL EXPLANATION.
SHUUU
HMM?
WHAT'S WRONG, NAGATO?
A RABBIT HAS APPEARED ON THE MOON.
?

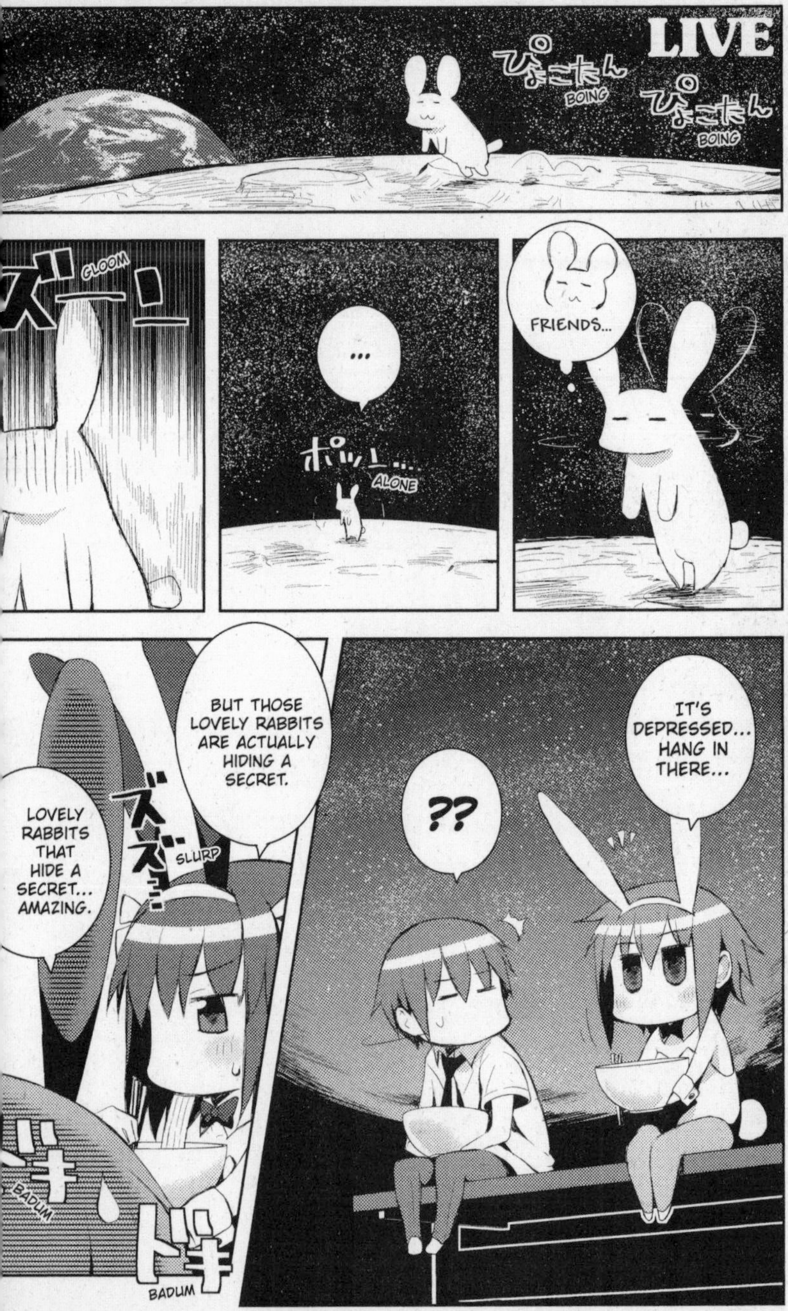
LIVE
ぴょこたん
BOING
ぴょこたん
BOING
FRIENDS...
...
ポッン...
ALONE
ズーン
GLOOM
IT'S DEPRESSED... HANG IN THERE...
??
BUT THOSE LOVELY RABBITS ARE ACTUALLY HIDING A SECRET.
ズズ
SLURP
LOVELY RABBITS THAT HIDE A SECRET... AMAZING.
ドキ
BADUM
ドキ
BADUM

•Moon Rabbit •Exists because Haruhi said so, Haruhi-quality to a T. Breathes through the oxygen concentrators in its ears and moves by kind of floating. Gets depressed when lonely. But not to the point where it will die.

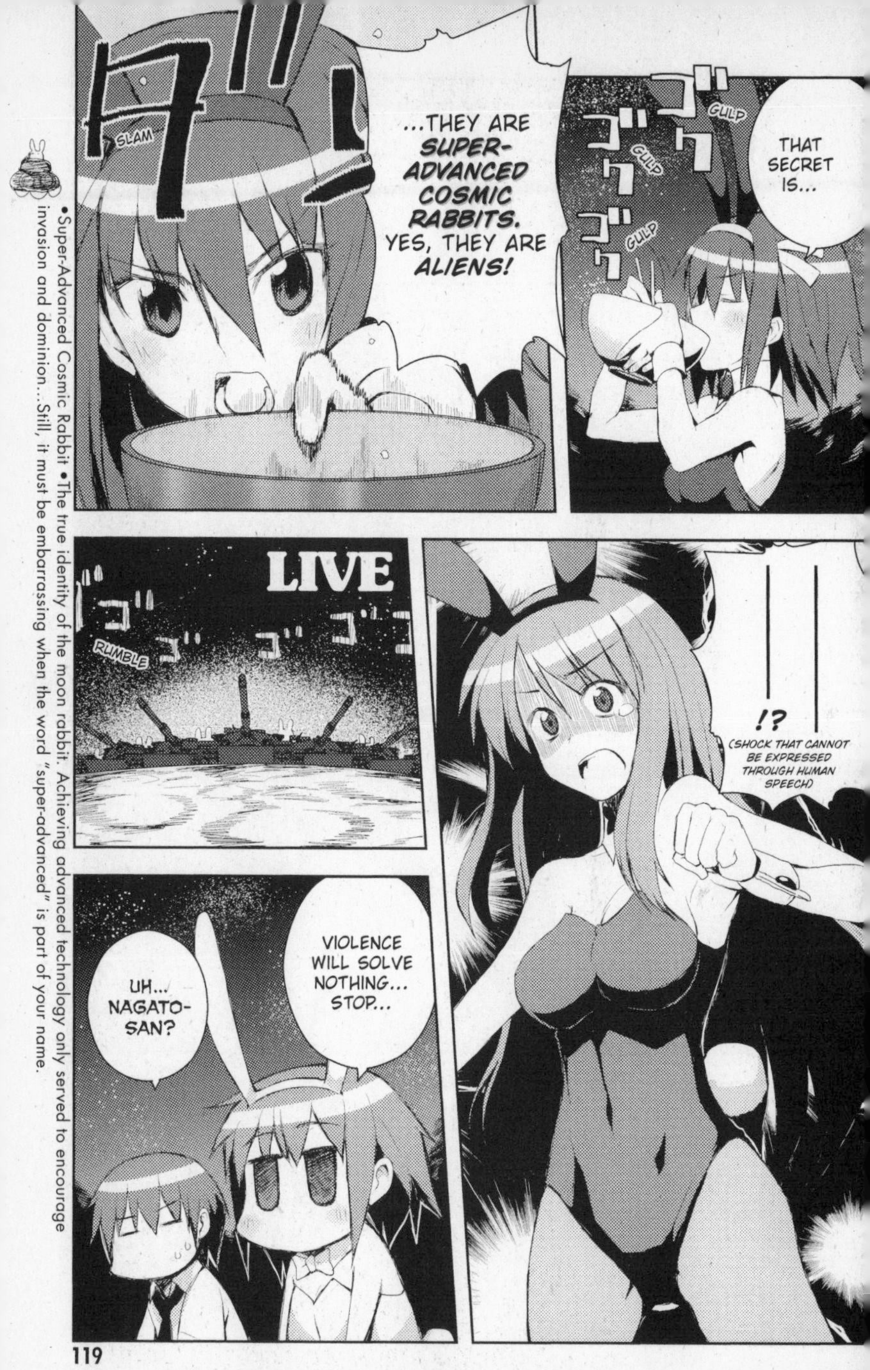
GULP
GULP
GULP
THAT SECRET IS...
SLAM
...THEY ARE SUPER-ADVANCED COSMIC RABBITS. YES, THEY ARE ALIENS!
!?
(SHOCK THAT CANNOT BE EXPRESSED THROUGH HUMAN SPEECH)
LIVE
RUMBLE
VIOLENCE WILL SOLVE NOTHING... STOP...
UH... NAGATO-SAN?

•Super-Advanced Cosmic Rabbit •The true identity of the moon rabbit. Achieving advanced technology only served to encourage invasion and dominion...Still, it must be embarrassing when the word "super-advanced" is part of your name.

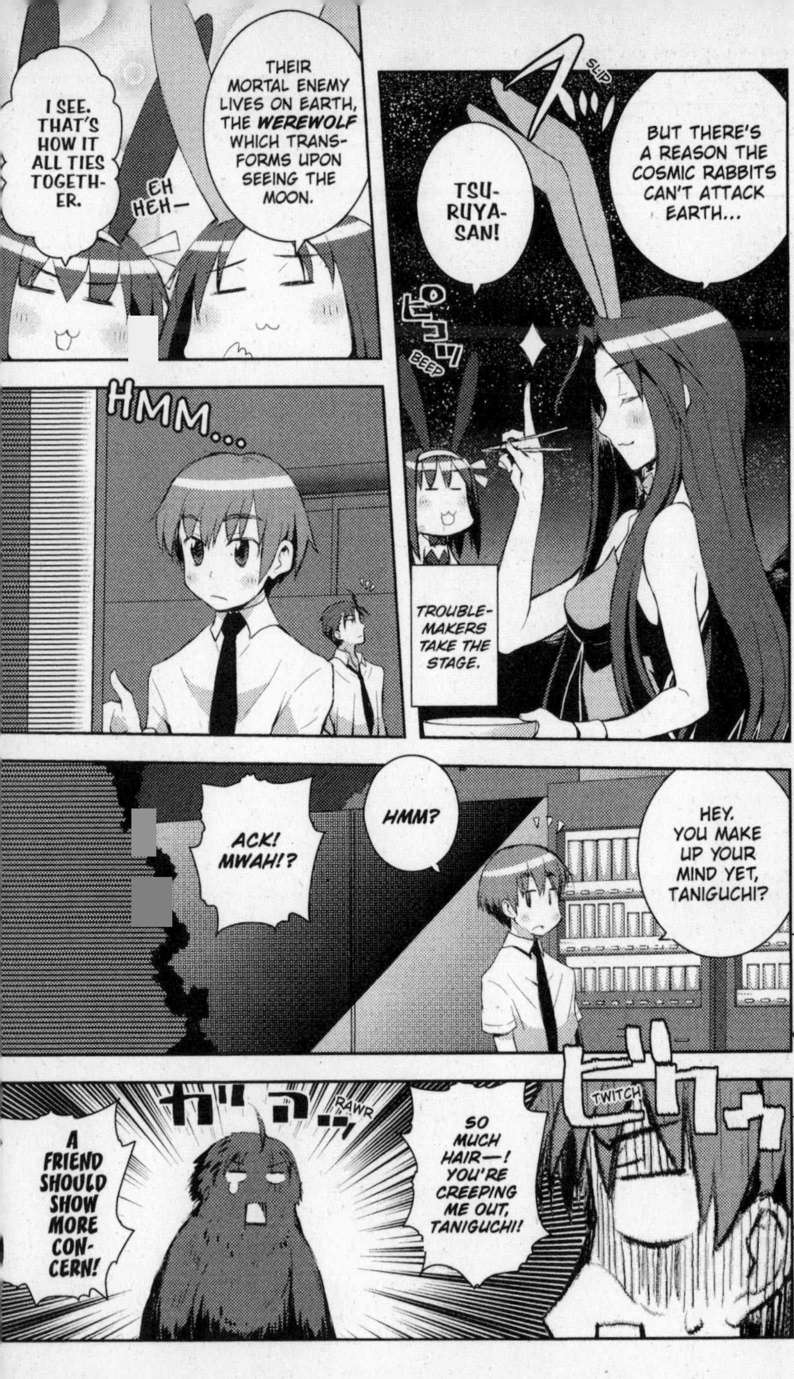
SLIP
BUT THERE'S A REASON THE COSMIC RABBITS CAN'T ATTACK EARTH...
TSU-RUYA-SAN!
BEEP
TROUBLE-MAKERS TAKE THE STAGE.
THEIR MORTAL ENEMY LIVES ON EARTH, THE ***WEREWOLF*** WHICH TRANS-FORMS UPON SEEING THE MOON.
EH HEH—
I SEE. THAT'S HOW IT ALL TIES TOGETH-ER.
HMM...
HEY. YOU MAKE UP YOUR MIND YET, TANIGUCHI?
HMM?
ACK! MWAH!?
TWITCH
SO MUCH HAIR—! YOU'RE CREEPING ME OUT, TANIGUCHI!
RAWR
A FRIEND SHOULD SHOW MORE CON-CERN!

•The Weird Werewolf •Taniguchi transforming into a wolf after seeing the moon. Though he looks more like an excessively hairy man than a wolf. Is this Haruhi's attempt at a kind gesture or just another aggravation...?

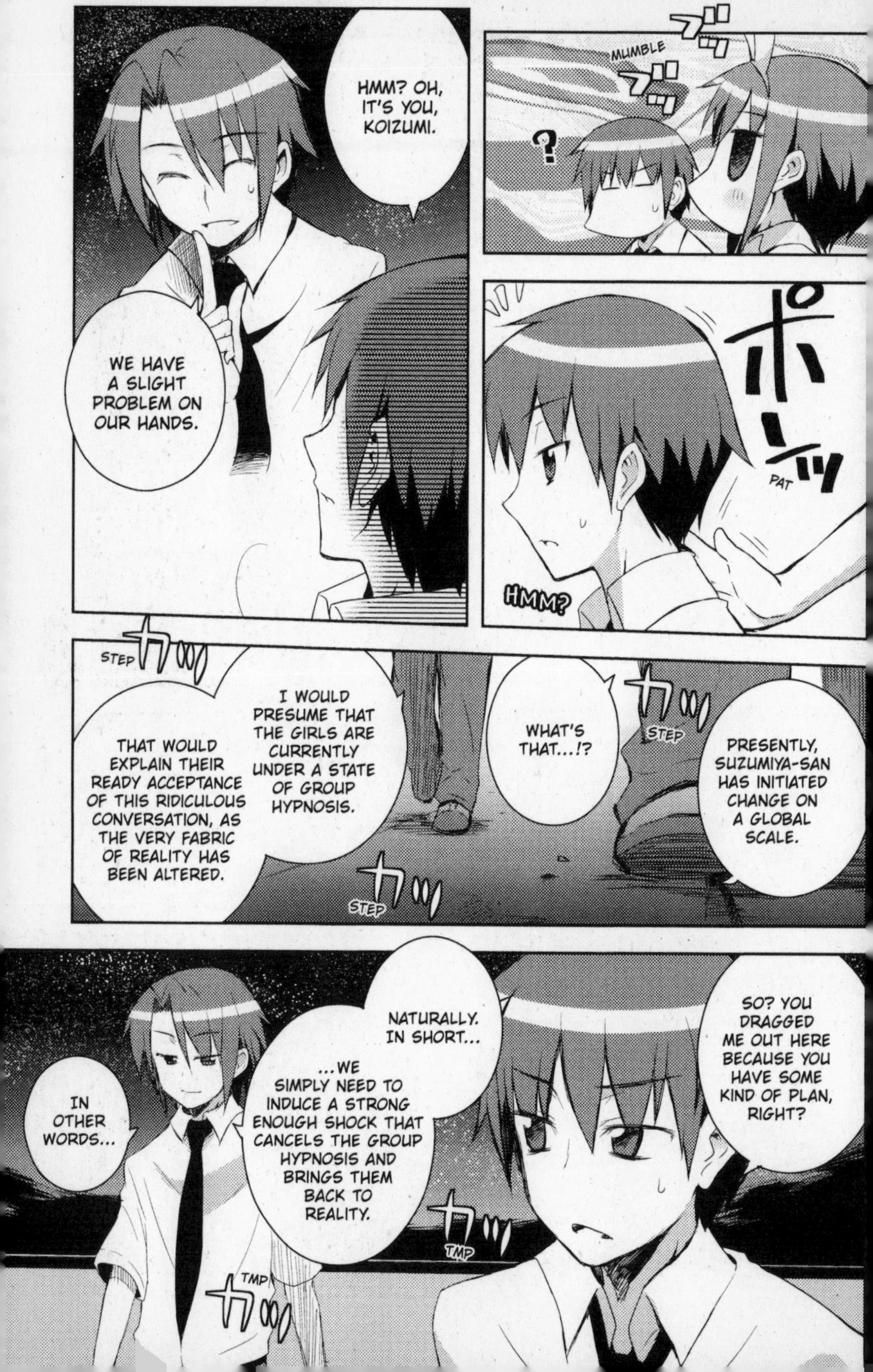
MUMBLE
?
PAT
HMM?
HMM? OH, IT'S YOU, KOIZUMI.
WE HAVE A SLIGHT PROBLEM ON OUR HANDS.
PRESENTLY, SUZUMIYA-SAN HAS INITIATED CHANGE ON A GLOBAL SCALE.
STEP
WHAT'S THAT...!?
I WOULD PRESUME THAT THE GIRLS ARE CURRENTLY UNDER A STATE OF GROUP HYPNOSIS.
THAT WOULD EXPLAIN THEIR READY ACCEPTANCE OF THIS RIDICULOUS CONVERSATION, AS THE VERY FABRIC OF REALITY HAS BEEN ALTERED.
STEP
STEP
SO? YOU DRAGGED ME OUT HERE BECAUSE YOU HAVE SOME KIND OF PLAN, RIGHT?
NATURALLY. IN SHORT...
...WE SIMPLY NEED TO INDUCE A STRONG ENOUGH SHOCK THAT CANCELS THE GROUP HYPNOSIS AND BRINGS THEM BACK TO REALITY.
TMP
IN OTHER WORDS...
TMP

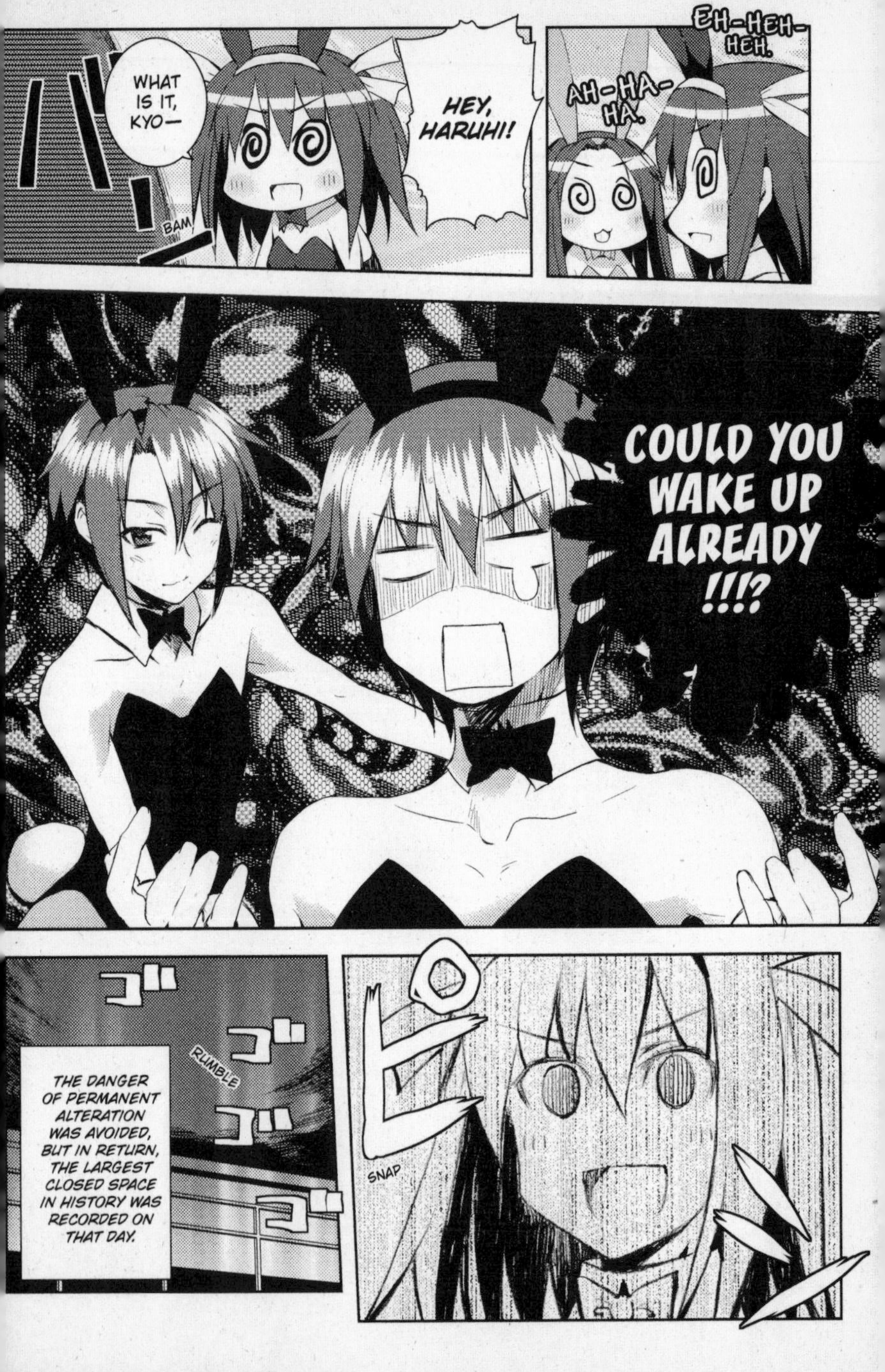
EH-HEH-HEH.
AH-HA-HA.
HEY, HARUHI!
WHAT IS IT, KYO—
BAM
COULD YOU WAKE UP ALREADY!!!?
SNAP
RUMBLE
THE DANGER OF PERMANENT ALTERATION WAS AVOIDED, BUT IN RETURN, THE LARGEST CLOSED SPACE IN HISTORY WAS RECORDED ON THAT DAY.

SHAMI

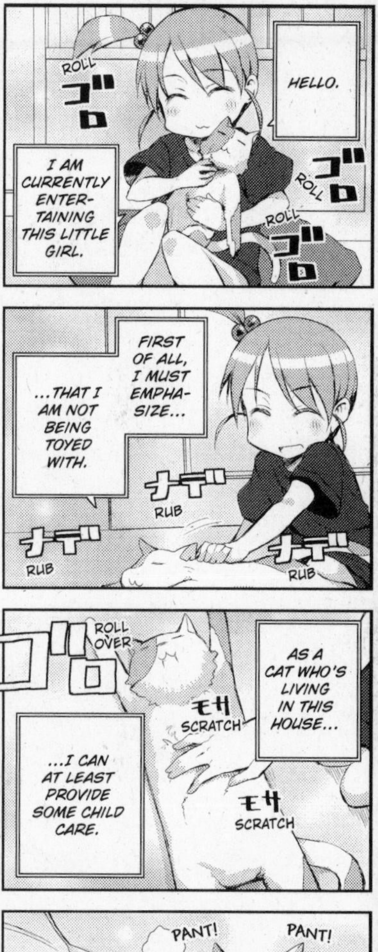
HELLO.
I AM CURRENTLY ENTERTAINING THIS LITTLE GIRL.
ゴロ ROLL
ゴロ ROLL
ゴロ ROLL
FIRST OF ALL, I MUST EMPHASIZE...
...THAT I AM NOT BEING TOYED WITH.
ナデ RUB
ナデ RUB
ナデ RUB
AS A CAT WHO'S LIVING IN THIS HOUSE...
ゴロ ROLL OVER
モサ SCRATCH
...I CAN AT LEAST PROVIDE SOME CHILD CARE.
モサ SCRATCH
PANT!
PANT!
HIS ARGUMENT WASN'T VERY CONVINCING.
フシャー BRUSH

TACKLE

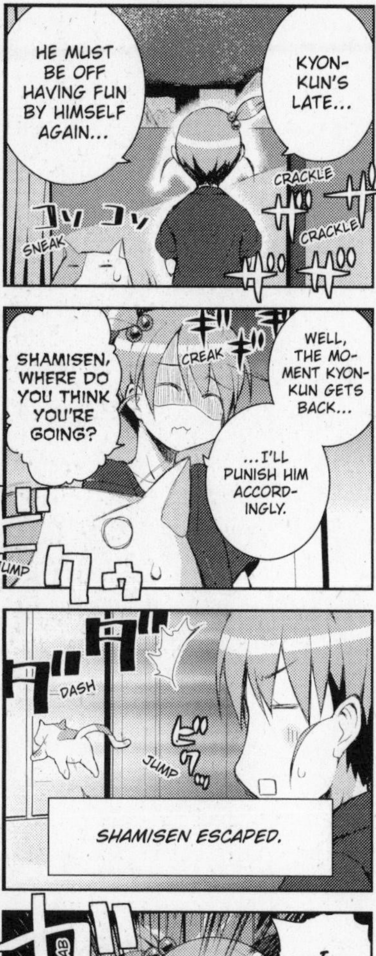
KYON-KUN'S LATE...
HE MUST BE OFF HAVING FUN BY HIMSELF AGAIN...
CRACKLE
CRACKLE
コソ コソ SNEAK
WELL, THE MOMENT KYON-KUN GETS BACK...
...I'LL PUNISH HIM ACCORDINGLY.
CREAK
SHAMISEN, WHERE DO YOU THINK YOU'RE GOING?
JUMP
DASH
JUMP
SHAMISEN ESCAPED.
I DON'T THINK SO!!!
GRAB
A TACKLE WORTHY OF FUTURE NFL CONSIDERATION, IF SHE WERE A BOY.

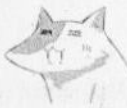

•Shamisen •A rare male calico. In this manga, he tries to sound like a gentleman.

•Kyon's sister •Kyon's sister. A girl who's willing to sacrifice her brother and Shamisen in the name of having fun.

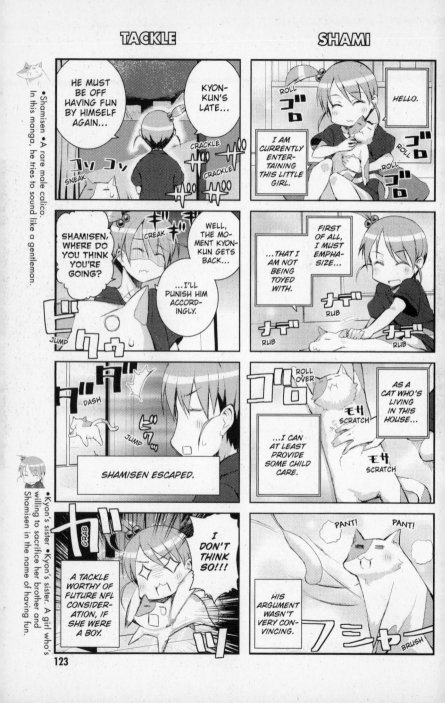

AMBUSH

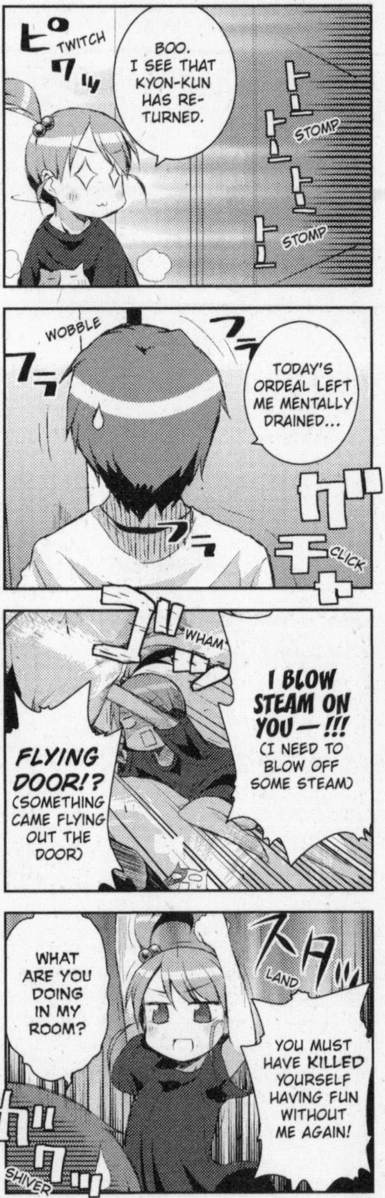
BOO. I SEE THAT KYON-KUN HAS RE-TURNED.
TWITCH
STOMP
STOMP
TODAY'S ORDEAL LEFT ME MENTALLY DRAINED...
WOBBLE
CLICK
WHAM
I BLOW STEAM ON YOU—!!! (I NEED TO BLOW OFF SOME STEAM)
FLYING DOOR!? (SOMETHING CAME FLYING OUT THE DOOR)
LAND
WHAT ARE YOU DOING IN MY ROOM?
YOU MUST HAVE KILLED YOURSELF HAVING FUN WITHOUT ME AGAIN!
SHIVER

SIBLING FIGHT

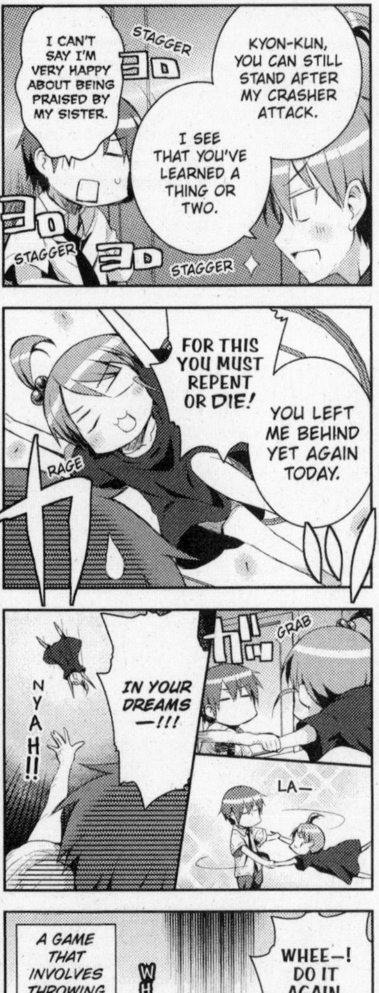
KYON-KUN, YOU CAN STILL STAND AFTER MY CRASHER ATTACK.
STAGGER
I CAN'T SAY I'M VERY HAPPY ABOUT BEING PRAISED BY MY SISTER.
I SEE THAT YOU'VE LEARNED A THING OR TWO.
STAGGER
STAGGER
YOU LEFT ME BEHIND YET AGAIN TODAY.
FOR THIS YOU MUST REPENT OR DIE!
RAGE
GRAB
IN YOUR DREAMS—!!!
NYAH!!
LA—
WHEE—! DO IT AGAIN, KYON-KUN.
WHAT?
A GAME THAT INVOLVES THROWING SOMEONE ONTO A BED.
PLOP

IDEA

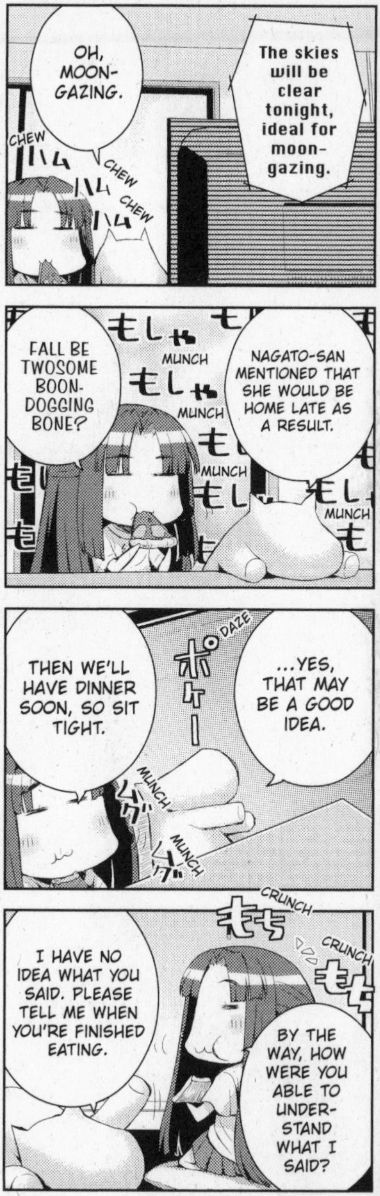
The skies will be clear tonight, ideal for moon-gazing.
OH, MOON-GAZING.
CHEW ハム
CHEW ハム
CHEW ハム
NAGATO-SAN MENTIONED THAT SHE WOULD BE HOME LATE AS A RESULT.
FALL BE TWOSOME BOON-DOGGING BONE?
MUNCH もしゃ
...YES, THAT MAY BE A GOOD IDEA.
DAZE ポケー
THEN WE'LL HAVE DINNER SOON, SO SIT TIGHT.
MUNCH ムグ
MUNCH ムグ
CRUNCH もち
CRUNCH もち
BY THE WAY, HOW WERE YOU ABLE TO UNDERSTAND WHAT I SAID?
I HAVE NO IDEA WHAT YOU SAID. PLEASE TELL ME WHEN YOU'RE FINISHED EATING.

PRACTICAL APPLICATION

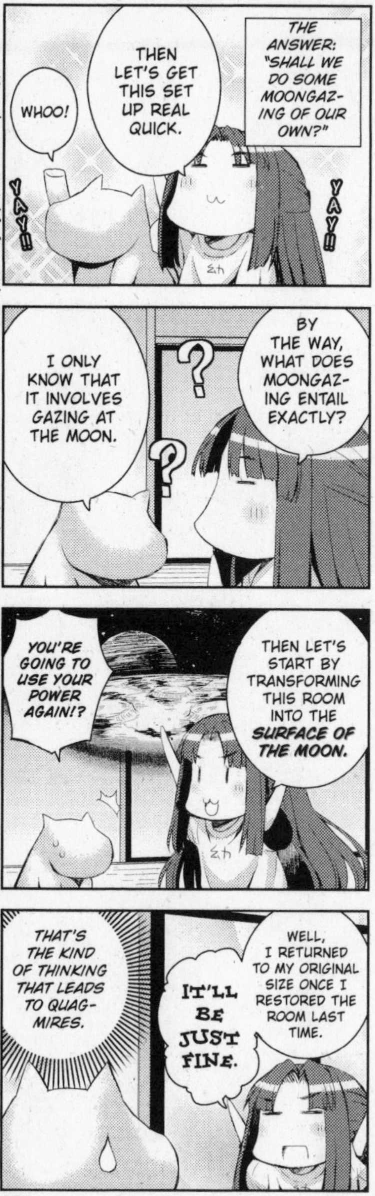
THE ANSWER: "SHALL WE DO SOME MOONGAZING OF OUR OWN?"
YAY!!
THEN LET'S GET THIS SET UP REAL QUICK.
WHOO!
YAY!!
BY THE WAY, WHAT DOES MOONGAZING ENTAIL EXACTLY?
I ONLY KNOW THAT IT INVOLVES GAZING AT THE MOON.
THEN LET'S START BY TRANSFORMING THIS ROOM INTO THE SURFACE OF THE MOON.
YOU'RE GOING TO USE YOUR POWER AGAIN!?
WELL, I RETURNED TO MY ORIGINAL SIZE ONCE I RESTORED THE ROOM LAST TIME.
IT'LL BE JUST FINE.
THAT'S THE KIND OF THINKING THAT LEADS TO QUAGMIRES.

•Kimidori-san •A life-form (dog) created from a balloon by Nagato. Has a rather irresponsible temperament.

•Achakura-san •Back in action after being destroyed and is crashing at Nagato's place. Recently discovered that she shrinks even more upon using her alien power.

MOONGAZING

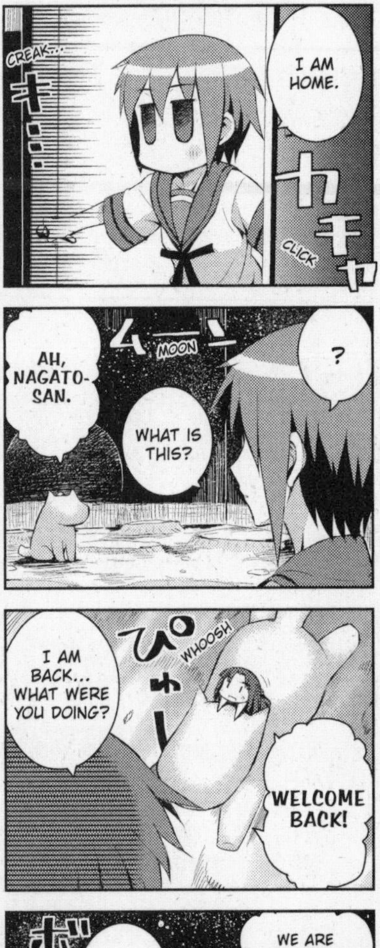
I AM HOME.
CREAK...
CLICK
?
MOON
AH, NAGATO-SAN.
WHAT IS THIS?
WHOOSH
I AM BACK... WHAT WERE YOU DOING?
WELCOME BACK!
WE ARE DEVOTING OURSELVES TO THE MOON. MOONGAZING FROM THE MOON ITSELF!
SO SMALL...
WHISPER
RAISE

LUNAR MARKETING

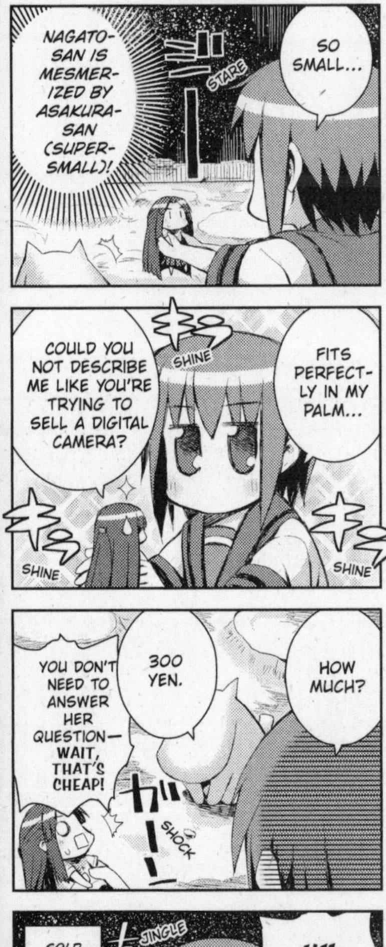
SO SMALL...
STARE
NAGATO-SAN IS MESMERIZED BY ASAKURA-SAN (SUPER-SMALL)!
FITS PERFECTLY IN MY PALM...
SHINE
COULD YOU NOT DESCRIBE ME LIKE YOU'RE TRYING TO SELL A DIGITAL CAMERA?
SHINE
SHINE
HOW MUCH?
300 YEN.
YOU DON'T NEED TO ANSWER HER QUESTION—WAIT, THAT'S CHEAP!
SHOCK
I'M CHEAPER THAN A NENDOROID DOLL!
JINGLE
SOLD ON THE SURFACE OF THE MOON.
COME AGAIN!

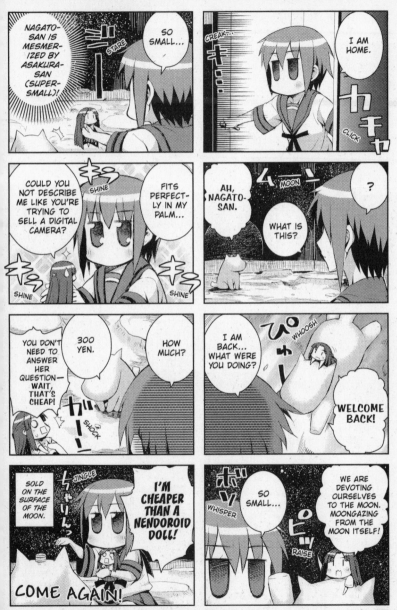

PLUS ONE

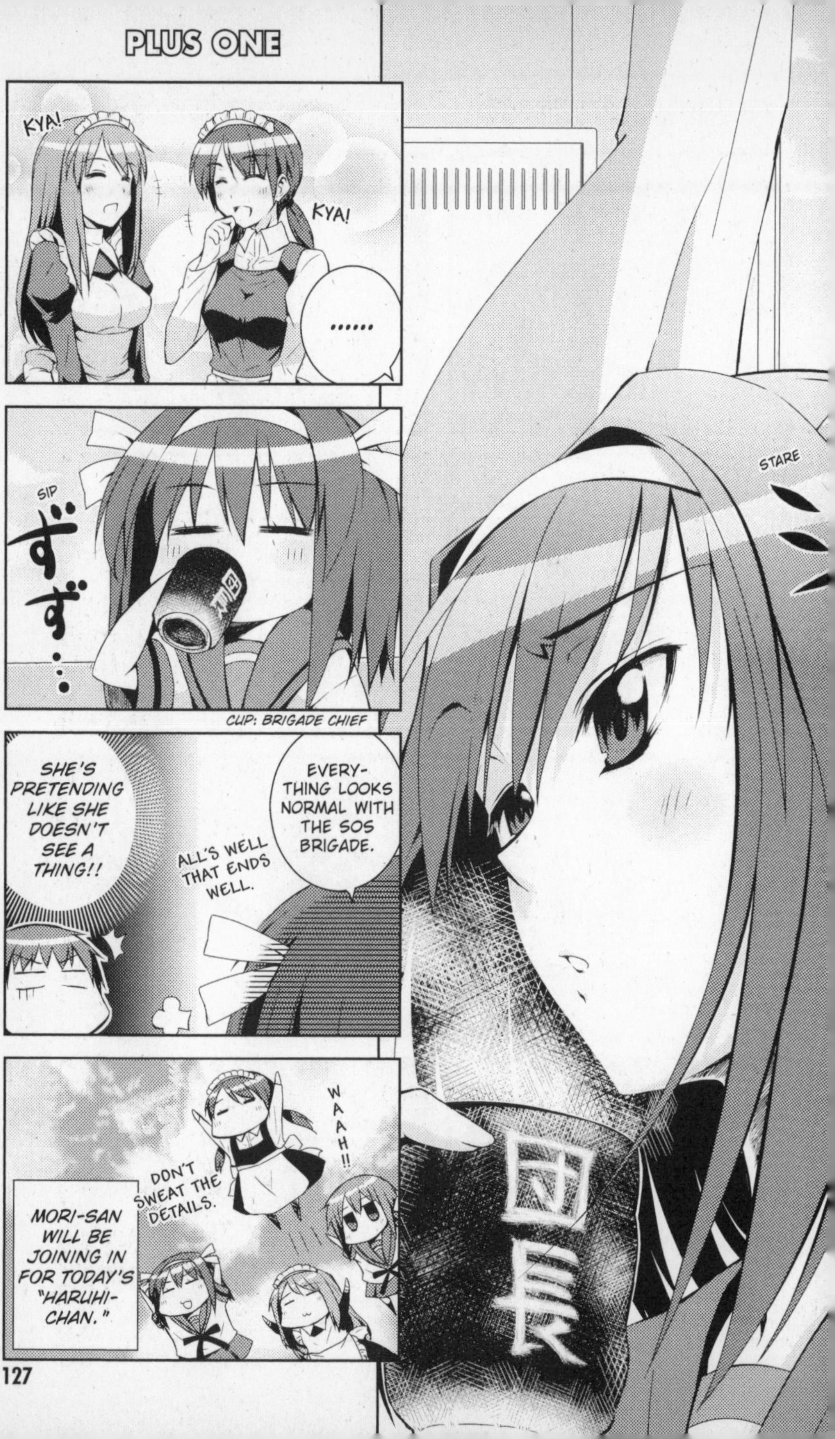
STARE
団長
KYA!
KYA!
......
SIP
ずず…
団長
CUP: BRIGADE CHIEF
EVERY-THING LOOKS NORMAL WITH THE SOS BRIGADE.
ALL'S WELL THAT ENDS WELL.
SHE'S PRETENDING LIKE SHE DOESN'T SEE A THING!!
WAAH!!
DON'T SWEAT THE DETAILS.
MORI-SAN WILL BE JOINING IN FOR TODAY'S "HARUHI-CHAN."

•Haruhi-chan •SOS Brigade brigade chief. Has no problem with Mori-san's presence since she's having fun.

•Kyon •Supposed to be the main character in this story. Too much verbal riposting and his eyes will roll back in his head.

•Mikuru-chan •Actually from the future. She seems to admire Mori-san as the ideal maid?

HOW TO POUR TEA

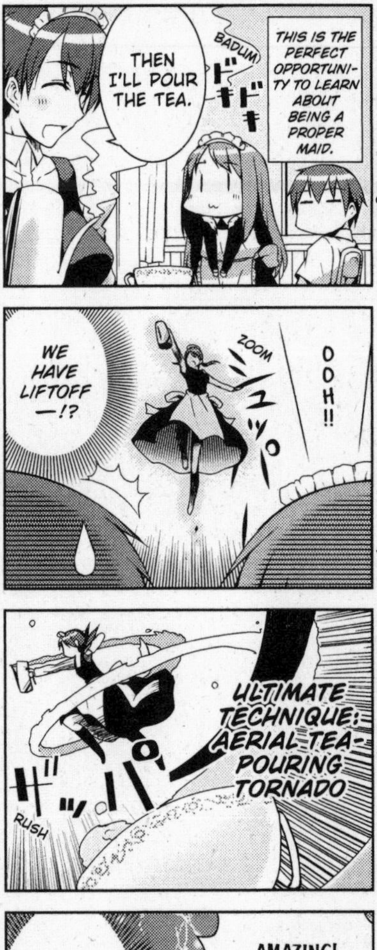
THIS IS THE PERFECT OPPORTUNITY TO LEARN ABOUT BEING A PROPER MAID.
BADUM
THEN I'LL POUR THE TEA.
OOH!!
ZOOM
WE HAVE LIFTOFF—!?
ULTIMATE TECHNIQUE: AERIAL TEA-POURING TORNADO
RUSH
AMAZING! SHE JUMPED SO HIGH TO INFUSE AIR INTO THE TEA!
ASAHINA-SAN SOUNDS LIKE A COMMENTATOR NOW.
TWITCH

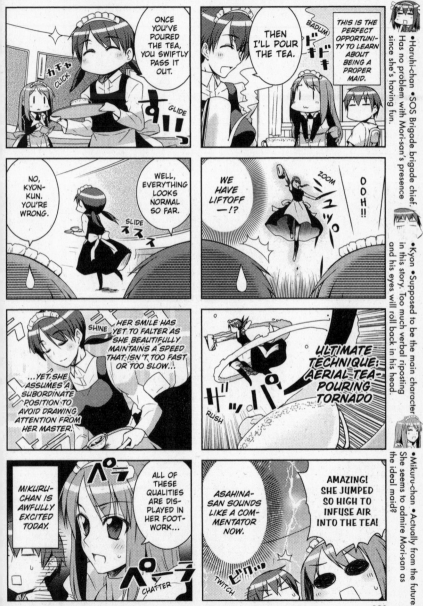

MAID STYLE

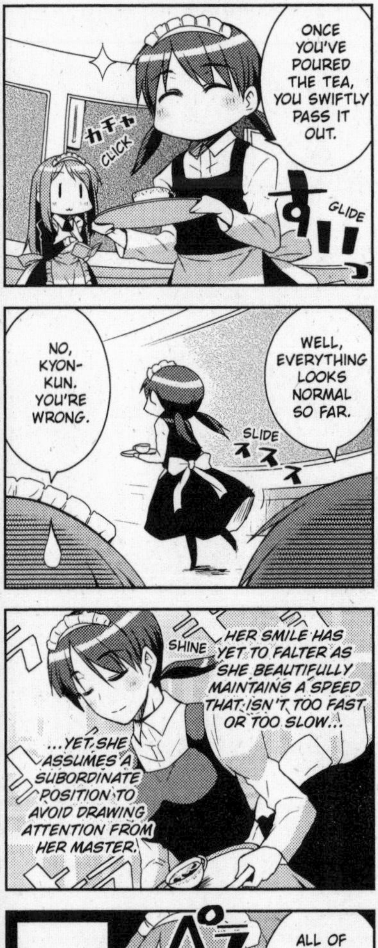
ONCE YOU'VE POURED THE TEA, YOU SWIFTLY PASS IT OUT.
GLIDE
カチャ
CLICK
WELL, EVERYTHING LOOKS NORMAL SO FAR.
SLIDE
NO, KYON-KUN. YOU'RE WRONG.
HER SMILE HAS YET TO FALTER AS SHE BEAUTIFULLY MAINTAINS A SPEED THAT ISN'T TOO FAST OR TOO SLOW...
SHINE
...YET SHE ASSUMES A SUBORDINATE POSITION TO AVOID DRAWING ATTENTION FROM HER MASTER.
ALL OF THESE QUALITIES ARE DISPLAYED IN HER FOOTWORK...
MIKURU-CHAN IS AWFULLY EXCITED TODAY.
CHATTER

LIKE A MASTER

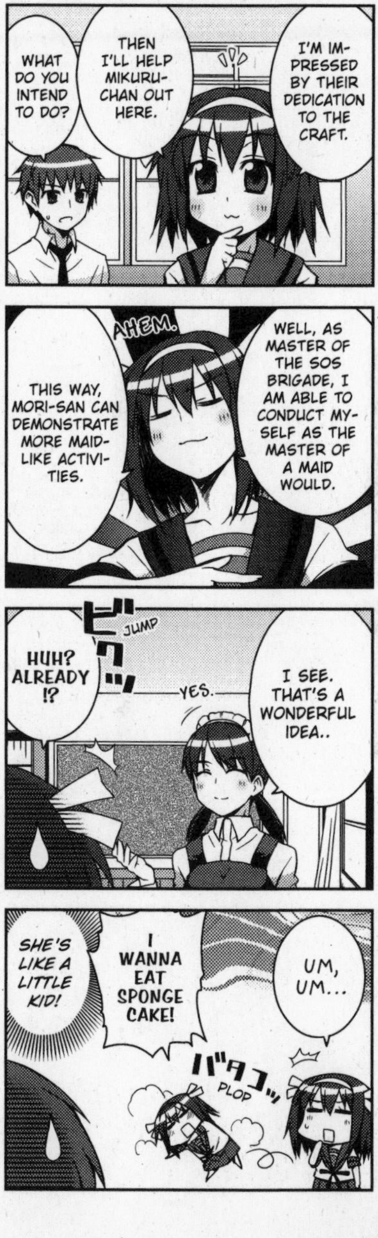
I'M IMPRESSED BY THEIR DEDICATION TO THE CRAFT.
THEN I'LL HELP MIKURU-CHAN OUT HERE.
WHAT DO YOU INTEND TO DO?
AHEM.
WELL, AS MASTER OF THE SOS BRIGADE, I AM ABLE TO CONDUCT MYSELF AS THE MASTER OF A MAID WOULD.
THIS WAY, MORI-SAN CAN DEMONSTRATE MORE MAID-LIKE ACTIVITIES.
I SEE. THAT'S A WONDERFUL IDEA..
YES.
ビクッ JUMP
HUH? ALREADY!?
UM, UM...
バタコッ PLOP
I WANNA EAT SPONGE CAKE!
SHE'S LIKE A LITTLE KID!

EXPRESS

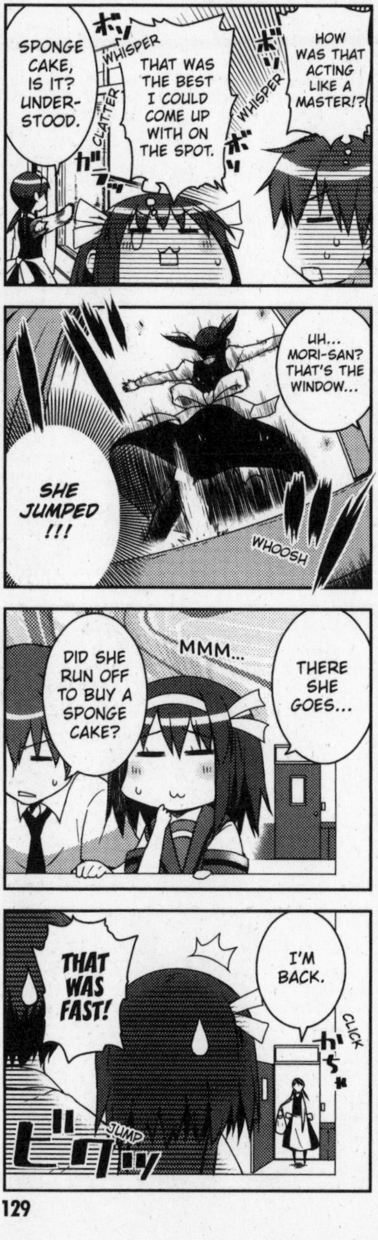
HOW WAS THAT ACTING LIKE A MASTER!?
ボソ WHISPER
THAT WAS THE BEST I COULD COME UP WITH ON THE SPOT.
ボソ WHISPER
SPONGE CAKE, IS IT? UNDERSTOOD.
ガタッ CLATTER
UH... MORI-SAN? THAT'S THE WINDOW...
WHOOSH
SHE JUMPED!!!
THERE SHE GOES...
MMM...
DID SHE RUN OFF TO BUY A SPONGE CAKE?
I'M BACK.
かちゃ CLICK
THAT WAS FAST!
ビクッ JUMP

•Mori-san •A member of the Agency Koizumi belongs to. A maid with superhuman abilities.

•Nagato •Actually an alien gamer. Doesn't do anything this time, so here you see her jumping.

CLEANING TIPS

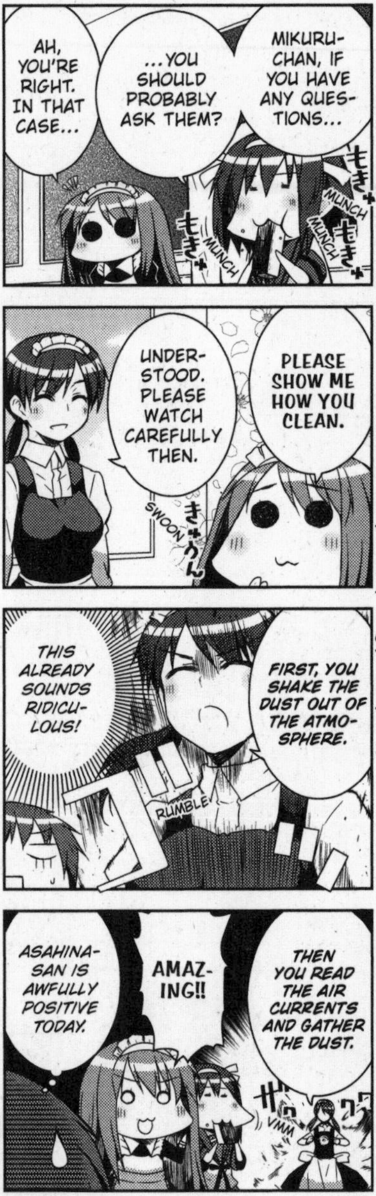
MIKURU-CHAN, IF YOU HAVE ANY QUESTIONS...
...YOU SHOULD PROBABLY ASK THEM?
AH, YOU'RE RIGHT. IN THAT CASE...
MUNCH MUNCH MUNCH
PLEASE SHOW ME HOW YOU CLEAN.
UNDER-STOOD. PLEASE WATCH CAREFULLY THEN.
SWOON
FIRST, YOU SHAKE THE DUST OUT OF THE ATMO-SPHERE.
THIS ALREADY SOUNDS RIDICU-LOUS!
RUMBLE
THEN YOU READ THE AIR CURRENTS AND GATHER THE DUST.
AMAZ-ING!!
ASAHINA-SAN IS AWFULLY POSITIVE TODAY.
VMM

FRUITS OF THE DAY'S LABOR

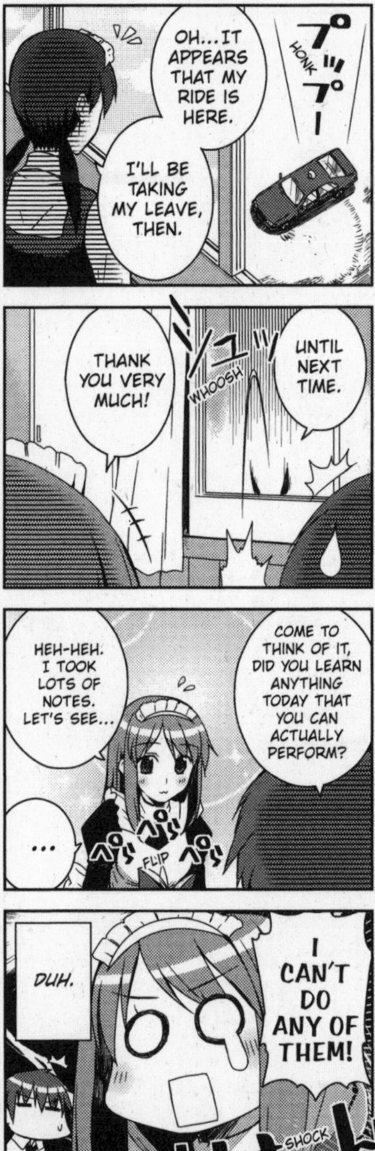
HONK
OH...IT APPEARS THAT MY RIDE IS HERE.
I'LL BE TAKING MY LEAVE, THEN.
WHOOSH
UNTIL NEXT TIME.
THANK YOU VERY MUCH!
COME TO THINK OF IT, DID YOU LEARN ANYTHING TODAY THAT YOU CAN ACTUALLY PERFORM?
HEH-HEH. I TOOK LOTS OF NOTES. LET'S SEE...
FLIP
...
I CAN'T DO ANY OF THEM!
DUH.
SHOCK

•Koizumi •An enigmatic transfer student who happens to be an esper. Loves to make a scene, but he's absent this time.

•Achakura-san •Back in miniature action after being destroyed. Surprisingly homey.

•Kimidori-san •A life-form created from a balloon by Nagato. Somewhat shameless.

THE BORED PERSON'S SOLUTION TO BOREDOM

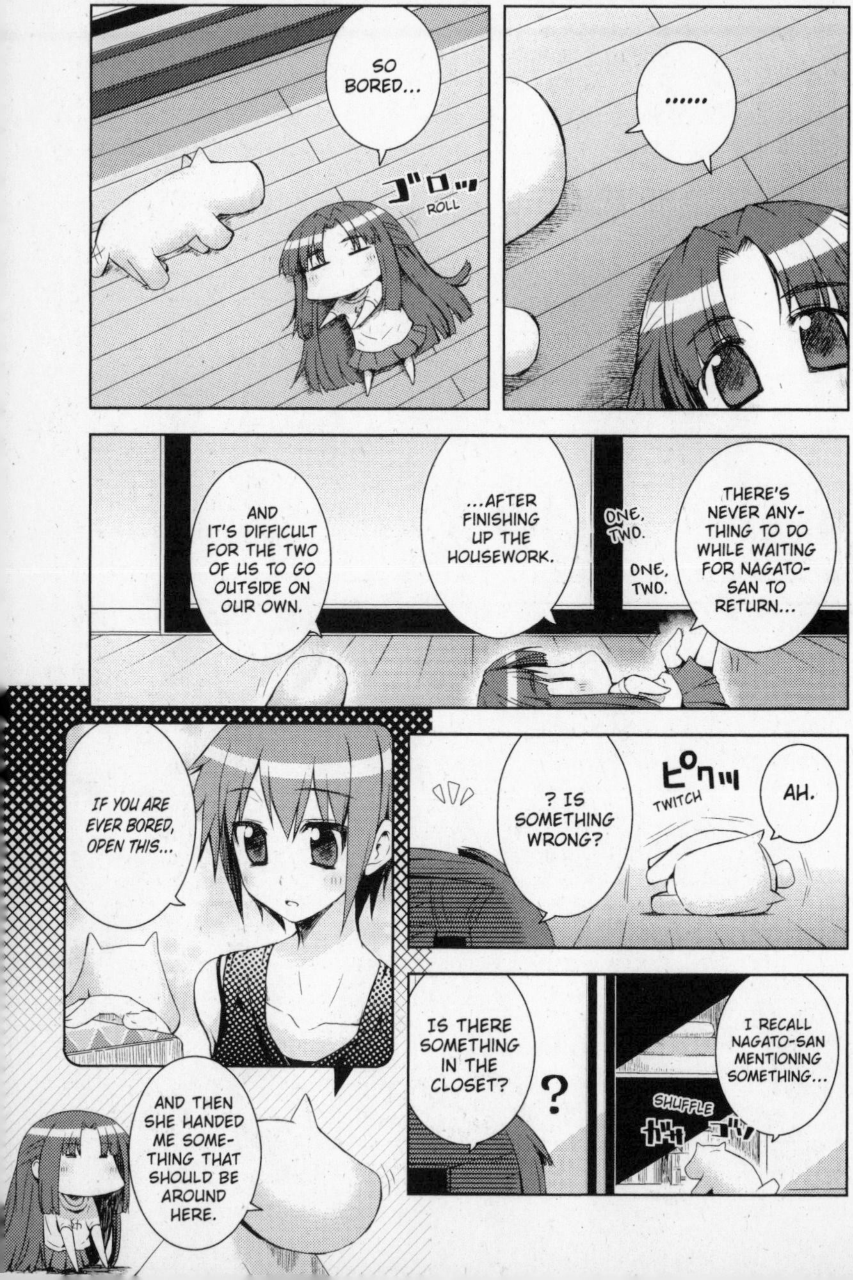
......
SO BORED...
ROLL
THERE'S NEVER ANYTHING TO DO WHILE WAITING FOR NAGATO-SAN TO RETURN...
ONE, TWO.
ONE, TWO.
...AFTER FINISHING UP THE HOUSEWORK.
AND IT'S DIFFICULT FOR THE TWO OF US TO GO OUTSIDE ON OUR OWN.
AH.
TWITCH
? IS SOMETHING WRONG?
I RECALL NAGATO-SAN MENTIONING SOMETHING...
SHUFFLE
IS THERE SOMETHING IN THE CLOSET?
?
IF YOU ARE EVER BORED, OPEN THIS...
AND THEN SHE HANDED ME SOMETHING THAT SHOULD BE AROUND HERE.

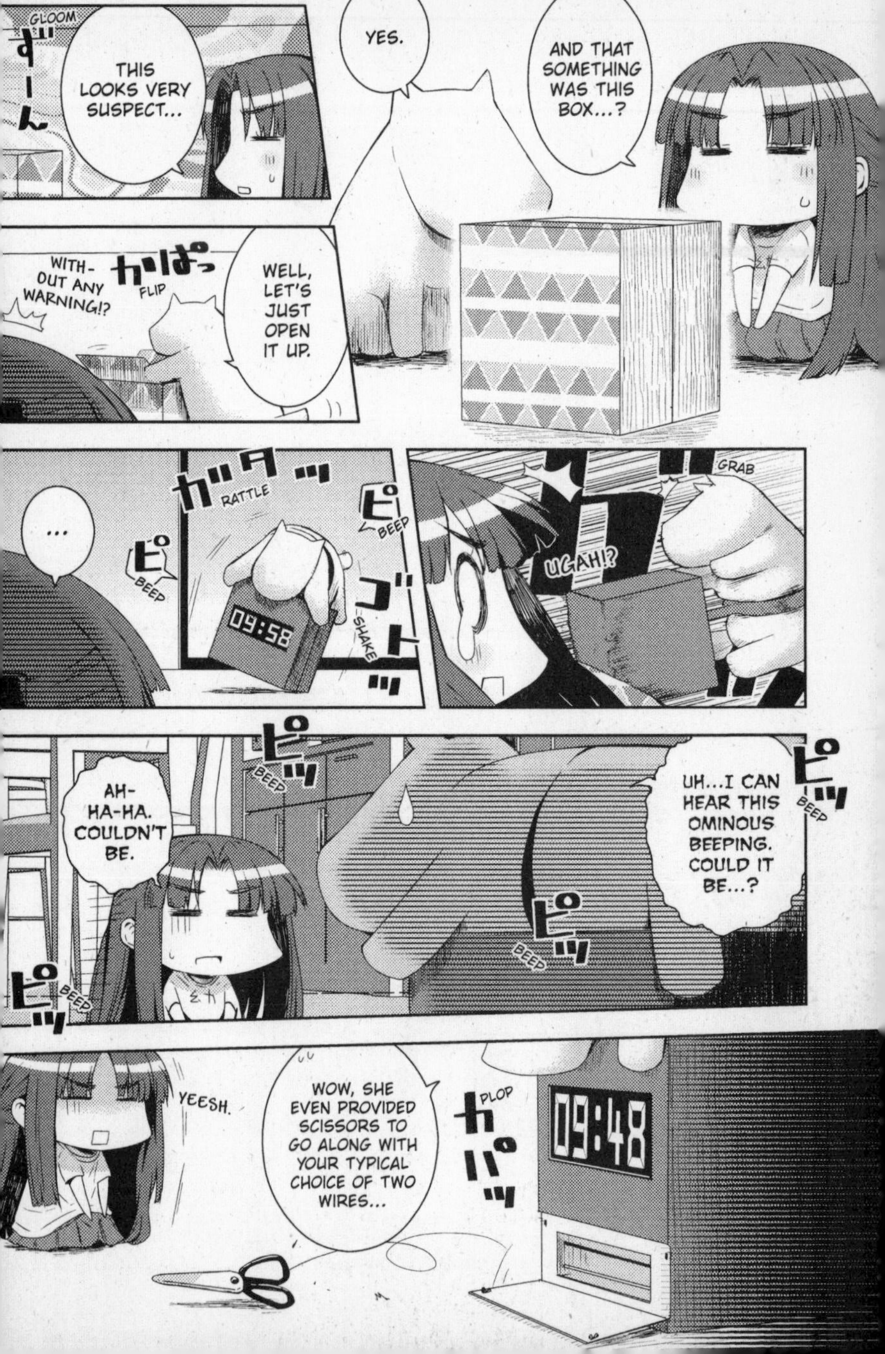
AND THAT SOMETHING WAS THIS BOX...?
YES.
GLOOM
ずーん
THIS LOOKS VERY SUSPECT...
WELL, LET'S JUST OPEN IT UP.
かぱっ
FLIP
WITH-OUT ANY WARNING!?
GRAB
UGAH!?
ガタッ
RATTLE
ピ
BEEP
ゴトッ
SHAKE
ピ
BEEP
...
09:58
ピッ
BEEP
UH...I CAN HEAR THIS OMINOUS BEEPING. COULD IT BE...?
ピッ
BEEP
ピッ
BEEP
AH-HA-HA. COULDN'T BE.
ピッ
BEEP
09:48
カパッ
PLOP
WOW, SHE EVEN PROVIDED SCISSORS TO GO ALONG WITH YOUR TYPICAL CHOICE OF TWO WIRES...
YEESH.

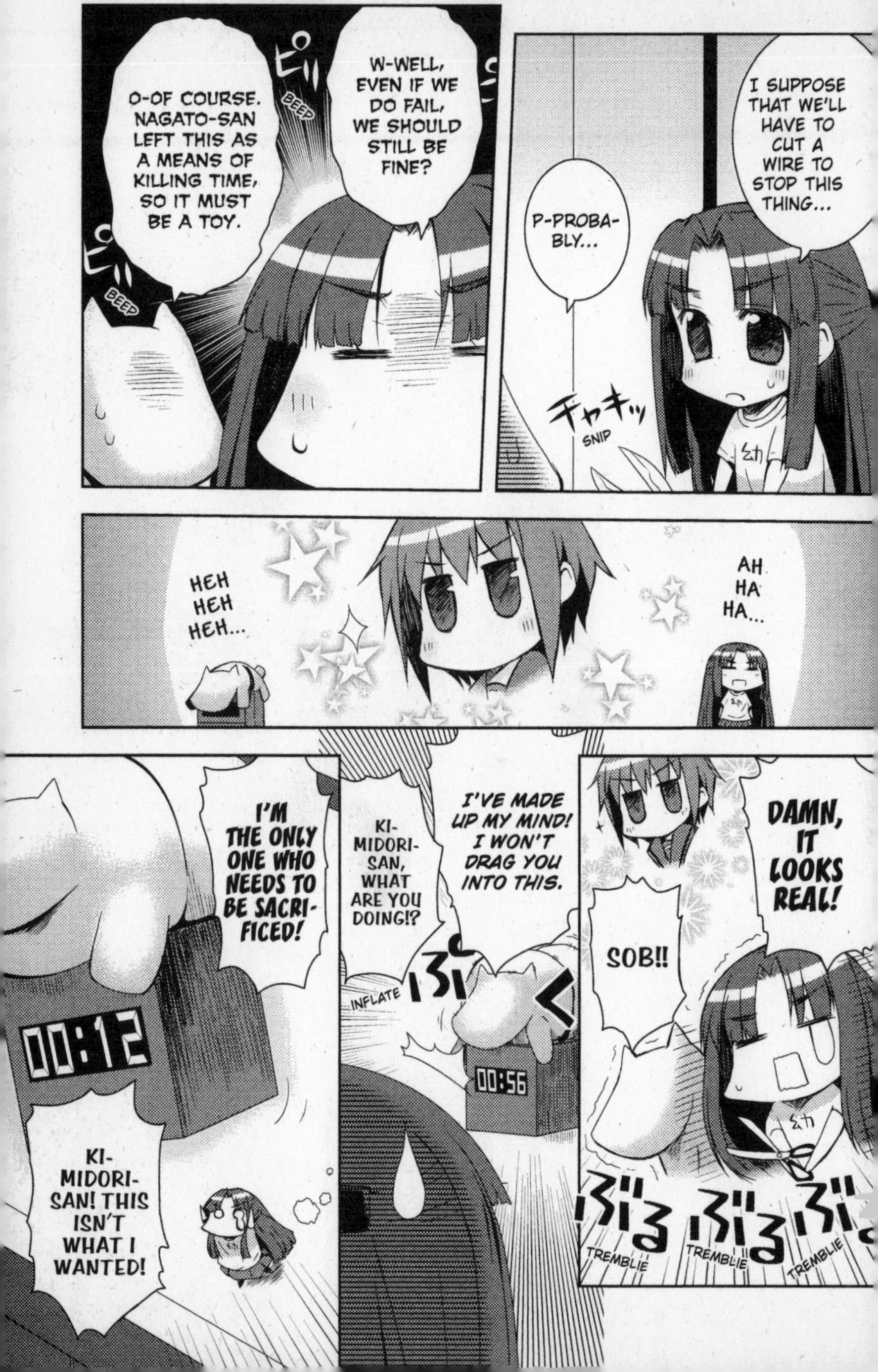

I SUPPOSE THAT WE'LL HAVE TO CUT A WIRE TO STOP THIS THING...
P-PROBABLY...
チャキッ
SNIP
W-WELL, EVEN IF WE DO FAIL, WE SHOULD STILL BE FINE?
ピッ
BEEP
O-OF COURSE. NAGATO-SAN LEFT THIS AS A MEANS OF KILLING TIME, SO IT MUST BE A TOY.
ピッ
BEEP
AH HA HA...
HEH HEH HEH...
DAMN, IT LOOKS REAL!
SOB!!
ぶるぶるぶる
TREMBLIE TREMBLIE TREMBLIE
I'VE MADE UP MY MIND! I WON'T DRAG YOU INTO THIS.
KI-MIDORI-SAN, WHAT ARE YOU DOING!?
ぷく
INFLATE
00:56
I'M THE ONLY ONE WHO NEEDS TO BE SACRIFICED!
00:12
KI-MIDORI-SAN! THIS ISN'T WHAT I WANTED!

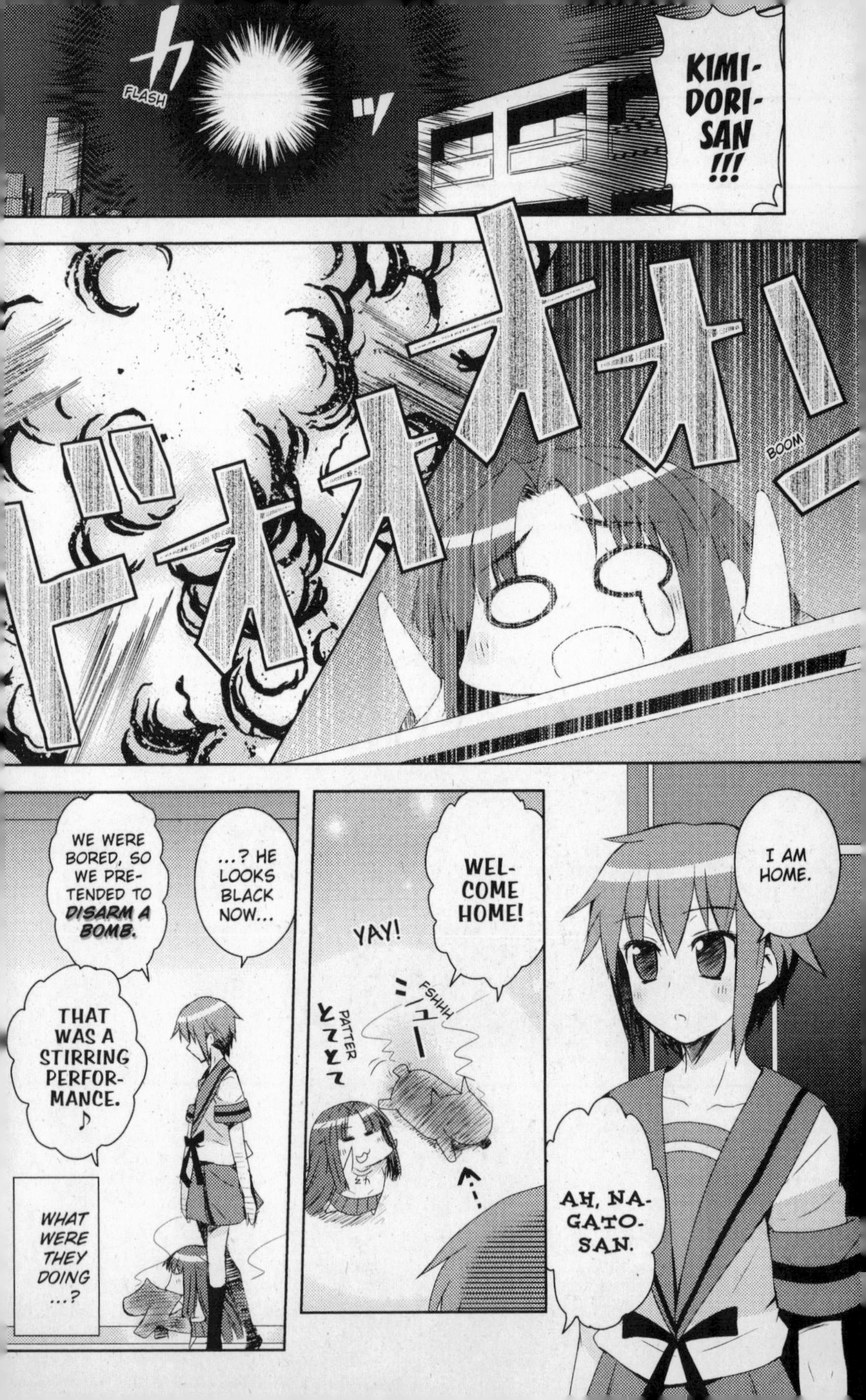
KIMI-DORI-SAN!!!
FLASH
BOOM
I AM HOME.
AH, NA-GATO-SAN.
WEL-COME HOME!
YAY!
FSHHH
PATTER
...? HE LOOKS BLACK NOW...
WE WERE BORED, SO WE PRE-TENDED TO *DISARM A BOMB.*
THAT WAS A STIRRING PERFOR-MANCE. ♪
WHAT WERE THEY DOING ...?

I WAS UNABLE TO
USE THIS DRAWING
STYLE IN AN ACTUAL
PANEL AS SHE WOULD
BE DIFFICULT TO
RECOGNIZE.

MORI-SAN WITH
HER HAIR DOWN.

TV

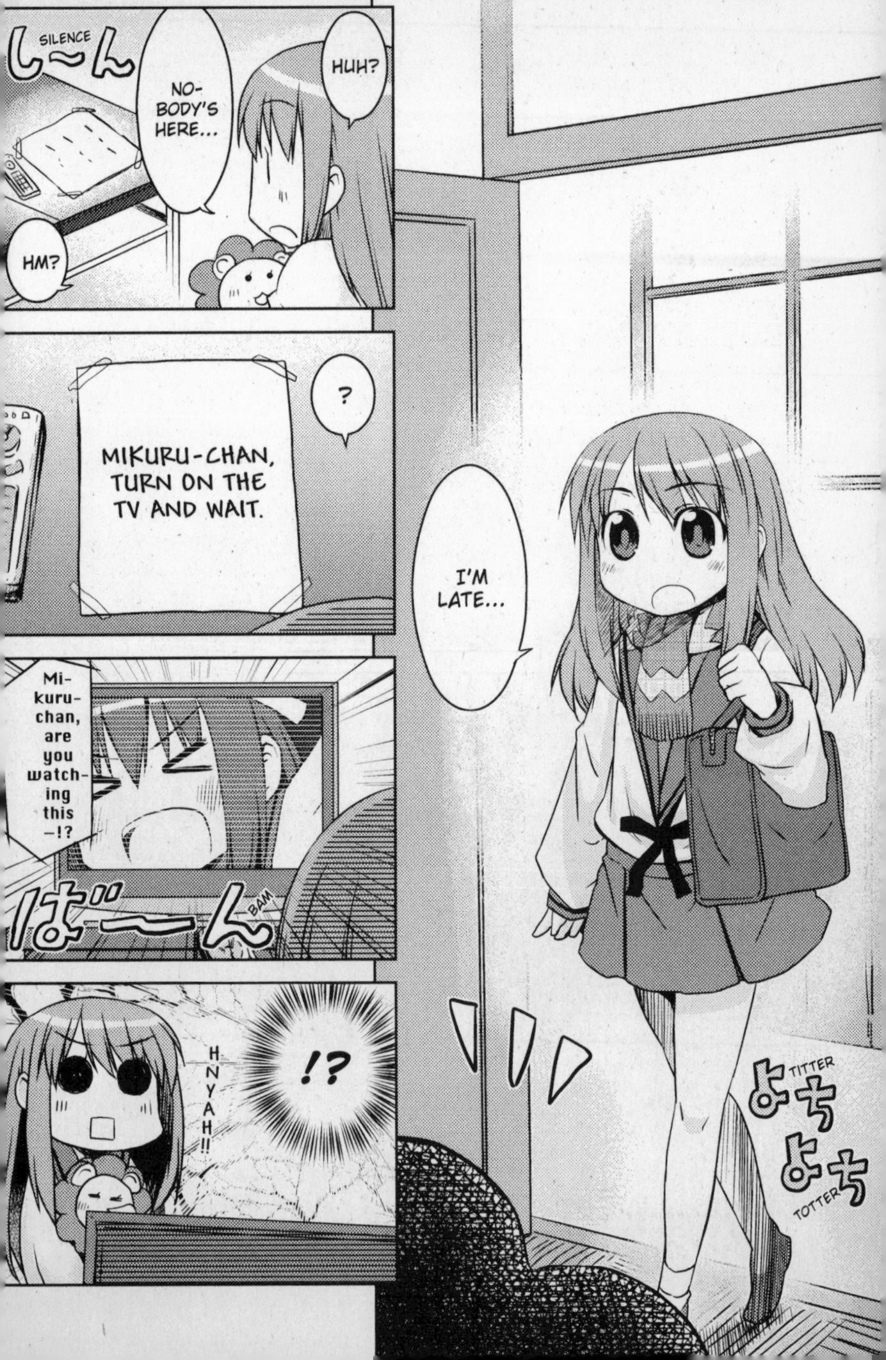
I'M LATE...
よち よち TITTER TOTTER
HUH?
NO-BODY'S HERE...
しーん SILENCE
HM?
?
MIKURU-CHAN, TURN ON THE TV AND WAIT.
Mi-kuru-chan, are you watch-ing this—!?
ばーん BAM
!?
HNYAH!!

INTRODUCTION

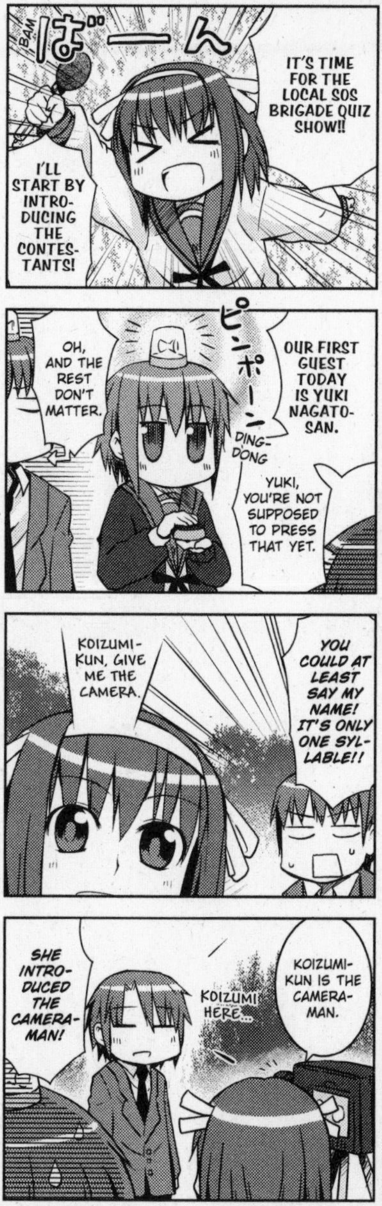
BAM
ばーん
IT'S TIME FOR THE LOCAL SOS BRIGADE QUIZ SHOW!!
I'LL START BY INTRODUCING THE CONTESTANTS!
OUR FIRST GUEST TODAY IS YUKI NAGATO-SAN.
ピンポーン
DING-DONG
OH, AND THE REST DON'T MATTER.
YUKI, YOU'RE NOT SUPPOSED TO PRESS THAT YET.
YOU COULD AT LEAST SAY MY NAME! IT'S ONLY ONE SYLLABLE!!
KOIZUMI-KUN, GIVE ME THE CAMERA.
KOIZUMI-KUN IS THE CAMERAMAN.
KOIZUMI HERE...
SHE INTRODUCED THE CAMERAMAN!

QUESTION

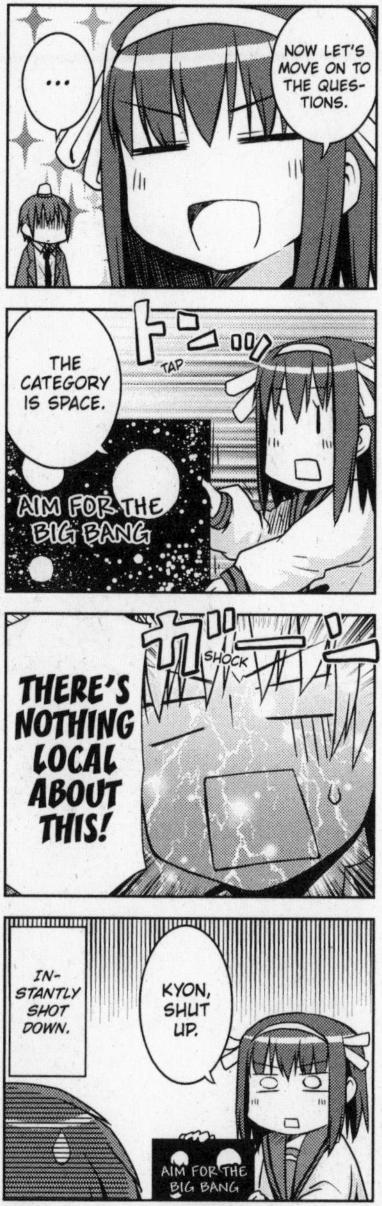
NOW LET'S MOVE ON TO THE QUESTIONS.
...
トン
TAP
THE CATEGORY IS SPACE.
AIM FOR THE BIG BANG
ガーン
SHOCK
THERE'S NOTHING LOCAL ABOUT THIS!
KYON, SHUT UP.
IN-STANTLY SHOT DOWN.
AIM FOR THE BIG BANG

LOCAL

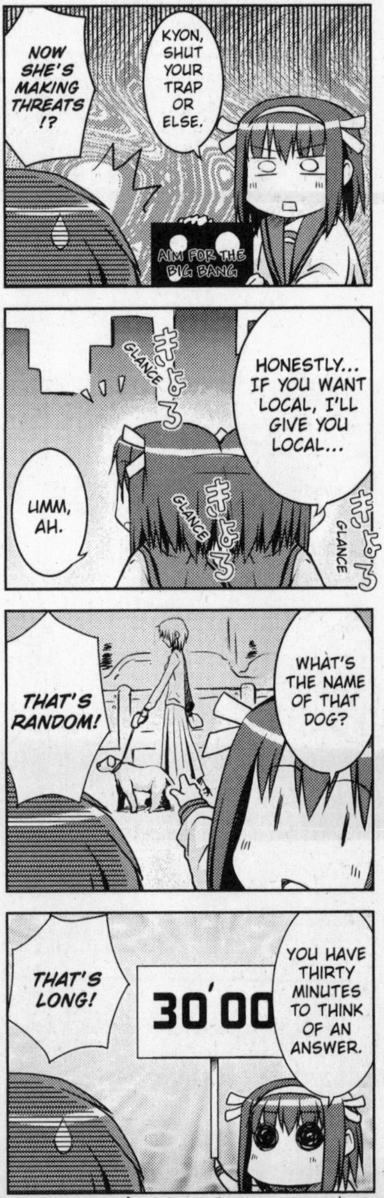
KYON, SHUT YOUR TRAP OR ELSE.
NOW SHE'S MAKING THREATS!?
AIM FOR THE BIG BANG
HONESTLY... IF YOU WANT LOCAL, I'LL GIVE YOU LOCAL...
きょろ GLANCE
きょろ GLANCE
きょろ GLANCE
UMM, AH.
WHAT'S THE NAME OF THAT DOG?
THAT'S RANDOM!
YOU HAVE THIRTY MINUTES TO THINK OF AN ANSWER.
30'00
THAT'S LONG!

ANSWER

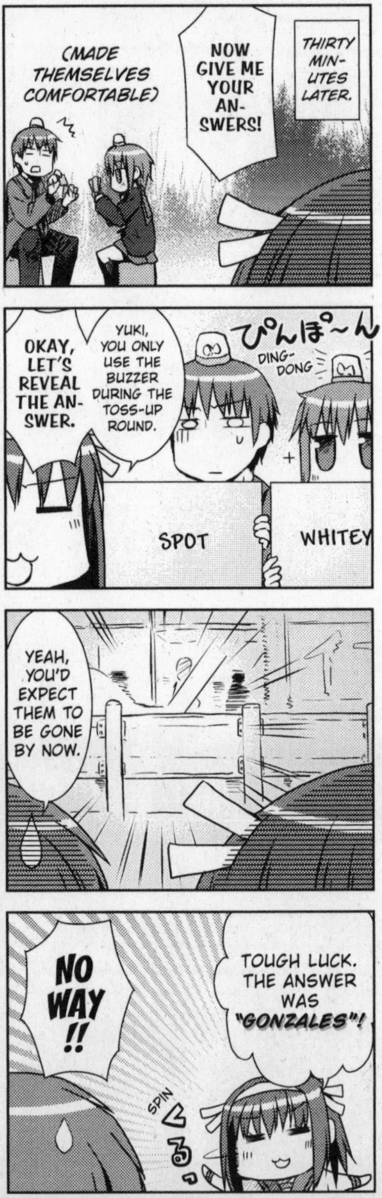
THIRTY MIN-UTES LATER.
NOW GIVE ME YOUR AN-SWERS!
(MADE THEMSELVES COMFORTABLE)
ぴんぽ～ん
DING-DONG
YUKI, YOU ONLY USE THE BUZZER DURING THE TOSS-UP ROUND.
OKAY, LET'S REVEAL THE AN-SWER.
WHITEY
SPOT
YEAH, YOU'D EXPECT THEM TO BE GONE BY NOW.
TOUGH LUCK. THE ANSWER WAS "GONZALES"!
NO WAY!!
くる SPIN る

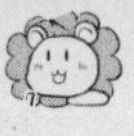
•Infinity Lion •Space creature that Mikuru-chan keeps as a pet after it was summoned by Haruhi.

FIREWORKS

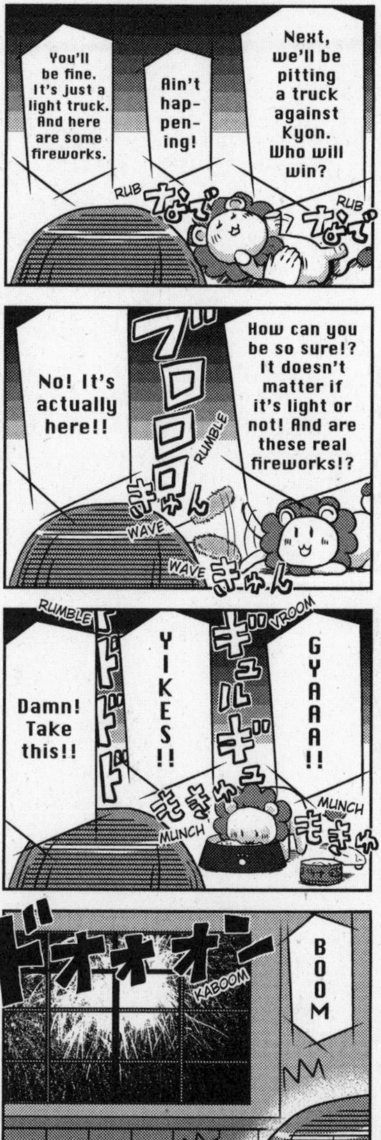
Next, we'll be pitting a truck against Kyon. Who will win?
Ain't hap-pen-ing!
You'll be fine. It's just a light truck. And here are some fireworks.
なで RUB
RUB なで
How can you be so sure!? It doesn't matter if it's light or not! And are these real fireworks!?
ブロロロ RUMBLE
No! It's actually here!!
きゅん WAVE
WAVE きゅん
GYAAAA!!
VROOM
YIKES!!
RUMBLE
Damn! Take this!!
MUNCH
MUNCH
BOOM
KABOOM

NO CLUE

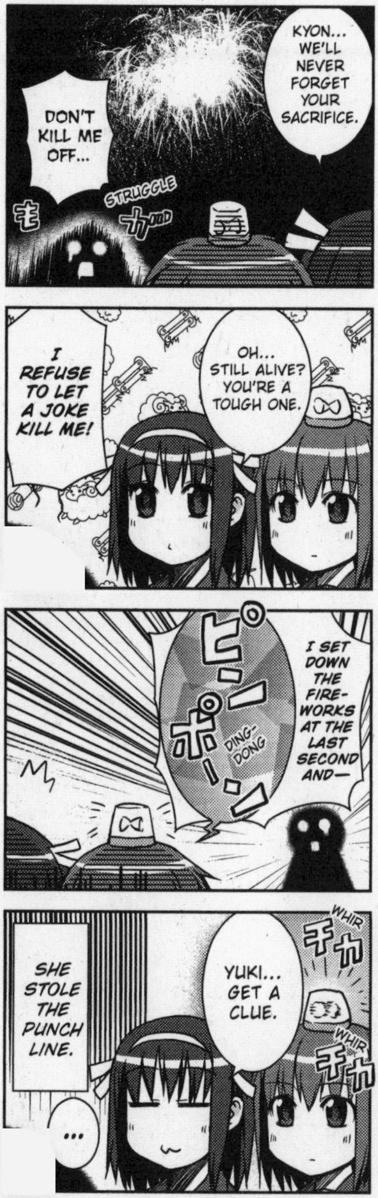
KYON... WE'LL NEVER FORGET YOUR SACRIFICE.
DON'T KILL ME OFF...
STRUGGLE
OH... STILL ALIVE? YOU'RE A TOUGH ONE.
I REFUSE TO LET A JOKE KILL ME!
I SET DOWN THE FIRE-WORKS AT THE LAST SECOND AND—
DING-DONG
WHIR チカ
YUKI... GET A CLUE.
WHIR チカ
SHE STOLE THE PUNCH LINE.
...

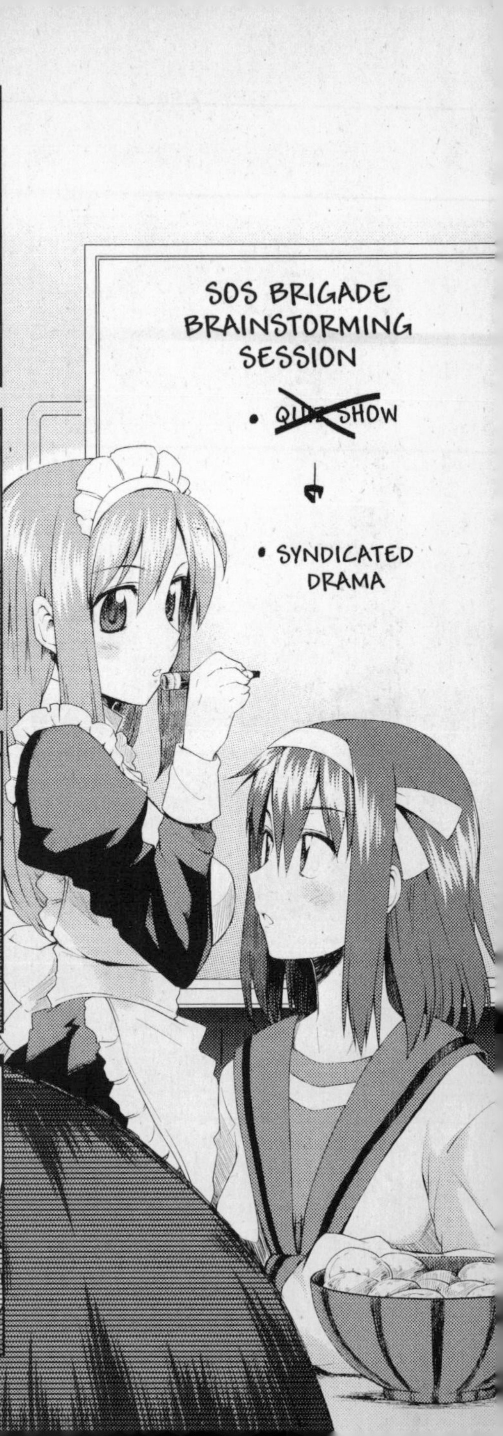
SOS BRIGADE BRAINSTORMING SESSION
• QUIZ SHOW
• SYNDICATED DRAMA

BRAINSTORM

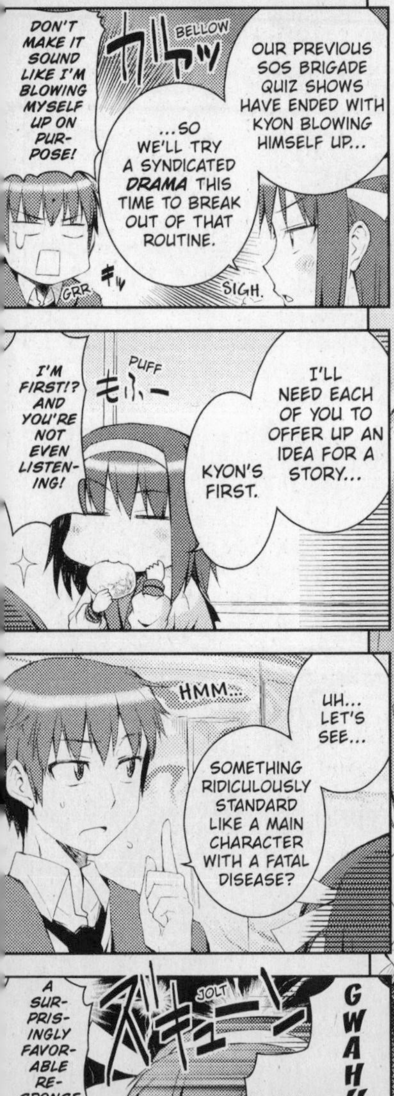
BELLOW
OUR PREVIOUS SOS BRIGADE QUIZ SHOWS HAVE ENDED WITH KYON BLOWING HIMSELF UP...
...SO WE'LL TRY A SYNDICATED DRAMA THIS TIME TO BREAK OUT OF THAT ROUTINE.
DON'T MAKE IT SOUND LIKE I'M BLOWING MYSELF UP ON PURPOSE!
SIGH.
GRR
I'LL NEED EACH OF YOU TO OFFER UP AN IDEA FOR A STORY...
KYON'S FIRST.
PUFF
もふー
I'M FIRST!? AND YOU'RE NOT EVEN LISTENING!
UH... LET'S SEE...
SOMETHING RIDICULOUSLY STANDARD LIKE A MAIN CHARACTER WITH A FATAL DISEASE?
HMM...
GWAH!!
N-NEVER THOUGHT OF THAT ONE...!
JOLT
A SURPRISINGLY FAVORABLE RESPONSE!?

SOAP OPERA

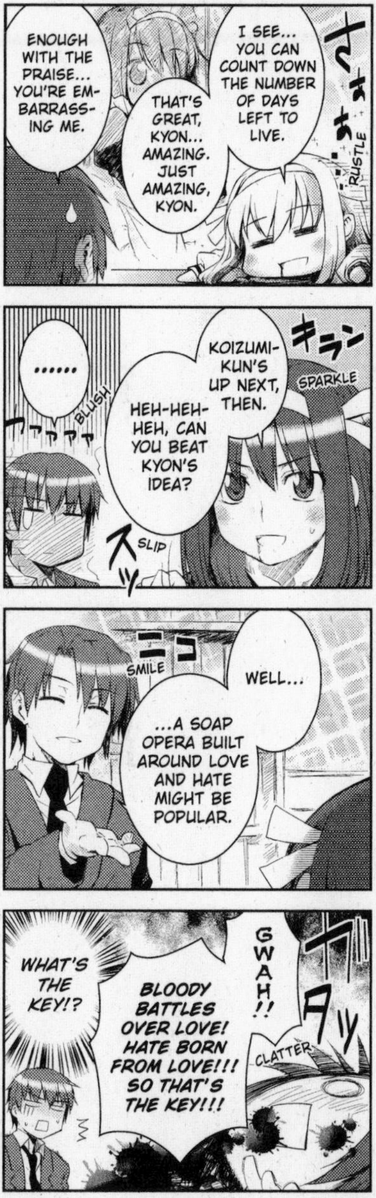
I SEE... YOU CAN COUNT DOWN THE NUMBER OF DAYS LEFT TO LIVE.
RUSTLE
THAT'S GREAT, KYON... AMAZING. JUST AMAZING, KYON.
ENOUGH WITH THE PRAISE... YOU'RE EM-BARRASS-ING ME.
SPARKLE
KOIZUMI-KUN'S UP NEXT, THEN.
HEH-HEH-HEH, CAN YOU BEAT KYON'S IDEA?
......
BLUSH
SLIP
WELL...
...A SOAP OPERA BUILT AROUND LOVE AND HATE MIGHT BE POPULAR.
SMILE
GWAH!!
CLATTER
BLOODY BATTLES OVER LOVE! HATE BORN FROM LOVE!!! SO THAT'S THE KEY!!!
WHAT'S THE KEY!?

DIGEST

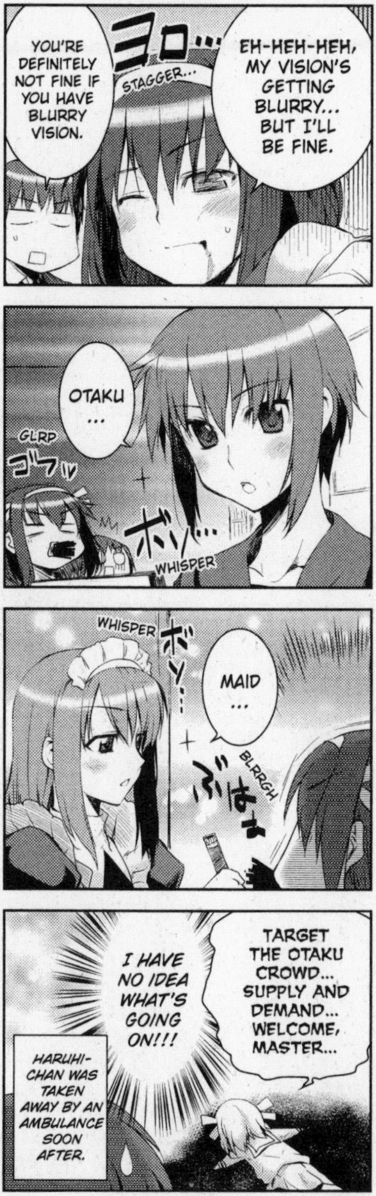
EH-HEH-HEH, MY VISION'S GETTING BLURRY... BUT I'LL BE FINE.
STAGGER...
YOU'RE DEFINITELY NOT FINE IF YOU HAVE BLURRY VISION.
OTAKU ...
WHISPER
GLRP
MAID ...
BLRRGH
WHISPER
TARGET THE OTAKU CROWD... SUPPLY AND DEMAND... WELCOME, MASTER...
I HAVE NO IDEA WHAT'S GOING ON!!!
HARUHI-CHAN WAS TAKEN AWAY BY AN AMBULANCE SOON AFTER.

FIGHTING

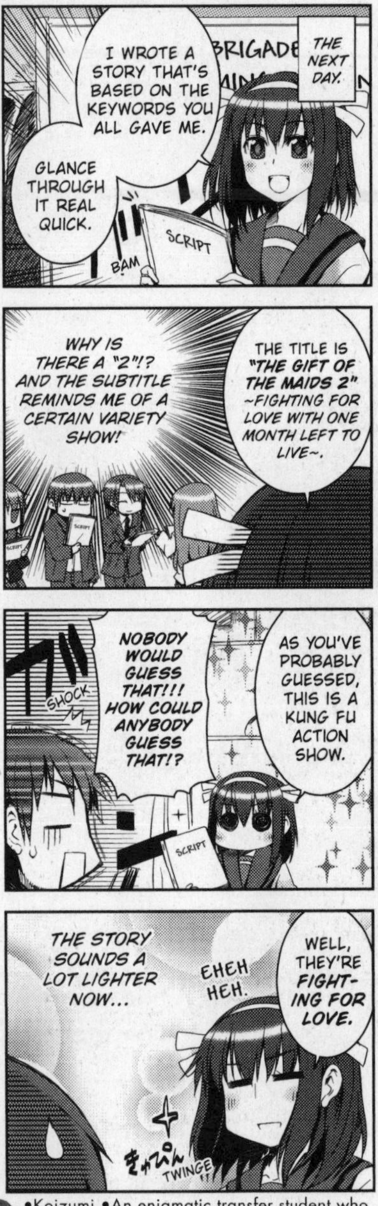
THE NEXT DAY.
BRIGADE
I WROTE A STORY THAT'S BASED ON THE KEYWORDS YOU ALL GAVE ME.
GLANCE THROUGH IT REAL QUICK.
BAM
SCRIPT
THE TITLE IS "THE GIFT OF THE MAIDS 2" ~FIGHTING FOR LOVE WITH ONE MONTH LEFT TO LIVE~.
WHY IS THERE A "2"!? AND THE SUBTITLE REMINDS ME OF A CERTAIN VARIETY SHOW!
SCRIPT
SCRIPT
AS YOU'VE PROBABLY GUESSED, THIS IS A KUNG FU ACTION SHOW.
NOBODY WOULD GUESS THAT!!! HOW COULD ANYBODY GUESS THAT!?
SHOCK
SCRIPT
WELL, THEY'RE FIGHTING FOR LOVE.
EHEH HEH.
THE STORY SOUNDS A LOT LIGHTER NOW...
TWINGE

REMAINING TIME

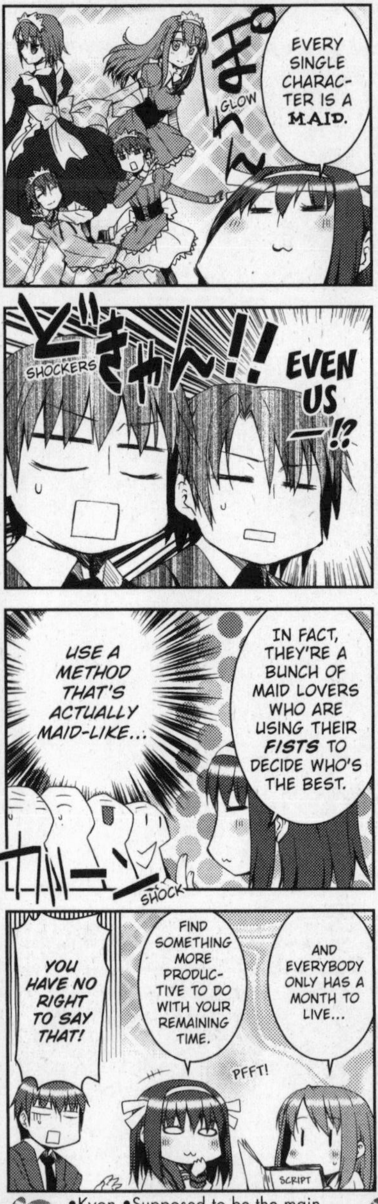
EVERY SINGLE CHARACTER IS A MAID.
GLOW
SHOCKERS
EVEN US—!?
IN FACT, THEY'RE A BUNCH OF MAID LOVERS WHO ARE USING THEIR FISTS TO DECIDE WHO'S THE BEST.
USE A METHOD THAT'S ACTUALLY MAID-LIKE...
SHOCK
AND EVERYBODY ONLY HAS A MONTH TO LIVE...
FIND SOMETHING MORE PRODUCTIVE TO DO WITH YOUR REMAINING TIME.
YOU HAVE NO RIGHT TO SAY THAT!
PFFT!
SCRIPT

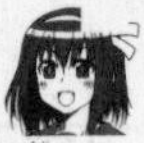

•Haruhi-chan •SOS Brigade brigade chief. Completely caught up in playing a TV producer?

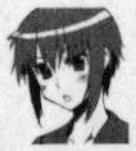

•Nagato •Actually an alien gamer. Rather interested in participating in Haruhi's ideas.

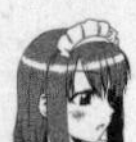

•Mikuru-chan •Actually from the future. Owner of the Infinity Lion "Infy."

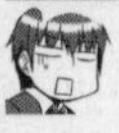

•Kyon •Supposed to be the main character in this story. Prefers looking at maid outfits to wearing them.

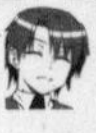

•Koizumi •An enigmatic transfer student who happens to be an esper. Knows his way around and avoids most of the damage Haruhi causes.

LOVE

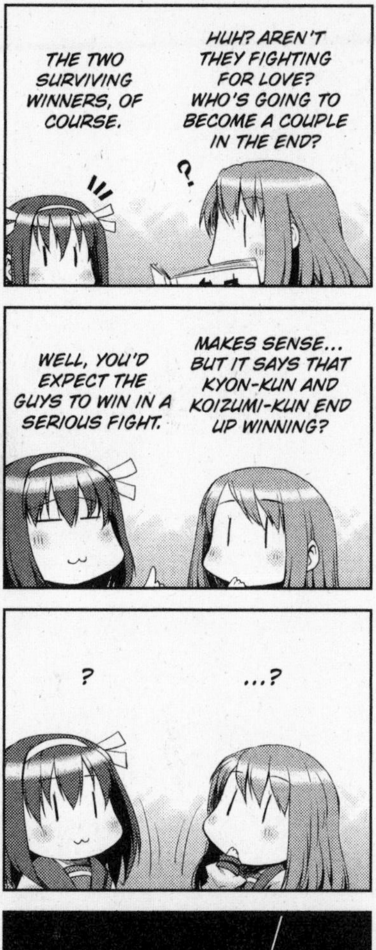
HUH? AREN'T THEY FIGHTING FOR LOVE? WHO'S GOING TO BECOME A COUPLE IN THE END?
THE TWO SURVIVING WINNERS, OF COURSE.
?
MAKES SENSE... BUT IT SAYS THAT KYON-KUN AND KOIZUMI-KUN END UP WINNING?
WELL, YOU'D EXPECT THE GUYS TO WIN IN A SERIOUS FIGHT.
...?
?
THERE YOU ARE, INFY.
PET PET
MIKURU-CHAN DIDN'T UNDER-STAND, SO SHE STOPPED THINKING ABOUT IT.

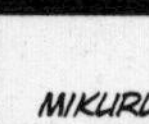
•Infinity Lion •Space creature that's grown attached to Mikuru-chan. Also serves as a scarf.

MEDICAL ENERGY

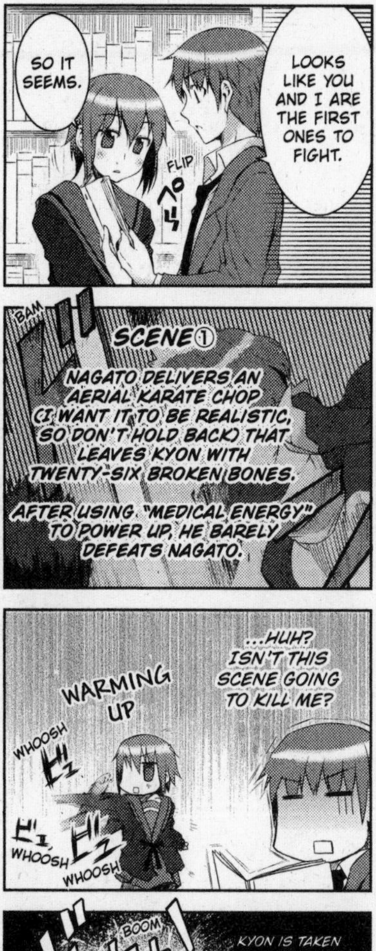
LOOKS LIKE YOU AND I ARE THE FIRST ONES TO FIGHT.
SO IT SEEMS.
FLIP
BAM
SCENE①
NAGATO DELIVERS AN AERIAL KARATE CHOP (I WANT IT TO BE REALISTIC, SO DON'T HOLD BACK) THAT LEAVES KYON WITH TWENTY-SIX BROKEN BONES.
AFTER USING "MEDICAL ENERGY" TO POWER UP, HE BARELY DEFEATS NAGATO.
...HUH? ISN'T THIS SCENE GOING TO KILL ME?
WARMING UP
WHOOSH
WHOOSH
WHOOSH
BOOM
KYON IS TAKEN OUT BY NAGATO'S AERIAL KARATE CHOP BEFORE HE USES THE POWER OF "MEDICAL ENERGY" (AN EXPLODING SPECIAL EFFECT) AND SCATTERS INTO THE SKY.
HE STILL BLEW HIMSELF UP IN THE END...

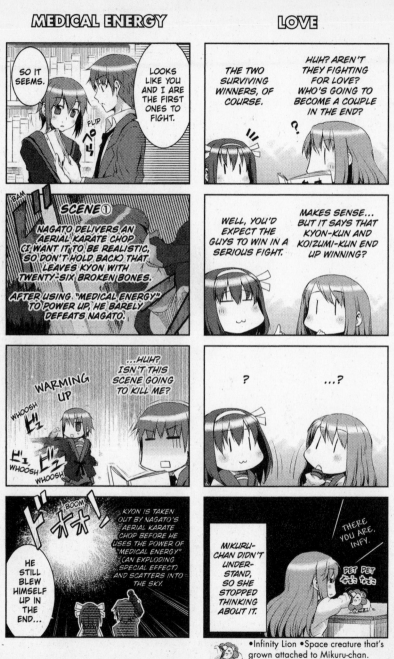

COOKING

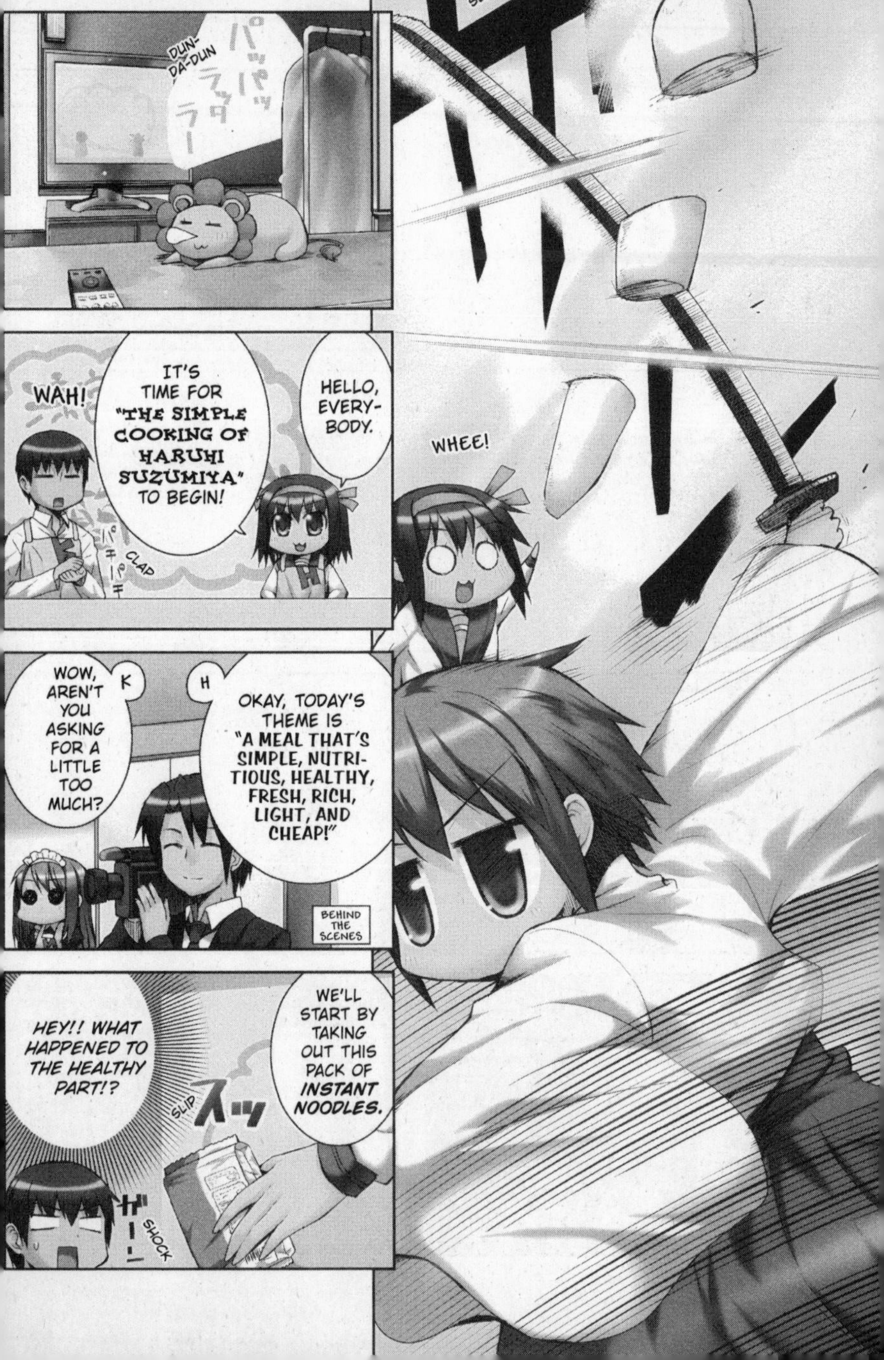
SLICE
WHEE!
DUN-DA-DUN
パッパッラッタラー
HELLO, EVERYBODY.
IT'S TIME FOR "THE SIMPLE COOKING OF HARUHI SUZUMIYA" TO BEGIN!
WAH!
パチパチ
CLAP
H
OKAY, TODAY'S THEME IS "A MEAL THAT'S SIMPLE, NUTRITIOUS, HEALTHY, FRESH, RICH, LIGHT, AND CHEAP!"
K
WOW, AREN'T YOU ASKING FOR A LITTLE TOO MUCH?
BEHIND THE SCENES
WE'LL START BY TAKING OUT THIS PACK OF *INSTANT NOODLES.*
SLIP
スッ
HEY!! WHAT HAPPENED TO THE HEALTHY PART!?
ガーン
SHOCK

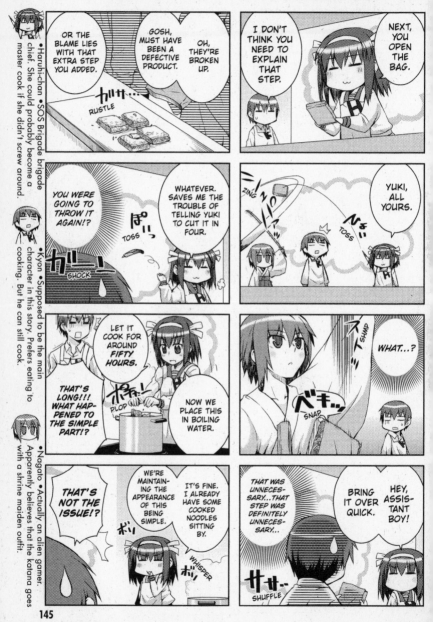

CUTTING JOB

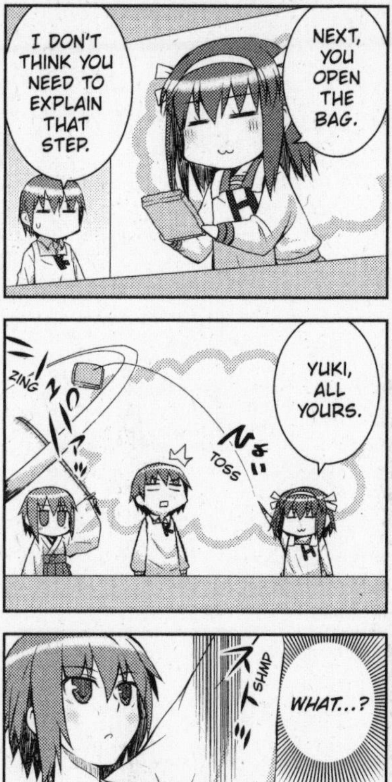
NEXT, YOU OPEN THE BAG.
I DON'T THINK YOU NEED TO EXPLAIN THAT STEP.
YUKI, ALL YOURS.
TOSS
ZING
WHAT...?
SHMP
SNAP
HEY, ASSISTANT BOY!
BRING IT OVER QUICK.
THAT WAS UNNECESSARY...THAT STEP WAS DEFINITELY UNNECESSARY...
SHUFFLE

SIMPLE

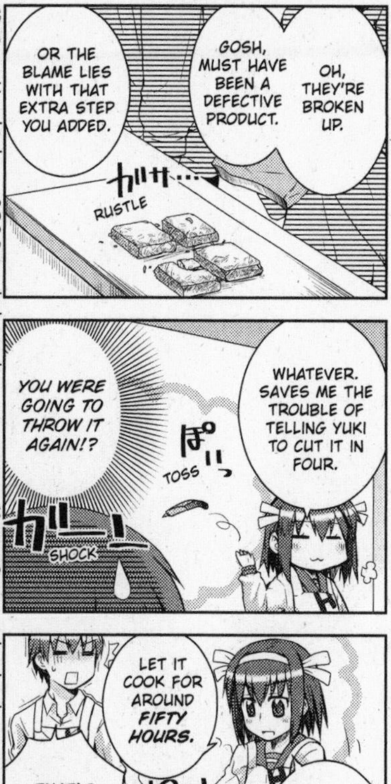
OH, THEY'RE BROKEN UP.
GOSH, MUST HAVE BEEN A DEFECTIVE PRODUCT.
OR THE BLAME LIES WITH THAT EXTRA STEP YOU ADDED.
RUSTLE
WHATEVER. SAVES ME THE TROUBLE OF TELLING YUKI TO CUT IT IN FOUR.
TOSS
YOU WERE GOING TO THROW IT AGAIN!?
SHOCK
NOW WE PLACE THIS IN BOILING WATER.
PLOP
LET IT COOK FOR AROUND FIFTY HOURS.
THAT'S LONG!!! WHAT HAPPENED TO THE SIMPLE PART!?
IT'S FINE. I ALREADY HAVE SOME COOKED NOODLES SITTING BY.
WE'RE MAINTAINING THE APPEARANCE OF THIS BEING SIMPLE.
WHISPER
THAT'S NOT THE ISSUE!?

•Haruhi-chan •SOS Brigade brigade chief. She could probably become a master cook if she didn't screw around.

•Kyon •Supposed to be the main character in this story. Prefers eating to cooking. But he can still cook.

•Nagato •Actually an alien gamer. Apparently believes that the katana goes with a shrine maiden outfit.

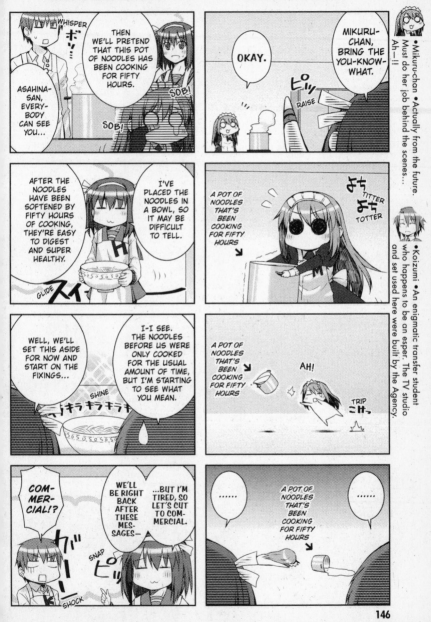

FIFTY HOURS

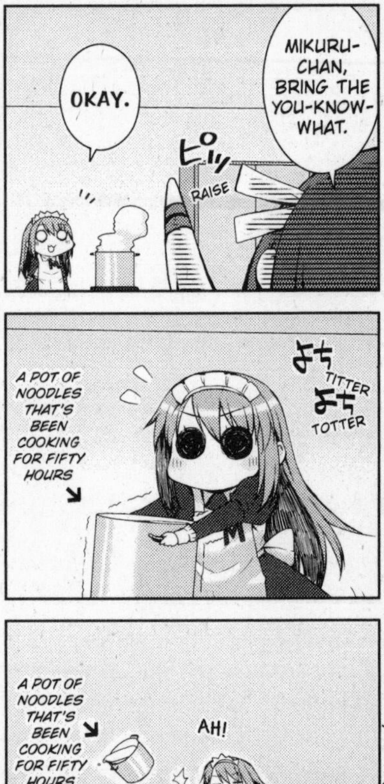

MIKURU-CHAN, BRING THE YOU-KNOW-WHAT.
OKAY.
ピッ
RAISE
よち TITTER
よち TOTTER
A POT OF NOODLES THAT'S BEEN COOKING FOR FIFTY HOURS
A POT OF NOODLES THAT'S BEEN COOKING FOR FIFTY HOURS
AH!
TRIP
こけっ
......
......
A POT OF NOODLES THAT'S BEEN COOKING FOR FIFTY HOURS

•Mikuru-chan •Actually from the future. Must do her job behind the scenes... Ah—!!

•Koizumi •An enigmatic transfer student who happens to be an esper. The TV studio and set used here were built by the Agency.

THREE MINUTES

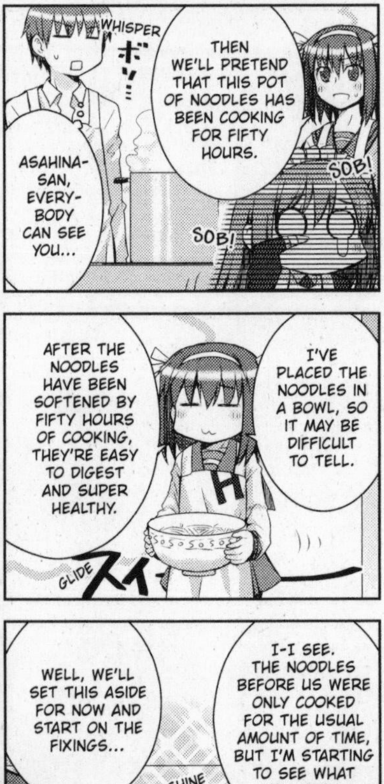

THEN WE'LL PRETEND THAT THIS POT OF NOODLES HAS BEEN COOKING FOR FIFTY HOURS.
WHISPER
ボソ…
ASAHINA-SAN, EVERYBODY CAN SEE YOU...
SOB!
SOB!
I'VE PLACED THE NOODLES IN A BOWL, SO IT MAY BE DIFFICULT TO TELL.
AFTER THE NOODLES HAVE BEEN SOFTENED BY FIFTY HOURS OF COOKING, THEY'RE EASY TO DIGEST AND SUPER HEALTHY.
GLIDE
スイー
I-I SEE. THE NOODLES BEFORE US WERE ONLY COOKED FOR THE USUAL AMOUNT OF TIME, BUT I'M STARTING TO SEE WHAT YOU MEAN.
WELL, WE'LL SET THIS ASIDE FOR NOW AND START ON THE FIXINGS...
SHINE
キラキラキラキラ
...BUT I'M TIRED, SO LET'S CUT TO COMMERCIAL.
WE'LL BE RIGHT BACK AFTER THESE MESSAGES—
COMMERCIAL!?
SNAP
ピッ
ガーン
SHOCK

AUTOMATIC KNIFE

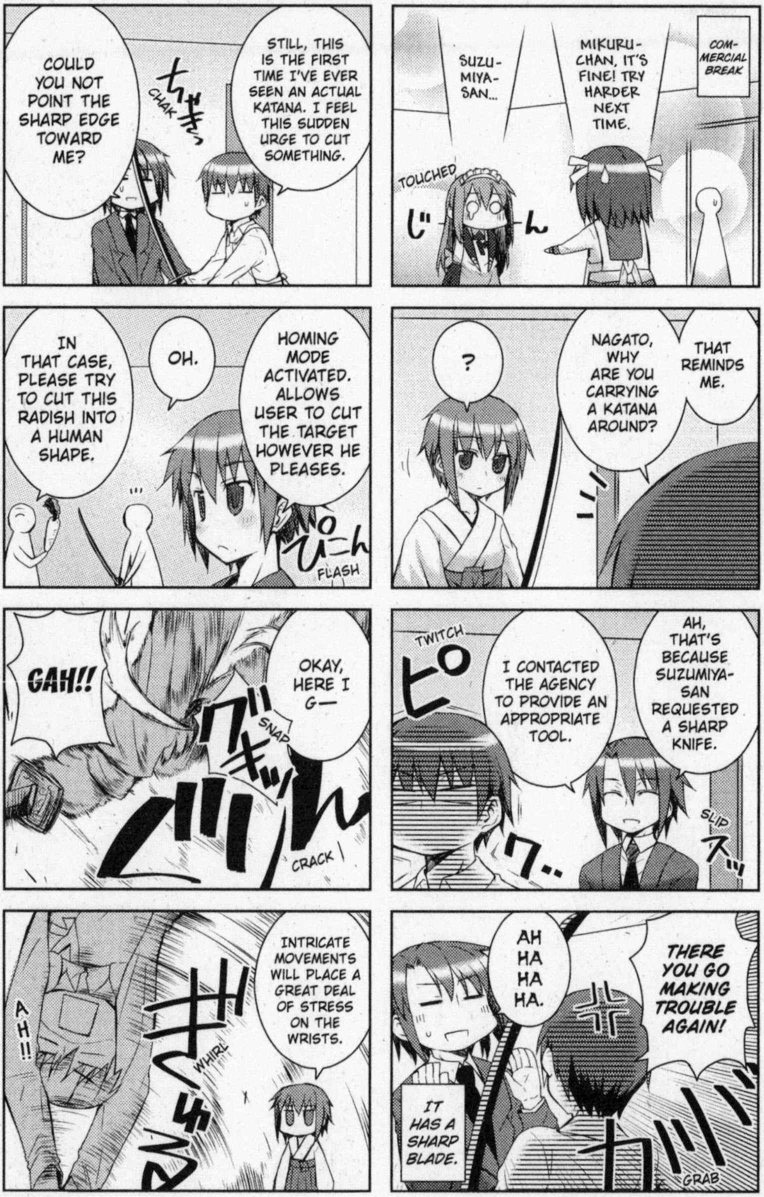
COMMERCIAL BREAK
MIKURU-CHAN, IT'S FINE! TRY HARDER NEXT TIME.
SUZUMIYA-SAN...
TOUCHED
THAT REMINDS ME.
NAGATO, WHY ARE YOU CARRYING A KATANA AROUND?
?
AH, THAT'S BECAUSE SUZUMIYA-SAN REQUESTED A SHARP KNIFE.
SLIP
I CONTACTED THE AGENCY TO PROVIDE AN APPROPRIATE TOOL.
TWITCH
THERE YOU GO MAKING TROUBLE AGAIN!
AH HA HA HA.
IT HAS A SHARP BLADE.
GRAB
STILL, THIS IS THE FIRST TIME I'VE EVER SEEN AN ACTUAL KATANA. I FEEL THIS SUDDEN URGE TO CUT SOMETHING.
CHAK
COULD YOU NOT POINT THE SHARP EDGE TOWARD ME?
HOMING MODE ACTIVATED. ALLOWS USER TO CUT THE TARGET HOWEVER HE PLEASES.
OH.
IN THAT CASE, PLEASE TRY TO CUT THIS RADISH INTO A HUMAN SHAPE.
FLASH
OKAY, HERE I G—
SNAP
GAH!!
CRACK
INTRICATE MOVEMENTS WILL PLACE A GREAT DEAL OF STRESS ON THE WRISTS.
WHIRL
AH!!

•Great Knife "Yuki" •Knife which automatically responds to its wielder's desire. Its powers from Nagato allow it to cut steel and bend the rules of the universe, so it is a blade to be feared.

A MASTER'S SKILL

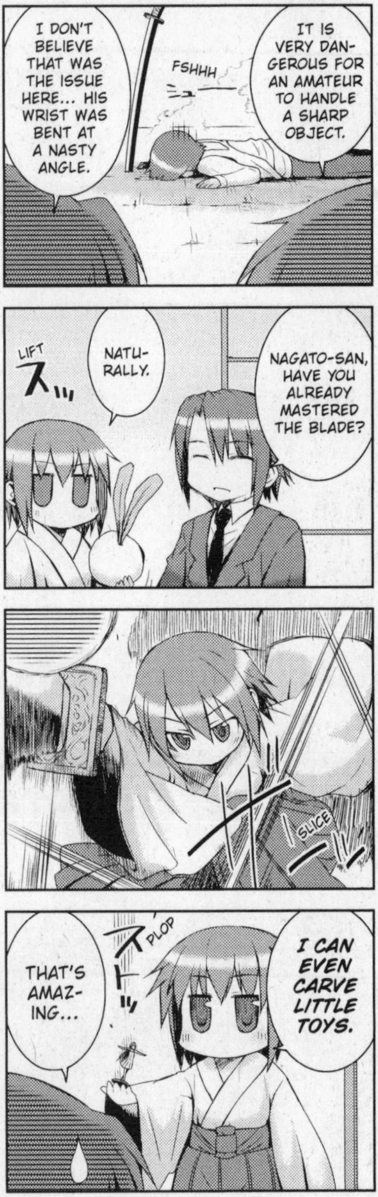
IT IS VERY DANGEROUS FOR AN AMATEUR TO HANDLE A SHARP OBJECT.
FSHHH
I DON'T BELIEVE THAT WAS THE ISSUE HERE... HIS WRIST WAS BENT AT A NASTY ANGLE.
NAGATO-SAN, HAVE YOU ALREADY MASTERED THE BLADE?
NATURALLY.
LIFT
SLICE
I CAN EVEN CARVE LITTLE TOYS.
PLOP
THAT'S AMAZING...

TRICK

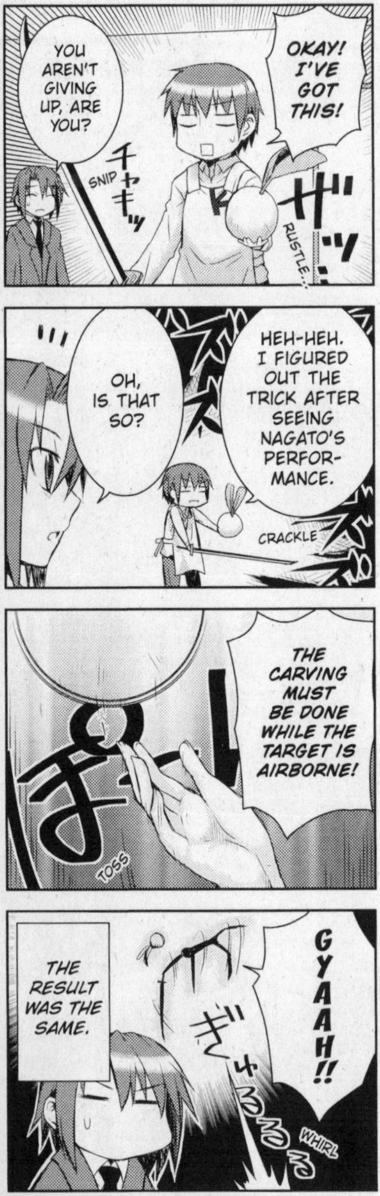
OKAY! I'VE GOT THIS!
YOU AREN'T GIVING UP, ARE YOU?
RUSTLE...
SNIP
HEH-HEH. I FIGURED OUT THE TRICK AFTER SEEING NAGATO'S PERFORMANCE.
OH, IS THAT SO?
CRACKLE
THE CARVING MUST BE DONE WHILE THE TARGET IS AIRBORNE!
TOSS
GYAAAH!!
THE RESULT WAS THE SAME.
WHIRL

FIXINGS

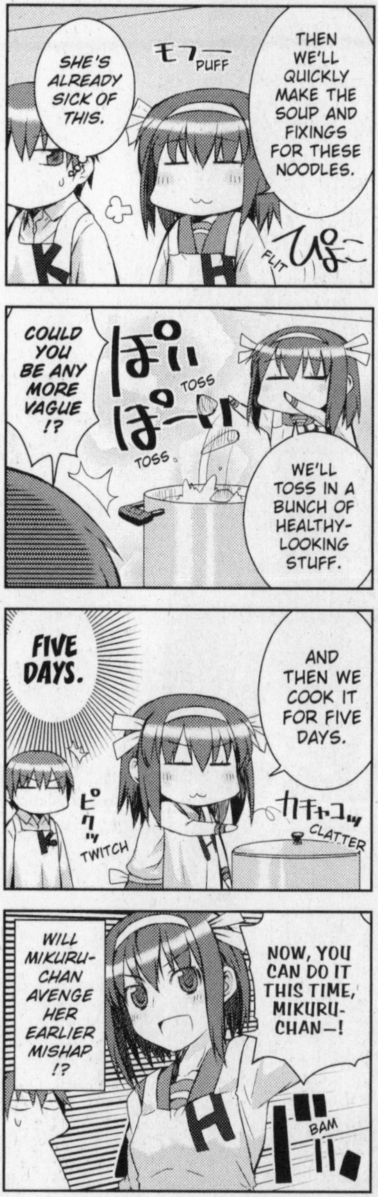
THEN WE'LL QUICKLY MAKE THE SOUP AND FIXINGS FOR THESE NOODLES.
モフー PUFF
SHE'S ALREADY SICK OF THIS.
FLIT
ぽい TOSS
ぽーい TOSS
WE'LL TOSS IN A BUNCH OF HEALTHY-LOOKING STUFF.
COULD YOU BE ANY MORE VAGUE!?
AND THEN WE COOK IT FOR FIVE DAYS.
FIVE DAYS.
カチャコッ CLATTER
ピクッ TWITCH
NOW, YOU CAN DO IT THIS TIME, MIKURU-CHAN—!
WILL MIKURU-CHAN AVENGE HER EARLIER MISHAP!?
BAM

FIVE DAYS

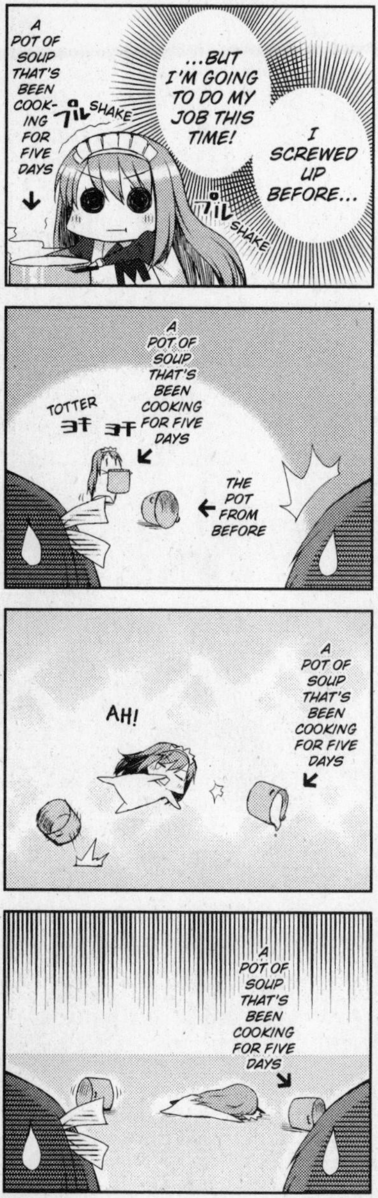
I SCREWED UP BEFORE...
...BUT I'M GOING TO DO MY JOB THIS TIME!
プル SHAKE
プル SHAKE
A POT OF SOUP THAT'S BEEN COOKING FOR FIVE DAYS
THE POT FROM BEFORE
A POT OF SOUP THAT'S BEEN COOKING FOR FIVE DAYS
TOTTER
A POT OF SOUP THAT'S BEEN COOKING FOR FIVE DAYS
AH!
A POT OF SOUP THAT'S BEEN COOKING FOR FIVE DAYS

UNIFORM

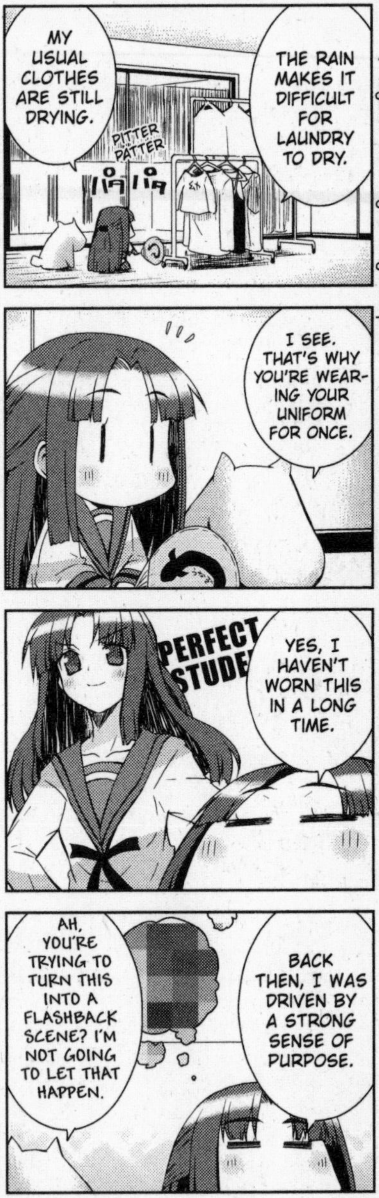
THE RAIN MAKES IT DIFFICULT FOR LAUNDRY TO DRY.
MY USUAL CLOTHES ARE STILL DRYING.
PITTER PATTER
I SEE. THAT'S WHY YOU'RE WEAR-ING YOUR UNIFORM FOR ONCE.
YES, I HAVEN'T WORN THIS IN A LONG TIME.
PERFECT STUDE
BACK THEN, I WAS DRIVEN BY A STRONG SENSE OF PURPOSE.
AH, YOU'RE TRYING TO TURN THIS INTO A FLASHBACK SCENE? I'M NOT GOING TO LET THAT HAPPEN.

PRIORITY

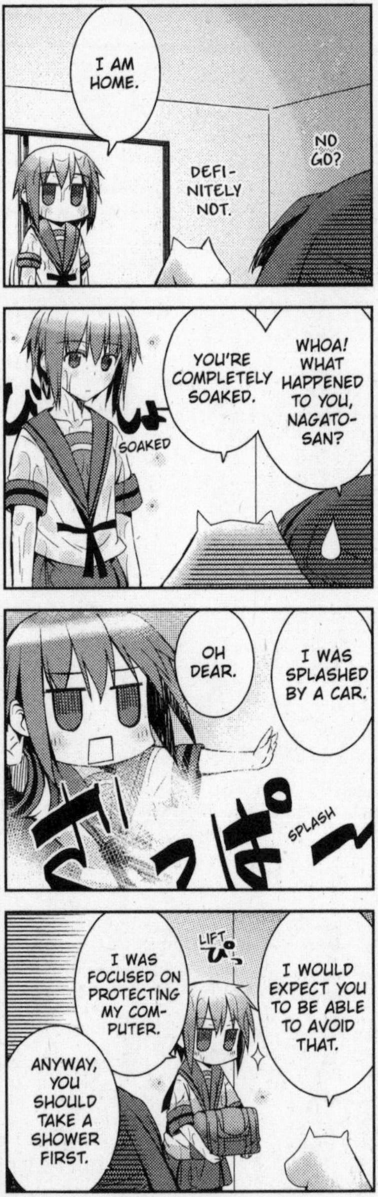
I AM HOME.
NO GO?
DEFI-NITELY NOT.
WHOA! WHAT HAPPENED TO YOU, NAGATO-SAN?
YOU'RE COMPLETELY SOAKED.
SOAKED
I WAS SPLASHED BY A CAR.
OH DEAR.
SPLASH
I WOULD EXPECT YOU TO BE ABLE TO AVOID THAT.
LIFT
I WAS FOCUSED ON PROTECTING MY COM-PUTER.
ANYWAY, YOU SHOULD TAKE A SHOWER FIRST.

•Achakura-san •Back in miniature action after being destroyed in her battle with Nagato. Crashing at Nagato's place.

•Kimidori-san •A balloon dog created by Nagato. His name comes from the color of his body.

SECRET MEASURE

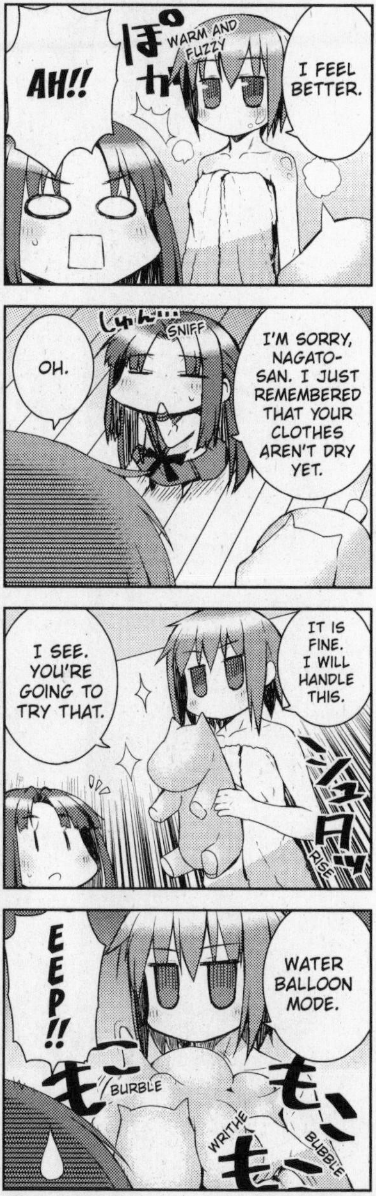
I FEEL BETTER.
ぽか
WARM AND FUZZY
AH!!
I'M SORRY, NAGATO-SAN. I JUST REMEMBERED THAT YOUR CLOTHES AREN'T DRY YET.
しゅん…
SNIFF
OH.
IT IS FINE. I WILL HANDLE THIS.
シュタッ
RISE
I SEE. YOU'RE GOING TO TRY THAT.
WATER BALLOON MODE.
もこ
BUBBLE
もこ
WRITHE
もこ
BURBLE
EEP!!

WATER BALLOON MODE

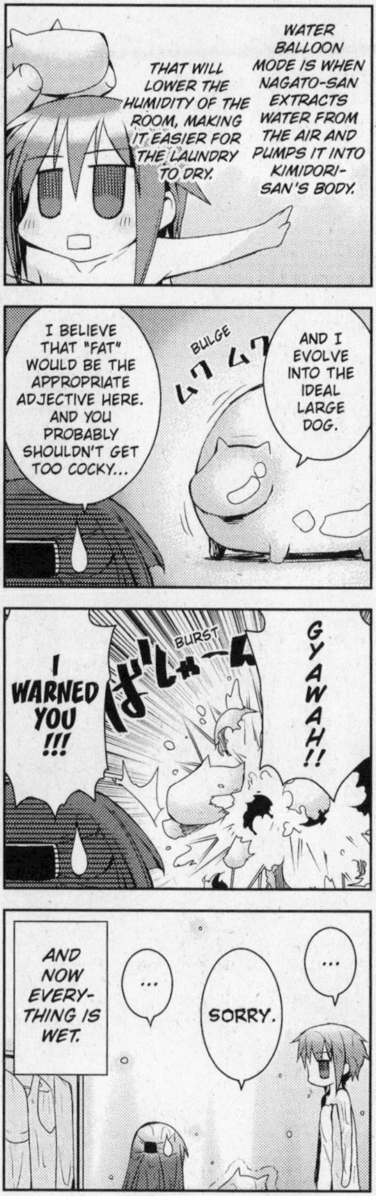
WATER BALLOON MODE IS WHEN NAGATO-SAN EXTRACTS WATER FROM THE AIR AND PUMPS IT INTO KIMIDORI-SAN'S BODY.
THAT WILL LOWER THE HUMIDITY OF THE ROOM, MAKING IT EASIER FOR THE LAUNDRY TO DRY.
AND I EVOLVE INTO THE IDEAL LARGE DOG.
ムク ムク
BULGE
I BELIEVE THAT "FAT" WOULD BE THE APPROPRIATE ADJECTIVE HERE. AND YOU PROBABLY SHOULDN'T GET TOO COCKY...
GYAWAH!!
ぱしゅーん
BURST
I WARNED YOU!!!
...
SORRY.
...
AND NOW EVERYTHING IS WET.

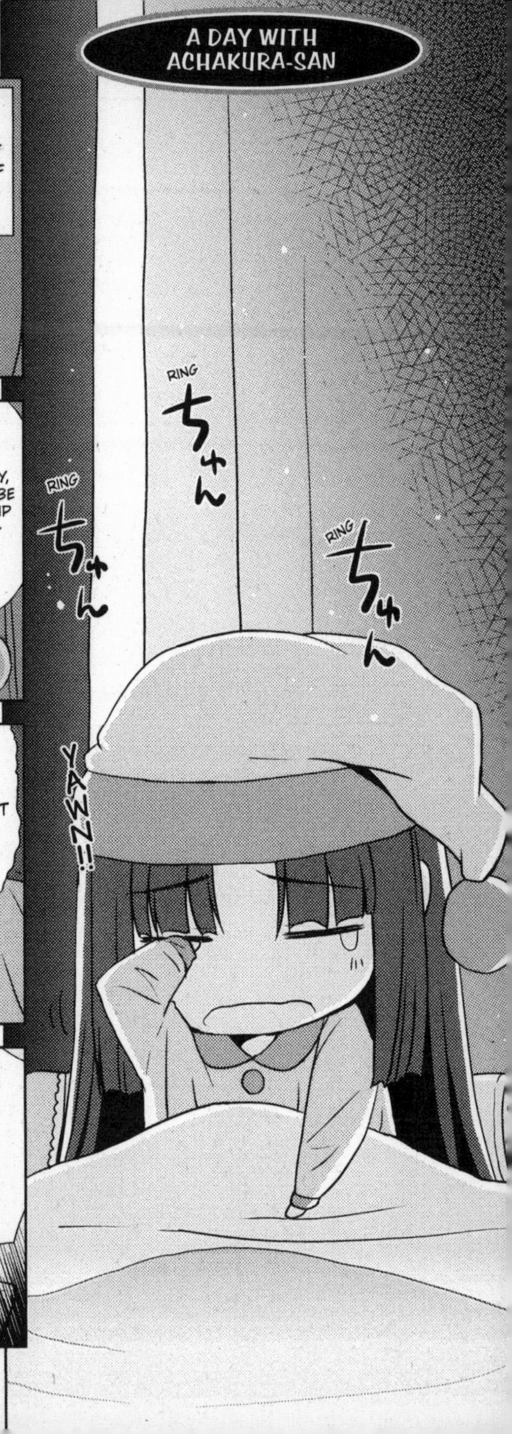
A DAY WITH ACHAKURA-SAN
RING
ちゅん
RING
ちゅん
RING
ちゅん
YAWN!!

MORNING

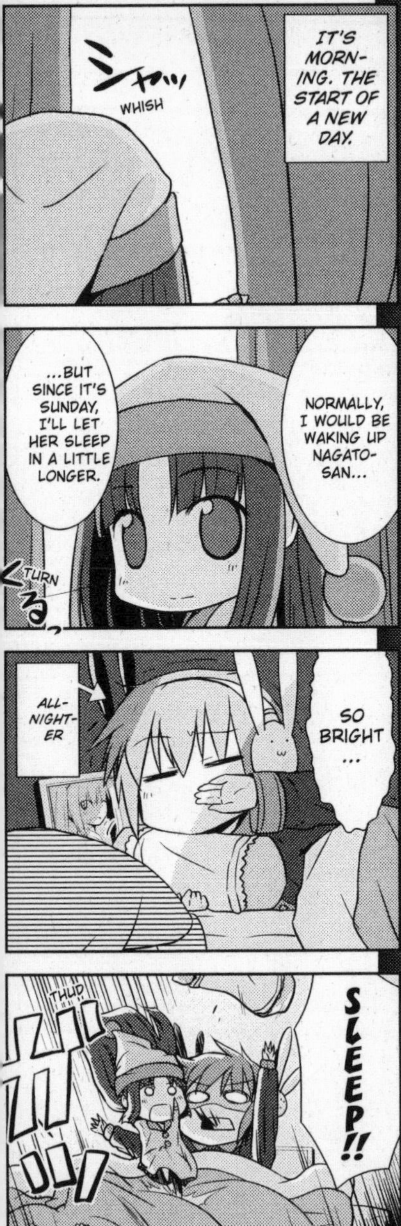
IT'S MORNING. THE START OF A NEW DAY.
シャッ
WHISH
NORMALLY, I WOULD BE WAKING UP NAGATO-SAN...
...BUT SINCE IT'S SUNDAY, I'LL LET HER SLEEP IN A LITTLE LONGER.
TURN
くるっ
SO BRIGHT ...
ALL-NIGHTER
SLEEEP!!
THUD
ガバッ

*THIS STORY TAKES PLACE SHORTLY BEFORE KIMIDORI-SAN WAS BORN.

IMPOSSIBLE

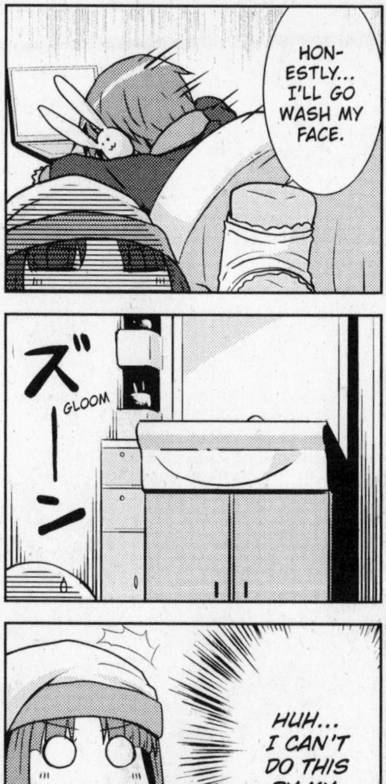
HON-ESTLY... I'LL GO WASH MY FACE.
ズーン
GLOOM
HUH... I CAN'T DO THIS BY MY-SELF?
THAT WAS A PRETTY STRONG KICK... SHE WON'T BE WAKING UP ANY TIME SOON.
ガラ
RATTLE...

SECRET ART

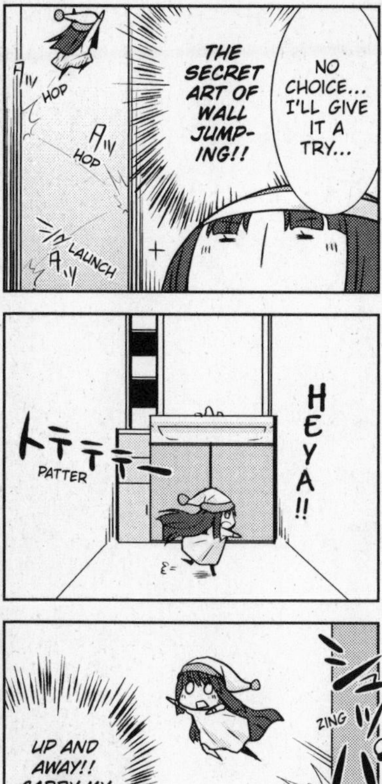
NO CHOICE... I'LL GIVE IT A TRY...
THE SECRET ART OF WALL JUMP-ING!!
HOP
HOP
LAUNCH
HEYA!!
トテテテー
PATTER
シュッパー
ZING
UP AND AWAY!! CARRY MY WISH(?) BEYOND THIS WALL.
ゴッ
THUD
GYAH!!

•Achakura-san •Back in miniature action. Lives with Nagato after being captured.

•Nagato •Hooked on games as of late. Toys with Achakura-san while observing her.

•Kyon •The main character in this story. This time, he only appears in the four-panel segment, and you really only see his back.

•Haruhi-chan •SOS Brigade brigade chief.
She doesn't engage in any bizarre activities
or go out of control this time.

WATERBOARD

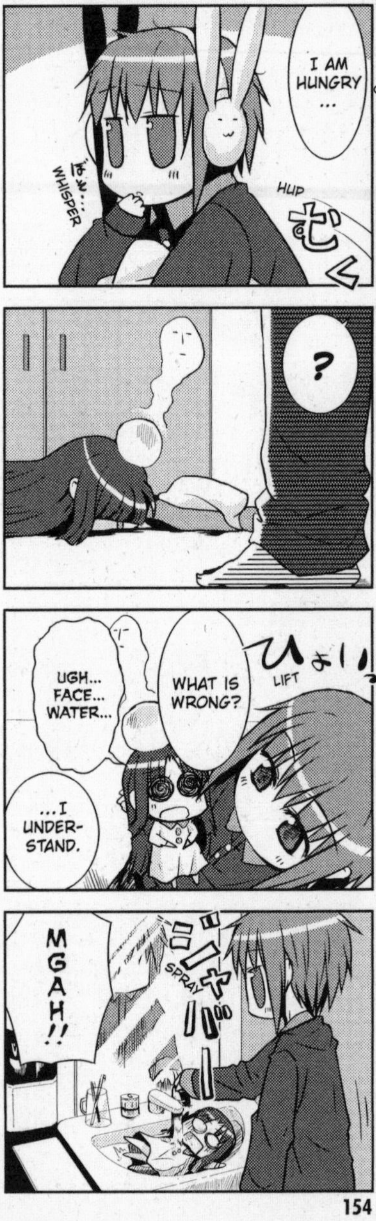
I AM HUNGRY ...
WHISPER
HUP
?
LIFT
WHAT IS WRONG?
UGH... FACE... WATER...
...I UNDER-STAND.
SPRAY
MGAH!!

PAYBACK

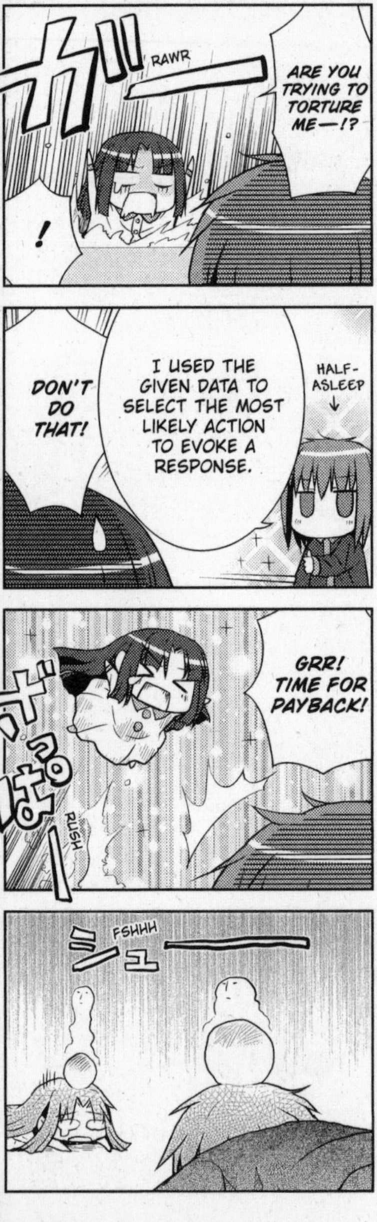
ARE YOU TRYING TO TORTURE ME—!?
RAWR
HALF-ASLEEP
I USED THE GIVEN DATA TO SELECT THE MOST LIKELY ACTION TO EVOKE A RESPONSE.
DON'T DO THAT!
GRR! TIME FOR PAYBACK!
RUSH
FSHHH

EXTRACURRICULAR ACTIVITIES

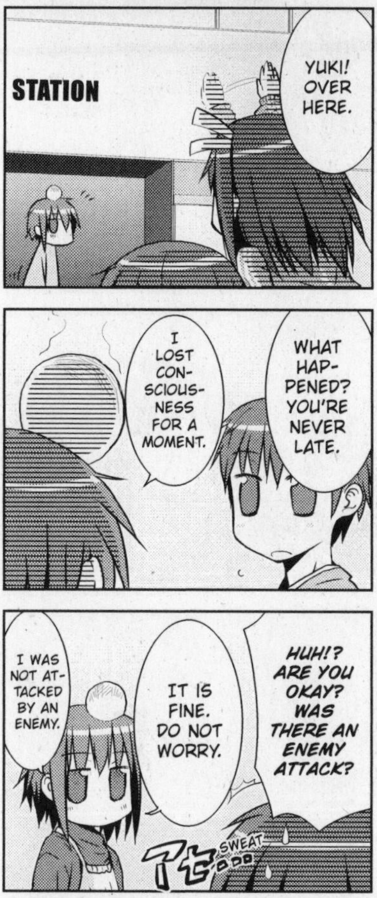
YUKI! OVER HERE.
STATION
WHAT HAPPENED? YOU'RE NEVER LATE.
I LOST CONSCIOUSNESS FOR A MOMENT.
HUH!? ARE YOU OKAY? WAS THERE AN ENEMY ATTACK?
IT IS FINE. DO NOT WORRY.
I WAS NOT ATTACKED BY AN ENEMY.
SWEAT
NO PROBLEM. I AM FUNCTIONING NORMALLY.
I'M OVER HERE...
YOU SURE ABOUT THAT?

CLEANING

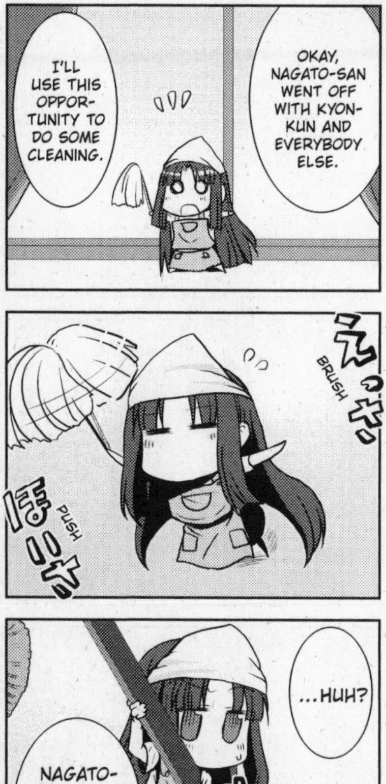
OKAY, NAGATO-SAN WENT OFF WITH KYON-KUN AND EVERYBODY ELSE.
I'LL USE THIS OPPORTUNITY TO DO SOME CLEANING.
BRUSH
PUSH
...HUH?
WHIR
NAGATO-SAN WENT TO SEE KYON-KUN, RIGHT...?
CAN I CALL MYSELF A MEMBER OF THE RADICAL FACTION WHEN I'M STANDING AROUND CLEANING!?
OOH!!

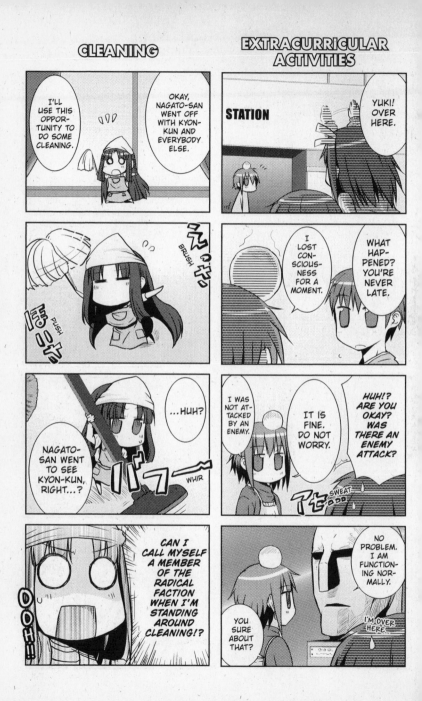

THE SECOND BARRIER

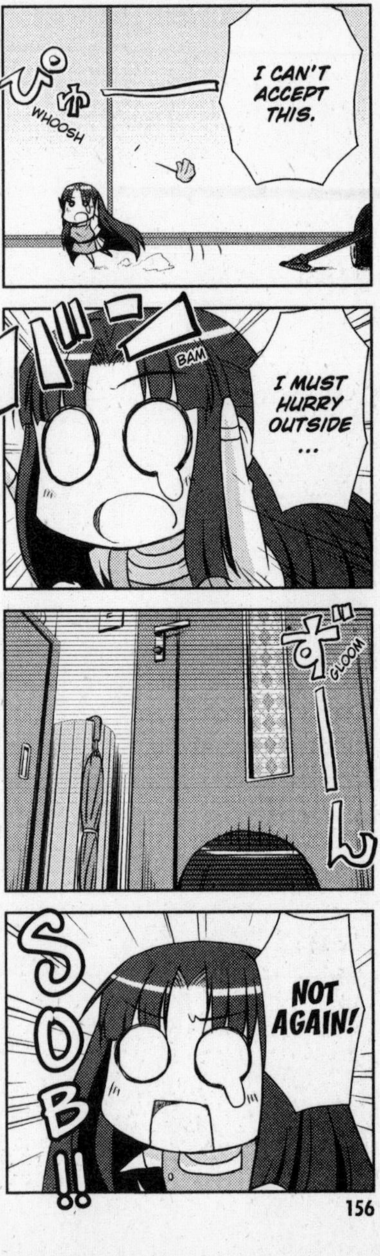
I CAN'T ACCEPT THIS.
ぴゅ
WHOOSH
I MUST HURRY OUTSIDE ...
バーン
BAM
ずーん
GLOOM
NOT AGAIN!
SOB!!

UMBRELLA AND ME

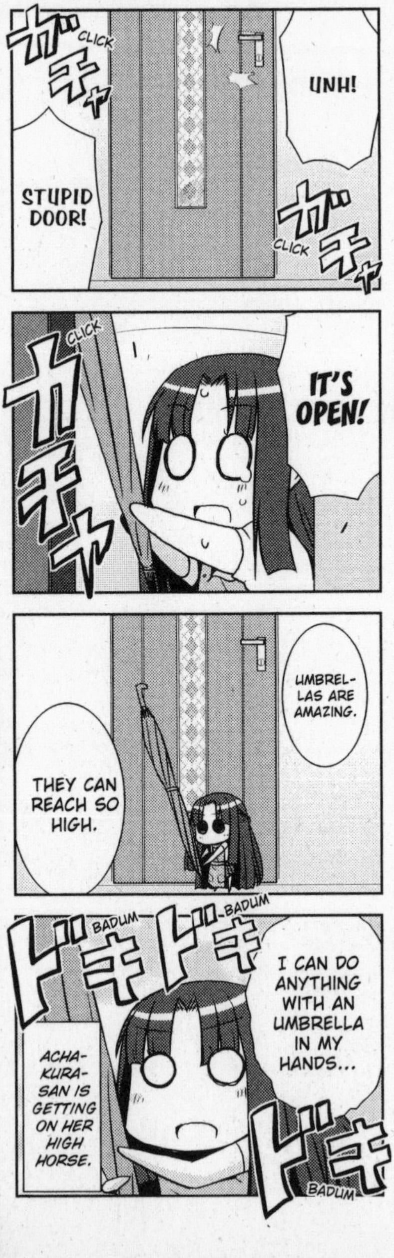
UNH!
ガチャ
CLICK
STUPID DOOR!
ガチャ
CLICK
IT'S OPEN!
カチャ
CLICK
UMBRELLAS ARE AMAZING.
THEY CAN REACH SO HIGH.
ドキドキ
BADUM BADUM
I CAN DO ANYTHING WITH AN UMBRELLA IN MY HANDS...
ACHAKURA-SAN IS GETTING ON HER HIGH HORSE.
ドキ
BADUM

NATURAL ENEMY

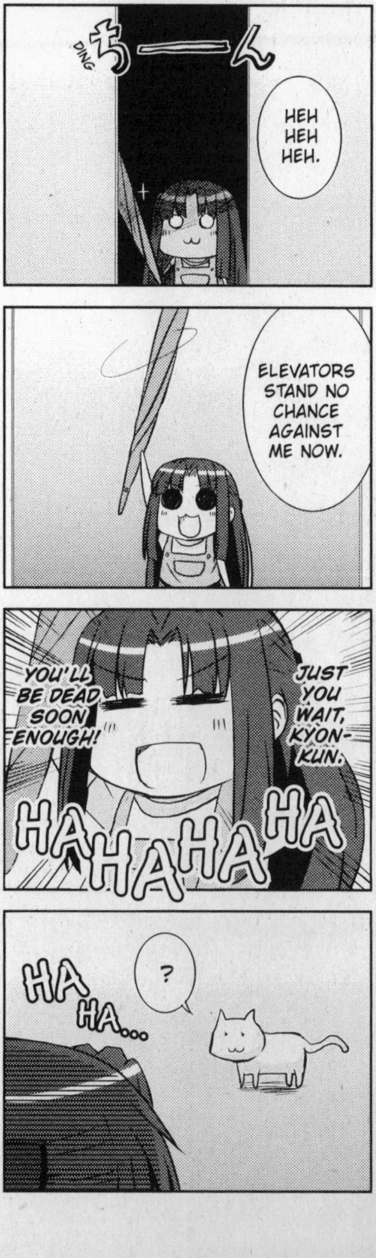
ち ーーん
DING
HEH HEH HEH.
ELEVATORS STAND NO CHANCE AGAINST ME NOW.
JUST YOU WAIT, KYON-KUN.
YOU'LL BE DEAD SOON ENOUGH!
HAHAHAHAHA
?
HA HA...

NATURAL ENEMY

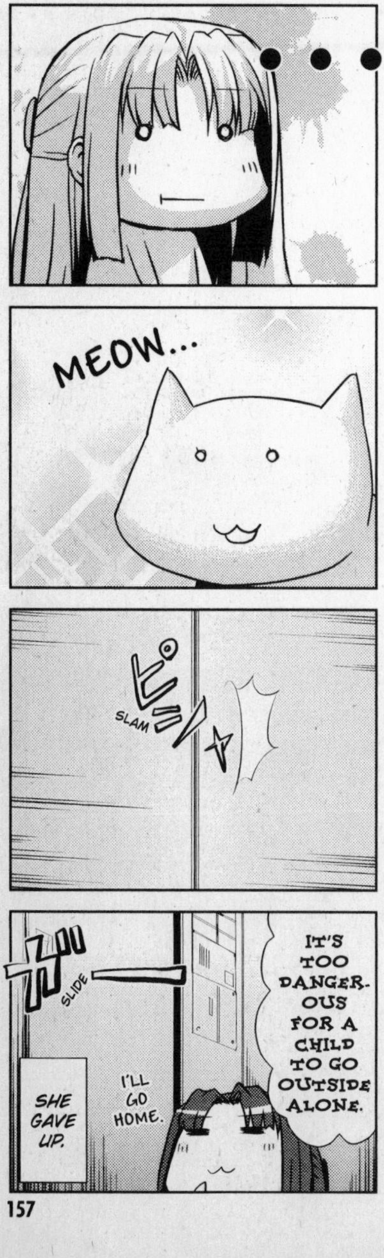
• • •
MEOW...
ピシッ
SLAM
SLIDE
IT'S TOO DANGER-OUS FOR A CHILD TO GO OUTSIDE ALONE.
I'LL GO HOME.
SHE GAVE UP.

SHOPPING

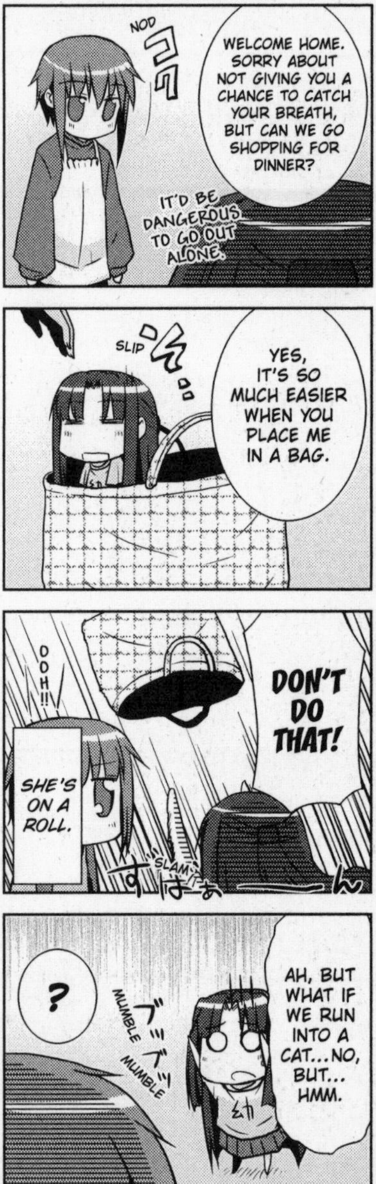
WELCOME HOME. SORRY ABOUT NOT GIVING YOU A CHANCE TO CATCH YOUR BREATH, BUT CAN WE GO SHOPPING FOR DINNER?
NOD
IT'D BE DANGEROUS TO GO OUT ALONE.
YES, IT'S SO MUCH EASIER WHEN YOU PLACE ME IN A BAG.
SLIP
DON'T DO THAT!
OOH!!
SHE'S ON A ROLL.
SLAM
AH, BUT WHAT IF WE RUN INTO A CAT...NO, BUT... HMM.
MUMBLE
MUMBLE
?

SUPERMARKET

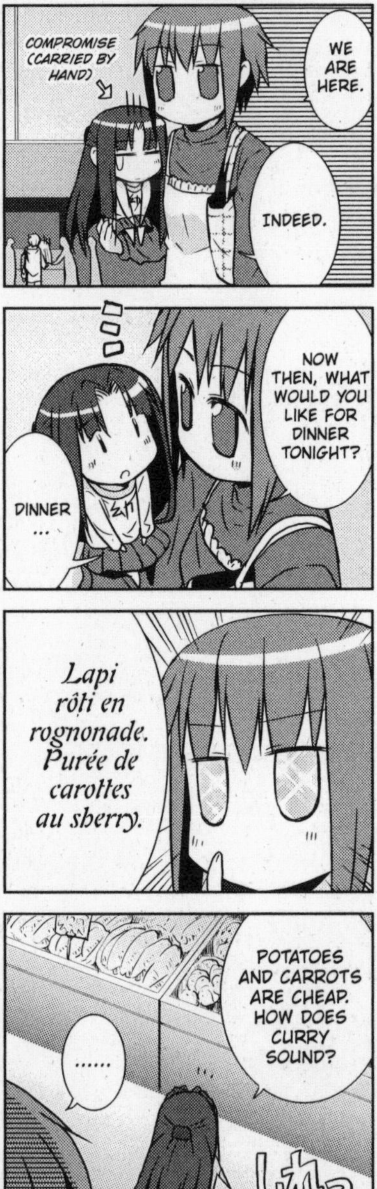
WE ARE HERE.
COMPROMISE (CARRIED BY HAND)
INDEED.
NOW THEN, WHAT WOULD YOU LIKE FOR DINNER TONIGHT?
DINNER ...
Lapi rôti en rognonade. Purée de carottes au sherry.
POTATOES AND CARROTS ARE CHEAP. HOW DOES CURRY SOUND?
......
SHRUG

SYNCHRONIZED

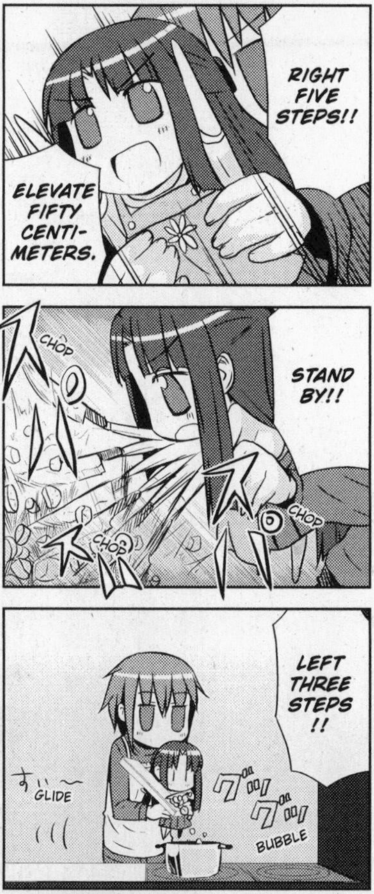
RIGHT FIVE STEPS!!
ELEVATE FIFTY CENTI-METERS.
STAND BY!!
CHOP
CHOP
CHOP
LEFT THREE STEPS!!
GLIDE
BUBBLE
OKAY, LET'S EAT!!
TREMBLE
ぷるぷる

GO TO BED

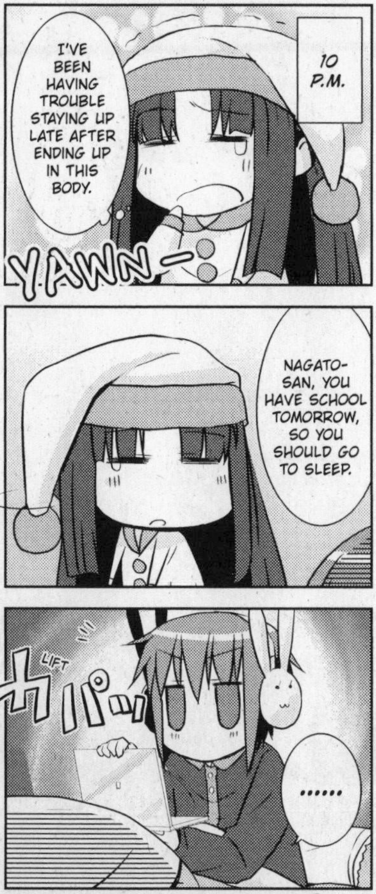
10 P.M.
I'VE BEEN HAVING TROUBLE STAYING UP LATE AFTER ENDING UP IN THIS BODY.
YAWN-
NAGATO-SAN, YOU HAVE SCHOOL TOMORROW, SO YOU SHOULD GO TO SLEEP.
LIFT
......
SNAP
GO TO SLEEP!!

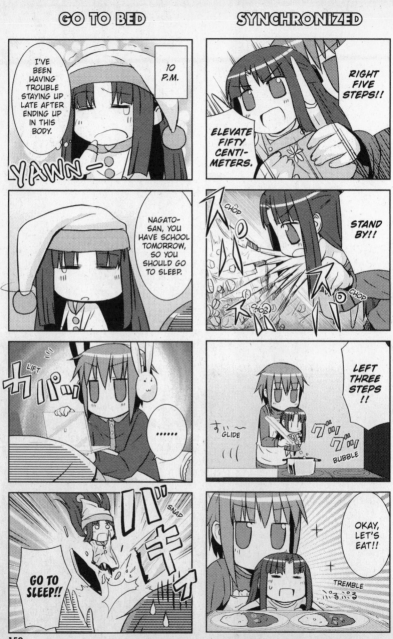

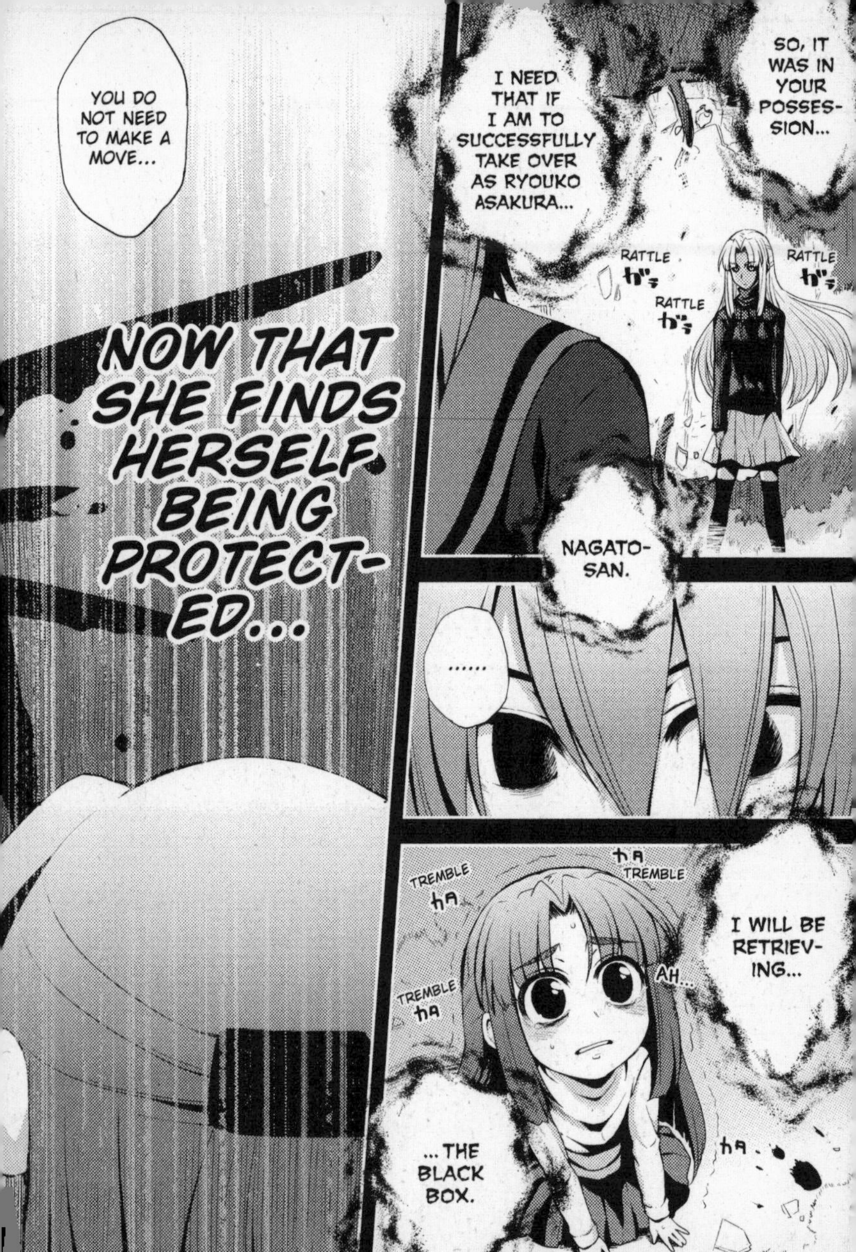
SO, IT WAS IN YOUR POSSESSION...
I NEED THAT IF I AM TO SUCCESSFULLY TAKE OVER AS RYOUKO ASAKURA...
RATTLE
RATTLE
RATTLE
NAGATO-SAN.
......
I WILL BE RETRIEVING...
TREMBLE
TREMBLE
AH...
TREMBLE
...THE BLACK BOX.
YOU DO NOT NEED TO MAKE A MOVE...
NOW THAT SHE FINDS HERSELF BEING PROTECTED...

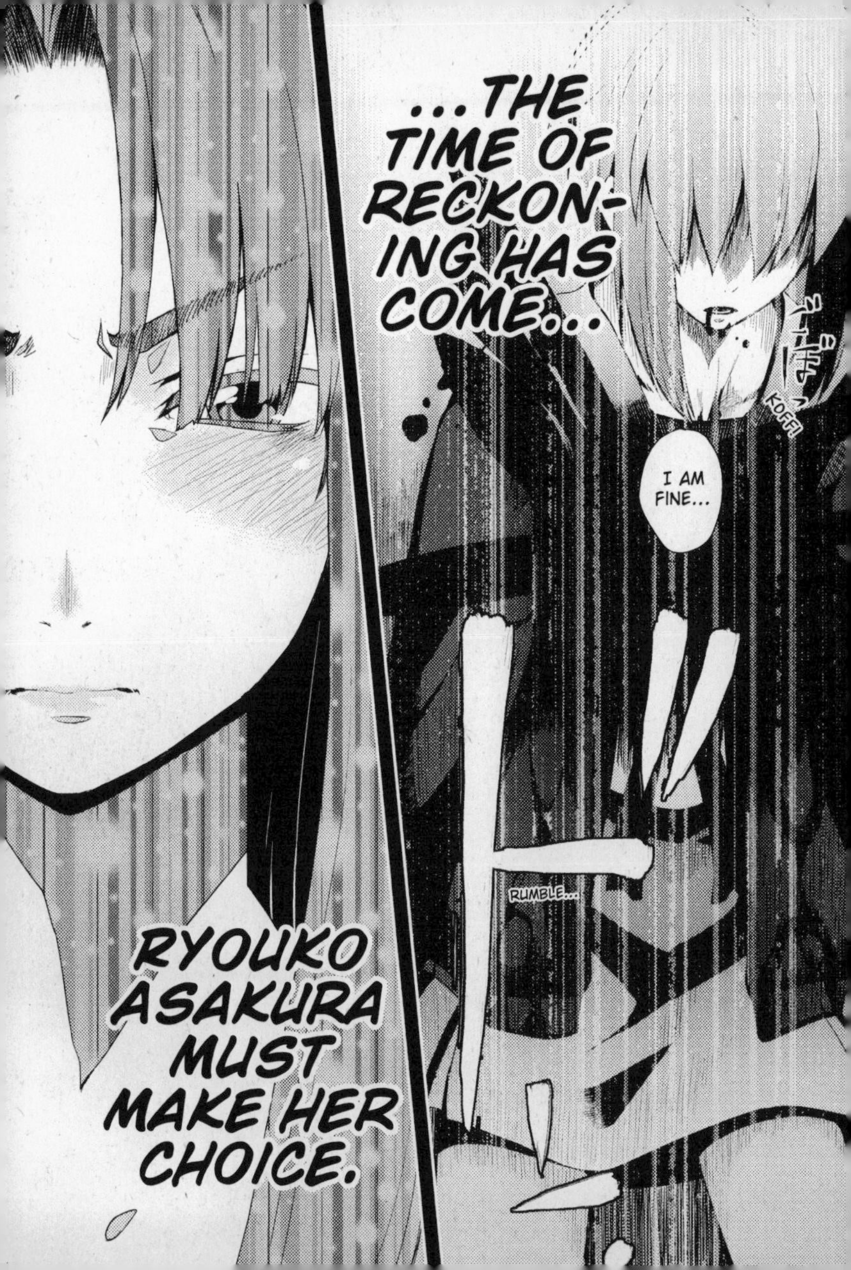
...THE TIME OF RECKONING HAS COME...
KOFF!
I AM FINE...
RUMBLE...
RYOUKO ASAKURA MUST MAKE HER CHOICE.

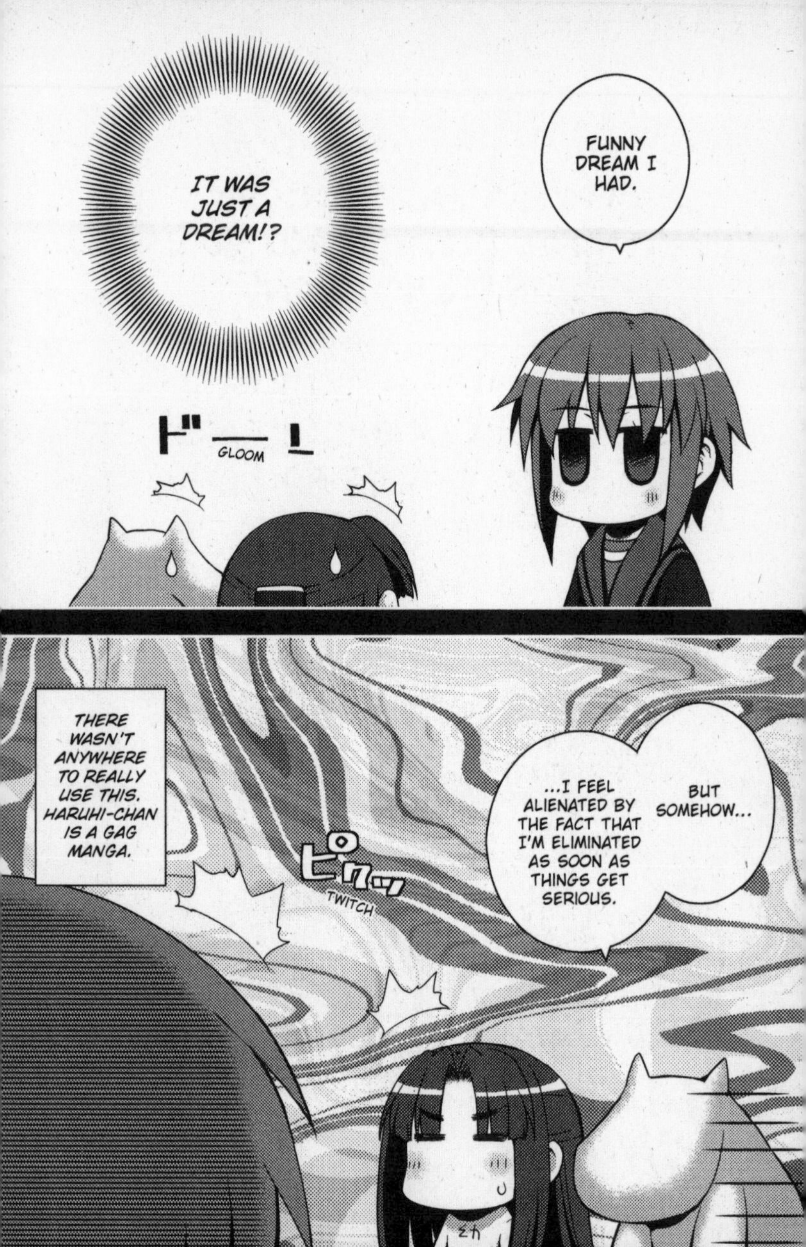
FUNNY DREAM I HAD.
IT WAS JUST A DREAM!?
ドーン
GLOOM
BUT SOMEHOW...
...I FEEL ALIENATED BY THE FACT THAT I'M ELIMINATED AS SOON AS THINGS GET SERIOUS.
THERE WASN'T ANYWHERE TO REALLY USE THIS. HARUHI-CHAN IS A GAG MANGA.
ピクッ
TWITCH

CONGRATULATIONS ON
PUBLISHING THE SECOND VOLUME
OF *HARUHI-CHAN*!

NAGATO AND ACHAKURA-SAN
REALLY WARM YOUR HEART.
AND MORI-SAN IS SO COOL!

いとうのいぢ

NOIZI ITO

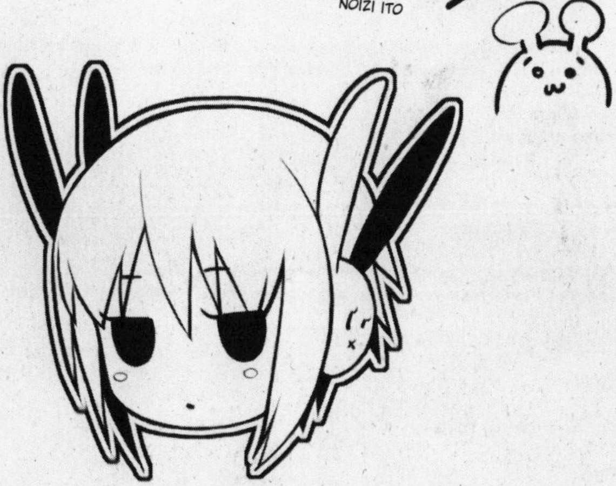

THE MELANCHOLY OF SUZUMIYA
HARUHI-CHAN
❷

Original Story: Nagaru Tanigawa
Manga: PUYO
Character Design: Noizi Ito

Translation: Chris Pai for MX Media LLC
Lettering: Hope Donovan

The Melancholy of Suzumiya Haruhi-chan Volume 2
© Nagaru TANIGAWA • Noizi ITO 2008 © PUYO 2008. First published in Japan in 2008
by KADOKAWA SHOTEN Co., Ltd., Tokyo. English translation rights arranged with
KADOKAWA SHOTEN Co., Ltd., Tokyo through TUTTLE-MORI AGENCY, INC., Tokyo.

English translation © 2011 by Hachette Book Group, Inc.

Yen Press
Hachette Book Group
237 Park Avenue, New York, NY 10017

www.HachetteBookGroup.com
www.YenPress.com

Yen Press is an imprint of Hachette Book Group, Inc.
The Yen Press name and logo are trademarks of Hachette Book Group, Inc.

First Yen Press Edition: May 2011

ISBN: 978-0-316-08958-6

10 9 8 7 6 5 4 3 2 1

BVG

Printed in the United States of America